The Catholic Studies Reader

CATHOLIC PRACTICE IN NORTH AMERICA

This series aims to contribute to the growing field of Catholic studies through the publication of books devoted to the historical and cultural study of Catholic practice in North America, from the colonial period to the present. As the term "practice" suggests, the series springs from a pressing need in the study of American Catholicism for empirical investigations and creative explorations and analyses of the contours of Catholic experience. In seeking to provide more comprehensive maps of Catholic practice, this series is committed to publishing works from diverse American locales, including urban, suburban, and rural settings; ethnic, postethnic, and transnational contexts; private and public sites; and seats of power as well as the margins.

The Catholic Studies Reader

EDITED BY JAMES T. FISHER
AND MARGARET M. McGUINNESS

FORDHAM UNIVERSITY PRESS
New York 2011

Portions of this chapter originally appeared in Margaret M. McGuinness, "A Place for Everything: Catholic Studies and Higher Education," *American Catholic Studies Newsletter* 35, no. 2 (fall 2008): 1, 7–10.

Fordham University Press also publishes its books in a variety of electronic formats. Some content that appears in print may not be available in electronic books.

Library of Congress Cataloging-in-Publication Data

The Catholic studies reader / edited by James T. Fisher and Margaret M. McGuinness.
p. cm.— (Catholic practice in North America)
Includes bibliographical references and index.
ISBN 978-0-8232-3410-3 (cloth : alk. paper)
ISBN 978-0-8232-3411-0 (pbk. : alk. paper)
1. Catholic Church—United States. 2. Catholics—United States—Intellectual life. I. Fisher, James Terence. II. McGuinness, Margaret M.
BX1407.I5C38 2011
282′.730904—dc22

2010053325

Printed in the United States of America
13 12 11 5 4 3 2 1
First edition

Contents

Acknowledgments

The editors gratefully acknowledge the generosity of John and Constance Curran, whose stewardship made this volume possible. We are also deeply thankful for the encouragement and friendship of Mark Massa, S.J., the Curran Center's founding director; Mark's successor as director of the Curran Center, Christine Firer Hinze; associate directors Angela Alaimo O'Donnell and John Seitz; and Maria Terzulli, the Curran Center's incomparable administrator.

The Catholic Studies Reader

Introduction

The Need for Catholic Studies

JAMES T. FISHER AND MARGARET M. McGUINNESS

Margaret McGuinness was a graduate student at Union Theological Seminary (New York) when Father James J. Hennesey's *A History of the Roman Catholic Community in the United States* was published in 1981, even as James Fisher was studying American cultural history down the New Jersey Turnpike at Rutgers. Although other scholars, including Notre Dame's Philip Gleason and Jay Dolan, were also writing about American Catholicism at this time, McGuinness's church history classes were paying very little attention to their work, focusing primarily on the U.S. Protestant experience. Hennesey's book convinced her that American Catholicism was a vital part of the U.S. religious landscape, but it also made her realize how many chapters were still missing from the story. She decided to write her dissertation on "something Catholic" (Catholic social settlements in the United States), as did a number of her contemporaries (Fisher wrote on the mid-twentieth-century Catholic counterculture), and a more complete picture of how American Catholics have lived and practiced their religion slowly began to take shape. Twenty-five years later, from McGuinness's vantage point as chair of the Religion Department at Philadelphia's La Salle University and coeditor of *American Catholic Studies* (formerly *Records of the American Catholic Historical Society of Philadelphia*), it is clear that one result of this scholarship has been the development of the emerging discipline of Catholic Studies.

To a certain extent, Catholic Studies has had a place in institutions of higher education as long as Catholics have had a sustained presence in American academia. The approach favored by scholars between 1890 and 1950, however, was very different from that of today's practitioners of Catholic Studies. The American Catholic Sociological Society (ACSS), for instance, was founded in 1938 to validate the importance of a distinctively Catholic sociology in what some scholars believed was an intellectual environment hostile to religion. Today's version of Catholic Studies would be virtually unrecognizable to the founders of ACSS and their colleagues. The "old" idea no longer carries much weight within most Catholic institutions of higher education. Most scholars working in Catholic Studies insist that the discipline be treated as a legitimate academic area in which men and women of all faiths (and none) are expected to produce scholarship respected by the academy.

Catholic Studies is an interdisciplinary program that includes, but is not limited to, theology, history, literature, political science, economics, sociology, fine arts, music, and social work. Courses defined as Catholic Studies enable students to explore the myriad ways in which Catholicism has informed people's lives and the world in which they live. Catholic Studies programs can be found at Catholic colleges and universities throughout the United States (there are at least forty-five of them), and a growing number of Catholic and non-Catholic universities have raised money for endowed chairs in this field. Because this is a relatively new program within the academy, however, faculty, administrators, and church leaders do not always agree on what constitutes this emerging discipline or under what circumstances it should be studied.

The establishment of Catholic Studies programs, at least at most Catholic colleges and universities, differs from that of other programs drawing faculty from multiple departments, such as American Studies, Black Studies, and Women's Studies. A number of Catholic universities began offering majors and/or minors (or certificates) in Catholic Studies as a response to *Ex Corde Ecclesiae*, the apostolic constitution on Catholic higher education promulgated by Pope John Paul II to remind faculty and administrators of the importance of maintaining a distinctively Catholic identity. Programs identified as "Catholic Studies" offer concrete proof (to bishops, alumni and alumnae, and donors) that a university's academic programs are situated within the larger Catholic intellectual tradition. "Of course we are concerned about our Catholic identity," the argument goes, "look at our program in Catholic Studies."

Not only do Catholic Studies programs bear witness to the mission of Catholic colleges, but they also help preserve and support the premise that an institution's Catholic identity is not confined exclusively to a theology or religious studies department. English, economics, political science, and sociology are all potential vehicles for informing undergraduates about Catholic teachings, life, and culture; in other words, Catholicism is taught across the curriculum. This sort of interdisciplinary approach allows nursing and allied health students to participate in discussions on when and how a dying individual should be kept alive, and it gives Catholic business schools the opportunity to offer accounting and finance majors an understanding of the Church's teachings on labor unions and the concept of a living wage. In the very sophisticated and specialized college and university of the twenty-first century, this curricular approach encourages all students to wrestle with important questions and issues in which Catholic thought and tradition has had significant input.

There is no clear consensus as to what constitutes a Catholic Studies program. Does placing existing courses under the heading "Catholic Studies" create an interdisciplinary area of study? Catholic universities, of course, require all students to complete a minimum number of religion/theology courses in order to graduate, but what other fields are important? Are there particular disciplines to which all Catholic Studies students should be exposed? Is literature more important than art; is art more important than sociology? The answer seems to depend upon the strengths and preferences of the faculty member administering the Catholic Studies program at his or her university.

Programs in Catholic Studies (major, minor, and/or certificate) seem to fit into one of three major categories. The first group established a program by gathering together relevant courses already being offered and, after assessing their relevance, cross-listing them under Catholic Studies. Philadelphia's La Salle University, for instance, allows students to earn a minor in Catholic Studies by electing six out of twenty-five possible courses, none of which have been designed specifically for the program. Some, such as "Visualizing the Sacred," are clearly related to the discipline. Others, such as "Social Welfare Policy," can appear to be a bit of a stretch unless the syllabus includes topics related to Catholic social thought.

Some Catholic colleges and universities, using the basic model exemplified by La Salle, have formalized the program's structure by connecting it to an institute of Catholic Studies. John Carroll University of

Cleveland, Ohio, requires students to complete eighteen credits for a concentration in Catholic Studies. Undergraduates choose one approved course from religion, philosophy, humanities, and natural or social sciences, in addition to an elective and a required seminar on great thinkers in the Catholic intellectual tradition. Each semester's relevant course offerings are listed by department on the institute's website to make it easier for students completing the concentration to plan their schedules.

A second model for Catholic Studies programs is offered at Anna Maria College in Paxton, Massachusetts, which offers neither a religion/theology nor a philosophy major but has developed a comprehensive major in Catholic Studies with three options from which students may choose: Catholic Intellectual and Cultural Heritage, Religious Education, and Pastoral Ministry. Rather than an introductory course in religion, majors are required to take a course called "Introduction to Catholic Studies." Upper-level courses include a capstone in Catholic Studies and a course requiring guided community service.

A third model, found at Fordham and Georgetown, allows students to choose from a "basket" of courses but requires an introductory course in Catholic Studies (in Fordham's case, American Catholic Studies). Georgetown students take a course called "Explorations in Catholic Culture," in addition to a second Catholic Studies course. Students at Fordham University are expected to complete a two-semester seminar in American Catholic Studies during their junior year along with four other courses (chosen from a list of forty-one) in order to receive a certificate in this area.

It is worth noting that some universities have deliberately chosen a fourth option: not to develop a program in Catholic Studies. Although it offers a doctorate focusing on the practice of theology in U.S. Catholicism, the University of Dayton consciously decided not to establish any sort of degree program in Catholic Studies, focusing instead, according to faculty member Una Cadegan, on a "General Education curriculum informed by Catholic intellectual tradition and supported by a significant proportion of the faculty."

The diversity among Catholic Studies programs at Catholic colleges and universities raises two questions that are relevant for the future development of this discipline. The first concerns the relationship between Catholic Studies and American Catholic Studies. Although it is generally agreed that a relationship exists between the two, there is less agreement about the nature of that relationship. American Catholic Studies, of course, fits rather neatly into the larger field of Catholic Studies, but it is not yet clear how these two disciplines will come together either in the scholarly community or in programs and institutes housed in colleges and universities.

Catholic Studies may be a broader field than one focusing on the interaction of a universal church with a particular culture, but several major Catholic universities have chosen to encourage and fund centers focusing on American Catholicism. Since its inception in 1975, the University of Notre Dame's Cushwa Center has become a central clearinghouse for studies in U.S. Catholicism. In more recent years, Fordham University's Curran Center for American Catholic Studies has become known for its wide variety of programs both inside and outside of the classroom. Not only can students complete a certificate program in this discipline, but the Curran Center also sponsors public events and lectures such as "'Re-mapping the Bronx': How Mexican Immigrants Are Transforming the Neighborhoods in Which They Live with Their Culture, Faith, and Social Organizations" and "Autism and Advocacy: A Conference of Witness and Hope." Centers and institutes focused on the more general theme of Catholic Studies have not yet achieved the status of those devoted to American Catholic Studies at Notre Dame and Fordham.

Two journals, *American Catholic Studies* and *U.S. Catholic Historian*, are dedicated to publishing in American Catholic Studies, but a comparable publication entitled *Catholic Studies* does not yet exist. Recognizing the interdisciplinary nature of the field, the editors of *American Catholic Studies* welcome submissions from authors writing in history, sociology, theology, architecture, art, cinema, music, popular movements, and other related areas. *U.S. Catholic Historian* publishes thematic issues related to all areas of American Catholicism. Neither journal, however, publishes articles focusing on Catholicism as it is studied and lived outside of the United States (although comparative pieces are considered). The presence of *American Catholic Studies* and *U.S. Catholic Historian*, along with the Cushwa and Curran centers, implies that this discipline has found a place within the academy. The broader field of Catholic Studies, however, may not yet have found its niche.

A second question is this: What is the relationship between Catholic Studies in Catholic colleges and universities and the Church of the future? Exposing undergraduates to Catholic theology and culture may serve a function at Catholic institutions of higher education, one viewed as crucial by administrators: helping to pass down the faith to the next generation of American Catholics. When courses incorporating Catholicism are offered on a regular basis, the current (and future) generation of undergraduates may learn something about the culture of Catholicism.

Whether Catholic Studies will play a role in preparing the lay leaders of the future remains to be seen. In 2005, thanks to a generous grant from the John and Constance Curran Charitable Foundation, Fordham University embarked on a multiyear study entitled "Passing on the Faith, Passing on the Church: U.S. Catholicism in a New Century." One of the project's three goals was an examination of the role Catholic Studies might play as "an emerging academic discipline and a source of intellectual revival in the church" (see www.fordham.edu/cs/study.shtml for a full discussion of "Passing on the Faith"). The subgroup charged with exploring this topic, recognizing that very little had been written about Catholic Studies and its role in "passing down the faith," decided that the publication of a collection of essays would both generate discussion about the place of Catholic Studies in higher education and offer a resource for faculty, administrators, pastoral associates, and directors of religious education. (The place of Catholic Studies in adult and continuing education is important, but outside the focus of this essay.) Scheduled to be published in 2011, as of this writing, the essays discuss a wide range of topics related to theoretical and practical aspects of Catholic Studies, as well as the role played by the discipline in Catholic and non-Catholic colleges and universities.

Catholic Studies courses have recently become a part of the curriculum of non-Catholic colleges and universities. In the last several years, Duke University, Hofstra University, and University of California Santa Barbara (UCSB), among others, have encouraged interested donors to endow chairs in this discipline. Catholic Studies positions at non-Catholic institutions serve a very different purpose from those at Catholic colleges and universities. The Catholic Studies chair at UCSB, for example, exists alongside endowed chairs in Tibetan Buddhist Studies, Sikh Studies, and Jewish Studies. Although courses relating to the tradition, beliefs, and practices of Catholicism may appeal to Catholic students interested in gaining a deeper understanding of their religion, professors are neither expected nor encouraged to view "passing down the faith" as a course objective. In addition, an endowed chair in Catholic Studies at non-Catholic universities does not imply the presence of a comprehensive program in the discipline. The chair holder may teach courses in Catholicism without administering a program or center of any sort.

Catholic Studies chairs at non-Catholic universities serve as a reminder of other issues that will need to be addressed as this emerging discipline finds its place in academia. The first has to do with the very definition of Catholicism. Julie Byrne, for instance, who holds the Monsignor Thomas J. Hartman Chair in Catholic Studies at Hofstra University, is currently studying what she calls "independent Catholics." These "other Catholics" consider themselves Catholic, but not Roman Catholic. Should Orthodox, Anglo-Catholics, Protestant Catholics, and separatist Catholics be included in Catholic Studies courses? It is a little easier, Byrne admits, to answer this question from the perspective of a non-Catholic university where a definition that is descriptive rather than prescriptive might be more appropriate. Catholic universities hoping to pass down the faith to the next generation may have different views on this subject. How much emphasis should be placed on Roman Catholic women priests, for instance, in a program dedicated to what is commonly viewed as "normative" Catholicism?

Second, should Catholic Studies be housed exclusively in religion or theology departments? Any program focusing on a particular denomination must certainly include theology, but Catholic Studies, by its very nature, claims to be about more than theology and the ways in which people practice their faith. It is about how men and women live their lives, make choices, choose people with whom to socialize, and respond to the challenges and opportunities of contemporary culture. It is worth noting in this context that even though chairs in Catholic Studies tend to be housed in religious studies or theology departments, a number of scholars who identify with this discipline are not theologians. Una Cadegan (University of Dayton) and Kathleen Sprows Cummings (University of Notre Dame), whose work focuses on American Catholic women, are members of American Studies departments; James O'Toole (Boston College), author of the recently published *The Faithful: A History of Catholics in America*, is in the history department; Barbara Mann Wall, an historian of Catholic nursing sisters, is a faculty member of the University of Pennsylvania's School of Nursing. Although none of these scholars are theologians, their work clearly contributes to our knowledge of the tradition and culture of Catholicism.

Catholic Studies is administered, structured, and envisioned differently in Catholic and non-Catholic colleges and universities throughout the United States. As the number of scholars whose work is classified as Catholic Studies continues to grow—and, given the number of graduate students writing dissertations in areas related to Catholicism, there is no doubt this will be the case—it is important that we come to at least some agreement on what it means not only to "do" Catholic Studies, but also to offer programs leading to majors, minors, or certificates.

Seventy years ago, the American Catholic Sociological Society was founded to enable and encourage the practice of sociology from a Catholic perspective. A good deal has changed during the intervening years. Universities once viewed as somewhat anti-Catholic now boast endowed chairs in Catholic Studies, and Catholic college and university faculty and administrators, who once assumed all students would graduate with a solid foundation in the teaching, tradition, and lived practices of Catholicism, now depend on Catholic Studies programs to convince themselves that at least some of their graduates will be qualified to assume leadership roles in the Catholic Church of the twenty-first century. There is certainly some tension existing between those promoting Catholic Studies solely as an intellectual discipline and those who believe it should be used as one of many vehicles by which the faith can be handed down to future generations. It is not too difficult to envision ways in which this tension can serve to sensitize those in non-Catholic and secular universities to the role this discipline plays in implementing the mission of Catholic colleges, while, at the same time, pushing those Catholic institutions who view Catholic Studies as a way to appease donors, bishops, and graduates worried about Catholic identity to recognize its validity as an academic discipline that can increase our understanding of the theology, culture, faith, traditions, and lived practices of Catholicism.

The essays in this volume are gathered around five interrelated, highly permeable themes critical to the practice and/or theory of Catholic Studies, an enterprise that until now has generated remarkably little self-conscious reflection on its origins, interdisciplinary character and prospects. The essays in Part I, "Sources and Contexts," treat some of the textual and contextual materials that fuel the dialogues between Catholic Studies and Catholic "tradition" on the one hand, and Catholic Studies and the secular realms of the humanities and social sciences on the other.

In "'The Story Is What Saves Us,'" Debra Campbell locates the tradition of American Catholic "life-writing" at the heart of Catholic Studies practice. From the earliest accounts of European explorers to dramatic nineteenth- and twentieth-century conversion narratives by notable Protestants to contemporary chronicles of faith lost or reclaimed, the stories told by American Catholics—sampled in "eleven exemplary works" selected for treatment by Campbell—chart the experience of a community so diverse its shared traditions are both inscribed and invented in these autobiographical narratives. The memoirs explored by Debra Campbell are deeply informed by their authors' personal religious experience and—more often than not—by their engagement with the vast "Catholic Intellectual Tradition," the title and subject of Mary Ellen O'Donnell's contribution. Her concise survey of that tradition runs from Augustine—whose spirit pervades the tradition of Christian "life-writing like no other"—through Thomas Aquinas, whose rediscovery by Church authorities in the late nineteenth century propelled "neo-Thomist" (or "neoscholastic") thought to Catholic intellectual dominance lasting deep into the twentieth century. O'Donnell envisions Catholic Studies as a mode of encounter with these canonical authors marked by openness and intellectual charity, driven by concerns of the present but engaged with the very different horizons of authors past.

In "Passing on the Faith," Sandra Yocum reconstructs debates over the nature of authentically Catholic "formation," both intellectual and spiritual, as conducted by elite figures in U.S. Catholic higher education during the first half of the twentieth century. Then as now a desire for integration and wholeness was widely shared; the most contentious issue pitted advocates of a rigidly neoscholastic formalism against others intent on producing young Catholic apostles infused with a radical zeal for social justice and openness to engagement with the non-Catholic world. These debates, which engaged leaders from Catholic women's colleges in addition to male clerics, belie the image of "Catholic unity" often ascribed to that era, a view promoted by some intent on making Catholic Studies a vehicle for retrieving the lost world of "integral" Catholicism.

David O'Brien's essay, "The (Catholic) Politics of Catholic Studies," extends Yocum's discussion into the post–Vatican II era, when ongoing internecine battles over the direction of the Church's intellectual apostolate assumed a much more overtly political character. O'Brien locates the movement for Catholic Studies programs at the heart of this political tumult, with the scramble for access to potential donors, the need to secure institutional and moral support and other pre-requisites for flourishing Catholic Studies programs now implicated in the cultural and religious politics of Catholic identity and mission, a struggle waged not only on campuses but also in the Church broadly construed. O'Brien urges Catholic Studies advocates to take responsibility for the history of these struggles "so as to uphold the precarious position that Catholicism makes intellectual claims."

The essays in Part II, "Tradition and Methods," treat questions fundamental in defining what Catholic Studies is, what it does, and what it means to precede "Studies" with "Catholic." In "Catholic Studies and Religious Studies," Ann Taves explores the concept of "tradition," a key term in negotiations to position Catholic Studies as an interdisciplinary field embedded in the spaces between well-established discourses of religious studies and theology. The relatively recent phenomenon that finds privately endowed positions in Catholic Studies ensconced in both public and private non-Catholic universities has created an unprecedented opportunity and challenge. Taves suggests that Catholic Studies scholars at secular institutions will inhabit a variety of stances in relationship to Catholic tradition. Students in turn will bring their own convictions, from religious doubt to ardent desires that coursework enhance personal faith formation along with intellectual growth. Taves herself avows a preferential option for exploring the meanings invested in religious traditions over judging claims made in their name, a practice that might flourish as one among a compelling variety of approaches embraced by scholars in Catholic Studies.

Just as Ann Taves urges Catholic Studies practitioners to carefully discern "who we are forming for what end," Jeannine Hill Fletcher, in "A Definition of Catholic," proposes a method of rigorous interrogation not only of "what is Catholic" but also "what Catholic is." Fletcher reminds us that the "Catholic" in Catholic Studies never represents the totality of personal and spiritual identity for Catholic persons: it constitutes but one element among many that contribute to forging personal, spiritual, and intellectual identities. The challenge for Catholic Studies, in Fletcher's view, is to generate scholarly and pedagogical practices that recognize the essentially hybrid character of "Catholic," an insight this systematic theologian intuitively shares with British scholar Paul Giles (author of the pioneering 1992 study *American Catholic Arts and Fictions*), who suggested in a 1999 essay that Catholicism in America flourishes "as a form of hybridity, modulating the very different (often antagonistic) forces with which it has come in contact."

In "Method and Conversion in Catholic Studies," Richard M. Liddy reminds us that the quest for a distinctly "Catholic Studies" method was anticipated in the groundbreaking work of the Canadian Jesuit Bernard Lonergan, particularly in his magisterial 1957 work *Insight: A Study of Human Understanding*, and in *Method in Theology* (1972). In this latter work, Lonergan called for "integrating studies," interdisciplinary works that linked theology with the "human sciences," a project of special relevance for contemporary Catholic Studies.

The authors of the essays in Part III, "Pedagogy and Practice," offer reflections drawn from their experiences of teaching in Catholic Studies settings. As Ann Taves reminds us, the location of Catholic Studies practice helps shape both the form and content of the enterprise. In "Catholic Studies in the Spirit of 'Do Whatever He Tells You,'" Una

Cadegan explains why the University of Dayton chose to feature "Catholic Studies without 'Catholic Studies,'" despite boasting perhaps the deepest concentration of scholars pursuing Catholic Studies topics of any university in the nation. Dayton's Catholic identity pervades the university's curricular and extracurricular life, in the spirit of its founders, French priests of the Society of Mary, a religious order dedicated to education in all fields including general and professional studies. The Dayton model, as Cadegan explains, affords all faculty members regardless of religious affiliation a direct investment in the university's mission.

At many other Catholic colleges and universities the primary challenge is to provide students with a concise, coherent introduction to Catholic tradition in a dedicated setting such as the Catholic Studies classroom affords. In "Afflicting the Comfortable," Margaret M. McGuinness advocates for a semester-long focus on the tradition of Catholic social teaching, an integral component of the Church's public mission for well over a century that remains dimly understood—if at all—by most Catholics and non-Catholics alike. This approach opens students to the intellectual and theological traditions underlying Catholic social teachings, which in turn find deep resonance among the large and growing cohorts of undergraduate students involved in community outreach and service learning programs. This Catholic social teaching model thereby bridges the divide between Catholic Studies and Catholic campus life.

In a similar spirit, Kathleen Sprows Cummings's essay "Teaching About Women, Gender, and American Catholicism" reveals how an undergraduate course on the history of American Catholic women provides students with an array of new perspectives from which to view women's experience in the Church. The course also introduces students to forms of gender analysis that illuminate uniquely Catholic phenomena—from the process of "making saints" to the monumental historic role played by women's religious communities to issues of race and ethnicity—employing methods drawn from a range of fields that support an interdisciplinary practice of Catholic Studies.

In "Visual Literacy and Catholic Studies," Catherine R. Osborne proposes that acquisition of visual literacy should enjoy a high priority in Catholic Studies practice, not simply because of the Church's familiar role in fostering visual arts but also because across much of Christian history, spiritually enriching visual materials were more accessible and more efficacious than written texts; these visual materials inspired theological reflection and helped shape Catholic devotional and liturgical practices. In treating religious architecture, Osborne further demonstrates how the construction of sacred space also shapes religious experience, modeling for readers opportunities for field work undertaken by students as an integral component of Catholic Studies pedagogy.

In Part IV, "Ethnicity, Race, and Catholic Studies," essays devoted to topics of race and ethnicity illuminate the relationships between older interdisciplinary fields and Catholic Studies, and offer pedagogical resources for deepening its inclusive, interdisciplinary character. These works also invite Catholic Studies practitioners to explore rich topical frontiers as yet unopened. In "We Have Been Believers: Black Catholic Studies," Diana Hayes and Cecilia Moore trace the evolution of a movement that originated in the late 1960s not among academics but among African American priests, brothers, and members of women's religious communities who had for too long endured the shared experience of institutional racism in the Church. Black Catholic studies enriched African American theology without being subsumed by it; the movement also deepened U.S. Catholic historical studies—as the authors note in an assertion rich in implications for Catholic Studies practice—by prompting a recognition that the "syncretism" marking African American Catholic devotional practices was not confined to the black Catholic experience. The adaptation of elements from other traditions was an integral feature of Euro-American Catholicism, which borrowed liberally from evangelical revivalism and other historically non-Catholic sources.

As Linh Hoang reminds us in his essay, "Asian American Catholic Experience and Catholic Studies," the presence of Asian American Catholic communities radically unsettles standard narratives of U.S. Catholic history, while shifting the contexts informing discussions of the contemporary Church. Yet just as U.S. Catholics have been notably hesitant to make the conceptual adjustment to fit these realities, as Hoang explains scholars in U.S. religious studies often discount Asian American Catholics, owing to a habitual if not exclusive focus in the religious studies academy on non-Christian Asian traditions. Hoang offers a highly compelling case for Catholic Studies engaged on two fronts simultaneously: alerting Euro-American Catholics to the salience of ethnicity in Asian American religious life while highlighting the *religious* identity of Asian American Catholics lest it remain overlooked in religious studies scholarship.

In "Working Toward an Inclusive Narrative," Kristy Nabhan-Warren offers a personal reflection on the kind of relationships scholars often share with the subjects of their work. Nabhan-Warren's ethnographic work among Hispanic Catholics transformed her understanding of the devotional practices found in the Hispanic communities in which she lived and studied. She discovered that her status as a non-Catholic was viewed as an asset by some of her interlocutors, who sensed that a sympathetic account of their experience told from a Catholic perspective might arouse suspicion in some readers. Nabhan-Warren's methodological self-awareness serves to reaffirm not only that interdisciplinary scholarship is arduous and complex, but also that Catholic Studies attracts practitioners from a wide array of backgrounds driven by intellectual curiosity and the desire to share meaningful stories.

Part V asks the question "Is there a 'Catholic Imagination'?" The notion of a uniquely "Catholic imagination" functions as both an article of faith among scholarly exponents of novelist/sociologist Andrew M. Greeley's dictum "Catholics imagine differently" and as the centerpiece of Catholic Studies' dominant mode of literary and theological analysis. Deeply grounded in the aesthetic philosophy of prominent neo-Thomists such as Jacques Maritain, a magisterial work (*The Analogical Imagination*) by the contemporary theologian David Tracy, and Greeley's prolifically feisty offerings, works treating the Catholic imagination have come to signal the most distinctive hermeneutic of Catholic Studies practice. Yet as the contrasting essays in this section reveal, the Catholic imagination is itself "imagined differently," reaffirming the varieties of religious and cultural experience that inspired Catholic Studies into being and sustain faith in its future amid a traumatic moment in the U.S. Catholic experience.

In "Seeing Catholicly," Angela Alaimo O'Donnell treats sacramental qualities and themes found among poets and novelists whose works constitute a kind of canon of the Catholic literary imagination. From the nineteenth-century English Jesuit Gerard Manley Hopkins to the mid-twentieth-century French novelist Georges Bernanos and American writer Flannery O'Connor, a writer of short stories set in the postwar American South, O'Donnell limns a spiritual aesthetic best conveyed perhaps in the words of a character dying young in Bernanos's celebrated novel *The Diary of a Country Priest*: "Grace is everywhere." As an accomplished poet herself, O'Donnell is particularly attuned to the subtle interplay of language and spirit; close readings as modeled in this essay open readers to that sense of "felt mystery" which Thomas J. Ferraro suggests Catholic Studies might restore to the practice of literary analysis.

In "Cultural Studies Between Heaven and Earth," Tom Ferraro suggests that vestiges of a Catholic imagination may be discerned in classic works of American literature authored by Protestants, and in particular the most canonical novel of all, Nathaniel Hawthorne's *The Scarlet Letter*. Ferraro enlists the intercession of Robert A. Orsi, perhaps the most influential figure in the field of American Catholic Studies, who in his own work has treated the interior religiosity and public devotional lives of urban Italian Americans—to provide a kind of Catholic Studies rereading of *The Scarlet Letter*. The playful quality of this exercise only enhances the sense that, to paraphrase Ferraro, American Studies has been "Catholicized" via works of Orsi, Ferraro himself, and others who explicitly treat issues that historically bedeviled Protestants, such as the body in its various guises and (in)capacities and the interplay of suffering, erotic desire, and spirituality. Tom Ferraro's notion that Catholic Studies at its best inspires scholars and teachers to "meditate then mediate" is affirmed and reaffirmed in the essays found in this volume.

In "Catholic Studies and the Sacramental Imaginary," Maureen H. O'Connell demonstrates how the "Catholic imagination" mode of interpretation might better serve what the philosopher Charles Taylor calls the "social imaginary," a complex notion distilled by O'Connell to represent the manner in which persons in community envision together social and political alternatives. O'Connell suggests that the prevailing Catholic "imaginary" has failed to fully engage the range of social injustices found in places like her native Philadelphia. Her account of that city's 2,800 wall murals—and her own engagement with these murals as sites of theological reflection and liberation praxis—represents a way of doing Catholic Studies that both draws on the approaches described in this volume and models a new kind of Catholic humanism. O'Connell's project is radically interdisciplinary as the work of a Christian ethicist drawn to works of visual art whose presence demands interpretive responses beyond the limits of "Catholic imagination" precedent, yet rooted in unfulfilled yearnings of Catholic activists in the tradition of the Catholic Worker movement, the liturgical movement, and the Catholic interracial apostolate, each of which sought an integration of faith, culture, community, and the work of social justice.

Catholic Studies is itself a legatee of the quest for an "integral" Catholicism. Some scholars in the field ardently seek to revive that tradition. Others honor their vocations in this evolving interdisciplinary enterprise by seeking to understand the various meanings of Catholic tradition to those who came before, and those present to us now and in the future. We hope to address the concerns of both kinds of readers in this collection, and to help predict and shape the course of Catholic Studies in years to come.

Part I: Sources and Contexts

1 "The Story Is What Saves Us"
American Catholic Memoirs

DEBRA CAMPBELL

I cannot totally grasp all that I am.

Saint Augustine

Autobiographical works such as Augustine's *Confessions* are the very foundation of Catholic Studies.[1] Even a cursory look at the footnotes in the comprehensive histories of American Catholicism published since the 1950s reveals how deeply our understanding of the evolution of Catholic life in North America is grounded in *life-writings*, an elastic term for personal narratives presented in a variety of genres and formats, from travel narratives and traditional memoirs to autobiographical fiction and specialized hybrids (conversion and departure narratives, "Why I am a Catholic" books, and so on). Life-writings are pervasive and various, yet they are frequently neglected as a separate topic in Catholic Studies. This chapter adopts an exploratory approach and examines some representative texts that belong in the emerging canon in the field of Catholic Studies, suggesting ways to think about these kinds of narratives in all of their diversity.[2] One of the primary functions served by life-writings in Catholic Studies is to remind readers from all denominations, vocations, and walks of life that the Catholic Church is a community composed of individuals whose identities are deeply informed by a common faith and sharply varying experiences of Catholic lived religion. When we try to make sense of the massive institutional presence and imposing intellectual heritage of *Catholicism*, it is crucial to keep the actual life experiences of Catholic *people* in mind.

There is a sense in which all life-writings belong in the category of travel literature. It is no coincidence that the metaphor of the pilgrimage (or journey) is so frequently invoked in discussions of autobiographical writings of all kinds, not just the ones that are explicitly spiritual.

Life-writings describe genuine movement from one place (emotional, intellectual, or spiritual state of being) to another. They attract a readership because others can identify with the places—and the experiences of displacement—that they describe. Often people read memoirs because they share the authors' hopes for a specific destination. This may explain the abiding popularity of the *Confessions* of Saint Augustine (354–430), bishop of Hippo in North Africa and pathbreaking Catholic theologian, with Catholics over the centuries. Scholars studying the genre of autobiography agree that the *Confessions* is a quintessential, precedent-setting work. It has had an especially important influence upon American Catholic life-writings. Despite the vast distance in time, space, and cultural experience between Augustine and American Catholics, the *Confessions* remains a touchstone for authors of Catholic memoirs into the present day.

In his introduction to *The Norton Book of American Autobiography* (1999), the literary historian Jay Parini refers to Augustine's *Confessions* in his account of the genesis of Benjamin Franklin's decidedly non-Catholic *Autobiography* (1791). Parini maintains that as an eighteenth-century autobiographer, Franklin had two possible models: the confession, pioneered by Augustine (in which "the writer reveals his inner torments or moments of ecstasy") and the memoir (where "the role of the individual on the great stage of history becomes the subject"). Parini emphasizes the significance of Franklin's decision to make his *Autobiography* a combination of the features of the private confession and the public memoir, with a touch of hagiography ("exemplary lives of the saints") incorporated as well.[3] The Catholic memoirs explored in this chapter, for the most part, share the hybrid nature of Franklin's famous autobiography. They combine features of the private confession and the public memoir, and they have frequently proved useful to subsequent generations of Catholics seeking examples of what it means to live the faith: in Augustine's famous metaphor from *The City of God* (427), to remain always a citizen of the heavenly city while living as a resident alien in the earthly city.

Eleven Exemplary Works

The history of American Catholic life-writings has yet to be written. This essay is based on the premise that we have much to learn from reading Catholic memoirs. The life-writings examined in this chapter were once widely read and occasionally controversial. They changed how readers thought about themselves and the Church. They prompted Catholics to speak out and to act. Unfortunately, most of these memoirs have slipped into obscurity; only Catholic historians read them. This chapter, addressed to a general audience, represents a plea to read these and other American Catholic memoirs and see where they lead us.

What follows is an overview suggesting some of the broad contours in its evolution from the colonial period through the twentieth century. By looking at even a small sampling of eleven exemplary works, chosen from the expansive and ever-growing collection of possibilities, one can gain some sense of how the form and function of these works have developed over time in response to the evolving shape, size, and status of the Catholic Church in America and to parallel changes in American literary and popular culture. Each of these memoirs serves to evoke for readers a distinct Catholic world. One task of the autobiographical writer is to create "a parallel world" out of the small portion of lived experience that is disclosed in a text, while a massive amount is "left out, left to challenge and subvert the text that appears on the printed page."[4] For authors of Catholic life-writings (and their readers), this act of creating a parallel world has frequently become an occasion for reflections on spirituality, God's presence, and the nature of the Church. This is why a self-consciously Catholic memoir is never simply a memoir. It always has other work to do. It opens up a whole range of experiences that otherwise would remain closed to us. Exposure to these personal narratives and the worlds that they reveal can make a profound difference in the lives and faith of Catholic readers, both "everyday Catholics" and those who would hope to lead the Church.

Adventures in the Unknown Interior of America (1542) was written by a Spanish soldier, a member of the landed gentry, Álvar Núñez Cabeza de Vaca (ca. 1490–1557). The genre is a product of its times: it is a travel narrative that was also a report from a subordinate to a patron. Cabeza de Vaca justifies his own actions as one of four survivors in an expedition (1527–37) of six hundred men sent to conquer the area between Florida and the Rio Grande. Interwoven into Cabeza de Vaca's rich and detailed descriptions of the various indigenous communities in which he found himself a prisoner, a servant, a trader of goods, and eventually a valued healer, one sees his spirituality evolving as he discovers in his healing rituals teachable moments for both sides. Cabeza de Vaca describes how he was transformed by his close encounters with non-Christian indigenous peoples, especially by his discovery of genuine compassion and morality where he had not been prepared to expect it. His success as a healer among the Indians increased his "gratitude to our Lord, Whose demonstrated mercy gave us conviction that He would liberate us and bring us to a place where we might serve Him."[5] What he saw and endured, including the brutality and immorality of his compatriots, in contrast to the morality and integrity of some of the natives, turned his world upside down, complicated his faith, and fed his hopes for an expanded multiethnic Christian community in the New World.

The *Autobiography* of the Dublin-born printer and publisher Mathew Carey (1760–1839) reflects the situation in which Catholics found themselves during the early decades of the new republic. Carey relates how he arrived in Philadelphia on November 1, 1794, "with about a dozen guineas in my pocket, without relation or friend." In Ireland he had been harassed and ultimately prosecuted because representatives of the Crown considered his published tracts and his newspaper, *The Volunteers' Journal*, treasonous. Thanks to a gift of four hundred dollars from the Marquis de Lafayette shortly after his arrival, as well as his marriage of almost thirty-nine years to the "industrious, prudent, and economical" Bridget Flahavan, Carey was able to establish himself in the publishing business and gradually to grow prosperous. He wrote a classic nineteenth-century memoir outlining the virtues necessary to become a self-made man in America.

Carey did not hide his Catholic faith, but neither was Catholicism the major element in his identity. He recounts an incident at his own dinner table, when he was entertaining "a highly respected citizen" and "longtime correspondent" who railed on at length about a service he had attended at St. Augustine's Church: "It is all show, all ceremony. There is no religion in it." When he had finished, Carey "smilingly" told his dinner companion that he was "at this moment surrounded by members of that Congregation." The "thunderstruck" guest apologized for having "made a most miserable display of illiberal prejudice." Years later they still laughed about the incident. Among the works Carey published were Catholic devotional books and the Catholic (Douay-Rheims) Bible, but his company was primarily known for non-Catholic political and literary works. His public profile outside of St. Augustine's Church was that of a concerned American, actively promoting the non-sectarian Sunday School Society of Philadelphia and relief work during the yellow fever epidemic of 1793. His memoir sought to show, by example, that "with unflinching perseverance and industry" and some timely assistance, a poor immigrant could make a home in America and build a "moderate fortune."[6]

Like Mathew Carey's *Autobiography*, *At the End of the Santa Fe Trail* by Sister Blandina Segale (1851–1941) originated in a request made to the author by the editor of a periodical. Sister Blandina's memoir is a revised version of a journal that she kept for decades so that she could share with another member of the Sisters of Charity, Sister Justina (her biological sister Maria Maddelena), her experiences as a "fit-in-to-any assignment sister"[7] in Colorado and New Mexico from 1872 to 1894. Most orders of women religious kept chronicles, which were rarely seen by those outside of the community. Memoirs written by individual sisters were more unusual; some might consider them an impediment to the selflessness sisters sought to cultivate. Sister Blandina's memoir was something of an anomaly when it was published in the *Santa Clara Magazine* from October 1926 through January 1931, but it was an idea whose time had come. Its popularity led to two book-length versions that appeared in different editions in 1932 and 1948.

At the End of the Santa Fe Trail provides a rare, detailed account of the workings of the Catholic Church on the frontier and the daily life of an immigrant sister engaged in building the fundamental institutions of any local community in the nineteenth century (schools, hospitals, and orphanages), without a budget, and with a mandate to make these institutions self-sustaining. Sister Blandina's often-cited references to her encounters with Billy the Kid, which have focused scholars' attention on inaccuracies in the text, are not the most important parts of the memoir. Her journal captivated readers because it answered questions that few knew enough to ask: how did sisters in the western territories achieve what they did with so few resources and in the face of serious obstacles stemming from their sex, their religion, and their poverty?

Above all, it is a tale of collaboration and improvisation, in which we see Sister Blandina building alliances with other sisters, local priests (especially Jesuits), and a broad circle of friends, including Jewish doctors, Protestant railway executives, law enforcement personnel, cowboys, and Native American and Hispanic working people.

The model of religious life embraced by Sister Blandina and the popularity of her memoir provide insight into the expectations of at least some of her readers, American Catholic women who entered convents in increasingly large numbers during the first half of the twentieth century. Sister Blandina fought tirelessly for social justice, confronting capitalists who sought to exploit the poor in frontier communities. She took risks, and she made practical decisions on site without having to consult her superior back in Cincinnati. She assumed responsibility for her words, decisions, and actions. Her motto was: "Do what you can for others in the position you find yourself. Leave the rest to God."[8]

Mathew Carey and Sister Blandina were Catholic immigrants who distinguished themselves in public service to their adopted land and published memoirs that were considered exemplary, even inspirational. Orestes Brownson (1803–76) produced an early example of a different type of American Catholic life-writing, the conversion narrative. North American Protestant conversion narratives had been published in abundance since the First Great Awakening in the 1730s, but there were virtually no American Catholic prototypes when Brownson's autobiography, *The Convert, or Leaves from My Experience*, appeared in 1857. *The Convert* traces Brownson's long, circuitous spiritual pilgrimage: his boyhood and adolescent attraction to various forms of Protestant Christianity during the age of heightened soul-searching and religious rededication known as the Second Great Awakening (ca. 1800–1830); time spent as a Universalist, then a nondenominational, preacher; ordination as a Unitarian clergyman; involvement in the Transcendentalist movement; and finally, conversion to Catholicism in 1844. Brownson entered the Church just as a massive influx of (primarily Irish and German) Catholic immigrants were changing the face of America and its Catholic community, provoking a strong adverse reaction from the anti-Catholic Native American Party. Brownson's religious experiences differed from those of the immigrant Catholics with whom he worshipped. Nonetheless, as a preacher, lecturer, and public intellectual, he felt called upon to be a defender of the Catholic Church and the spiritual legacy it contained for people of all classes and ethnicities.

The Convert, which combines intellectual biography with Catholic apologetics, became the model for an entire subgenre of Catholic memoirs aimed at showing how arguments for the uniqueness of the Catholic Church have proved persuasive to men (and occasionally women) of intellect and experience. Because he wrote in a time of escalating nativism, and because his own non-Catholic friends tended to be skeptical of his strong defense of Catholic teachings and authority, Brownson took pains to explain that *The Convert* was "no work of fiction," but rather an "honest book." He was especially concerned to show that it was not written under any form of coercion, but instead represented

> the free production of my own mind, the free expression of my own honest convictions as formed by my experience, the inspiration of grace, and the teachings of Catholic faith and theology, and may be taken by my readers as a specimen of that freedom which Catholicity secures to all of her children.

Brownson, a celebrity convert, used his autobiography as an opportunity to address some of the negative stereotypes clinging to the Catholic Church in his time. He admitted that he had not "found the Catholic population perfect," but added that in his thirteen years as a Catholic, he had encountered "a continued succession of agreeable surprises." He had discovered a Catholic community that was "superior to what I expected, more intellectual, more cultivated, more moral, more active, living and energetic."[9]

One way to understand the changes at work within the American Catholic community during the first half of the twentieth century is to turn to the bumper crop of Catholic life-writings published from the late 1940s through the 1950s, but reflecting an earlier experience. This unique historical moment in the immediate wake of the Second World War witnessed the culmination of American Catholic confidence, visibility, mobility and prosperity, a trend already evident by the First World War. The number of readers interested in Catholic narratives sharply increased during these years, in part the long-term result of a decision made at the Third Plenary Council of Baltimore in 1884, when the American Catholic bishops proclaimed that each parish should have its own school. The priority placed upon Catholic education by the clergy and sisters, and by an ambitious Catholic community with fresh memories of the immigrant experience, gave rise to a building boom by midcentury. Newly constructed parochial schools, colleges, convents and seminaries reinforced the sense of Catholic presence in America, as did the increasing visibility of Catholic memoirs being reviewed in Catholic and secular newspapers, magazines, and journals.

We will examine five works from this period, all highly acclaimed by contemporary Catholic reviewers: *The Manner Is Ordinary* (1957) by John LaFarge, S.J.; *Memories of a Catholic Girlhood* (1957) by Mary McCarthy; The *Long Loneliness* (1952) by Dorothy Day; *Color Ebony* (1952) by Helen Caldwell Day; and *The Seven Storey Mountain* (1948) by Thomas Merton. A close reading of these personal narratives suggests that while the changes in Catholic aspirations and visibility after the Second World War appeared dramatic and sudden, they had their roots in developments that were at least several decades old, and teachings that were even older.

John LaFarge, S.J. (1880–1963), wrote his autobiography, *The Manner Is Ordinary* (1957), toward the end of a long career as a Catholic journalist working under various titles in the editorial offices of the Jesuit journal *America* from 1926 until his death. LaFarge's readers find themselves in the presence of a seasoned raconteur who shares stories about his boyhood and adolescence in a Catholic family living among the WASP elite in Newport and Manhattan, his undergraduate years at Harvard, his seminary education at Innsbruck, and his subsequent life as a Jesuit priest. LaFarge's background was out of the ordinary: he was a born Catholic whose convert mother was the great-great granddaughter of Benjamin Franklin. His father, an artist also named John, was frequently absent; his surrogates and his son's mentors included Henry Adams, Theodore Roosevelt, and Henry James. LaFarge spent his Harvard years (1897–1901) trying to build community among the isolated Catholic students with projects such as a clothing drive, the proceeds of which were sent directly to Mrs. Booker T. Washington, wife of the president of the Tuskegee Institute.

Family friends in high places in America and Europe gave LaFarge rare opportunities to see the Catholic Church from the inside and also to explain its policies and teachings to a broad spectrum of non-Catholics on both continents. In *The Manner Is Ordinary*, LaFarge recalls meeting all of the popes from Leo XIII (1878–1903) to Pius XII (1939–58). He recounts how his work as a parish priest on the Maryland shore from 1911 to 1926 led to the establishment on Pentecost Sunday 1934 of the New York Catholic Interracial Council, as well as to many speeches and several book-length treatments of racism and the Church. In 1938, while LaFarge was visiting Italy, Pope Pius XI arranged for a one-on-one meeting with him to discuss the race question. In June 1942, when A. Philip Randolph of the Brotherhood of Sleeping Car Porters organized a massive demonstration at Madison Square Garden, LaFarge was the only white man invited to speak.

LaFarge was at his most prophetic in his treatment of the clear, organic relationships among his interests in race relations, rural poverty, liturgical reform (including liturgical art and music), Catholic education, and the effort to combat the political, social and spiritual effects of Nazi and Communist totalitarianism. A trip to Europe in 1938 to attend the International Eucharistic Congress in Budapest gave him the opportunity to reflect upon the convergence of these apparently disparate questions in his vision and his spirituality. Close to twenty years later, he vividly recalled that at seeing firsthand how Hitler "had successfully managed to sweep away the impressive structure of German Catholic church organizations, I was convinced that the Church, if it was to stand up against organized assaults of our times, must encourage its members to return to a deeper source of collective strength." LaFarge believed that education and liturgical reform constituted the keys that unlocked the resources necessary to fight injustice, racism, and poverty. In response to the accolades from guests at a testimonial dinner for him held at the Waldorf-Astoria in New York in 1952, LaFarge acknowledged that it had hurt him when a colleague once referred to him as "a champion of lost causes," but the way in which he said it signaled to the audience that he knew that the causes so dear to his heart could no longer be dismissed as lost. These causes continue to present challenges for the Church: LaFarge's autobiography provides historical perspective that is critical to a contemporary understanding of American Catholic responsibilities in the areas of race, poverty, and liturgical reform.[10]

If LaFarge's narrative conforms most closely to the model of the memoir, in which we see an individual's life and actions against the backdrop of history, *Memories of a Catholic Girlhood*, published in the same year by Mary McCarthy (1912–1989), is pure confession, full of inner trials and triumphs, carefully preserved in stories that at first seem almost too personal to be shared with the reading public. One can understand why *Memories* elicited a variety of strong reactions when it first appeared in print, just as it does half a century later. Most striking is the author's voice, which combines the precocious Catholic schoolgirl's insistence upon telling the absolute truth with the middle-aged professional writer's profound sense of the ironies inherent in her own narratives. In a review published in the *Saturday Review*, Phyllis McGinley underscored the usefulness of irony in *Memories*: "truth, no matter how plain or unvarnished, is also so multiple-faced that few can see it whole."[11] Between the ages of six and seventeen, McCarthy experienced so many different facets of the American Catholic Church that her images of it become kaleidoscopic.

Her earliest impressions, gleaned from her convert mother and indulgent invalid father, left her with a strong belief that it was "a special treat to be a Catholic, the crowning treat and privilege." Her Grandmother McCarthy, the matriarch of a prosperous Catholic family in Minneapolis, embraced a "blood-curdling" Catholicism that arose out of competition, mutual suspicion, and sometimes contempt between Catholics and Protestants, feelings intensified in an age of escalating immigration. For Grandfather McCarthy, a successful Catholic businessman, faith centered upon possible cures for his rheumatism in pilgrimages to the shrine of St. Anne de Beaupré. At her parochial school, St. Stephen's, in Minneapolis, McCarthy and many of her classmates thrived in the "competitive atmosphere" promoted by the sisters who taught them. She sought to excel in every way possible: academic work, sports and devotion: "I felt my religion very intensely and longed to serve God better than anyone else. This, I thought, was what He asked of me."

In 1923, when her Protestant grandfather brought her back to Seattle and enrolled her in an exclusive Sacred Heart convent school at Forest

Ridge, McCarthy encountered yet another face of the Church, which required that she, too, present another face and jettison the one that had worked so well at St. Stephen's. At Forest Ridge, the nuns cultivated the girls like exotic flowers so that their intellectual gifts and spiritual discipline were carefully balanced and students prepared for the various responsibilities awaiting them. *Memories* reaches a crescendo in McCarthy's account of her loss of faith in a carefully prepared dispute with a Jesuit chaplain at Forest Ridge, but some of McCarthy's most passionate writing is reserved for her detailed explanation of why she is "not sorry to have been a Catholic," replete with cherished details of her life before she left the Church in her early teens. Here, the middle-aged McCarthy, who elsewhere proudly proclaimed herself a lapsed Catholic, describes a profoundly Catholic way of being in the world ("a straining against reality, a rebellious nonconformity") not confined to the institutional Church but available even to those who feel they must move beyond it.[12] McCarthy broke new ground in articulating a post-Catholic consciousness that growing numbers of born Catholics were to embrace in subsequent decades. Although she never intended her memories to be therapeutic for others—and would have recoiled at the thought—her narrative, especially her fully developed sense of the ironies of Catholic life, has provided respite for other casualties of the Church's growing pains and served as a model for future female Catholic memoirs.

Dorothy Day (1897–1980) begins her autobiography, *The Long Loneliness* (1952), by reflecting upon the visceral experience of going to confession: the sights, sounds, smells, and feel of the many confessionals she has known. She concedes that "going to confession is hard. Writing a book is hard, because you are 'giving yourself away.'" She openly acknowledges her limitations, and this confession becomes a prayer: "I can only write of myself, what I know of myself, and I pray with St. Augustine, 'Lord, that I may know myself, in order to know Thee.'" Like many authors of conversion narratives, she divides her life into two parts, before and after, but in the telling we see that the reality was more complex: twenty-five years spent "floundering," then her first steps toward conversion, and finally, over five years later, the new life that conversion is supposed to bring.

The years of floundering and restlessness were also hardworking and productive, years of commitment and sacrifice, spent at the University of Illinois, in the New York editorial offices of *The Masses* and *Call*, and in prison after the Washington women's suffrage march (1917) and the raid on the IWW headquarters in Chicago (1923). They were busy, intermittently happy, years, punctuated by intense conversations and celebrations in Greenwich Village bars, the publication of a novel, *The Eleventh Virgin*, in 1924 (and talk of a movie contract), serious relationships, and finally, the birth of a baby, Tamar Teresa, in 1926. Day insists that she "came to know God" only after she had experienced "a whole love, both physical and spiritual." Day's decision to have Tamar baptized came easily, an outgrowth of her newly discovered love of God. Her own road to baptism was more difficult and protracted.

The Long Loneliness is not an idealized, or even conventional, conversion narrative. Day's reception of the sacraments brought her "no particular joy"; she had to leave her two "loves" behind: her common-law husband, Tamar's father, Forster Batterham, who refused to stay with her if she converted, and her friends on the political Left, whose beliefs and affiliations were roundly condemned by the Church (and vice versa). In December 1932 she was sent by *Commonweal* to cover a Communist hunger march in Washington, D.C. Watching the demonstration clarified what had been frustrating her about her life since her conversion. She compared her "summer of quiet reading and prayer," in all of its "self-absorption," with the efforts of Communists, "in their struggle, not for themselves but for others."[13]

The final section of *The Long Loneliness* describes Day's collaboration with the French peasant and social reformer, Peter Maurin, and how in May 1933 they launched the *Catholic Worker*, a newspaper dedicated to spreading the radical ideas within the Catholic tradition in an American society that was thoroughly unfamiliar with them. The newspaper, and the Catholic Worker Houses of Hospitality, where volunteers lived in solidarity with the poor, suggested an alternative Catholic vision and made it possible for volunteers (priests, sisters, and substantial numbers of Catholic college students) to combine their faith with strenuous work and study aimed at promoting social justice. For decades *The Long Loneliness* has propagated this vision for a diverse readership. In 1983, three years after Day's death, Dale Vree, who had participated in the

Berkeley Free Speech Movement in the mid-1960s and later moved to East Germany because of his Marxist-Leninist sympathies, recalls how Day's life and her memoir had gradually transformed his consciousness:

> Too many of us start out with a strong faith, which leads into social action, which then results in an erosion of that faith and a co-optation by secular forces. But Dorothy Day's life is a monument to the truth that this need not—and must not—be so. Social action and basic faith commitment are not in a zero-sum relationship. Consequently, Dorothy Day's story is not a period piece; rather, it is a beacon in the dark.[14]

In 1951, the year before the publication of *The Long Loneliness*, another Catholic Worker memoir appeared in print: *Color Ebony*, written by Helen Caldwell Day (1926–), an African American convert who had begun working in the Mott Street House of Hospitality in 1947. The author was only twenty-six, but she had a compelling story to tell: a peripatetic Southern girlhood as a child of divorce and as the daughter of a professor at Bishop College, a "Negro college" in Marshall, Texas; the move north in 1945 to study at the Harlem Hospital School of Nursing; conversion to Catholicism in the mid-1940s during nursing school; a brief, unhappy marriage to a navy man, George Day, and the birth of a son, who contracted polio; her own struggle with tuberculosis at a sanatorium in New York State; and finally, a move back south to Memphis, where she established the Blessed Martin Catholic Worker House in 1951. *Color Ebony* and its sequel, *Not Without Tears*, show how the Catholic Workers provided an island of hope for Day, as she sought to alleviate the effects of racism in the lives of poor blacks and dared to name the racism in her newfound church. In an especially powerful passage, she describes her response to a priest in Holly Springs, Mississippi, who insisted that he was being "prudent" in segregating his parish, "trying to help the Negro and keep down racial friction."

> The only thing he forgot was that that kind of prudence has no place in the Mystical Body of Christ, in the life of the Church. He forgot that the Church is *One*, Holy and Universal, and that the Mass is for all, so that no baptized person can be lawfully forbidden to hear and offer it, to satisfy the prejudices of a few, or of a majority.[15]

The Seven Storey Mountain is a conversion narrative written by Thomas Merton (1915–68), a brilliant, worldly, restless young man with a cosmopolitan past and literary ambitions who entered the Trappist Monastery of Our Lady of Gethsemane in Kentucky on December 10, 1941, three days after the bombing of Pearl Harbor. Toward the end of the book, Merton describes his entry into the cloister for the first time, accompanied by two fellow postulants: "We handed over our fountain pens and wristwatches and our loose cash to the Treasurer, and signed documents promising that if we left the monastery we would not sue the monks for back wages for our hours of manual labor."[16] Apparently handing over the pen was strictly symbolic: Merton, who had already been working in a variety of genres, including poetry, novels, criticism, and even "anti-autobiography,"[17] never stopped being a writer. His first volume, *Thirty Poems*, half of which were written in the monastery, was published in 1944. During the next two years, he produced the initial draft of *Seven Storey Mountain*, along with many other poems and articles, all of which were first scrutinized by Trappist censors. *Seven Storey Mountain* appeared in print in 1948, with blurbs from Evelyn Waugh, Clare Booth Luce, Graham Greene, and Bishop Fulton Sheen on the dust jacket. Within a year it had sold more than 600,000 copies in hardcover; millions more copies in many editions have been sold since.

Merton explains that the Trappists had not always encouraged monks to write; he had entered at a special moment in the history of the order, a time of growth and experimentation within the American Trappists, when their houses were crowded and new daughter communities were being launched. (The popularity of his memoir added, at least temporarily, to the growth and overcrowding.) It was also a transitional moment in the life of the American Catholic Church. Merton's own story and the way he told it—sometimes the romantic, sometimes the smart-aleck, sometimes the overly reverent convert, writing under the towering influence of Augustine's *Confessions*—resonated with the postwar American Catholic reading public. Soon Merton came to see the book as a piece of literary and spiritual juvenilia, his own penance to endure, but American Catholics would not forget the book that helped them to envision a new way of being Catholic, something that bridged the gap between the theology and popular culture of the High Middle Ages and that of the late 1940s in America. Historian Mark

Massa aptly describes this complex (and unintended) feat: "Merton *revealed* American Catholicism to itself, articulating 'what we may sense but cannot say,' leading the Catholic community to a future with new possibilities."[18]

For all of its resonance with Augustine's *Confessions* and Benedictine monastic traditions that appeared distinctly—even refreshingly—alien within the American landscape, Merton's *Seven Storey Mountain* constituted a new kind of Catholic memoir; it raised expectations for a Catholic renewal movement, whose shape and possibilities remained enticingly shrouded from view. Just over a decade later, on January 25, 1959, the recently consecrated Pope John XXIII revealed his intention to call the Second Vatican Council (1962–65), which set in motion several years of wide-ranging, unprecedented, open-ended conversations within the Church in Rome and around the globe. These conversations were just as important to the future of the Church as the thick tome of formal documents produced by the Council. Two very different memoirs, both published by Doubleday in 1972, bear witness to the changing expectations and expanding conversations within the American Catholic Church in the wake of the Council: *Bare Ruined Choirs*, by Garry Wills (1934–), and *Private Faces/Public Places*, by Abigail McCarthy (1915–2001).

Readers saw that they were in for a new kind of Catholic life-writing even before they turned to the introduction to *Bare Ruined Choirs*. The subtitle, "Doubt, Prophecy, and Radical Religion," marked this Catholic memoir as entirely new terrain, a narrative synchronized with the unrest within American culture in ways that were startling and provocative. The dust-jacket photo of Wills, shirtsleeves rolled up, sporting stylish sideburns, is credited to *Playboy*, where one of the chapters, originally entitled "Sex and the Single Priest," had first appeared. *Bare Ruined Choirs* is a perfect example of the hybrid nature of autobiography underscored by Jay Parini: it is a deeply personal narrative that captures a liminal moment in the lives of Wills's generation of American Catholics and assorted fellow travelers. With empathy and historical seriousness that is all the more impressive because it is being applied to the confusions and pain of the present moment and very recent past, Wills depicts the emotional and spiritual roller coaster ride of the Catholic liberals between the Council and the early 1970s. He starts with Norman Podhoretz's prediction that the decade would be American Catholics' turn to "make it," and he sifts through some of the contradictory evidence: "President Nixon was ingratiating himself with the Knights of Columbus, and promised aid to parochial schools—just as those schools were closing, nuns leaving them, orthodox parents objecting to things taught in them." He concludes: "The Catholics' hour had come, though they did not seem to know it; had come, too late, just as their church was disintegrating."

There is a sense in which the entire volume is a memoir, a narrative of Wills's travels through the strange country inhabited by post–Vatican II Catholics in the early 1970s, with special emphasis upon points of intersection between religious elation and confusion and their secular counterparts. The first chapter, "Memories of a Catholic Boyhood," a version of which had appeared in *Esquire* in 1971, has long enjoyed a special status as a stand-alone memoir, with its own niche in the canon of American Catholic life-writings. The title hearkens to Mary McCarthy's in important and complex ways. Like McCarthy, Wills takes great pleasure in explaining the nuance of Catholic difference in the Church before the Council, and describes a communal version of McCarthy's private sense of loss at leaving the sanctuary provided by the pre–Vatican II Catholic Church. But in the place of McCarthy's personal confession, Wills provides us with the memoir of a generation. "To recover a world," Wills insists, "you must recreate what childhood was like in that world."

This is the agenda in "Memories of a Catholic Boyhood," narrated, hauntingly, in the first person plural. "We grew up different," he begins. "There were some places we went, and others did not—into the confessional box, for instance. There were also places we never went, though others could—we were told, from youth, to stay out of non-Catholic churches." Wills revels in the details of his Catholic boyhood, knowing they would mean very little to Catholic boys of the present day, and conveys the feelings that came (and went) with the now abandoned rituals he describes. He recalls that, as a boy, and an altar server, he had learned to speak "a different language from the rest of men," something extending beyond the Latin of the Mass and into the realm of scholastic theological jargon. It was empowering on a very deep level: "To know the terms was to know the thing, to solve the problem." And it left his boyish self with a certainty: "the real was what always was: it was eternal, unchangeable, like the church."

Building upon the meticulously detailed and evocative memoir in the first chapter, Wills shows, in subsequent chapters, what happens when one travels through the Church of the early 1970s, armed with the premises gleaned from his Catholic boyhood. By the end of the book, one is ready for his parting shot:

> The path to one's buried self runs through the unearthing of one's corporate past, however that has (like all our private pasts) been betrayed, its vision lost, its call unheeded. The best things in the church, as in a nation, or in individuals, are hidden and partially disowned, the vital impulse buried under all our cowardly misuses of it. . . . Life's streams lie far down, for us, below the surface of our lives—where we must look for them. It is time to join the underground.[19]

Abigail McCarthy's *Private Faces/Public Places* speaks from the same pivotal moment in American Catholic history and conveys a parallel sense of loss. On one level it is the story of a Catholic marriage—between the author and Minnesota senator and 1968 presidential hopeful Eugene McCarthy—written in the immediate wake of their separation in 1969 after twenty-four years together. This story is important in itself, because it helps readers to understand how a lay couple with a certain kind of Catholic education, including undergraduate degrees from (and some teaching experience at) the College of St. Catherine's and St. John's University in Minnesota in the late 1930s and early 1940s, embraced currents of Catholic Church renewal during the decades leading up to the Second Vatican Council. McCarthy was teaching high school German and English in Mandan, North Dakota, immediately after her college graduation in 1936, when she first became interested in the liturgical movement and its connection with the vision of human solidarity inherent in the doctrine of the Mystical Body of Christ. She spent long hours in lively conversation with her parish priest, Father Hildebrand Eickoff, a German Benedictine with ties to

St. John's Abbey, in which they discussed not only liturgical renewal but also the latest works in Catholic history and biography.

Abigail McCarthy's memoir parallels Mary McCarthy's when she explains how, in her friendship with Father Hildebrand and later her marriage, she learned to make the transition between a variety of alternate Catholic worlds. In conversations with Father Hildebrand, she first learned to negotiate the chasm between St. John's and her alma mater, the College of St. Catherine, whose successful accreditation, Phi Beta Kappa chapter, and genuine academic seriousness elicited "sly male ragging" in the prefect's rooms frequented by Eugene McCarthy when he was a teacher at St. John's. Later, after her marriage, she would briefly enter another distinctive Catholic world, the utopian Catholic Rural Life movement, which established small farm communities in the hopes of strengthening faith and marital love against the onslaughts of an increasingly secular America. She would encounter still other Catholic worlds, each with its own challenges, which became occasions for growth as a person and in her faith. She recalls a moment in the late 1940s, when the family lived in faculty housing (converted barracks) at St. Thomas College in St. Paul. A European professor remarked upon the abundance of young Catholic faculty children and suggested that Europeans did not adopt as uncritical a view of magisterial teachings on birth control as American Catholics apparently did. Looking back upon this conversation, Abigail McCarthy recalls how shocking it was for her to hear a teacher of natural law at a Catholic college question Vatican pronouncements on contraception at a time when "one's stand on birth control was almost the touchstone of one's Catholicity."

Private Faces/Public Places is full of incidents like this one, which illuminate moments when the author's consciousness changed and new possibilities opened up. There is an undercurrent of loss, especially in the section on the breakdown of the marriage at the center of the narrative, but more often, the reflections on change in the Church strike a positive note. McCarthy recalls how wholeheartedly professors and students at her college embraced the "Catholic Renaissance" in the late 1930s and early 1940s. She shares how it *felt* to be a Catholic college student in those heady days: "To be a Catholic no longer meant that one kept one's religion in one mental compartment, one's secular knowledge in another. . . . To be a Catholic now meant that one was part of a worldwide community which shared a splendid heritage of arts and letters and in which tremendous intellectual effort was being put into the restructuring of human society to cope with modern evils."

One of the most powerful passages in the memoir recounts an extremely private moment of recognition in the early 1940s: the author's discovery of an entirely new dimension of existence while studying for her M.A. in literature. McCarthy was reading a borrowed copy of the *Autobiography of St. Teresa*, "smuggled out of some seminary library" by a graduate school acquaintance at a time when mystical writings were not usually assigned readings at Catholic colleges or even graduate schools. (For her readers in the early 1970s, McCarthy explains that the personal narratives of the mystics had been considered dangerous reading, only to be pursued "under guidance." Historian Christopher Dawson, who was especially respected in Catholic circles at mid-century, treated mystical writings as volatile, a kind of "dammed-up energy" produced during decadent eras when "religion was excluded from the mainstream of history.") Abigail McCarthy remembers exactly where she was ("that narrow little room at Mrs. McClure's") and precisely how she felt ("shaken and fascinated") when she first opened the *Autobiography*. She explains: "I knew that one met and experienced God in prayer and in the sacraments, but that there could be this naked, blinding experience of the Divine was frightening."[20] Writing her memoir, she took care to describe this private encounter alongside the public ones in Washington, Minnesota, and in Rome during the Second Vatican Council. Taken together, both kinds of encounter flesh out what it meant to be an American Catholic woman in the pivotal years between the Depression and the early 1970s.

Late-Twentieth-Century Reflections

One form of life-writing that emerged in the wake of the Second Vatican Council explores the relationship between individual life experience and *being* Catholic. Before the Council, it was most often converts who wrote "Why I Am a Catholic" books, with a strongly apologetical purpose. Brownson's *The Convert* is a classic prototype of this sort of memoir in the North American setting. In the postconciliar era, when public disputes about the future direction and policies of the Church were accompanied by individual soul-searching concerning the meaning and expressions of Catholic identity, readers were anxious to hear, and some authors willing to explain, why, and on what terms, they *remained* Catholic. At the same time, following in the tradition of Mary McCarthy, others addressed why, and under what conditions, they had decided to leave the Church or some specific enclave within it. What follows is by no means exhaustive but intends to show how this kind of writing evolved in the decades following the Council, and how it remains alive, proliferating and mutating in the twenty-first century.

Peter Occhiogrosso's *Once a Catholic* (1987) suggests what happens to the "Why I Am a Catholic" book in the 1980s: the scope is enlarged to include practicing and lapsed Catholics, and the mix is intended to remind readers of the intellectual and cultural diversity within the American Catholic community. The "Introit" begins with a quotation from Robert Hoyt, founding editor of the *National Catholic Reporter*: "I think it has always been the case that everyone defined Catholicism for himself or herself, and there are millions and billions of Catholicisms running around embodied that don't fit the standard operating definition."[21]

Once a Catholic, based upon the author's extensive interviews with twenty-six well-known Catholics and ex-Catholics—writers, activists, entertainers and artists—seeks to explore the ways in which Catholic education, training, and piety are permanently inscribed upon those who have been raised in the faith, regardless of the disparate paths they choose in later life. The interviews, skillfully edited by Occhiogrosso, clarify what Catholic identity means to a broad spectrum of post–Vatican II public figures ranging from Sister Joan Chittister to Frank Zappa. They also allow us to listen in on an impassioned conversation underway among American Catholics in the immediate wake of the Council, as they debated issues ranging from ritual and theology to celibacy and abortion.

Occhiogrosso's interviews raise, and partially answer, one question asked with increasing urgency from the late 1960s onward: now that they worshipped in English, ate meat on Fridays, and decided for themselves whether to use birth control, were Catholics *really* that different from other Americans? Garry Wills addressed the question by examining his Catholic boyhood. In 1972, the year *Bare Ruined Choirs* was published, a diverse group of Catholic scholars, including Gregory Baum, Rosemary Ruether, David O'Brien, Charles Curran, Monika Hellwig, and Richard McBrien, attended a summer conference where they shared papers that explored the connections between their life stories and what Baum chose to call their "styles of thought." Baum reflects upon the cumulative impact of the conference presentations, which taught the participants "that much more is hidden in our lives than we at first realize. We have to be taught to take our own experience seriously." The conference participants had discovered how reflection upon their own pilgrimages represented "a way to self-knowledge, and beyond that, an entry into wisdom." Nonetheless, Baum observed, "while the way we think is determined by biography, our thoughts remain free, which here means dependent on the unaccountable moments when we are being addressed by God's word."[22]

Almost thirty years later, in March 2001, a group of historians who "were born into Catholic families and thus had been 'touched by Catholicism'" met at Cornell University with a parallel agenda in mind. In his introduction to a collection of essays produced by this group, Nick Salvatore, one of the organizers, explained his desire to explore how "the consciousness developed in the home" affected the historical vision of those who were raised as Catholics, regardless of whether they remained practicing Catholics.[23] This collection illustrates how effectively even specialized and specifically focused life-writings can evoke the many different worlds that Catholic writers call *home*. It also reminds us that one of the most important preoccupations of Catholic life-writings in the late twentieth century is the Catholic family and the distinctive—but by no means monolithic—experience of Catholic boyhood and girlhood.

Garry Wills showed us his boyhood in meticulous detail, but his family experience remains shrouded from view. Other late-twentieth-century male Catholic memoirs pay more attention to family dynamics. In *Frank and Maisie* (1985), Wilfrid Sheed, son of Maisie Ward and Frank Sheed, Catholic publishers and street preachers, confesses that "because their Catholic publishing seemed almost as bizarre as their

Catholic tub-thumping," he embraced "the delicate pleasures of outsiderness at an early age." Writing in middle age, he asserts: "Religion as such strikes me as a desperate attempt on the part of mankind to bore itself to death in expiation of some forgotten excitement." But he proceeds to insist that his family life (which by any external standard can only be said to have been saturated with Catholicism) "was a whole life and a merry one. . . . It was simply the thing we did." In *Days of Obligation* (1992), Richard Rodriguez speaks of the ways in which his parents' two very different stories of emigration from Mexico in the 1920s become the foundation for his hyphenated identity and politics, especially his own internalized (and eventually published) arguments with Mexican Catholicism. This does not mean that he makes any attempt to jettison his connection to the Church. Everyday events constantly remind him how Catholic he is; for example, contemplating a mirror his decorator had bought from the estate sale of a recent AIDS casualty, his mind instinctively turns to Augustine's meditation on evil. James Carroll's *An American Requiem* (1996) represents a classic in this subgenre, which Sheed's subtitle names a "memoir with parents." In early manhood, Carroll set himself the challenge to be true to his two selves. One was the "Outstanding Air Force ROTC Cadet" from Georgetown, poised to follow in the footsteps of his military father, whose "belief in the world of hierarchy was total," and "defending it was his one real passion, his vocational commitment, and his religious duty." The other self was a Vietnam War protester, tending toward the priesthood and the life of a writer. At the Paulist novitiate at Mount Paul, he recognized his story, and his inner dividedness, in Augustine's self-questioning in the *Confessions*: "Where could my heart flee from my heart?" He embraced the answer implicit in Augustine's text: "instead of escape, try expression."[24]

Catholic women's memoirs written during the same period describe departures from the Church in young womanhood, which would be reversed in middle age. Patricia Hampl, whose birth in 1946 places her in the vanguard of Catholic baby boomers, shares a familiar scenario in a chapter of her memoir *I Could Tell You Stories* (1999) entitled "The Mayflower Moment: Reading Whitman During the Vietnam War." She refers to her family "enacting the classic Vietnam-era battles and arguments, ornamented in our own baroque Catholic way where hierarchy was the whole point." During this tumultuous era, her Sunday morning declaration to her father that she "wasn't going to Mass anymore, ever" was practically a punctuation mark, rather than a separate sentence of its own. It was about the war, and about the "lozenge of personal revolution" (the Pill) that she ("an earnest communicant") had ingested with tea, chocolate cake, and a Reuben sandwich at Brother's Delicatessen in downtown Minneapolis. In another memoir, *Virgin Time*, she describes her protracted pilgrimage back into the Church, but on her own terms.[25]

Mary Gordon's memoir *The Shadow Man* provides another version of the female Catholic baby boomer's departure from the Church. Gordon, like Hampl, left because she needed a freedom of expression (sexual, political, and intellectual) that was unavailable to young Catholic women in the late 1960s. For Gordon, the journey back into the Church required that she uncover the secrets that her father, who died when she was seven, left behind when he had entered the Church in 1937. It also required that she rebury him, literally and metaphorically. Her account of preparing the service provides us with a rare glimpse of what the return of faith actually looks and feels like. A priest friend who agreed to officiate at the reburial service helped her select the prayers from the *Modern Order of Ritual* and its older Latin predecessor. Gordon reflects upon what the rituals mean to her:

> There is no way that the words I have chosen can be of use without the structure or the semblance of belief. I don't know what I believe about the fate of the life these bones represent. But the form of belief seems deeply precious, irreplaceable. The form can contain more than most forms, and is therefore conducive to more beauty, more truthfulness.

Gordon examines her conscience ("Is this a hateful, a cowardly, hedging of the bets?") and ends with an affirmation of faith: "Whatever it is, I will not give up these forms, these words."[26]

Looking Ahead

This chapter represents one small step, a recommendation that the still evolving field of Catholic Studies take memoirs seriously. Any field that is grounded in historical and literary studies must come to recognize the importance of life-writings, for these provide the details and texture of life and linger over aspects of life that official records and histories based upon them neglect entirely. Those interested in lived religion in the past must pay special attention to autobiographical works because they are the most immediate points of contact with it. Artifacts are evocative, but there is no substitute for recollections that pin down their specific meaning in the life of an individual. We must be clear: such memories are not infallible or uninflected. They are not videos of the past. Still, they are precious for all that they tell us about the subjects' ways of being in their world. Even the choice of words or structure can point readers back to the lived experience and provide us with the right questions to ask about it.

All of these basic arguments concerning the value of life-writings apply to secular memoirs as well as Catholic ones, but there are also specific reasons why autobiographical writings are of fundamental importance to Catholic Studies, whose emergence coincided historically with the public recognition of the many silenced voices in the Church, past and present.[27] The close reading of Catholic life-writings does more than provide texture and detail for our historical renderings of the Catholic Church. It is also itself an act of re-creation (or expiation) for the silences that the narratives begin to fill. In a meditation on vocation toward the beginning of *An American Requiem*, James Carroll insists that "the story is what saves us."[28] One does not need Garry Wills's pre–Vatican II Catholic education to know what "the story" is; the subtext of every Catholic memoir is that our stories and "the story" are forever in dialogue.

2 The Catholic Intellectual Tradition

A Classification and a Calling

MARY ELLEN O'DONNELL

"Just as we reject the principle of divorcing faith and works, so we reject the principle and the practice of divorcing the life of faith and the life of study," wrote Father Leo Ward of the University of Notre Dame in 1961.[1] Describing the ideal for the Catholic school, Ward's rejection invites reflection on Catholic intellectual life. However, this comment, which might galvanize Catholic professors who perceive themselves as exemplars of the ideal, might also solicit quite a different reaction from those outside the professionally academic arena. The public perception of Catholicism does not always incline toward a scholastic tradition. Thomas Landy writes, "To many Americans, a 'Catholic intellectual' is regarded at least as an enigma, if not a full-fledged oxymoron. Numerous critics have asserted that 'real' Catholics are not able to think independently, and are thus not capable of being legitimate intellectuals."[2] For some, the Catholic intellectual tradition is the most engaging aspect of the religious heritage, boasting such famed thinkers as Augustine and Thomas Aquinas. For others, the combination of "Catholic" and "intellectual" yields little more than a paradox. This spectrum of possible assumptions regarding the concept of "the Catholic intellectual tradition"—from its enduring and characterizing capacity to its apparent impossibility—exemplifies the complicated nature of my subject. Depending on whom you ask both inside and outside the faith, the Catholic intellectual tradition can seem a vital and lasting part of this religion or a nonsensical contradiction of terms.

Is there Catholic intellectualism? Is it a religious practice? How does intellectual work function within ecclesiastical structures? My interrogation of the Catholic intellectual tradition relies on a historiographical approach to scholarship that addresses this tradition as a categorical problematic. Numerous volumes have been written attempting to define the Catholic intellectual tradition, creating competing views of its position and merits within a broader religious tradition. This classificatory literature offers a useful evidentiary source for the multifaceted character of the Catholic intellectual tradition and its contemporary observers.

My essay begins with a brief consideration of reasons for the divergence of opinion on the concept itself among contemporary individuals. How might the same descriptor provide a vocational call for some and cause for scoffing by others? Perhaps I should not proceed without the following disclaimer: I firmly espouse the notion of the Catholic intellectual tradition and recognize it as a dynamic, living and rich heritage that persists and evolves. Convinced of and committed to this aspect of Catholicism, I first turn to those who challenge it in order to examine how anyone might designate "Catholic" and "intellectual" as mutually exclusive. I realize that any person connected to such bastions of Catholic education as the Catholic University of America, the University of Notre Dame, or Fordham University would deem this preposterous. With much of the Catholic intellectual tradition inarguably entrusted to them to be passed on, these institutions take seriously the tradition's past and, more pressing, its future.

Still, despite the success and reputation of these academies, the terms "Catholic" and "intellectual" are discretely separated and opposed by many. With this contention acknowledged and briefly explored, I will move to consider the limitations of this response to the Catholic intellectual tradition and shift the focus to the tradition's entrenched history, vibrant present, and promising future. I will first address the complicated nature of the label "tradition" in this context and some motives for constructing this rhetorical category. I will then examine the multiple dimensions of this assembled "tradition." How is it defined? Who plays a role in it? What are the key people and events that scholars have highlighted for its development? How does it take shape today? I conclude with a look at the challenges the Catholic intellectual tradition faces and the directions it might pursue in the future.

Defining the Catholic Intellectual

In *Catholic Intellectual Life in America* (1985), Margaret Mary Reher emphasizes a crucial factor in contemporary challenges to the concept of the Catholic intellectual: the Enlightenment. This eighteenth century movement that began in Europe and was adopted in North America has defined the Western conception of the intellect.[3] She writes, "The rallying cry of the Enlightenment was 'Have the courage to use your own understanding.' This extended into the area of religion. Not doubt but dogma became the intellect's most dreaded foe."[4] Indeed, a religious institution with a clearly denoted hierarchy and source of authority could be perceived as limiting one's ability to use her own reason according to Enlightenment ideals. The message of the Enlightenment, with its focus on the individual's rational capacity, brought into question how a person might fully embrace the Catholic Church and yet simultaneously trust his own understanding, even if it might conflict with the answers that came from "above." Certainly, the authority of the Church and its hold on doctrine are usually the first sources for challenging the Catholic intellectual tradition. In *Language, Religion, Knowledge*, James Turner writes, "In the past century we have grown used to thinking of faith and knowledge as mutually exclusive, almost contradictory, even hostile. So we fear that, in the end, no church would really release its universities from the fetters of doctrine to pursue knowledge. At the back of our minds we suspect that a Catholic university cannot really disentangle itself from the heavy hand of ecclesial authority—the long, legendary shadow of the Inquisition—without disengaging itself with Catholicism."[5] To be a Catholic intellectual might seem, to some, a contradiction because of this alleged competition between one's ability to think on her own and still be a fully faithful member of the Church. The defining element of a questioning and expansive nature among intellectuals could, according to some, undermine the distinct and unchanging structure that, for them, has characterized the Catholic Church.

These disparate allegiances—the individual pursuit of the enlightened mind and full sacramental membership in an institutional church—were pitted against each other by secular thinkers primarily to distinguish an emerging epistemology from an existing theology. In defining the parameters for legitimate knowledge, influential cultural figures made certain God, the idea of God and organizations based on such a notion, would remain well outside endeavors related to epistemology. This discourse, then, made the Catholic life ostensibly divorced from what was taking hold as the perceived genuine participation in the life of the mind.

The other challenge to the concept of the Catholic intellectual tradition pertains not to organizational structure but rather to religious practice. Margaret C. Jacob describes another result of this era upon the attitude toward religion: "The religiosity of the educated began to seem distant from the public displays, processions, and bell ringing of an earlier age and from the ornate Catholicism practiced at the time in southern Europe and transmitted to Latin America by the Spanish and Portuguese. Religion in general was becoming more private than public, more individual than collective, and thoughts rather than ornate ceremonies began to define the believer."[6] Indeed, powerful Enlightenment thinkers did find a way to be religious, though their religion took a distinct form. In rather general terms, such religiosity precluded the materiality and ceremony so closely associated with Catholic practice and adopted a more cerebral quality.[7] Minds, rather than bodies, became the primary agents in religious experience. This observable shift has affected the way many today respond to religious practice. While scholars in the last few decades have been working to uncover the depth and richness of material culture in religion, for the lay (particularly secular) observer, any kind of attention to objects and artifacts might hint at superstition and naïveté among practitioners. The attention Catholics pay to the physical world in the sacraments and through sacramentals has contributed to the perception that they might not meet criteria to be considered intellectuals.

The problem with these challenges, of course, is the false dichotomies they draw and the exaggerated assumptions they impose. Indeed, the Catholic Church functions as an institution with a hierarchical structure and levels of authority. However, that does not mean that its members are mindless robots whose every thought and action are preemptively assigned. This global religious tradition with its millennia of history boasts a wide range of thinkers who certainly did not always agree, and who pondered the strong and complicated connections between faith and reason. Contributions by Catholics in philosophy, theology, literature, science, and the arts can hardly be disputed. Furthermore, most thinkers today would not last long by denying the importance of their physical conditions in this good postmodern world.

Material circumstances and all that they offer and prohibit occupy a secure place in contemporary scholarship. While the Enlightenment's criteria for an intellectual might still have a stronghold on public opinion in the West, the movement never quite achieved its goal of excising the body from the human experience, even one invested in reason. So how could anyone perpetuate these false dichotomies and exaggerated assumptions to dispute the concept of the Catholic intellectual?

One possibility is the very functioning of the university and its distinct disciplines. It has effectively perpetuated a perceived split between Catholic faith and intellectual life. James Heft helpfully explains this phenomenon when he writes, "In the academy today, these two dimensions—religious faith and scholarship—often occupy two different compartments, hermetically sealed off from each other, so as to prevent the alleged distortion of objective scholarship by subjective faith."[8] With the university's intentional separation of faith from scholarship, one must crisscross boundaries to be both a believing practitioner and an intellectual. Once again, these constructed boundaries have shaped the perception that a person can only exist on one side or the other of a posited "intellectual" divide.

The intensive categorization and criteria for the intellectual that developed out of Enlightenment discourse and these resulting boundaries ultimately created the need for a consideration of a separately designated Catholic intellectual tradition. In a way, the assembled boundaries have led to the need for the very concept of a Catholic intellectual tradition. Richard Liddy articulates the problem. He writes, "A curious aspect about the phrase 'the Catholic intellectual tradition' is the possible implication that there could be any kind of genuine Catholic tradition other than an intellectual one."[9] His remark raises this question: What is the need for rhetorically carving out one part of the tradition and labeling it intellectual? Perhaps it does create a challenging quandary for determining what fits within and what falls outside this category, but its establishment seems to offer a clear rebuke to any suggestion that Catholics do not fit the developing model of the intellectual. By recognizing their own intellectual tradition, Catholics can acknowledge the dominating Enlightenment standards and demonstrate that their own past and present provide a rival for that ideal type.

So how have Catholics constructed this category? It is important first to notice the potential pitfalls identified in the literature about the Catholic intellectual tradition. Richard Liddy explains, "The problem with our ordinary thinking about the Catholic intellectual tradition . . . is that we tend to think of it, as we tend to think of all tradition, as just about the past."[10] Liddy's observation emphasizes the natural tendency to consider tradition by looking backward. He steers us away from the temptation to define the Catholic intellectual tradition by listing names or citing texts. Such a list would inevitably suggest that the tradition itself is dead. Monica Hellwig similarly warns that this tradition "cannot be reduced to a treasury of deposits from the past."[11] So, if it is not merely a history of thinkers and a collection of their writings, to what does the Catholic intellectual tradition refer? These two scholars have responses. Liddy notes, "The point of any authentic tradition is to change us in the present so that we can articulate the authentic meanings of the tradition in the future. If we read Augustine or Aquinas, and we are not changed so that we think or act differently, then we water down their meaning. We reduce them to our own narrow horizon."[12] Hellwig similarly asserts, "Perhaps the most fruitful way of thinking about the Catholic intellectual tradition is in terms of two aspects: the classic treasures to be cherished, studied, and handed on; and the way of doing things that is the outcome of centuries of experience, prayer, action and critical reflection."[13] The Catholic intellectual tradition does not simply provide an inheritance of wisdom, but rather it calls people to think and act differently.

But just *what* is it? Unmistakably, both Liddy and Hellwig suggest a kind of forward-moving process when it comes to this tradition, but they and their fellow scholars of Catholic intellectualism also fully acknowledge and appreciate a collection of individuals and an historical body of work that launched (and has sustained) this process. To understand the construction, development and future of the Catholic intellectual tradition, then, one must identify the defining characteristics that make works and people consistently worthy of this category in scholarship about the topic. A survey of the emerging canon indicates the following criteria for regular inclusion in the Catholic intellectual tradition: (1) membership in the Church and a commitment to Catholicism as an institutional space and (2) a deliberate use of reason to achieve a rational and organized consideration of the faith. This second criterion eschews any boundary placed between reason and faith to show how they cannot only coexist but can even complement one another.[14] Within these parameters, many Catholics have gone one step further by offering a reasoned proof for the existence of God. Others have contributed reflections about the complex relationship between the life of the mind and the life of the spirit. These inclusive requirements offer basic guidelines for anyone looking to the past to determine the shape of this Catholic intellectual tradition. The individuals whom scholars have classified within it are the public intellectuals whose work introduced something new to the ongoing conversation about faith and reason.

These requirements have allowed for the construction of a canon, but as Liddy and Hellwig warn us, the tradition does not end with voices from the past. I will examine the ways that criteria have expanded over time, particularly the last two centuries, and the innovative ways Catholics are contributing to an evolving Catholic intellectual tradition. Before I consider these more recent developments, though, I will survey the constructed catalog of thinkers who have been charged with proving the longstanding tradition of the Catholic intellectual.

Construction of a Catholic Intellectual Canon

It should come as no surprise that the beginning of the Catholic intellectual tradition has been traced to the earliest members of the Church itself, including the apologists who worked to make sense of Christianity to believers and nonbelievers alike. First- and second-century thinkers such as Tertullian, Origen, and Clement laid the groundwork for understanding that revelation might provide the ultimate source of wisdom and that reason can helpfully enlighten matters of faith. It was Saint Augustine, however, who is most often credited with beginning the Catholic intellectual tradition, centering his own narrative of faith within the contours of philosophical thought. Greatly influenced by Saint Ambrose and the Platonist thinker Plotonius, and moved by Saint Paul's Letter to the Romans, Augustine became a Christian. He was soon ordained a priest and then Bishop of Hippo in 395. His attitude toward faith changed over time: initially he resented the blind faith that the Church called for, but later he discerned that one needed to believe in the Word of God before one could ever hope to understand it. One of the most essential themes in Augustine's writings is the ultimate importance of God's grace. Arguing against heretics, Augustine contended that human beings were by nature sinful people who could be redeemed only by God's sovereign grace. In his most influential works, *Confessions* and *City of God*, Augustine works to answer the question of where human beings might find the happiness they seek. In the end, he determines that only God offers true happiness. William A. Herr succinctly explains Augustine's conclusion:

> As rational beings we desire knowledge, we want to understand things; and we can be content with nothing less than the answer to all questions and the explanation of all things, which is God. . . . Just as the mind seeks a permanent object of knowledge, such as the ideal Forms of Plato, so the heart seeks a permanent object of desire. Or, as Augustine puts it, our hearts were made for God, and they are restless until they rest in Him.[15]

The bishop's examination into and conclusion about human beings' need for knowledge and the answer Augustine finds in God leaves little doubt as to why he offers a solid beginning for those distinguishing a Catholic intellectual tradition. His writing indicates an awareness of and appreciation for the complementary aspects of human nature: reason and faith.[16]

The next figure often included in this tradition builds on Augustine's philosophical approach to understanding belief in God. Writing long after Augustine in the eleventh century, Saint Anselm of Canterbury embraced the idea that reason could help explain Christianity. He wanted to understand the faith systematically. His most significant contribution was that which is known as an ontological argument for the proof of God's existence in the philosophy of religion. He claimed that God is that than which nothing greater can be conceived. The priority given to reason over revelation in his proof makes Anselm a key figure for piecing together the longstanding intellectual heritage among Catholics.[17]

From Anselm, this quick tour of Catholicism's intellectual past moves to what has been deemed the golden age of the Catholic intellectual tradition: the medieval period. With the beginning of the modern university during these centuries, religion and scholarship came together in an official way through this institutional setting. They emerged mostly out of monastic and cathedral schools and initially were constituted mainly by clergy. While many universities existed throughout Europe, during the Middle Ages, the most important was the University of Paris, and it became something of a model for others. The study of theology in these settings consisted of close readings of both scripture and the writings of church fathers; however, at the base of all study was firm belief in the tradition and faith in the authority of the Church.[18]

The celebration of this time period as a golden age helpfully illustrates the criteria for constructing the Catholic intellectual tradition. First, it boasts the emergence of "scholasticism," an intellectual movement named after the "schoolmen" who embraced reason's capacity for understanding human nature and supernatural truth. Intellectual historians highlight the rationalism that dominated the age. Furthermore, this period witnessed institutional establishments all over Europe that provided the space and opportunity to apply reason specifically to matters of faith. It became as much a lifestyle as a course of study for many. However, the most important element noted about this epoch points to the influence of Aristotelian thought, which took hold during these centuries, most famously by Thomas Aquinas. Not everyone so quickly embraced Aristotle's line of thinking, but eventually its widespread influence required at least a response to it.

By the twelfth century, the works of Aristotle had instigated a new mode of questioning. With all of his works translated, making them newly accessible in the West, Aristotle provided an updated methodology for thinking about religion, and the schoolmen were widely studying it. Because of this curiosity about Aristotle and the new availability of his works, in the thirteenth century, Aristotelian thinking was an established part of university studies. Out of it emerges, arguably, the most influential person in the Catholic intellectual tradition: Saint Thomas Aquinas, born in 1225. A Dominican friar and student of Albert the Great at the University of Paris, Thomas Aquinas was determined to establish a systematic way of recognizing the complementary relationship between faith and reason. Basing his approach on the work of Aristotle, Aquinas set out to offer a rational basis for Christianity. Initially, this embrace of Aristotle was thought problematic. The famous Greek's philosophy contradicted Christian belief in some regards, most importantly with reference to creation. Moreover, the translations of Aristotle's works were usually grouped with interpretations by Arabic thinkers, most famously Averroes, a Muslim philosopher who studied Aristotle's works within the context of Islam. Therefore, Church officials outlawed instruction of certain elements of Aristotelian thinking. Aquinas was caught up in this condemnation of Aristotelian thinking during his career, but he managed to escape the excommunication that others did endure. (Such reactions by the Church throughout history do contribute to the anti-intellectual impression about Catholics. As we see clearly in this example, though, the hierarchy is not the only member of the tradition, and its members often come around to see the wisdom they were missing.) The Catholic Church finally realized that its harsh response was erroneous and eventually came not only to accept it but to insist fully upon its teaching only a few centuries later. This occurred in its most official form through the 1917 Code of Canon Law, established by Benedict XV, which required all theology and philosophy courses in Catholic institutions to include Thomism, the philosophical movement based on Aquinas's teachings.

Beyond his participation in this controversial Aristotelian interest, Thomas Aquinas pushed Catholic intellectualism to a new level of philosophical inquiry. Among his prolific works, his two best-known writings are the syntheses he produced titled *Summa contra gentiles* and *Summa Theologiae*. The first offers a defense of the faith, while the second, his main work, provides a comprehensive theology. Both are based on metaphysical methodology learned from Aristotle. His latter work treats an enormous range of topics pertaining to God and human beings, including the Trinity, creation, grace, incarnation, the sacraments, and resurrection. The most famous of his topics focuses on the existence of God and provides the cosmological argument for God's existence. Aquinas offers a proof that God exists based on causality. He argues that all beings are contingent, that is, that they rely on something else for their existence. Since this chain of dependency cannot continue ad infinitum, there must be a first cause, an unmoved mover. This, he claims, is God.[19]

While the case of the "unmoved mover" remains a staple in most philosophy courses, Aquinas's effect far surpassed his specific arguments. His method and philosophical foundation fundamentally influenced Catholic thinking and even its doctrine. By integrating Christian teaching with Aristotelian reasoning, he provided the soundest basis to date for reasoned reflections on belief in God. He showed that one can reason from the existence of the world to the existence of God, and that this move did not depend on individual faith or subjective experience. This intellectual approach spawned the field of natural theology, which, at its most basic conception, relies on the notion that God has provided reason so that human beings might come to know and understand the world around them. Aquinas's dependence on reason in the work of religious faith makes him the ultimate candidate for inclusion in a Catholic intellectual tradition. In fact, he becomes the exemplary model and his teachings over time became the basis for the theological and philosophical movement known as Thomism, which has surfaced and been adapted in important ways since the thirteenth century. The basic elements of Thomism state that while human beings cannot fully grasp supernatural truths (such as the Trinity) by way of natural reason, there is no opposition between natural reason and God-given faith. In fact, when rightly ordered, reason leads one to truth and ultimately to God. This line of thinking has outlined the terms of the conversation so that even much later thinkers who did not adopt Aquinas's theories had, in some way, to respond to this intellectual's premises. Though some of Aquinas's contemporaries, such as Bonaventure and Duns Scotus, also receive notable mentions in the Catholic intellectual tradition, their attention to experiential knowledge and ethical principles, respectively, do not earn the same status for progress of the Catholic intellect. Indeed, Aquinas is deemed the superb example of this constructed golden age with its legacy of the university and the celebrated life of the mind.[20]

The century following Aquinas, however, witnessed much debate and struggle over Christian theology and the philosophy that was developing in the universities. Scholasticism, the intellectual approach used by Aquinas and many others, briefly lost its stronghold in certain European countries. A humanistic approach, championing the individual capacity of the human being and challenging the clericalism that had characterized the Church, was beginning to take hold. This fueled Martin Luther's attack on the Catholic Church that spurred the Protestant Reformation. As scholar Jude P. Dougherty notes about Martin Luther, "Sworn enemy of Scholasticism, he once remarked that God had sent Aristotle as a punishment for the sins of mankind."[21] Luther's influence largely affected the direction of what has been classified the Catholic intellectual tradition. Not only did the Reformation period witness this challenge to the value and power of reason, but it also eventually led to a Protestant intellectual tradition against which the Catholics might continue to define themselves.

Indeed, during the Reformation itself, Catholics had to assert themselves against this powerful force. With many influential people deeply invested in challenging the Church, Catholics were called to affirm their faith in the institution. In contemporary scholars' catalog of the Catholic intellectual tradition, two men who endured these circumstances are credited with remaining faithful to the Church while maintaining the importance of reasoned study: Desiderius Erasmus (d. 1536) and Sir Thomas More (d. 1535). Close friends, these two shared an interest in exploring the influence of religious faith on scholarly work and community.[22] While Erasmus is usually depicted as the humanist intellectual and More as the self-sacrificing man of God, both men validated scholarship as a religious pursuit. Historian Constance Furey describes More's position: "A life of study could be a religious life for men and women alike, so long as they embraced it as an alternative to worldly values and calculations." She notes Erasmus's stance as well: "Erasmus, speaking from the position of a full-time scholar, was even more explicit that the work of scholarship was salvific. . . . The work scholars did was religious work."[23] Both figures were deeply invested in creating scholarly communities for such work. Until his death, Erasmus remained a committed humanist and Catholic. Initially torn about the Protestant Reformation, Erasmus did come to oppose Martin Luther. Thomas More, however, has earned the reputation of a more devotional person. He faced a particularly harsh encounter with the English Reformation when, as part of the court of Henry VIII, he refused to disavow the authority of the Catholic Church and was martyred as a result. Erasmus's and More's inclusion in this assembled Catholic intellectual tradition offers solid examples of people fully engaged in a life of study and fully involved in their social and political surroundings. They deliberately, even under harsh circumstances, persisted in their Catholicism. Additionally, they offer alternatives from the rather dominant Thomistic persuasion in their more humanistic approaches.

The decades that followed the Reformation eventually led to a renewal of Thomistic thought among Catholics. This played out particularly among different religious orders. While Dominicans had always held fast to Thomism, new orders founded during the Catholic revival of the mid–sixteenth century adopted Saint Thomas as their official teacher. Ignatius of Loyola, founder of the Jesuits in 1540, included requirements for reading Aquinas and Aristotle in the Jesuits' studies of theology and philosophy. Variations on Aquinas's teachings did differentiate certain orders and even spurred new tangential movements. However, at their bases, they mutually held Thomistic thought. During the Council of Trent, the meeting of bishops called in 1545 to clarify and unify Catholic doctrine and teaching, discussions depended greatly on the work of Thomas Aquinas.[24]

The problem with much of this attention to Aquinas, however, was that the Church, having endured serious threats and challenges, felt somewhat vulnerable and protective of its position in Christendom. As a result, the focus on Thomistic theology and philosophy became more of a comfortable default position where the Church could feel safe without pushing further in intellectual inquiry during the centuries that followed the Reformation. It was not only Martin Luther's actions in the sixteenth century that had this impact. Facing the scientific and philosophical innovations in work by the likes of Galileo, Isaac Newton, John Locke, and later Immanuel Kant, among many other Enlightenment thinkers of the seventeenth and eighteenth centuries, the Church became defensive about its claim to truth and retreated from intellectual engagement with the times.

The nineteenth century produced a significant turn in Catholic intellectual life and a zealous revival of Thomistic thought, especially toward its end. Movements occurring in Europe and the concurrent developments in the United States combined to create a volatile era in what has emerged as the Catholic intellectual tradition. Having endured the effects of the Reformation, the Enlightenment, and the French Revolution in Europe and facing mounting challenges in the United States on account of their associations with former colonial forces, Catholics in the West had their work cut out for them in pursuing their intellectual heritage. Still, they rose to the occasion, but not without significant adversity. In the United States, the difficulty came from both sides: the American "natives" and the Vatican. As part of a large organization with allegiance to a leader in Europe, Catholics in the United States did not garner a lot of credibility among American intellectuals who were basing their new nation on Enlightenment ideals that questioned authority and embraced freedom from doctrine.[25] Likewise, the Vatican did not allow for any kind of adaptations to these new social and political circumstances. Despite such substantial challenges, there were a few prominent American Catholics who adopted Enlightenment principles and worked to bring them into accord with Catholic values. In the late eighteenth and early nineteenth centuries, Archbishop John Carroll, the first in the United States, and Bishop John England of Charleston worked to show that the American republicanism supported by Enlightenment ideals could mesh with a newly developing American Catholicism. This created significant upheaval and led to what has been deemed the Americanist controversy. In the end, the Vatican denounced any effort by Americans to withdraw from the authority of the Church, and it minimized the independence these Catholics sought for their national religious setting.[26]

While Archbishop Carroll did not ultimately succeed in his attempts for governing authority in the United States apart from Rome, he did achieve success in another area that continues to affect American Catholic intellectual life: the establishment of the first Catholic college on American soil. Georgetown College was intended to produce an American-born clergy as well as to offer a Catholic education in the Jesuit tradition. While its development and Carroll's participation are not without controversy regarding their contributions to American Catholic intellectual life, Catholic higher education in the United States, begun with this institution, constitutes a major aspect of the constructed Catholic intellectual tradition.[27]

Carroll's and his contemporaries' efforts to achieve a level of separation from the Holy See in Rome epitomizes the kind of threats the Church was sensing during this period. Bishops overseas seeking a new level of self-sufficiency only further evidenced that the Pope's authority could be questioned. The threat was perceived to be building throughout the first half of the nineteenth century, so, at that point, Pope Pius IX began a concerted effort to strengthen papal authority and looked to the Jesuits to help him do so. The Jesuits, longstanding supporters of Thomism, embraced it and used it for this purpose. Eventually, Pius IX's successor, Leo XIII, made it official. During his pontificate, Leo XIII institutionalized Thomism in a way no one had done to date. In his encyclical *Aeterni Patris* (1879), Leo "mandated a return to the thought of Aquinas himself as the authoritative Catholic response to the intellectual challenges of modernity."[28] In many ways, this papal act determined Catholic intellectual life for the next century and a half. Many followed this lead and celebrated what Thomas Aquinas had done for Catholicism. Influential leaders such as Isaac Hecker (b. 1819), convert and founder of the Paulist order; Etienne Gilson (b. 1884), a preeminent French historian; Jacques Maritain (b. 1882), philosopher and French ambassador to the Vatican; and Karl Rahner (b. 1904) embraced Thomism and encouraged its vitality among Catholic intellectuals for many decades. Their names are requisite in any discussion of the Catholic intellectual tradition.[29] The Vatican itself also continued to bolster the movement. In 1914, Pius X commanded that ecclesiastical institutions granting pontifical degrees use Aquinas's *Summa Theologiae* as a textbook. In 1917, the Code of Canon Law from Benedict XV required all theology and philosophy courses in Catholic institutions to include Thomism. This combination of mandates from Church authorities and wise individuals genuinely interested in Aquinas's teachings yielded a boom for Thomism. It hit its peak in the United States in the decades between the world wars, which witnessed not only its diffusion in universities and seminaries but also in established Catholic periodicals such as the lay-founded *Commonweal* and the Jesuit-run *Thought*.[30] It is difficult to underestimate the effect of Thomistic philosophy and theology, particularly on the development of American Catholicism throughout the twentieth century. Indeed, any consideration of a Catholic intellectual tradition must take seriously the embrace of Thomism and the varied ways it has been used and adapted. Its philosophical grounding and its celebration of reason alongside faith have put this movement at the heart of the assembled Catholic intellectual tradition.

This quick tour through two millennia of Catholic intellectual history features only a small selection of the major names and trends that have attracted significant scholarly attention in a formation of the Catholic intellectual tradition, but it offers a sampling of those most frequently invoked for the canon of Catholic intellectualism. These figures evidence the common criteria of a complicated link between faith and reason. Of course, much of their work leans toward theological and ecclesiastical topics. Certainly, these categories have shaped much of the discourse about Catholic intellectuals, but they cannot claim a monopoly. This becomes particularly apparent when the period under consideration is narrowed to the last two centuries. Significant scholarship has been dedicated to intellectual life as it has developed in the more recent era. Certainly, theology and ecclesiology surface prominently in such investigations, but the intellectual label is more broadly applied than it often is for pre-nineteenth-century thinkers.

New Categories for the Catholic Intellectual

In *Catholic Converts: British and American Intellectuals Turn to Rome* (1997), Patrick Allitt focuses on the primacy of converts during his period of interest—at least in the English-speaking world. He begins his preface with the following: "Nearly all the major Catholic intellectuals writing in English between 1840 and 1960 were converts to Catholicism. Having been raised outside the Catholic faith, they enjoyed greater educational advantages than their born-Catholic contemporaries and developed a spirit of intellectual adventurousness."[31] Applying this interpretive lens, he offers a new factor in the effort to assemble the major players in the Catholic intellectual tradition. In fact, his portrayal of these rather recent converts emphasizes their own motivation for establishing the intellectual respectability of the tradition, among both born Catholics and those outside the fold. In this way, Allitt shows their investment in and contribution to Catholic intellectualism. In *Catholic Intellectuals and the Challenge of Democracy* (2002), Jay P. Corrin examines Catholics' encounter with modernity and democracy up through the middle of the twentieth century. He writes, "This book describes the struggles of progressive and reactionary Catholic intellectuals to adjust their religious views to the dynamics of social change, from the French Revolution to the rise of the twentieth-century dictators. Those who tried to accommodate their faith with political and social democracy were the true precursors to what Pope John XXIII referred to as *aggiornamento*, the task of the bringing the Church up to date with the times."[32]

Certainly, every Catholic intellectual's thinking has been influenced by his or her social and political surroundings, but these most recent centuries, and their accompanying modernity, have posed a distinct set of problems for Catholic thinkers. Corrin's work places the confrontation with these problems squarely within the purview of the Catholic intellectual, effectively making it another feature of this tradition. Other historians further limit their scope to the situation in the United States and the political, cultural, and social circumstances specific to its development. Margaret Mary Reher's *Catholic Intellectual Life in America* (1985) charts major figures beginning in 1780 until 1985. Her study takes up a chronological trajectory that follows episcopal response to the Enlightenment through to the romanticism of Orestes Brownson and Isaac Hecker to the development of the Catholic University to the social thought of Dorothy Day and the move toward pluralism. John McGreevy's work *Catholicism and American Freedom* (2003) offers an intellectual history of American Catholics from the mid–nineteenth century through the end of the twentieth focused primarily on social and political issues, such as slavery, education, and abortion. Narrowing the scope to this country and its particular circumstances, these surveys piece together a local Catholic intellectual tradition identified within the United States.

Another important expansion of this category beyond theology and ecclesiology has been the scholarly attention to American Catholics' participation in arts and literature. In recent historiography, the imagination has become an important piece of Catholic intellectualism, especially in the United States. One of the fascinating consequences of this development in the ongoing construction of a Catholic intellectual tradition is its ability to embrace the physical and aesthetic elements that had otherwise been cast aside as anti-intellectual. The claim that film, art, fiction, and poetry that deal with Catholic topics or emerge out of a Catholic milieu boast thoughtful, reflective, even philosophical dimensions pushes the boundaries of this tradition. The most comprehensive of such works, Paul Giles's *American Catholic Arts and Fictions: Culture, Ideology, Aesthetics*, makes the claim that "we can analyze the internal consistency of Catholic culture and its power to shape thought in the world." Analyzing such figures as F. Scott Fitzgerald, Walker Percy, Flannery O'Connor, Mary McCarthy, Allen Tate, and Francis Ford Coppola, Giles explores a wide variety of thinkers whose works offer a variety of perspectives for observing this religious heritage.

Other works such as Anita Gandolfo's *Testing the Faith: The New Catholic Fiction in America* (1992) and Ross Labrie's *The Catholic Imagination in American Literature* (1997) focus only on literature as a rich resource for gauging the Catholic intellectual milieu in the United States since the end of the nineteenth century. Arnold Sparr limits his research to the mid–twentieth century in *To Promote, Defend and Redeem: The Catholic Literary Revival and the Cultural Transformation of American Catholicism, 1920–1960* (1990). In this study, Sparr directly addresses the frustration American Catholics felt about their second-class role as citizens and intellects in the United States, felt particularly acutely in the 1920s after the unsuccessful presidential campaign of Catholic Al Smith. Sparr argues that this frustration sparked a revival that intended to reclaim intellectual status in the United States. This revival, he explains, would recover tradition and neoscholasticism, and it would take form through literature. Finally, in one other notable work, the Catholic imagination draws attention for its influence in the making of American films. In *Afterimage: The Indelible Catholic Imagination of Six American Filmmakers* (2000), Richard Blake considers the importance of theological concepts such as the sacraments and mediation as they contribute to the artistic work of making movies. This kind of study highlights the expansion of the Catholic life of the mind as it has been addressed in recent scholarship. Such works offer a sampling of this growing attention to imagination in the construction of the Catholic intellectual tradition.

While the worlds in novels and movies have been hospitable to this heritage, the spaces that the Catholic intellectual tradition seems to occupy most comfortably, according to its creators, continue to be institutions of higher learning. Writing specifically about Catholic universities and colleges in the United States, Monika Hellwig calls them "a major factor in the study and handing on of the Catholic intellectual and cultural tradition."[33] Indeed, it cannot be overestimated how crucial such institutions remain in the construction and continuation of a Catholic intellectual tradition. Catholics invested in this tradition, particularly those in the United States, perceive the Catholic university as the model for the balanced life of faith and intellectualism. Still, just as challenges to the viability of Catholic intellectualism provoked a close examination and assembly of this separate intellectual tradition, doubts about the identity, purpose, and legitimacy of the Catholic university have incited much reflection on the function and vitality of these institutions.

Many edited collections and individual monographs have been devoted to the problematic of the Catholic university. Longtime president of the University of Notre Dame Theodore Hesburgh, C.S.C., edited a collection titled *The Challenge and Promise of a Catholic University* (1994). In this volume, men and women, ordained and lay, all with some affiliation to Notre Dame, describe the character and mission of their Catholic university. After nearly thirty essays, Father Hesburgh summarizes:

> Most basically, this is a place where reason and faith intersect and influence each other, even reinforce each other, as they grapple with all of the problems that face the transmission and growth of knowledge and the multiplication of new and complex moral problems. . . . All this is not characteristic or expected of all universities, but taken together these essential aspects of Notre Dame do begin to describe the challenge and promise of a Catholic university. . . . It is not that all must be philosophers and theologians but all should have some concern about the philosophical and theological implications of all human intellectual activity.[34]

With the criteria of the Catholic intellectual tradition at the heart of their mission and identity, then, Catholic universities and colleges bear much of the burden of keeping the tradition alive and encouraging its growth and development. Many intellectuals within that setting have publicly accepted this responsibility as a kind of vocation. For example, in the preface to their collection *Examining the Catholic Intellectual Tradition*, Anthony Cernera and Oliver Morgan affirm "the need to lift up, transmit, and develop the Catholic intellectual tradition as central to the task of Catholic higher education."[35] As a result, they have published their volume with the intention of communicating to competent and open-minded yet unaware colleagues in these institutions the content and value of the tradition. Theologian Lawrence Cunningham reflects on his passionate dedication to inspire in students the kind of love for learning he has enjoyed. After many decades teaching in secular universities, he felt grateful for his move to Notre Dame, where he feels free to embrace his Catholicism and yet also to feel challenged intellectually by his colleagues in an ecumenical setting. He writes, "In a setting like Notre Dame we might aspire to connect learning with the pursuit of the Christian life itself. . . . What is important is that a place like Notre Dame provides the home where such an exercise of joining life to learning is possible, even if we fail to exercise that possibility to its fullest."[36] He realizes that not everyone perceives such gravity in their work or feels ready to meet that high standard: "I doubt that most of us always think of our work as a vocation to holiness or feel ourselves quite up to the demands that such a calling makes on us." However, he does not want this to discourage professors in Catholic institutions, for the ultimate example in his eyes faced the same dilemma: "As he began his university career, Thomas Aquinas must have felt the same way."[37] Carrying on this legacy, for Cunningham, gives his life meaning, purpose, and, what is most important, holiness.

The challenges and uncertainties surrounding this endeavor have led to recent institutional developments among these Catholic colleges and universities. On an individual basis, some schools have established offices of "mission" and "identity." Varying slightly by institution, these new offices normally have a staff whose responsibility involves clarifying and maintaining the Catholic identity of the school and its participation in the heritage of a particular order—Jesuit, Lasallian, and so on. Consistently among their aims is to understand, celebrate, and promote the continuation of a Catholic intellectual tradition through the institution's work. Another notable development was the founding of

Collegium, a national organization of Catholic colleges and universities. Established in 1992, it has aimed to respond to the challenges of upholding faith-based missions and of recruiting faculty who could both "articulate and expand the vision of the Catholic intellectual tradition."[38] It sponsors annual summer colloquies for faculty and advanced graduate students who gather both for dialogue on this boundless subject and for development of their own vocation to participate in it. With such attention to the mission and vocation of this work, Catholic colleges and universities aim to connect faith and intellect.

Contemporary Directions for Catholic Intellectual Life

With teachers and scholars committing themselves to inheriting and sharing the Catholic intellectual tradition, we might assume that what has been assembled will continue to evolve and mature. However, the nature and contours of this developing tradition have been brought into question by some of these inheritors. The first concern might be the conspicuous gender imbalance in the constructed canon. Ursula King, a Catholic academic who was educated and has taught in institutions outside the United States, expresses dissatisfaction with the tradition and issues a challenge for its continuation. She writes, "Women of the twentieth century have . . . considerable difficulty in identifying with many aspects of the intellectual life as previously conceived. Until very recently, intellectual life, and especially theology, have been understood in an entirely andocentric way because most of this life, throughout most of the history of the Church, has been deeply embedded in a rigidly patriarchal framework."[39] Certainly, as the category of Catholic intellectualism has been constructed in most scholarship, women rarely find a place among the intellectual giants so often heralded. However, as historians, theologians, teachers, and ministers look to this category, they must appreciate that this heritage has been built upon nominations. The major figures of this identified Catholic intellectual canon have been selected and upheld. Thus, part of Ursula King's challenge speaks directly to those of us participating in this construction. It becomes our job to inscribe women into the picture. As more scholars pay closer attention to the contributions of women before the mid–twentieth century, for example to the theological and intellectual underpinnings of mystics such as Julian of Norwich, Teresa of Avila, and Catherine of Siena, we continue to learn about the influence of women whose rich intellectual participation in Catholicism has long been overlooked.

With such increasing research, this very type of historiographical essay will necessarily change for an accurate depiction of the perceived canon. With an eye toward more contemporary contributions, we note that the last several decades have witnessed changes in women's participation in this Catholic heritage—exciting indications for the expansion of the Catholic intellectual tradition for the future. Indeed many of those "women of the twentieth century" whose trouble King has identified discovered a new thread in Catholicism that has opened promising doors for engagement.

The increasing number of women teaching in theological institutions and seminaries and the development of feminist theology since the mid–twentieth century point toward a new horizon for the Catholic intellectual tradition. As more women enter the field of theology, their influence on this heritage continues to grow. Since the founding of the first graduate theology program for women at St. Mary's College in 1943 in South Bend, Indiana, by Sr. Madeleva, women have been seeking formal theological training. (This American academy came even nine years before Pope Pius XII founded an institute in Rome to prepare women to teach theology.) Sr. Madeleva's insightful action marks an important moment for the recognized participation in academic theology among women. Numbers of women committed to theological training have consistently increased since then.[40] Further, women theologians have been effectively organizing and galvanizing each other for their role in this intellectual work in recent decades.[41] These advances hold great promise for the impact of women on this part of the Catholic heritage.

Growing numbers and increasing motivation also reflect the tremendous success of feminist theology. In the chapter "New Foundations: Catholic Women Reshape Theology" in her book *Good Catholic Girls: How Women Are Leading the Fight to Change the Church*, Angela Bonavoglia provides a helpful introduction to this growing discipline and its tremendous effect upon the field. Providing a case study of feminist theologian Elizabeth Johnson, that chapter outlines some of the major changes in the field that range in areas from biblical study to sexual ethics to liturgy. First, though, Bonavoglia notes that such changes have been noticed: "Esteemed theologian David Tracy believes that feminism's encounter with religion has produced an 'intellectual revolution.'"[42] This revolution's beginnings are most notably credited to Rosemary Radford Reuther, Elisabeth Schüssler Fiorenza, and Mary Daly, who established feminist theology as a viable approach to the study of God and humanity.[43] Much of their pioneering work began as they earned doctoral degrees and continued in their prominent roles at institutions including Claremont Graduate Theological Union, Harvard Divinity School, and Boston College, respectively. When it comes to defining feminist theology, Elizabeth Johnson offers the phrase "from the perspective of women and women's flourishing."[44] As the Catholic intellectual tradition continues to evolve, its survival will require the inclusion of this vibrant innovation. As such efforts take root and grow, the Catholic intellectual tradition can begin to respond to Ursula King's first concern.

Beyond the role of women in this intellectual heritage, King issues three other distinct challenges to the Catholic intellectual tradition. She issues a "global challenge," encouraging Catholics to take an even more prominent role in addressing social problems around the world. She issues a "gender challenge," pushing Catholics to appreciate the full humanity of men and women. Finally, she issues a "spiritual challenge," urging Catholics to embrace the full range of human experience. King writes, "We possess a gloriously rich intellectual inheritance in Catholicism, but Catholics will have to wrestle with decisive new challenges during the next millennium—the tradition cannot remain intact without some profound changes. Yet is has the resources to respond to the new circumstances and contexts of a new era."[45] She concisely articulates the problem and the promise of the Catholic intellectual tradition: it has a deep and rich history on which to rely, but for it to survive and grow, it requires close attention, action, and change. This animating call echoes the work of Richard Liddy and Monica Hellwig, who warn that the Catholic intellectual tradition does not simply provide an inheritance of wisdom but rather calls people to think and act differently. To sustain itself and be sustained, this heritage must extend beyond libraries and directly impact Catholic life in the present in all its complexity.

As noted earlier, academic practice does not address the full range of contributions by Catholics to form an intellectual tradition. With this in mind, I nominate one woman whose work evidences a fervent commitment to both faith and intellect. Author Mary Gordon's fiction, essays, and memoirs richly depict the struggles and joys of an American Catholic experience. Established in the American intelligentsia as a professor of English at Barnard College and a member of the American Academy of Arts and Letters, Gordon constantly invokes her Catholic faith and identity in her work, highlighting the equally impressive forces of that faith and the intellect. In an interview with Bill Moyers in his series *Faith and Reason*, Gordon emphasizes the role of questioning in her faith-life: "The ability to question, the ability to take a skeptical position is absolutely central to my understanding of myself and my understanding of myself as a religious person. It's very important to experience doubt. I think faith without doubt is just either nostalgia or a kind of addiction. And I'm not interested in that."[46]

The life of the mind, a questioning and curious mind, remains a critical aspect of Mary Gordon's faith. It seems impossible for her to maintain one without the other. Still, as champions of the Catholic intellectual tradition would insist, Gordon intends for her work to do more than provide an opportunity for self-reflection. It intends to call on others to think and act differently. In the interview, she explains, "the work of the writer is always, to use a religious term, incarnational. How do we witness to the mix of being human? How do we witness to the inherent contradiction of being human? And also, I believe that if a writer can do her or his work, it is to try to imagine the other."[47] Finally, this motivation is deeply rooted in her own reading of the Gospels, as she notes, "if reading the Gospel means anything, if Jesus means anything, it's about seeing everybody, every human being as Jesus. That's what makes sense. That—therefore, every human being is of enormous value. Every human being is sacred." Embracing the intellectual work of the writer and academic, Gordon demonstrates how that part of her life remains in constant conversation with her Catholic faith. Outside any department of theology or philosophy and unconcerned with neoscholasticism or Thomism, Mary Gordon demonstrates one way that contemporary Catholics are living the intellectual life. Through her literature, as well as her contributions as a public intellectual, Gordon offers an example of how the thinking Catholic continues to wrestle with elements of faith in one's own social and cultural circumstances. Furthermore, and perhaps more importantly, Gordon's work as a Catholic intellectual invites her readers and listeners to engage in this active reflection as well. Indeed, such active reflection continues to be the real work of the Catholic intellectual. The gift and burden of this Catholic intellectual tradition as it has been constructed, then, calls upon its creators and inheritors not only to model a life that embraces mind and spirit but also to inspire other Catholics to do the same.

3 Passing on the Faith

Training the Next Generation of American Practicing Catholics

SANDRA YOCUM

How to pass on "the faith"? We certainly are not the first generation—and I hope not the last—to ask this question. One can find evidence of such concerns, sometimes oblique, other times explicit, in Paul's letters, among the earliest extant Christian writings. A host of difficult questions came early to those communities that the first apostles founded. What does it mean to believe in the name of Jesus Christ, the one who was crucified, the cruelest, the most despised, the most shocking form of empire-orchestrated execution? What does it mean to believe in the one whose tomb was discovered empty, who appeared as the Risen One to his disciples? What is essential to this faith received from the earliest apostles, and what not? Does the faithful disciple follow the intricacies of the Jewish law, especially as practiced by the Pharisees? What does it mean to baptize in the name of the Father, Son, and Holy Spirit? Who exactly is this Jesus who is called the Christ? What are the core teachings, the required practices?

To pass on the faith—if only it were as easy as passing a note, a checklist of what one must believe, such as a creed. Yet, as Nicholas Lash points out in introducing his text *Believing Three Ways in One God: A Reading of the Apostles' Creed*, those who think that a creed is "a list of theses, a catalogue of chapter headings for a textbook of theology" are seriously mistaken. He describes the creed rather as a kind of summation of the biblical narrative. "What the Scriptures say at length, the Creed says briefly." Lash's description of reciting the creed makes clear that this seemingly unremarkable activity of recitation implies far more than most participants fully comprehend. "To say the Creed is to confess, beyond all conflict and confusion, our trust in One who makes and heals the world and who makes all things one"—though we confess this One in "three ways."[1] So even that succinct declaration, the Creed, requires far more than passing on a list for recitation.

Surely in hearing the phrase "passing on the faith," images of more than a list of beliefs pass before the eyes of the hearers' imaginations. "The faith," after all, points to a way of life—a life embedded in a community beyond any single individual or any particular place or time—but always manifest, always lived as a way of life in particular times and places. Those who have some interest in passing on the faith to the next generation in this time and place may want to claim the United States of the early twenty-first century to be the absolute worst time and place to pass on the faith. And no doubt it is the most difficult, at least for those who live in the early twenty-first century, since it is the time and place in which they are called to the task. After all, Christians from earlier times and places had only to deal with persecutions, martyrdoms, changes in empires, collapses of social structures, invasions, crusades, Christian schisms, not to mention plagues, minimal education, poverty, economic upheavals and transformations, protesting Christian reformers, revolutions, and antichurch movements. This potentially endless list makes clear that others long before the twenty-first century believed with deep conviction that theirs were the most difficult circumstances ever imaginable to pass on the faith.

Readers who open a volume dedicated to explorations of "Catholic Studies" may be surprised or even uneasy to see an essay considering how to "pass on the faith." Admittedly, Catholic Studies functions at times as a kind of quarantining of Catholicism's influence in the university setting. Some view the pursuit of Catholic Studies as more akin to a postmortem than a celebration of generativity. Others may want to protect Catholic Studies from the vagaries of confessional or catechetical ideologues. Yet, as I will argue, "passing on the faith" is a complex process that depends upon a wide-ranging, multidisciplinary intellectual engagement. The best of Catholic Studies can contribute to "passing on the faith" in such a way that the "next generation" engages in the rich complexities of faith as believed and practiced over a long history filled with the false and the true, the bad and the good, the ugly and the beautiful.

What follows is an exercise in Catholic Studies with a focus on more recent history in the United States of those who, in a sense, offered their own version of Catholic Studies with an eye toward "passing on the faith" to their "next generation." Even within this relatively limited focus, the subsequent discussion offers only some glimpses of a few of the last century's American Catholics who made concerted efforts to provide guidance in passing on the faith to the next generation—with a decided focus on forming "practicing Catholics." My purpose is not to argue for the superiority of any one of these efforts but to present a kind of network of strategies that emerged in the first half of the twentieth century. The hope in presenting these various strategies is to illuminate how these past efforts continue to shape current debates about passing on the faith.

The presentation of the strategies will unfold in three major sections. The first draws from discussions that occurred beginning in the 1920s through 1940 concerning how to educate college students in the Catholic faith, recognizing this particular group as an emerging coterie of Catholic intellectuals who could bring to bear influence on their own community and, more significantly, beyond that community in an effort to wrest the social order from secularism and restore it to its authentic foundation as Catholic/Christian. These discussions focus on teaching religion or theology. The second section offers an alternate approach to "passing on the faith," with a focus on the aesthetics of faith. That section will focus on two women who were among the most influential exemplars from the twentieth century. One is perhaps far too familiar, Dorothy Day. The other, Sister Madeleva Wolff, C.S.C., is familiar to very few. The third section will then offer some observations and conjectures on how the current next generation encounters the passing on of faith with a brief return to the theological query of what is the faith one hopes to pass on.

Winning the Minds and Hearts of Lay Catholics in the Classroom

The familiar narrative of twentieth-century Catholicism often points to the Second Vatican Council as the definitive movement when Catholics began to engage the modern world. American Catholics were, according to this story, located in a ghetto, a self-enclosed enclave that protected them from Protestant wiles and the even wilier modern, secular world (often described as the logical consequences of Protestantism's emphasis on personal judgment in matters of faith). Whatever the truth of the ghetto/ fortress narrative, it has too frequently led to overlooking how Catholics for most of the twentieth century were engaged in American culture and even adapted certain modern strategies to critique and reject what they perceived to be undermining the faith. A principal site for this engagement was the college religion or theology classroom. At least five approaches can be found.

Option 1: "Forming Practical Catholics"

One person who significantly shaped the debate on teaching the faith to college students in the first half of the twentieth century was John Montgomery Cooper, a priest of the diocese of Washington, D.C., and professor of religion and later anthropology at the Catholic University of America. Cooper's quest for excellence in the "religion course" began when he was assigned to teach the subject, first in high school and later at Catholic University. In fulfilling the assignment, he, like most Catholic teachers of religion, discovered his seminary education to be of little use. Seminary theology as Cooper had learned it was highly abstract and speculative in character. Cooper, while professing respect for this intellectual enterprise, felt certain that Catholic college students' minds and hearts would be captured only by "religion," by which he meant a lived faith.

The priest-educator drew upon resources other than neoscholasticism. The most important came from the rapidly emerging social sciences—psychology, sociology, and anthropology. He adapted these disciplines' inductive methods to inform his religion courses' content and pedagogy. His own classroom served, de facto, as a laboratory for experiments in effective teaching of religion. In 1923, he published a sort of lab report in four articles in *The Catholic Educational Review.* Each featured a description of a different religion course: apologetics, history, morality, and ascetics. In these articles, Cooper explained very clearly his use of an inductive approach. For example, he explicitly stated that his approach to and content in the advanced religion course in morals featured the "outgrowth of numerous informal conferences with other teachers working actively in the field and of the writer's personal experience and experimentation during thirteen years with college classes in religion and the same number of years with high school religion classes."[2] Similar methodological claims appeared in the other articles.

Cooper adopted the general term "religion" to identify the college courses he had developed. "Religion," not "theology," formed "practical Catholics." Cooper's distinction set the terms of the debate over college theology through the 1930s and into the 1940s. His influence is partially explained by his location at Catholic University, the nation's premier Catholic graduate school. More significantly, his critique had real merit, and he offered a genuinely viable alternative

The 1923 *Catholic Educational Review* series makes Cooper's commitment to the U.S. context of his time abundantly clear. His explanation of a course in apologetics, a frequent focus of Catholic religion classes, illustrates his American predilections. Cooper explicitly historicized and thereby relativized apologetics, identifying it as "the chameleon among the theological sciences, ever changing color to match the kaleidoscopic changes on the screen of human thought and human error."[3] The topics about which Catholics of the 1920s must have some knowledge range from birth control and eugenics to social justice for laborers. Rather than filling students' minds with a list of objections to contemporary practices, however, Cooper favored discussions of positive Catholic positions to depict the Church as "a living, energizing active organism in our contemporary civilization" whose dogmas had contributed to the increase of human happiness.

The dynamic interaction between Cooper's desire to teach a religion course that evokes religious commitment, even fervor, and his confidence in the effectiveness of inductive approaches to content as well as pedagogy is perhaps nowhere more evident than in his approaches to a course in church history. Identifying the Church as "the mystical body of Christ," Cooper characterized "her history [as] the record of the energizing of the spirit of Christ through His mystical body." He explicitly objected to those whose historical work was an exercise in nostalgia or a long story of decline from that greatest of all centuries, the thirteenth: "We are the children of our times. The thirteenth was a great century, but we are living in the third decade of the twentieth. And we judge institutions less by what they have done or left undone in the past than by what they are actually doing or leaving undone in the present." His inductive predilections manifested themselves in his organizing the course in "reverse chronological order" because of its superior pedagogical impact.[4]

His article on the morality course seems particularly bold in its criticism. He explicitly repudiated the manuals, or as he described them, "textbooks of such arctic temperature" caused by their "dominantly intellectualist" approach. The seminary-inspired manuals fail to address the concerns of 99 percent of the boys and 100 percent of the girls who "live their span of life as laymen and lay women in the world." Cooper, using images from medicine and psychology, queried his readers: "Shall our instruction in moral hygiene and health be confined to the microscopic examination of nocuous moral bacilli?" He preferred to focus upon what makes "the ideal practical Catholic layman and laywoman" using Jesus, the "Great Exemplar," as the model of the moral life.[5]

Cooper sought to create courses that would produce noticeable, even measurable effects in his students. The yet unmentioned fourth article in the 1923 series best illustrates Cooper's crafting courses as religious formation. This article featured "ascetic theology," which "is our Catholic science and art of character building and soul-training, our technic of moral and religious pedagogy." Comparing soul-training to athletic conditioning, Cooper referred to "coaching rules" that promised students a victory "in the game of Catholic living." His sources for developing the "technics" even include the pragmatist William James, whom Cooper acknowledged by quoting from his "brilliant chapter on 'Habit.'" This favorable judgment of James illustrates just how distinctive Cooper's approach was in comparison to the neoscholastics' deductive methods. These four articles served as a preview of his four-volume *Religion Outline for Colleges*, a textbook series adopted by about half of Catholic colleges, as reported in 1940s National Catholic Education Association surveys. How effectively they were used is unknown.[6]

Option 2: Training in the Theological Sciences

Voices other than Cooper's were being raised on the religious education of Catholic college students. In 1939, the National Catholic Alumni Federation held a conference, "Man and Modern Secularism." In the 1940 printed form, the subtitle "Essays on the Conflict of Two Cultures" reveals the analytical framework for the conference. Two orderings of reality, one Catholic, the other secular, are locked in struggle as each attempts to occupy various cultural spaces in which only one can fit. The essays follow a logical progression, from historical roots of the two cultures to their differing philosophical bases, and finally propose practical means for promoting Catholic culture. The essays' authors even introduce a certain complexity in admitting the possibility of "authentic secularism" and the inclusion of "genuine American democratic values," both as animating forces in the Catholic culture. The laity's education in theology emerges as key to creating a Catholic culture effective in countering secularism.

Not surprisingly, one theological approach championed was the strictly neoscholastic, with its focus on right thinking leading to right actions. Reverend Gerald B. Phelan, president of Toronto's Institute of Medieval Studies, argued for introducing courses beyond catechesis, "a thorough and systematic training in the science of revealed truth in order to appreciate the 'Gift of God' . . . Catholics' crucial role in winning the war between the two cultures requires them to judge moral issues, both personal and social, from "a deep foundation of theological learning."[7] He then chose another architectural image to reiterate its absolute necessity. "Theology, being the highest wisdom, is the architectonic science par excellence, the keystone of the Arch of Christian learning."[8] Without this keystone, the beautiful edifice of Catholic education would collapse. Theology for an enlightened laity is no luxury; it is essential.

Phelan then called for an innovation: "a positive and vigorous policy on the part of university authorities to encourage laymen and laywomen who have the ability and inclination to follow advanced courses in theology to enroll in the theological department of the university," a need especially acute for enthusiastic, Catholic-action-inspired youth. To fail to place theology at the center of a Catholic curriculum leaves "in the language of the Holy See a *corpus truncatum*, a headless body."[9] The image of such a corpse contrasts with that of the increasingly popular image of the Church as Mystical Body of Christ, engaged in the reconstruction of the social order. While Cooper had invoked this image in his account of teaching church history, Phelan used it to reinforce the necessity of exposure to authoritative teaching in theology.

What is crucial in Phelan's discussion is his insistence that lay men and women should have access to theological studies, a discipline previously preserved for the ordained.

A subsequent speaker, Reverend Francis J. Connell, C.Ss.R., S.T.D., then a professor of theology at Mt. St. Alphonsus, Esopus, New York, placed democratic ideals sorely threatened in 1939 under the protective embrace of the Mystical Body: "In a world that is becoming keenly conscious of the need of democracy to offset the steady growth of economic and civil totalitarianism the doctrine of the Mystical Body proclaims the noblest type of liberty, equality and fraternity ever realized on this earth." Connell carefully circumscribed this participatory democracy within the Church's hierarchical framework even while situating it in its local surroundings: "The nature and the extent of each one's participation in the apostolate depend on his particular abilities, his surroundings, the special needs of the time, and above all, the plan of activity laid down by the hierarchy."[10] His analysis belies ecclesial-political tensions between the centripetal forces of clerical authority and the centrifugal force of localized lay activities.

Connell insinuates an important pedagogical position in his seemingly matter-of-fact appeal to the "doctrine of the Mystical Body" rather than simply "the Mystical Body." Educating Catholic youth against modernity's errors meant forming their minds with correct teaching from which would follow appropriate Catholic Action. He aspired to form Catholics able to demonstrate to the agnostic and even atheist "that religion is something about which one can reason as unsentimentally as about mathematics or chemistry." Even beyond producing the savvy apologist, he imagined advanced courses forming students who might launch "a brilliant literary career in the service of Christ and his Church" or a life of political influence as "statesman or judge," or a life of public service as social worker.

Connell's commitment to this kind of education is evident in his active participation in the revision of the Baltimore Catechism (1941). At the Catechetical Congress in Philadelphia, November 15–18, 1941, Connell, now a professor in the Catholic University of America's Graduate School of Sacred Theology, made clear to his audience "that a catechism is not a text-book of religion. A text-book is supposed to contain substantially all the required matter for a certain course of instruction;

whereas a catechism contains only an undeveloped sketch of Catholic doctrine." Connell saw the Baltimore Catechism as singular in making the fundamentals of faith accessible to everyone, but he, not unlike Cooper, identified the pivotal role of the catechist who "must interpret and clarify the explanations of the catechism, solve the difficulties that may arise in the child's mind, supplement the content of the catechism with additional material suitable to the intellectual abilities of the grade she is teaching." Connell asserted that these catechists (whom he identifies as women) "must have a considerable knowledge of scientific theology," a knowledge that "must be far more comprehensive than that of the average lay Catholic," including "terms and definitions frequently used in theological manuals."[11] Connell's comments reveal how scholastic thought undergirded even the most basic catechetical resource text, the Baltimore Catechism. Though the laity who taught religion relied heavily upon the catechism, few had familiarity with the scholastic superstructure that buttressed each answer. His observations about the limits of the catechism seem to align with the limits in the classroom since too few had the ability to clarify, and even fewer were able to supplement, the catechism.

Option 3: Training Catholic Adventurers

Other conference participants offered real alternatives to the scholastic approach. The rhetoric of the Reverend Martin C. D'Arcy, S.J., head of Fordham University's Philosophy Department, stands in marked contrast to Connell's measured discourse. The Jesuit called for a "militant Catholicism" so that "the many-splendored beauty of Christ, can be made real and attractive to the youth of the age in which we live." D'Arcy seemed to have in mind the preparation of a more daring breed of Catholic youth fired by the tremendous upheavals occurring in the world of 1939. To educate for militancy in such a world, Catholics must transform the academic liberal ideal, love of learning for its own sake, by providing it with its proper Christian end, contemplation. At the same time, they must transform the revolutionary ideal of social change by providing the proper goal, "the bringing of the Kingdom of Heaven on earth, and to seek an ordered beauty, the ordered city of God."[12]

The Catholic militant featured in D'Arcy's essay participates in a kind of modern Catholic adventure involving brains, passion, and daring actions in overcoming all modernity's obstacles to Catholic conviction. These youthful protagonists know no reason for fear in a world where "grace perfects human nature and elevates it," and they become "the gestures of [Christ's] victorious love . . . His continued life on earth." D'Arcy demanded Catholic educators impress upon their students the ideal of a contemplative active in the world. "Catholic education, therefore, should give a buoyant, almost laughing faith and courage, a faith which is infectious, which rejoices in obstacles, in slaying dragons, in smiting evil, and sees the world not as an occasion of sin but of virtue and of love."[13] Connell depicted the lay apostle in the world as modern schola, calmly revealing point-by-point the errors of every opponent. This protagonist pales in comparison to D'Arcy's world-loving, countercultural dragon slayer. Yet, it must be reiterated that both agreed on proximate and ultimate ends, a Catholic transformation of the natural world in light of its supernatural ends. The differences lie in the means to these common ends.

Option 4: Forming Catholics for Ordinary Time

The National Catholic Welfare Conference's Director of the Education Department, Reverend George Johnson, highlighted the importance and challenge of childhood instruction in effecting early formation of the college-aged. Focusing upon elementary education, Johnson emphasized its context, the parish, "a natural unit of living. The children going to Mass on Sunday, seeing funerals and weddings and all the rest of the ordinary life of people, are getting a foundation in citizenship of the right kind." Johnson's description serves as a reminder that ordinary Catholic life encompasses even the Catholic intellectual who engages the world first and foremost as a member of this local community. The neighborhood demands engagement with the world through active participation in "the ordinary life of people." "If children grow up in the atmosphere of the parish, they are held close to the Church in society, thus leavening the whole mass."[14] Johnson, like all the other participants, appealed to the dominant American narrative by touting citizenship even as he qualified its Catholic expression by adding the phrase, "of the right kind." The "right kind" of freedom comes to individuals in knowing where they came from, where they are going, and how they can get there. Such knowledge requires no college degree since it can be discovered in, through, with, and from a community of learning open to all Catholics, the parish.

Option 5: Theology for Laity

John Courtney Murray, S.J., as often seemed to be the case among U.S. Catholic intellectuals of the last century, had the last say at the conference and in the essay collection. His oddly titled "Necessary Adjustments to Overcome Practical Difficulties," appears to be extemporaneous remarks at the conference. Reminiscent of Cooper, he argued against seminary theology as an appropriate model for an "effective program of Catholic action." Reflecting the precise distinctions of his scholastic training, his reasoning hinges on correctly identifying the purpose of a theology for the laity. College students need an education in "the livability of the Word of God as kept and given us by the Church; in other words, that our courses of theology must be wholly orientated toward life."[15]

Murray also displayed a certainty similar to Connell in identifying a fundamentally rational quality of Catholicism. Theology should

> emphasize the value of the truth in life . . . that the Catholic religion is an objective thing, or rather that the Catholic religion is essentially a theology; in other words, it is a vision of God. It is not an instrument of humanitarianism; it is not even primarily an instrument for the constitution of a social order, it is first and foremost a vision of God . . . that comes to us in a very definite way . . . in the concrete facts of a history; a history, namely, of a human life, the life of Christ; hence we have in basic Catholicism, two values: first, its objectivity; secondly, that it is historical; and of the ensemble of those two values results a third, that Catholicism is essentially a social thing.[16]

From Murray's perspective and that of the other participants, it is a social reality inclusive of ways of knowing and acting, in other words, of living.

Murray closed his essay noting that changes in theological education are symptomatic of broader changes in Catholic social relationships, particularly between the clergy and laity: "if Catholic action means anything, it means that that which the Church emphasizes has changed." If the defense against Protestantism meant emphasizing hierarchical authority, Catholic action meant "that now the Catholic emphasis rests upon the unity of the Church teaching and the Church learning, between the hierarchy and laity." He suggested that the most effective way to create a theology course for the laity is to ask them what they want. Citing the quote "*Nos sumus Christi ecclesia*," Murray's final line proclaims: "it is right that those of us who teach should learn from those of you who learn from us."[17] His conclusion about theology stands in sharp contrast to the apologetics course Connell described. Yet, in this case, their agreement had farther-reaching effects than their disagreements. Both agreed that laypeople in the modern age need a familiarity with theology in some form—a major change in Catholic culture as the theologically informed intellectual elite expanded beyond the clergy. For Murray, the task of "passing on the faith" is rooted in intellectual work with an eye toward the practical Catholic.

An Aesthetics of Faith: The Art of Appreciation

One might argue that the most effective way to examine the formation of practicing Catholics is to look at practitioners. Dorothy Day and Sister Madeleva Wolff, C.S.C., were contemporaries of the ensemble of men just considered. The former is, of course, the leftist activist who converted to Catholicism and, with the French-born itinerant lay preacher Peter Maurin, founded the Catholic Worker movement. Grounded in the practices of the spiritual and corporal works of mercy and shaped in and through Catholic liturgical and devotional practices, the Catholic Worker movement displayed its commitments in founding houses of hospitality and self-sufficient farms (what Peter Maurin called agronomic universities). Key to propagating the movement was "round table discussions for clarification of thought" and the publication of a newspaper bearing the title *The Catholic Worker*.

The other woman may be less familiar. A Holy Cross sister, Sister Madeleva Wolff served as president of Saint Mary's College in Notre

Dame, Indiana, from 1934 until her retirement in 1962. She, too, had a remarkable life; she was the first woman religious to graduate with a doctorate from the University of California, Berkeley—in her case, in English. She was a published poet whose work appeared in popular magazines as well as literature anthologies used in Catholic schools. During her tenure as Saint Mary's president, besides transforming the undergraduate curriculum and campus life, she founded the Graduate School of Sacred Theology (1943), the first to grant Roman Catholic women doctoral degrees with theology as its content. Her essay "The Education of Sister Lucy" is credited as the inspiration for the much praised and at times maligned Sister Formation Movement. In addition, she was a popular public speaker whose last public talk, shortly before her death, considered William Golding's recently published novel *Lord of the Flies*. Her talk bore the title "The End of Innocence," ironic in its timing at the beginning of the 1960s. She died suddenly in 1964 after a brief illness.

Each of these women has distinct but overlapping courts of influence, traces of which are evident in contemporary Catholicism. Certainly both were committed to education in their own way. In a collection, *On Pilgrimage*, a rendering of her 1948 journal, from which the quotes for this essay are taken, Day writes of the conversion of Douglas Hyde, an English communist who converted to Catholicism. His conversion came when reading for research purposes an English Catholic newspaper, *The Weekly Review*. She observes of her own journalistic efforts: "Maybe if we keep on writing and talking, there will be other conversions like Mr. Hyde's. It was reading an article that got Father Damian his help Brother Joseph, at Molokai. It was reading that converted St. Augustine. So we will keep on writing."[18] She continues, "And talking, too. . . . One needs to talk to convey ideas." Day saw herself as educator, principally through practicing the spiritual work of mercy, teaching the ignorant.

Sister Madeleva returns to a familiar trope in answering the question, "Why Do We Educate Our Daughters?" "Briefly, we educate them for exactly the reason for which God made them: to know, to love, to serve, to glorify Him now and forever. To achieve this we use the avenues proper to education, the avenues of their minds." She then provides examples of knowing God through "His world, His universe." She commends to her audience students who "have tried to understand, with reverence, the cumulative and unfolding patterns of existence, through the cultures, the sciences, the histories, the arts of peoples." Madeleva continues, "We trust that they will love with wonder the mysteries among which they move: the sacramental vocation of water without which we cannot have life of any kind anywhere; the momentous marriages of the elements; the secrets of atomic existence, of all existence; the mystery and validity of thought. . . . We want them to continue to love, to think, to wonder, to explore their own inheritances as children of God."[19]

Here, in Madeleva's words (not unlike Murray's), are hints of a "still more" to the faith that she and Day sought to pass on to the next generation. They had a deep appreciation for the aesthetics of faith, how beauty mediates the true and the good of the faith to those awake to the world around them, and both of these women were certainly awake to the world around them.

Dorothy Day loved to quote Dostoevsky: "The world will be saved by beauty." In her 1952 autobiography, *The Long Loneliness*, Day pointed to the beauty of creation—the beach, the sea, a garden on Staten Island—but the beauty of creation in her daughter's birth is part of what awakened in her a longing for God and eventually led her to the Catholic Church. Day's sense of beauty was not limited to bucolic settings, seascapes, or newborn daughters. Her aesthetic sensibilities had been formed in the cityscapes of Chicago and New York City and honed in the realities of Saint Joseph's House of Hospitality.

In assisting her daughter Tamar and her rapidly growing family in rural West Virginia, Day writes in ways that seem to intermingle the bucolic with the madcap. One early March morning, she speaks to her readers. "(I must grab the chance to write while I may), and the pails of water are heating on the stove. Since we have not washed since Saturday, there is a great wash for today." She describes two of her granddaughters "eating peanuts and singing happily"; one's voice resembles "a Chinese singer, having a particularly plaintive wail that delights her heart." She then jumps to recollections of yesterday's baptism of the new grandchild, with the two singing peanut-eaters "mumbling" their own creed while priest and sponsors recited clearly the Apostles' Creed. She criticizes other priests she has heard mumble their words, recalling that "'hocus-pocus' . . . is a corruption of the sacred words, 'Hoc est corpus meum.'" Then she abruptly observes, "Meditations for woman, these notes should be called, jumping as I do from the profane to the sacred over and over. But then, living in the country, with little children, with growing things, one has a sacramental view of life. All things are His, and all are holy."[20]

The city proved equally susceptible to her sacramental view. She wrote on September 19, of that same year, on the feast of St. Januarius, "In New York these last few days, around the corner from us on Mulberry Street, there is a fiesta, a feast, celebrated every year with bands and processions [and] feastings around open charcoal fires, where sausages are roasted on spits, huge pots of grease in which pieces of dough wrapped around pot cheese are French fried, corn is boiled." Day complains of the noise that accompanies it and contrasts it to the delicious quiet of West Virginia. But her rich description belies her complaints and affirms that sacramental view.

Madeleva's aesthetic sensibility had been shaped in rural Wisconsin, the flatlands of South Bend, Indiana, and the high desert of Salt Lake City. She lived in what by comparison is the far more rarefied world of a women's college. Her poetry, as here in "Mirrors," gives a glimpse of her own aesthetic sense:

I seek you always. Have I never seen you?
Let's ask if any bird has seen the air,
Or flower the light, though these are everywhere.
Choose any veil you will. Set it between you
And my beholding. Know it shall not screen you
From me. What occult vestures you may wear,
Too dread or dull or difficult to bear,
Are mirrors meaning naught unless they mean you.

Is beauty something I cannot discover?
Is truth a thing that only children know?
Are you not mine who are the whole world's lover?
Can I not find you in all winds that blow,
In the wild loneliness of lark and plover,
In slender shadow trees upon the snow?[21]

The image of the mirror, of course, is replete throughout spiritual writings. Paul speaks of looking through a mirror darkly; Clare of Assisi writes of Christ as the mirror in which she sees herself. For Madeleva, all she sees around her is a mirror of "the whole world's lover"—her lover, God.

Like Day, Madeleva placed her embrace of the world around her in the light of God in Christ. Hers, too, was marked by Incarnation. She had a phrase that guided her attempted attitude toward this world she loved: "relaxed grasp." And she provides a glimpse of its practice in her "Ballade on Eschatology,"[22] with the parenthetical title "(For the Hero of the Habitually Relaxed Grasp)."

Detachment is a virtue, teachers say.
Then let me practice it without regret.
What do I hold beyond this short today?
What cherish that I shall not soon forget?
These small things upon which my heart is set
Are matters for a heart's relinquishings.
One ultimate matter do I cleave to yet;
This, I shall not forget the four last things.

Remembrance, in a thief's unnoted way,
Filches from me with neither leave not let
My thousand petty deities of clay.
Perhaps my eyes are still a little wet;
Perhaps my heart may still a little fret.
Detachment is the stuff of sunderings.
Time, so they tell me, is a brave asset.
And I shall not forget the four last things.

Your voice, your eyes,—or are they blue or gray?
The day we said good-bye, the day we met;
Hills we have walked, birds, flowers, our work, our play;—
Memory, how do you aid me and abet?
Time closes round me with impalpable net.
I'll not advert to clay or crowns or wings.
I have no thing to lose, all things to get,
For I shall not forget the four last things.

Envoi
Lord, though by mortal tyrannies beset,

Immortal freedom in my wild heart sings,
A pauper comes to pay a pauper's debt.
God, I shall not forget the four last things.

Of course, the four last things are death, judgment, heaven, and hell. And perhaps few had in mind these four last things in considering passing on the faith to the next generation of practicing Catholics—practicing out of fear of a punishing God—though this is hardly the anticipation voiced by the wild-hearted Madeleva.

The aesthetics of faith, the beauty of faith, bursts forth for Madeleva and for Dorothy out of the love of God. Yet this love was not of a sentimental kind. Dorothy, in one of her many somber moments on her 1948 pilgrimage, recollects this experience. "One time I was traveling and far from home and lonely, and I awoke in the night almost on the verge of weeping with a sense of futility, of being unloved and unwanted. And suddenly the thought came to me of my importance as a daughter of God, daughter of a King, and I felt a sureness of God's love and at the same time a conviction that one of the greatest injustices, if one can put it that way, which one can do to God is to distrust His love, not realize His love. God so loved me that He gave His only begotten Son."[23] Knowing their end was not limited to this world allowed Dorothy and Madeleva to embrace the world in its myriad of details—to mourn losses, to delight in its many joys. It is this love that allowed both to delight in the details of the world given to them. It was in the fierceness of their love for God that the world's beauty emerged, which Madeleva held in delight with her relaxed grasp and Day enjoyed in all its richness as a practice of voluntary poverty. And they dedicated themselves to passing on this deep love in God's beauty to whoever might come their way.

The Generations of the Twenty-first Century

What do all of these observations have to do with passing on the faith to the next generation – the next generation in the twenty-first century? And more relevant to this essay's context, what do these observations have to do with an academic program called Catholic Studies? Does the role of Catholic Studies have anything to do with engaging students according to their needs inductively, with a focus on the "ideal practical layman and laywoman," or teaching them "the game of Catholic living"? Or can Catholic Studies in the twenty-first century in any way provide opportunities to explore Phelan's "thorough and systematic training in the science of revealed truth" to produce Connell's Catholics who can demonstrate "that religion is something about which one can reason as unsentimentally as about mathematics or chemistry "? Or is it possible that Catholic Studies might inspire D'Arcy's world-loving, countercultural dragon slayer? Or is there any place in Catholic Studies for Father Johnson's Catholics active in their parish, that "natural unit of living" where they might participate in "all the rest of the ordinary life of people"?

The only appropriate response to each question is, "Yes, of course, but not without attention to 'Necessary Adjustments to Overcome Practical Difficulties.'" Like all good practitioners, Catholics need to understand the game in practice and in theory. They need a bit of the daring adventurer while rooted in a local community in which they can continue to practice the game—a home field advantage of sorts. Catholic Studies gives a certain freedom to explore multiple facets of things Catholic in ways that no single discipline can address. Of course, Catholic Studies serves multiple purposes within an academic setting, and one certainly does not need to be a practitioner, aspiring or otherwise, to engage in Catholic Studies. Yet, Catholic Studies can be a rich resource for students interested in broadening their Catholic horizons.

Catholic Studies offers at least the condition for the possibility of deepening students' intellectual engagement with Christian faith and practice as it has developed over two millennia. It provides alternatives to and critical engagement with popular culture's multitude of options for defining "the faith." In a set of recent high school seniors' applications for a college scholarship with a focus on fostering vocations, the applicants responded to a question in which they were asked to cite a book other than the Bible that had shaped their faith life. Among the fifty-plus submitted for review, very few duplicates appeared. In light of what was previously said, it is interesting to consider how their choices coincide—or not—with the varied approaches that emerged in the previous century. Perhaps John Montgomery Cooper would give a nod to the student who mentioned *Seven Healthy Habits for Highly Effective*

Teens or the two who lauded Rick Warren's *The Purpose Driven Life*. Or he might have been relieved that as least some sought the "Great Exemplar" in reading Weber and Killgallon's *The Life of Christ* and Albert Nolan's *Jesus Before Christianity*, or even Charles Sheldon's classic *In His Steps*. Certainly Phelan and Connell would give a special cheer for the single student who mentioned the *Summa*, but would have also found satisfaction in the two who mentioned *Evangelium Vitae* or others who drew from the "new apologetics" *Catholic Beliefs and Traditions Ancient and Ever New*, as well as Amy Welborn's *Prove It! Church*. And Father D'Arcy might have been heartened to hear a student refer to Myles Connolly's *Mr. Blue*, a modern-day Saint Francis; Frank Mercadante's *Positively Dangerous*; Richard Foster's *Celebration of Discipline*; or the most intriguing, at least by title, *Jesus Freaks* by dc Talk and the Voice of the Martyrs. Still Cooper, Phelan, Connell, and D'Arcy might shudder at the shallowness of some of these selections—their flirting with America's primal religion, Gnosticism,[24] or their succumbing to religion as commodity.

Some selections resonated with those drawn to the aesthetics of faith. Certainly Sister Madeleva Wolff and Dorothy Day would have loved to see Dante mentioned, or Therese's *A Story of a Soul*, or perhaps even the contemporary contemplative, Joanna Weaver's *Having a Mary Heart in a Martha World*. Neither would have objected to Madeleine L'Engle's *A Ring of Endless Light*, Antoine de Saint-Exupéry's *The Little Prince*, or Victor Frankl's *Man's Search for Meaning*. It is hard to determine what they would have made of those who mentioned Mitch Albom's *The Five People You Meet in Heaven* or *Tuesdays with Morrie*. And it is even more uncertain what they might have said about three students' selections; each mentioned a Dan Brown novel, one his *Angels and Demons* and two *The Da Vinci Code*, as formative of their faith.

The question remains how much of what is offered the next generation does justice to the richness of Catholicism as an intellectual tradition, a tradition worthy of a distinct academic program. In "Necessary Adjustments to Overcome Practical Difficulties," Murray cautions that Catholicism "is not an instrument of humanitarianism; it is not even primarily an instrument for the constitution of a social order, it is first and foremost a vision of God." Such cautions align with those who are skeptical of faith's compatibility with the intellectual. Believers as much as nonbelievers are among these skeptics. Some would simply point to the myriad of opportunities on most campuses that allow students to participate in the practice of the faith in ways that Father Johnson would find at least vaguely familiar. Students speak fondly of their experience with youth ministry in their parishes or the profound impact various retreats have made. Some participate in liturgy through music ministry or as lectors or Eucharistic ministers. One can observe an increase in undergraduates' attendance at daily Mass, a few organize communal praying of the rosary or Eucharistic adoration—and yes, some get quite nervous about such trends—predicting a return to the pre–Vatican II days. Others have found service commitments or immersion trips as their principal expression of faith.

On the University of Dayton campus, not unlike many college campuses, a small cohort of students has given evidence of some interest in the intellectual dimensions of faith. Catholic Life is a student-organized group that focuses on a more intellectually based approach to faith based upon the official catechism and provides alternative social activities. Over the last decade, the number of religious studies majors has tripled. Yet, all of these practices of a minority require more study to understand how they are and are not simply variations on what is occurring in the wider culture and in what way they reflect a nostalgia for a prior time among people under forty who have no direct knowledge of the world to which they wish to return.

How do such practices inform engagement in the many challenges that these young people face in a world with a globalized economy, in a world where terrorism remains a constant psychological when not an actual physical threat? How is the Christian message heard in a media-saturated world that purposefully appeals to a sense of cynicism, cruelty, and vengefulness, or a world where analysts speak of younger people as understanding portable communication and entertainment as their birthright. The multidisciplinary nature of Catholic Studies offers a site for such explorations. Such multidisciplinary and at times interdisciplinary approaches can also capitalize on the younger generation's ability to adapt, to be multilingual at least in their ability to move across different types of cultures within the English-speaking United States. Their interests and curiosity include an openness at times to the varied beauty of diverse cultures and religious traditions.

Still, some of the "practical" difficulties remain. The eclectic approaches associated with Catholic Studies can further the dislocation of cultures and religious forms of life so that they become one more consumer choice, each one more exotic than the previous one. Surely an analogous dislocation affects students' sense of belonging and actively participating in "Catholic faith." This dislocation is further complicated by a Church struggling with internal splits over issues such as women's role, sexuality, and governance, with scandals, and with frequently less than inspiring leadership. And certainly a robust Catholic Studies program would necessarily explore such divisive and controversial issues. Still, there remain plentiful exemplars of the fully and critically engaged—those who aspire to the heroic and find their inspiration in the lives of other believers. Certainly, John Paul II, whose intellectual acumen is matched by his deeply formed spiritual life, has had a notable impact. Yet, even with John Paul II, the line between Christian hero and media celebrity is not always clear, a topic that invites analysis within a Catholic Studies context.

These brief descriptions, replete with dialectical dynamics, highlight the complexities of how contemporary situations intersect in contemporary students' lives and provide the context for the opportunities and challenges posed to any Catholic Studies curriculum. Given all that has been written here, the question remains what exactly is this faith to be passed on to the next generation and what does that task have to do with a multidisciplinary and interdisciplinary academic program called Catholic Studies. The simple answer is that the possibilities are seemingly endless, from the pragmatic, inductive approaches of a Cooper to the systematic approaches of a Connell to the inspiring narratives of a D'Arcy. Of course, there are also the more sophisticated analyses of a Murray and the aesthetics of a Madeleva and Dorothy Day. Catholic Studies provides the context to explore the wide and varying approaches to the faith that has been passed to the next generation.

Such exposure to the varied engagements with Catholicism is not for the purposes of a nostalgic restoration of a narrowly defined Catholicism. It is more about discovering possibilities in a critically expansive manner. It is more like what Thomas Merton wrote in *Conjectures of a Guilty Bystander* in concluding a section he entitled "Truth and Violence: An Interesting Era": "The Gospel is handed down from generation to generation *but it must reach each one of us brand new, or not at all* [*sic*]." What is being handed down to the next generation? What is it hoped that they will practice? To continue from Merton, "What makes the Gospel news?" His answer: "The faith . . . this new birth in the Spirit, [that] opens up a new dimension in which time and eternity meet, in which all things are made new: eternity, time, our own self, the world around us." He continues, "The Gospel is the news that, if I will, I can respond now in perfect freedom to the redemptive love of God . . . in Christ, that I can *now* rise above the forces of necessity and evil in order to say 'yes' to the mysterious action of Spirit that is transforming the world even in the midst of the violence and confusion and destruction that seem to proclaim His absence and His 'death.'"[25] Merton's own vision is predicated on his wide-ranging reading habits from the most ancient to the most contemporary of authors, Catholic and otherwise. His voracious reading habits are a kind of model of Catholic Studies.

A friend of mine told me a tale from his parish that suggests a certain urgency in providing a more intellectually rooted passing on the good news. He had gone to the parent's meeting for those with children preparing to receive their First Communion. The woman in charge of the catechesis announced to the parents that the emphasis for the children was to be "fun" and that they were intent, as she put it, on avoiding "all that yucky stuff"—which seemed to refer to the Catholic understanding of the Real Presence as Christ's Body and Blood. The power of the teaching of the Real Presence had somehow been reduced to something "yucky." This reduction stood in startling contrast with the following day's office of reading for the Feast of Saint Albert on November 15. The thirteenth-century theologian and teacher of Thomas Aquinas wrote the following about the Eucharist in a commentary on Luke's Gospel:

> There is nothing we can do that is more sweet. What could be sweeter than that in which God reveals all his sweetness to us? . . . For this sacrament begets love and unity. Is it not the greatest proof of divine love that Christ gives himself as food? It is as though he were saying: "I love them so much, and them me, that I want to be within them, and they want to receive me so as to be one body with me."[26]

The medieval teacher offers a vision of Eucharist that is neither esoteric nor yucky.

Catholic Studies provides opportunities for students to come to know the works, the lives, the perspectives of those who drew from and engaged in the Catholic intellectual tradition. It offers opportunities to explore those who defended "the faith," expanded the possibilities of faith's engagement in worlds unimaginable in the first century, and found in Catholic beliefs and practices a lens through which the world's beauty becomes recognizable. Catholic Studies can enrich Catholic engagement in quotidian dimensions of faith, the ordinary lives of Catholics, some of who might participate in the annual celebration of *Triduum*. As they engage in the passing on faith, those who have taken advantage of exploring Catholic Studies might recognize the rich possibilities laden in the second reading on Holy Thursday, taken from Paul's First Letter to the Corinthians (11:23–26).

> Brothers and sisters:
> I received from the Lord what I also handed on to you,
> that the Lord Jesus, on the night he was handed over,
> took bread and, after he had given thanks,
> broke it and said, "This is my body that is for you.
> Do this in remembrance of me."
>
> In the same way also the cup, after supper, saying,
> "This cup is the new covenant in my blood.
> Do this, as often as you drink it, in remembrance of me."
> For as often as you eat this bread and drink the cup,
> you proclaim the death of the Lord until he comes.

If Catholic Studies could contribute to passing on this one thing, this action, these words, to the next generation, then those who heard these words might receive them as gift to be cherished, remembered, and studied. Such reception might be without sentimentality as a vision of God in all its truth, goodness, and beauty that reflects the sweetness of God's deep and abiding love for us in the intellectual explorations of the academy and rugged urban landscapes surrounding a Catholic Worker House. Such study might bring to mind others who have enacted the eating, the drinking, and the proclaiming a death that brings life and still more life that comes in every time and place and will come again. Catholic Studies offers one avenue for exploring the possibilities and the limits of each generation's passing on of such a faith. To pass on that faith, despite all the limitations of each generation's expression of that faith, would be to pass on a faith that invites practice until God makes it perfect.

4 The (Catholic) Politics of Catholic Studies

DAVID O'BRIEN

Catholic Studies, the interdisciplinary study of Catholicism, seems a simple idea, and a useful one. Yet support for reflective intelligence about Catholicism has proven controversial in the Church and in the academy, even in academies sponsored by the Church. This volume describes the emergence of interest in Catholic Studies, including initiatives to establish Catholic Studies centers and academic programs in Catholic colleges and universities. These impressive projects, however, have yet to realize their potential or meet the very real need for institutional support for research and teaching on matters related to Catholicism. Only a limited number of Catholics are convinced of the usefulness of Catholic Studies, even fewer of the need for investment in developing Catholic scholarship. Research and teaching about Catholicism requires resources, human and material, and that support has proven hard to come by.

This essay will provide a short commentary on the development of Catholic Studies in the United States over the last three decades. We will focus attention on the way in which debate about Catholic Studies has been an important factor in the development of American Catholic institutions and ministries, and self-understanding, since the Second Vatican Council (1962–65).

The American Catholic Context

The Catholic politics of Catholic Studies are embedded in a network of contested questions, some related to the Second Vatican Council, some to the role of religion in American life, some to the present state and future prospects of the Catholic Church in the United States. Much has been written about the ideas behind Vatican II renewal and the now-dominant moves to "reform the reform," but very little has been said about the way ideas are translated into policies by internal politics. Even scholars well aware of the role of power and politics in church history seem wary of assessing politics in the contemporary Catholic Church, much less taking a deliberate part in those politics. Yet the recent history of episcopal appointments, liturgical texts, sacramental practice, and parish and diocesan finances make it clear that internal church politics play a very important role in shaping American Catholic life. And among the elements so shaped is Catholic cultural and intellectual life, including Catholic Studies. While Catholicism as a historical and contemporary fact is reason enough for scholars and teachers in many fields to pay attention to Catholics and their church, the prospects of Catholic Studies will be determined in large part by the decisions made by individual Catholics and by Catholic institutions.

Catholic Studies questions are engaged and contested in three institutional centers. One is Catholic higher education, where Catholic Studies is most discussed, and practiced. There the politics of Catholic Studies have emerged from sometimes bitter debates about the specifically Catholic responsibilities of Catholic colleges and universities. The second institutional location for Catholic Studies is in the growing number of Catholic Studies programs and chairs in other academic centers, public and private. There the politics of Catholic Studies engages larger questions of the role of religion in American culture and in American academic life. The third location for Catholic Studies is the Church, its monasteries, convents, seminaries, elementary and secondary schools, religious education programs and social and pastoral ministries. Included here would be independent associations such as Catholic publications, learned societies, and freestanding centers which take an interest in Catholic intelligence and imagination. Catholic Studies issues are openly debated and negotiated in the academy, and there are modestly politicized factions of Catholic theologians, but, despite their enormous pastoral importance, they are not very visible in the life of the Church. Yet it is there, as American Catholics decide for themselves what role reflective intelligence will play in the life and work of their church, that the question of Catholic Studies will in the end be resolved.

In each setting the presence, absence, and quality of Catholic Studies results from decisions, by individuals, committees, governing boards, officials, and benefactors. For two thousand years Catholicism has been an interesting and influential presence, and some scholars and teachers are naturally drawn to its study. But few regard the outcome of Catholic history as a matter of serious personal or historical significance, so they play only a minor role in the politics of Catholic Studies. Catholic Studies, like everything else Catholic, is shaped in large part by those who care about Catholicism, regard it as crucially important for the human family, and accept some responsibility for its future.

Some years ago Nathan Hatch, formerly provost at the University of Notre Dame and now president of Wake Forest University, told his fellow American evangelical Christians that the very possibility that their descendents might have an intelligent faith depended upon their willingness to invest substantial human and financial resources in serious study.[1] Similarly, support for Catholic Studies, including but not limited to theology, is a measure of commitment to intellectually serious Catholicism in the American future. Less obvious is that that support also measures the capacity of the Catholic community to take responsibility for its own history.

Some Personal Notes

I have been both a supporter and practitioner of Catholic Studies.[2] I was trained in American political history, but I stumbled into the history of American Catholicism early in my career. With similar lack of deliberation, I became engaged in a variety of movements and projects aimed at strengthening the public life of the American Catholic Church in social ministry, politics, pastoral reform, and higher education. In academic affairs I had the good fortune to work closely with the Association of Catholic Colleges and Universities (ACCU) and with a number of Jesuit academic projects, including the first National Seminar on Jesuit Higher Education. In these forums and in many publications I made the argument that the future of the American church was a matter of shared responsibility and, in the future as in the past, deliberate action would be needed if the American Catholic community was to flourish.[3]

It was in this context that I urged consideration of Catholic Studies as a practical strategy for solving problems related to the mission and identity of Catholic colleges and universities.[4] In 1995 I assisted the Association of Catholic Colleges and Universities (ACCU) in organizing a conference of college and university presidents designed to encourage consideration of Catholic Studies and partnerships with agencies of Catholic social ministry. With support from the Lilly Endowment and in partnership with the pioneering Catholic Studies program at the University of St. Thomas in Minnesota, I organized the first national conference on Catholic Studies in 1997. I also have had the opportunity to visit many Catholic colleges and universities and have been impressed by their prosperity, intellectual vitality, and determination to be faithful to their religious heritage.

In that same period I joined others to advocate establishment of a freestanding Institute for Advanced Catholic Studies to strengthen Catholic scholarship and encourage renewed commitment to intelligent faith throughout the American Catholic community. This project was brought forward by a group of the country's most distinguished Catholic scholars, including Francis Oakley, president of Williams College; Judge John Noonan, who delivered a powerful address on the project at Harvard; and Jil Ker Conway, prizewinning writer and former president of Smith College. Led by Michael Lacey, at that time director of American programs at the Woodrow Wilson International Center for Scholars, and Rev. James Heft, S.M., provost and University Professor of Faith and Culture at the University of Dayton, and with the help of a generous grant from an anonymous donor to be used as seed money, the organizers canvassed bishops, university presidents, foundations, and potential donors across the country. Despite making a strong case for the project as beneficial for the Church, for higher education, and for American society as a whole, the leaders were not able to generate the support needed for the major center they envisioned. A scaled-down version of the Institute, led by Rev. Heft, is currently located at the University of Southern California and has carried out some significant interfaith and interdisciplinary research projects.[5] Advocates of Catholic Studies and supporters of Catholic intellectual and cultural life have been sobered by that experience.

The limited achievements of the Institute mirror the modest role played so far by campus-based Catholic Studies programs.[6] The still-nascent Institute has done fine work; there has been a slow but steady growth of Catholic Studies centers, programs, and endowed chairs; and connections between colleges and universities and local churches are sometimes quite strong. Some creative and mutually beneficial connections between the Church and academic institutions have sparked some interest in renewing serious Catholic intellectual life. For example, Catholic overseas relief and domestic social action agencies such as Catholic Relief Services and the Catholic Campaign for Human Development have assigned staff to develop partnerships with Catholic higher education. Campuses boast expanding and ever more sophisticated programs of community-based learning and community service, including projects related to civic engagement, all of which provide rich experiential foundations for Catholic Studies. Such initiatives also provide opportunities for collaboration between Catholic higher education and Catholic pastoral and social ministries, turning the Catholic affiliation of academic institutions from a nagging problem into a set of enriching resources for the intellectual, cultural, and educational life of the college and university. But far more important than the role of Catholic Studies in easing the chronic obsession of academic leaders with institutional identity is its role in the continuing search for strategies and resources to enhance Catholic imagination and intelligence, a goal that requires engagement throughout the Catholic community.

A final personal word: After thirty-five years of working with Catholic institutions and agencies, I am convinced of the importance of internal Catholic politics. Things happen or do not happen because some individuals or groups work hard enough, or intelligently enough, to make them happen. This is obvious to scholars who have studied the Church or other institutions, but American Catholics with few exceptions remain remarkably innocent about the life and work of their church.[7] Perhaps the most important single fact about the politics of Catholic Studies is the passive role played by Catholic academic and intellectual leaders. Anyone even slightly familiar with contemporary Catholicism in the United States would be struck by the distance between Catholic ideas and Catholic practice. The most striking example in this context is the all but consensual emphasis on theological reflection and the absence of structured opportunities for such reflection in parishes, dioceses, agencies, and institutions.

Theologians are particularly invested in these gaps because the very nature of their vocation requires not only commitment to values of intellectual freedom and shared responsibility for Catholic self-understanding, but also participation in the life of the Catholic Church. In a word, to carry out their work theologians, and the Catholic academic institutions where the vast majority work, have a heavy stake in church reform; the Catholic intellectual vocation cannot be fully carried out unless the Church has room for serious scholarship and intelligent reflection. As I wrote in 1996, "Catholic higher education has an enormous stake in church reform toward collegiality and shared responsibility, including continued development of a strong national episcopal conference, and better mechanisms of consultation and shared responsibility at the diocesan level."[8] In the absence of such mechanisms, usually centered on parish and diocesan pastoral councils and independent boards of trustees for Catholic institutions, the dialogue between faith and culture that defines Catholic intellectual life, and Catholic Studies, can hardly flourish. Yet William Shea is the only American Catholic theologian I know of who has argued that theologians (and by implication other Catholic scholars) have to act politically if they are to maintain what Shea calls their "balancing act" between academic and ecclesiastical responsibilities. "Theologians must learn to act politically," Shea wrote in 1986. "It takes a strategy and relentless pressure if the ecclesiastical mountain is to be moved."[9]

Catholic Higher Education

The politics of American Catholicism and the need for deliberation and strategic action to support Catholic Studies is clearly evident in Catholic higher education. There, in a few short years after Vatican II, a genuine revolution took place as religious communities entrusted their colleges and universities to independent boards of trustees.[10] Academic leaders attempted to secure their role as universities by insuring institutional autonomy and academic freedom, while continuing to affirm their Catholic identity. American bishops welcomed the new arrangements, but the Vatican never accepted them and, together with a growing number of Catholics in the United States, regularly questioned how the colleges and universities continued to carry out their Catholic responsibilities.[11]

The structural changes in Catholic higher education reflected the wider experience of Catholic Americanization.[12] As more and more Catholics, with the benefits of increased education, took positions of responsibility in all sectors of American life, they tended to leave the tight networks of ethnic neighborhoods and urban parishes for the thinner associational life of the suburbs. Despite learned predictions to the contrary, Mass attendance, financial support, and vocations to the priesthood and religious life flourished for two decades after World War II. But profound changes were taking place below the surface, changes that would become evident when the American Catholic community began to implement the renewal mandated by the Second Vatican Council. Evangelical piety modified liturgical and catechetical practice, and Catholics increasingly insisted on the central role of conscience in moral decision making. Church leaders, concerned with the increasingly independent laity, tried for a generation to develop structures of shared responsibility that would enlist the Catholic people in the process of renewal and reform. But in the 1980s, that strategy was challenged by new leaders who hoped to restore Catholic unity, identity, and distinctiveness by reasserting clerical authority and emphasizing pastoral practices and moral issues that separated Catholics from other Americans. With that change, the dialogue between faith and culture seemed less important, and it became harder to maintain creative connections between Catholic academic institutions and other segments of the Church. Catholic Studies, proposed in the context of post–Vatican II renewal and reform, seemed attractive in the new setting less as a resource for an Americanized Catholic laity than as a project to sustain Catholic distinctiveness. As such, it would become less useful to Catholic academic institutions fully committed to sharing responsibility for American intellectual and cultural life.

Historian Philip Gleason located the Catholic academic revolution in this trajectory of American Catholic history,[13] arguing that separate incorporation and the multiple adjustments that accompanied it cost the Catholic colleges and universities their integrity as Catholic institutions. He has written that those who shaped Catholic higher education for the last thirty years were hell-bent on "assimilation" and "Americanization" and unwittingly gave away the Catholic game by imitating secular academia, hiring anybody who showed up with a good degree, and turning their backs on neoscholastic philosophy. The "secularization" of Protestant-sponsored colleges at the turn of the twentieth century seemed now to have been repeated by Catholic colleges and universities.[14] The Americanization of people and institutions was a story mainly of loss and defeat. Catholics who saw events this way hoped that Catholic higher education might salvage its Catholic integrity by the intervention of the Pope, and recent history seemed to fulfill their expectations. As Gleason put it: "*Ecclesiastical authority* [has now helped] stem what might have become an unintended slide into the kind of secularization experienced by Protestants a century ago."[15]

Others offered an alternative historical assessment. Drawing on Catholic social teaching, Vatican II's "Pastoral Constitution on the Church in the Modern World," and the 1974 Jesuit commitment to faith, justice, and the poor, many hoped that American Catholic higher education would renew its sense of Catholic mission by making its own the Church's newfound sense of shared responsibility for the fate of the human family. Gleason saw these "justice and peace" proposals as the only serious alternative to the recovery of identity by the reassertion of Catholic doctrine and ecclesiastical authority.[16] Jesuit institutions in particular have attempted to embody a sense of social and intellectual solidarity and place research and teaching in Catholic institutions at the service of church and society. In this setting, Catholic Studies is considered an academic strategy for bringing Catholic religious, intellectual, and cultural resources to bear on contemporary experience, and allow that experience to challenge and enrich Catholic faith and the life and work of the Church.

The argument between conflicting views of Catholic colleges and universities, and of Catholic theology and Catholic Studies, then, is at least in part an argument about Americanization. If Americanization is understood primarily as a process of secularization, then the proper response is to reaffirm distinctive Catholic truths and ecclesiastical responsibilities as Gleason proposes. If, as the earlier generation saw it, Americanization was a process of liberation leading to new responsibilities for the common life, then new educational and pastoral strategies similar to those adopted in most of Catholic higher education would be required. It is an old and important debate, resolved at the end of the nineteenth century with an option for the Church with accompanying subcultural strategies that effectively deprived lay experience of religious meaning. The same argument arose with the revival of Americanism in the post–World War II period, and it continues to dominate Catholic politics today.

This argument about the trajectory of American Catholic history is crucial to the politics of Catholic Studies. The decline of Catholic Americanism and the rise to dominance of subcultural and countercultural language and strategies has drained the foundations of Vatican II reform, relocated the American church's center, long represented by Joseph Cardinal Bernardin, and badly weakened the intellectual foundations of the Catholic academic revolution. Leaders such as Theodore M. Hesburgh, C.S.C., longtime president of the University of Notre Dame, and Rev. J. Bryan Hehir, architect of the public theology of the U.S. bishops as they wrote remarkable pastoral letters in the 1980s, followed the modified Americanist vision of Jesuit theologian John Courtney Murray. Murray understood the dialogue of faith and culture to involve a bilingual approach that allowed for faithful Christian discipleship and responsible American professionalism and citizenship. Murray's disciples knew there were critics of that approach, both radical Catholic advocates of nonviolence and the option for the poor, and conservatives convinced that the Church gave up too much when it accompanied its people into the pluralist, secular centers of national life. But they held to that Catholic vision of a "vital center" as appropriate to the historical experience of American Catholics who, as faithful citizens, now bore a full share of American public responsibility.

Advocates of this position found themselves on the defensive as the leaders of the Catholic Church, headed by Pope John Paul II, identified key moral issues such as abortion as definitive for faithful Catholics. At the same time, American neoconservatives rediscovered John Courtney Murray as a churchman and a Catholic first of all. In their hands, natural law could be used selectively to validate countercultural assaults on questions of sexuality while restraining the critical voice on economic and military questions. Few noticed the spillover into Catholic higher education, whose mission rested on the idea that the Christian was a "citizen of two cities" and in each city pursued a genuine Christian vocation.

I have argued with Philip Gleason and others for many years. I would tell the story of Americanization not in the passive voice of accommodation and cultural surrender, but in the active voice of liberation, solidarity, and shared responsibility. The movement of American Catholics from margin to mainstream was and remains good news, and the decision made by religious orders of men and women to accompany them on that journey was appropriate. The world Catholics created for themselves as they left their subcultures behind blurred boundaries but enlarged imaginations and expanded responsibilities. The now-dominant story about Catholic integrity at risk usually, but not always, uses countercultural language for subcultural purposes. It is a form of identity politics. The Americanist story, in contrast, values Catholic faith and tradition but acknowledges a full share of responsibility not only for American political and social life, but for intellectual life and culture as well. It differs from neoconservative views by insisting on civic as well as religious responsibility to maintain a critical voice about economic and social life, and to challenge the autonomy of the state on democratic, not just religious grounds. Most of all it affirms a deeper solidarity than that allowed by modern-day liberals or neoconservatives. The Second Vatican Council placed the dialogue of faith and culture in the context of solidarity: "the joys and the hopes, the griefs and anxieties, of the men [and women] of this age, these too are the joys and hopes the griefs and anxieties of the followers of Christ."[17] In this setting, Catholic intellectual life, and Catholic Studies, are solidarity in practice, and there is little room for pastoral or cultural strategies designed to set faith against a culture that, for better or for worse, is now our own.

Catholic Studies

If a board of trustees and administration of a Catholic college or university were to decide that they should take decisive action to preserve their institution's Catholic identity and provide an education suitable for lay Catholics, what should they do? Catholic Studies is the most interesting "practical action" proposed in answer to such questions.

Catholic Studies refers to interdisciplinary programs focused on Catholicism in some combination of:

Catholicism as an object of study, as in courses in history and the social sciences;

Catholicism as a perspective on human experience, a critical voice in many disciplines and programs, often labeled "Catholicism and" a particular subject matter;

Catholicism as a source of inspiration and integration for the academic vocation, either the learning experience of undergraduate students or the intellectual life of faculty and staff. This adds a pastoral element to academic programs, assisting students, scholars, teachers, and others to connect their faith and their work.

Catholic Studies chairs that offer students, Catholic or not, opportunities to encounter Catholic ideas exist at a number of non-Catholic institutions. Ordinarily, these emphasize Catholicism as an object of study, though many institutions have welcomed theologians whose work involves personal engagement with the Church and with Catholic doctrine.

At least twenty Catholic colleges and universities now have Catholic Studies centers dedicated to engaging issues of faith and learning central to institutional mission. Centers sponsor lectures, workshops, and forums designed to familiarize faculty, staff, and students with Catholic traditions and contemporary ideas and practices. Some support undergraduate programs that offer students the opportunity for a more systematic examination of Catholicism.

The most ambitious of these programs is at the University of St. Thomas in Minnesota.[18] Students can major or minor in Catholic Studies, and many double-major, allowing the University to develop courses in Catholic thought directly related to the student's major. There are opportunities for study in Rome, service at a local Catholic Worker house, and community prayer and worship. The Center offers summer seminars for interested faculty to foster engagement with the Catholic tradition and encourage the integration of faith with the work of teaching and research. While there is a strong base in philosophy and theology, substantial collaboration has taken place with the arts, sciences and other humanities. Most notable are undergraduate and graduate programs on "faith and the professions," with special attention to the school's huge MBA program. The St. Thomas program has sponsored national and international conferences on faith and business. The university has won a substantial endowment for a Center of Catholic Studies that will oversee these and other curricular and faculty development programs, house a chair in Catholic Studies, and publish a journal on Catholic intellectual life, *Logos*.

Whereas St. Thomas links it programs directly to institutional mission and has developed programs of worship, prayer, and service for students in the field, other programs have a more exclusively academic rationale. In some institutions, Catholic Studies takes advantage of a postmodern interest in situated learning, a rationale that is also attractive for proponents of Catholic Studies in non-Catholic university settings. As Georgetown's John Pfordresher put it, the program's rationale is "similar to that which underpins Women's Studies and Afro-American Studies." He continues: "The Catholic Church, regarded as a complex historical phenomenon affecting virtually every aspect of human thought and activity, is a subject worthy of sustained, informed, objective study both by the research scholar and the undergraduate student." Catholic Studies in this model indirectly fosters Catholic intellectual life, and in many cases it provides a home for Catholic scholarship, no small matter.

Other programs seek to offer faculty and students the opportunity to develop a more reflective faith while consciously engaging the Catholic tradition and in some cases taking responsibility for it. Emphasis on the academic vocation informs the Collegium program of summer seminars for graduate students and faculty as well as many campus-based programs that offer ongoing opportunities for prayer, reflection, and dialogue.[19]

All of these centers and programs, many still only modestly funded and staffed, demonstrate how strategic action can reinsert religious thought into campus culture in ways that enrich intellectual life and indirectly stimulate pedagogical and curricular innovation. On each campus the point these projects make is crucial: Catholic intellectual life is serious, important, and a necessary and valued part of the culture of this particular institution. Indeed a case can be made that the Catholic identity and responsibility of particular institutions will remain the rhetoric of mission statements if it does not influence the research choices, intellectual, and vocational self-understanding, and classroom presentations of the faculty. But for this influence to become real there must be a preliminary stage of dialogue, hardheaded analysis, and reflection. Only with the backing of a center or institute where this critical assessment can take place and large questions of religion and modern life are engaged will Catholic Studies courses and programs have a chance to be vital centers for these institutions.

Whether emphasis is placed on academic examination, dialogue, or spirituality, the purposes of all Catholic Studies programs include:

To insure, as a minimum, that interested students and graduate students can learn about the Catholic tradition and about the contemporary Church. Both are necessary. When only the tradition is mentioned, it leaves the impression that Catholicism was once an important element of Western culture, and thus deserves attention, but also leaves a second impression of an interesting, if archaic, museum.

To initiate and sustain constructive dialogue on matters of significance to the larger academic community. No word is more widely used to describe the method of connecting faith and scholarship than *conversation*. Making conversation happen is an important part of the Catholic Studies agenda. If the conversation gets serious, it will involve substantive Catholic analysis of both the discipline and its objects, a tougher agenda than it might appear. But, on the Catholic campus, placing human and financial resources behind that agenda could persuade faculty and staff that the institution's Catholic heritage and affiliation is an asset rather than a lingering problem.

In Catholic colleges and universities there is a third objective, to foster research and teaching that serve the needs of the Church, makes the university a place where the Church does its thinking, and upholds the precarious principle that Catholicism makes intellectual claims. This means both the personal issue stated by Nathan Hatch—will our children have the possibility of serious

Christian thinking?—and the larger issue of an intelligent church with the resources to conduct its affairs and pursue its mission in an effective way.

Finally, Catholic Studies initiatives are designed to provide Catholic scholarship with a home, and material support. The need to do this is well recognized in theology, less recognized in other areas. Seminaries and religious orders that played such an important role in preserving the intellectual tradition in the immigrant church can no longer do the job alone. Somewhere, some people must make Catholic scholarship and intellectual life their personal responsibility.

Catholic Studies programs also help meet some pressing practical needs in Catholic higher education. For example, if they come into existence with the endorsement of faculty and trustees through the ordinary procedures of academic governance, they give concrete, practical expression to the community's affirmation of its Catholic identity. In addition, interdisciplinary programs, including but not limited to theology and religious studies, can lift part of the burden of multiple expectations from those departments. After separate incorporation, academic leaders promised to develop strong theology programs to insure the academic presence of Catholicism. Often these departments are expected to foster the academic study of religion, provide a home for authentic Christian theology, Catholic and ecumenical, promote orthodox Catholic teaching, enable students to make sense of religious experience (one of the last academic homes for "seekers" one chair reported), introduce courses on non-Christian and non-Western religions, and sustain continuing dialogue on ethics and moral theology with other departments and schools. The universal presence in Catholic higher education of vital departments of theology and religious studies testifies to the continuing Catholic commitment of trustees and faculty, but the time has come to share many of these responsibilities more widely across the institution.

Perhaps most important, Catholic Studies programs create a center of responsibility for Catholic intellectual life. Nervous administrators sometimes worry that such a program would constitute an admission that Catholicism is not already an integral element of every department and program, but experienced faculty and staff know that what is everyone's responsibility ends up as no one's responsibility.

Finally, Catholic Studies programs offer a strategy for dealing with the contentious hiring question. If the community determines it needs such a program, then clearly faculty will be needed in many departments to participate in that program, and the Catholic interests of candidates becomes a legitimate matter for consideration.

Problems for Consideration

As noted earlier, the achievements of Catholic Studies are modest. These initiatives have faced a number of obstacles:

The Catholic "culture wars" have made both Church officials and academic leaders nervous about initiatives that use the title "Catholic." Ecclesiastical moves to assert power over institutions and over academic theology have had the effect of stimulating reemphasis on institutional autonomy and academic freedom, and on academic self-governance, a factor long ignored in the Catholic politics of Catholic higher education. There are many signs that faculty are less resistant to initiatives of this sort than in the past, but, ironically Catholic faculty worry that Catholic Studies could provide institutional cover for the reassertion of Catholic orthodoxy in campus culture and politics.

Resource limitations on each individual campus produce hesitation about new projects which lack external funding, leaving Centers and special programs dependent on "soft" money or the voluntary support of interested parties such as the sponsoring religious community. It is rare for Catholic Studies initiatives to arise from the community as a whole through the normal procedures of academic governance, often a prerequisite for incorporation into the standard budget.

Colleges and universities zealously defend their independence from one another, even when related to sponsoring religious communities, and they jealously guard their alumni and donor lists, as Lacey and Heft found out. As a result they have chosen to work together effectively to secure public support and to deal with the challenge of ecclesiastical intervention, but so far Collegium is their only cooperative project related to Catholic Studies.

Academic professionalization in all fields, even theology, places severe practical limitations on scholars and teachers interested in relating their work to specific communities, projects, or movements.

Aside from these matters of external understanding and support there are unresolved questions facing those committed to Catholic Studies programs. For one thing, is Catholic Studies a scholarly field or an animating center for Catholic intellectual life, a tension comparable to that between theology and religious studies. In recent years, Catholic colleges and universities have usually combined theology and religious studies with an increasingly lay and academically professional faculty. The differences, often conflicts, between theology and religious studies are felt in all academic settings, not just Catholic, but they were made more severe among Catholics by the well-publicized moves by Catholic authorities to assess the orthodoxy and even revoke the tenure of academic theologians. Lay faculty trained in theology acknowledge accountability within their discipline, not to ecclesiastical authorities, and they have none of the opportunities for training in a variety of sacred fields and spiritual formation available to the clerical and religious counterparts. Yet, like colleagues in other fields of study, faculty in theology and religious studies, lay or religious, often wanted to say both/and rather than either/or to the debate between inquiry carried on within the framework of faith, and inquiry about religion carried on with reference to methods and standards of evidence characteristic of other academic disciplines. To put this another way, everyone sees the value in drawing non-theologians into conversation about religion and intellectual life, but only as programs get started does it become clear that Catholic Studies faces many of the same issues that have plagued theology and religious studies departments.[20] For example: does Catholic Studies mean courses and research projects about Catholicism, or does it involve an interdisciplinary engagement of the community in its own faith tradition?

At Holy Cross College our mission statement, adopted by the community after four years of discussion, claims that "in a special way, the

College must enable all who choose to do so to encounter the intellectual heritage of Catholicism, to form an active worshipping community, and to become engaged in the life and work of the contemporary church." Is Catholic Studies about the first of these purposes only? If the other two purposes should also be involved, particularly in an undergraduate setting, how are they to be approached in ways consistent with sound academic policy? But if they are left out, does that choice not risk leaving theology to the experts and confirming the unintellectual drift of popular piety?

Second, there is the "let them do it" problem, what Thomas Landy calls the potential "ghettoizing of Catholic identity."[21] Just as Catholic academic matters in the past were left to theology, might the same not happen with Catholic Studies, substituting one kind of marginalization for another? This problem might be addressed as it often is with Women's Studies and Peace Studies: that such programs offer concentrations for students with a special interest in these matters and they also have the responsibility to promote attention to these matters throughout the life of the institution.

Finally, there is the Catholic element of Catholic Studies. Theologian David Hollenbach has argued that Catholic colleges and universities would do well to consider the virtue of solidarity, the common good. There is a social solidarity, he argues, which means that academic work must be done within the horizon of the option for the poor. And there is an intellectual solidarity, which means pursuit of the academic vocation in the horizon of the human community's search for meaning and value. According to Hollenbach, intellectual solidarity requires us to "take pluralism to conversation." Hollenbach believes that the most serious conversationalists are religious communities that uphold substantive notions of human good, and the university is the place for that conversation to begin, its public responsibility if you will.[22] Absent something like this very Catholic solidarity, and Catholic Studies will easily become one more reflection of Catholic retrenchment.

Here is the heart of the call to Catholic Studies, I think. Intellectual solidarity draws those of us who are Catholics to consider that our problems, the problems that draw us to Catholic Studies, are everyone's problems. It draws Catholic higher education to recover a mediating stance that rejects confessionalism, that is higher education without diversity, and mere sponsorship, higher education without religion. Catholic intellectual life, carried on within this horizon, faces directly the challenge of modernity to religion. The phrase "Catholic intellectual," according to James Turner, "if not downright oxymoronic to non-Catholics, connoted a strong person who read Thomas Aquinas and papal encyclicals while harboring deep suspicions of Sigmund Freud and John Locke. This character might be bright, even interesting as a curiosity, but certainly was not someone to engage in debate about contemporary sociology or recent literary criticism." Vatican II may have "exploded the cozy nest within which this odd bird was hatched," Turner continues, but from the debris few recognizable Catholic intellectuals, as distinct from "intellectuals who happen to be Catholic," have arisen. Turner is not surprised, because "Catholic universities have rarely fostered scholarship that plunges Catholicism into the pluralistic intellectual life of our times . . . and Catholic colleges have seldom encouraged their students to think seriously and flexibly about the relationship of their faith to the novels they are reading or the chemistry they are studying." But none of this is inevitable: "No Christian people has a richer intellectual tradition. But to activate that tradition in the lives of Catholics, to fulfill its mission to the church, Catholic higher education needs to make a dual move: back to the intellectual resources of Catholicism and out into the larger world of modern knowledge, so as to bring each to bear upon the other."[23] In the end, that is not a bad assignment for Catholic Studies.

Conclusion

It is the height of folly to think that any organization, including the Church, will act intelligently, or that the quality of its cultural life will be adequate to the scope of its mission, unless intelligent people are dedicated to devoting at least some of their time and talent to it. So the politics of the Catholic Studies question seems relatively clear. Will Catholic scholars, writers, and artists be persuaded to participate more energetically and constructively in the Church's public life and ministry and thereby create a network of Catholic intellectuals in many fields and disciplines who will share in the task of making the Church's contribution to American culture more creative and effective? Of course, this is not the only question. Certainly bishops should affirm and support intellectuals and artists. They in turn should cooperate with bishops in reforming seminary education and ministry training. Academic leaders, trustees, administrators, and benefactors should support scholars working within the Catholic tradition and helping to meet the needs of the Church. But all these turn upon a more fundamental question facing all Catholics, including artists and intellectuals. The promise of American Catholicism's remarkable history will bear fruit only if serious people, mature enough to ride out the tensions and ambiguities present in their moment in history, decide to devote a portion of their talent and energy to the Church, specifically to the intellectual life of the Church, its cultural enrichment, and its dialogue with the larger society. If they do so and engage the politics that arise from their vocation, Catholic intellectual and cultural life, and Catholic Studies, will flourish.[24]

Part II: Traditions and Methods

5 Catholic Studies and Religious Studies

Reflections on the Concept of Tradition

ANN TAVES

Although most of the chairs and programs established in Catholic Studies in recent years have been established in Catholic colleges and universities, an increasing number are appearing in non-Catholic institutions both private and public. Some of the latter have been established as interdisciplinary chairs or programs without any special relationship to religious studies; others, such as the new chairs at Hofstra and UC Santa Barbara, are located in departments of religious studies alongside endowed chairs in other religious traditions, such as Tibetan Buddhist Studies, Sikh Studies, and Jewish Studies. At UCSB, where the Department of Religious Studies has been organized on an area-studies model (for example, Religions of South Asia, Religions of North America, Religions of the Mediterranean World), the endowment of a series of chairs in particular traditions sparked a yearlong faculty discussion of how the study of traditions might relate to the study of religions in areas or regions.

In reflecting on those conversations, I was struck by the need for more sustained reflection on the concept of "tradition" within the context of religious studies. In those conversations, I used "traditions"—perhaps naively—as a loose synonym for "religions" as in "religious traditions" or as a way to refer to variants within a religion, as in, for example, Christian or Buddhist or Islamic traditions. Although I was not assuming that the boundaries of "a tradition" were clear-cut or undisputed, colleagues and doctoral students raised questions that seemed to equate studying traditions with advocating for a tradition or promoting traditionalism. In contrast to other concepts routinely used by scholars of religion, such as sacred, myth, ritual, and religion, I realized that we apparently had less scholarly distance on the concept of "tradition."

A search of the literature revealed that this is indeed the case. The concept of tradition has not been the focus intense discussion among scholars of religion in the same way that, say, myth or ritual or experience has been. Recently, however, there has been renewed interest in the term.[1] This new work evinced a fairly high level of frustration with defining the term beyond the bare etymological meaning of "things handed down." The best of the new work on the subject suggests these difficulties arise because the term is "an object of intense partisan struggles and ideological distortion," a conclusion that will surprise few Catholics. Claims regarding tradition, these scholars suggest, mark a site of struggle. If this is the case, and I think it is, then we can anticipate that there will be no easy way to separate the normative and descriptive aspects of tradition and that any attempt to do so will presuppose a point of view.[2]

Although "tradition" is a site of struggle, we can gain greater clarity if we distinguish between several different ways we use the term and, thus, several different kinds of sites where struggle can take place. The sociologist Edward Shils makes the helpful distinction between a tradition as a thing that is handed down from the past to the present and a tradition as a "chain of transmitted variants, as in the 'Platonic tradition' or the 'Kantian tradition.'"[3] We can distinguish, in other words, between references to particular traditions, such as apostolic succession, and the Catholic tradition as distinct from (say) the Protestant tradition. Tradition in either sense can be a site of struggle, as various parties argue over what counts as apostolic succession or over what counts as Catholic tradition. We can also distinguish between tradition in either of these senses and explicit appeals to tradition as a means of legitimation, alongside or in opposition to appeals to scripture, reason, science, and so forth. Here the struggle is more likely to be over what counts as a means of legitimation. We can distinguish these three senses of tradition as tradition_T (T = things handed down), tradition_L (L = lineage or chain of variants), and tradition_A (A = source of authority or legitimation).

These distinctions can help us to clarify similarities and differences between Catholic Studies in the context of religious studies departments in secular universities and Catholic Studies in the context of Catholic universities. First, Catholic universities are related in some way to the Catholic Church and, thus, are positioned within the Catholic tradition$_L$. Although what it means to be positioned in this way is debated, Catholic scholars teaching in Catholic universities typically presuppose that Catholic Studies can or should play a role in defining how the Catholic tradition$_L$ is or ought to be understood. Doing so may involve making appeals to tradition$_A$. In secular universities, Catholic scholars teaching in the area of Catholic Studies may want to define the Catholic tradition$_L$ and may make appeals to tradition$_A$ when doing so. This, I assume, is what some of my colleagues feared would be entailed in studying the Catholic or any other tradition$_L$ within the context of religious studies. This, however, is not how I understand what it means to do religious studies.

Second, academic disciplines can be thought of as similar in some ways to traditions$_L$. Academic disciplines, like traditions$_L$, are sites of struggle. Scholars argue over what it means to do religious studies or history or sociology, and they may appeal to disciplinary traditions$_A$ when doing so. In this essay, I will argue that we can and should distinguish between doing religious studies and doing theology and that this distinction gives rise to two distinct ways of doing Catholic Studies. Whether or not we can legitimately distinguish between religious studies and theology is an issue over which much ink has been spilled in religious studies, with some arguing that the two can and should be rigidly separated and others that this is not only impossible but also undesirable.[4] I am of the school, or tradition if you will, in religious studies that thinks that the two can and should be distinguished. In contrast to some who argue for this distinction, however, I understand doing theology and doing religious studies to involve specific roles or stances that scholars can take in relation to their subject matter regardless of their religious beliefs. Scholars can shift roles or positions as desired, but they should signal their intent to their audience or readers when they change roles.[5]

We can use the act of defining the key terms that constitute a discipline or tradition$_L$ to locate the boundary between the inside and the outside of the discipline or tradition$_L$. By key terms, I mean what others have referred to as "constitutive terms," that is, the terms without which the discipline or traditions$_L$ in question would not exist.[6] The constitutive term for the study of religion is "religion" or "religious studies." The constitutive term for the study of spirituality is "spirituality." For the study of history, it is "history." And so on. I think that with respect to traditions the situation is quite parallel. The constitutive term for Christianity is "Christian." In other words, for Christianity to exist as a living tradition$_L$, we have to ask, "What does it mean to be a Christian?" Likewise for (say) Catholicism to exist as a living tradition$_L$, we have to ask what does it mean to be Catholic or for Judaism, Jewish; or Islam, Muslim, and so on. The idea of a living tradition, in other words, presupposes something that is being kept alive through a transmission process. Though we do not normally refer to "living disciplines," we can extend the concept to disciplines as well. The key distinction then is between those who treat the tradition or discipline as a set of human beliefs and practices that can be understood historically and those who actively seek to keep a tradition or discipline alive in the present by defining what it means to for it to live in the present.

In this essay, my aim is to advance religious studies as a "living discipline" that studies (among other things) living (and dead) traditions$_L$ historically. As historians, we neither seek to keep traditions alive nor to "kill" them, but rather to observe and analyze the processes that those who identify with them employ to maintain and transform them. I am hoping, in other words, to advance religious studies as a discipline by defining it as a discipline that, among other things, studies traditions$_{L,}$ without attempting to define what is authentically traditional (what counts as a tradition$_L$). I will elaborate on this in relation to "the Catholic tradition$_L$" and debates over the meaning of tradition within Catholicism.

Positioning oneself either inside or outside a particular discipline or tradition results in both gains and losses. If we refrain from defining "Catholic" and, thus, from defining "the Catholic tradition$_L$," we can position ourselves so as to analyze and observe struggles over the meaning of tradition$_L$ over time with an eye to comparing the way that "traditions$_L$" are made and unmade in various contexts. Refraining from defining what counts as "the tradition$_L$" in a particular context frees us to compare underlying processes of interest to scholars in religious studies and the wider university. If we enter into the definitional process, we add our voice to the mix of voices struggling to define what it means to be Catholic. In doing so, we contribute to processes of reflection that are of deep concern to those who identify with the tradition$_L$. From a religious-studies perspective, particularly religious studies in the context of a public university, I do not think it is our task to enter into Catholic struggles to define "the Catholic tradition$_L$," but instead to study the definitions of those who are actively engaged in those struggles in order to advance our understanding of how religious communities constitute and maintain themselves over time. A religious-studies approach to tradition$_L$ allows us to do three things: elaborate a non-essentialist understanding of tradition$_L$ and tradition$_T$ appropriate to the study of religions, study Catholicism as a tradition$_L$ that has been created and maintained through intensive reflection on the meaning of tradition, and position the current move toward "Catholic Studies" reflexively with respect to Catholic efforts at self-definition. Doing these things will help us to integrate Catholic Studies into the study of religion as defined here; they may or may not further the interests of Catholics as Catholics.

A Non-Essentialist Understanding of Tradition

Taking a non-essentialist stance relative to tradition$_L$ and tradition$_T$ means understanding tradition$_L$ and tradition$_T$ as historically constructed products of contestation rather than as guarantors of truths revealed at the beginning and handed down over time. Viewing tradition$_L$ and tradition$_T$ in this way undercuts tradition$_A$ as a source of authority relative to other sources of authority. It is precisely this undercutting of claims based on tradition$_A$ that has allowed historians to investigate how traditions$_L$ and traditions$_T$ have emerged, developed, and been maintained (or not) over time.[7] Scholars standing both inside and outside of traditions$_L$ have used historical methods to undercut the legitimacy of claims based on tradition$_A$. When insiders to a tradition$_L$ use history to undercut claims based on tradition$_A$, they typically go on to argue for what they consider to be a more legitimate understanding of the tradition$_L$ based on either a different understanding of tradition$_A$ or on other sources of authority recognized by the tradition$_L$.[8] In so far as scholars of religion position themselves outside of traditions$_L$, they can compare the way in which traditions$_L$ and tradition$_T$ have been historically constructed. Many within religious studies would argue that such comparative work is a distinctive task of religious studies.

We can illustrate the distinction between these approaches by considering the concept of apostolic succession. The idea of apostolic succession is a tradition$_T$ within the Catholic and Anglican traditions$_L$, which claims that there is a line of succession that can be traced through successive bishops back to the apostles. Historians would argue that lines of succession that run from historical bishops back to the apostles were retrospectively constructed, given the historical evidence that the role of the monarchial bishop emerged gradually over the course of the first two centuries of the common era.[9] Recognizing this, however, allows us to examine the way in which the idea of apostolic succession was derived from the idea of apostolic authority and utilized in the construction and defense of what came to be called "orthodoxy." While apostolic succession per se is a Christian concept, scholars of religion can and have compared it with notions of authentic transmission in other traditions as part of an attempt to understand how orthodoxies are created.[10]

Benedict XVI, drawing on *Dei Verbum*, the Second Vatican Council's Dogmatic Constitution on Divine Revelation, draws a similar distinction between historical and theological method in his recent *Jesus of Nazareth* (2007). Historical methods, he argues, must leave the past, including the past attested to by the Bible, in the past. Historical methods cannot make "the biblical word . . . into something present *today*." Historical methods treat "biblical words . . . as human words" and the biblical texts as composites made up of texts written, rewritten, and combined over time to create "scriptures." With respect to "all efforts to know the past," he concludes, we must bear in mind that "we can never go beyond the domain of hypothesis, because we cannot bring the past into the present."[11] To bring the past into the present, we must make theological claims that position us within a tradition$_L$. Thus, as Ratzinger points out, the idea of "the unity of Scripture," that is, the unity of the Old and New Testaments, is a specifically Christian theological claim, based on a Christological hermeneutic. "This Christological hermeneutic, which sees Jesus Christ as the key to the whole [of scripture] and learns from him [that is, Jesus, in post resurrection appearances recounted in the gospel of Luke] how to understand the

Bible as a unity, presupposes a prior act of faith."[12] Only some first-century Jews believed that Jesus was the Messiah, and the rabbinic tradition, which emerged alongside Christianity during the first centuries of the Common Era, argued for a very different scriptural hermeneutic based on Mishnah and Talmud. While historians do not dispute that some first century Jews believed Jesus was the Messiah, they cannot as historians interpret the history of this period in light of that claim. For historians, the early Jewish Christians' claim that Jesus was the Messiah is simply one claim among many.

Catholic theologians also distinguish between general definitions of tradition that can be applied to any religion and definitions that presuppose specifically Christian claims. So, for example, Yves Congar, O.P., distinguishes between tradition$_{[T]}$ in its total meaning as the "transmission of an object to another person" and tradition as understood in the context of "revealed religion and Christianity itself." In the latter context, he distinguishes between apostolic tradition and ecclesiastical tradition with a range of subspecifications under each.[13] Gerald O'Collins, S.J., provides a general definition of tradition$_{[T \text{ or } L]}$ as "as a human reality [that functions] to secure a society's continuity, identity and unity. Traditions$_{[T \text{ or } L]}$ fashion *the bond between successive generations* in a society." A specifically Christian understanding of tradition, he indicates, presupposes "the saving [or foundational] revelation of God . . . in the history of Israel and then definitively in the life, death and resurrection of Jesus Christ."[14]

Those who position themselves within a tradition$_L$ take up a different set of questions from those who position themselves within religious studies. Within a tradition the basic question has to do with keeping a living tradition alive. From within the Christian tradition in particular the question is:

> How can we be sure and ensure that the original, foundational revelation remains living and effective in the present Church? To put matters more precisely: In the life of Christianity how does one generation know that, as it expresses and transmits to another what it has experienced of the divine self-communication, there will be real continuity between the foundational revelation which occurred then and the dependent revelation which takes place now? How does it

> know that there will be no loss of essential identity in re-enacting the basic experience of God's self-communication in Christ?[15]

From within a tradition$_L$ the central questions have to do with the authenticity and legitimacy of what is transmitted from the past to the present. The key question is what counts as tradition$_T$ and on what grounds.

To sum up: Traditions$_L$ generally posit some originary event (for example, the crucifixion and resurrection of Jesus or the Buddha's enlightenment) as revelatory of Truth or Reality and seek to bring this past event into the present. Bringing the past event into the present often involves tradition$_T$, that is, the handing down of something from the past to the present. Claims that a specific formulation of tradition$_T$ authentically transmits the past to the present are sometimes backed by references to tradition$_A$. Those outside the tradition$_T$—and this includes historians in their role as historians—are not in a position to decide if any particular formulation of tradition$_T$ authentically transmits the past to the present. Neither are they in a position to decide what counts as an authentic representation of a tradition$_L$, since doing so relies perforce on claims regarding tradition$_T$.

Scholars who routinely define a tradition for the purposes of teaching and research may view this last claim as overly strong. Definitions that seem neutral enough on the surface, however, break down under scrutiny. If, for example, we define Christianity as a chain of transmitted variants that descend from the figure of Jesus, how do we as scholars decide which variants (actually) descend from Jesus? Do we count as variants Glenda Green's *Love Without End* (1998), which she claims is based on her visitations with Jesus, *A Course in Miracles*, teaching recounted to Helen Schucman by an inner voice that she identified as the voice of Jesus, or *The Book of Mormon*, which Latter-day Saints view as "another testament of Jesus Christ"? While these claims are contested, each would count as a variant in so far as someone claims to have handed down something from the past to the present. In the case of Glenda Green and Helen Schucman, each claimed that the still-living Jesus directly handed down his words to her (that is, via oral transmission). In the case of Joseph Smith and *The Book of Mormon*, we have "another testament" having to do with Jesus Christ that Joseph

Smith and the communities descended from him claim was written by ancient prophets, edited by the historian-prophet Mormon, and translated by Joseph Smith. Deciding which variants actually descend from Jesus requires scholars to tacitly accept or reject claims regarding tradition$_{T}$, that is, that the apostle Paul really heard the voice of Jesus, but Glenda Green and Helen Schucman did not. Making such claims tacitly aligns us with definitions of Christianity advanced by particular groups or individuals and not others.

Scholars use various techniques to signal their intent to distance themselves from contested claims such as these. Sometimes they use the idea of "orders of discourse" to distinguish between their use of a term and the way others use it.[16] Scholars of religion often distinguish between the first- and second-order use of terms. In so doing, they intend to distinguish between terms that are used within a community, in accordance with the underlying presuppositions of the group, and terms that have been, in many cases, abstracted from particular contexts, more or less "scrubbed" of particularistic presuppositions, and put to use as generic concepts that can be utilized across a range of traditions.[17] Any number of basic terms in the study of religion have undergone such a process, including "religion," "religious experience," "ritual," "myth," "spirituality," and "mysticism," though scholars continue to debate to what extent the terms still reflect the presuppositions of the contexts that generated them.

In a recent essay, Gavin Flood argued for a distinction between first, second, and third order discourses, in order to distinguish between discourse at the level of practice (first order), theological reflection on practice from within the tradition (second order), and reflection on first-and second-order discourses from a comparative perspective from a position outside any particular tradition (third order).[18] Whether we distinguish between one or two (or more) levels of discourse within a tradition is not as crucial to my argument as noting the difference between the use of a concept that is bounded by the presuppositions of a religious group and a concept that scholars seek, however successfully, to purge of group-specific presuppositions in order to use it to examine similar phenomena across groups. Adopting a distinction commonly employed by anthropologists, we can refer to the former as the *emic* and the latter as the *etic* use of the term. Though there has been some scholarly reflection on the concept of tradition in this more generic (etic) sense, an etic approach has not been as thoroughly assimilated into religious studies as it might be.

Much of the scholarly frustration with the concept of tradition has arisen from two sources: the inability to differentiate between different ways of using the term, that is, between tradition$_T$, tradition$_L$, and tradition$_A$, and the inability to reliably signal the shift from an emic to an etic perspective. If, as I have suggested, historical methods tend to undercut tradition$_A$ and historians and religious studies scholars as such have no basis for determining what "counts" as a link or chain or variant and, thus, what counts as either tradition$_T$ or tradition$_L$, then one way to mark the shift from an emic to an etic use of the term lies in incorporating the contested character of what counts as tradition into the etic definition itself. Put simply, if we define tradition$_T$ etically as any thing that someone *claims* is handed down from the past to the present, we have a basis for proceeding that positions us within the discipline of history but does not require us to align ourselves with any particular group or individual.

The insertion of "someone claims," thus, historicizes the claims and makes it clear that traditions$_{[T]}$ are not given but actively constructed and as highly contested as the traditions$_{[L]}$ that presuppose them. The simple assertion of agency (someone claims) into the definition shifts our attention away from figuring out if something is (authentically) traditional or not and focuses it instead on the struggle over what counts as tradition$_{[T \text{ or } L]}$ within various communities or groups and on what grounds (including tradition$_A$). Building on Shils, this definition, thus, makes no statement about:

What is handed down
How long it has been handed down
How it has been handed down—whether orally or in written form or through imitation
Who makes the claim
What justification they advance for their claim
Whether it was actually or authentically handed down
Whether it was good or bad that it was handed down

The insertion of "someone claims" also provides a way to signal that we are positioning ourselves etically—that is, outside the traditions$_L$ in question and, thus, a means of clarifying some of the confusions that have surrounded the use of the term.

The Study of Catholicism as a Tradition

An upper-division undergraduate course I teach titled "Church, State, and the Construction of Orthodoxy" illustrates the historical, religious-studies approach that I consider appropriate in the context of a religious studies department in a secular, public university. The course surveys the emergence and development of the Catholic Church as a transnational institution with a particular focus on how its centralized authority structure emerged in conjunction with the definition, maintenance, and transmission of "orthodoxy" and through interaction with the political order. Histories of Christianity or Catholicism that seek to keep the tradition alive typically assume that Jesus was the Messiah and presuppose Jesus' life, death, and resurrection as originary events, as revelation or manifestations, that is, of the living Word. Histories that begin in this way presuppose that true teachings were revealed at the outset and then defended against heretics (false teachings) that emerged in response. In this view, it is assumed that orthodoxy existed from the beginning independent of heresy, and that, if orthodoxy could be protected from heresy, it could be passed on more or less unchanged.

From a strictly historical vantage point, of course, this cannot be presupposed. Then and now people disagree over whether Jesus was *the* true Messiah, *a* true Messiah, a false messiah, a failed messiah, or whether there were, are, or will be any messiahs at all apart from human longing and imagination. Historians as such cannot judge the question but instead explore these various beliefs about messiahs and their consequences. So the course I teach does not start from the premise of truth revealed in the originary events of Jesus' life, death, and resurrection, but rather with what the surviving texts reveal about the range of reactions to Jesus that emerged among those who followed him and those who did not. From this starting point, we do not see revealed truth battling heresies cropping up on every side, but rather a diversity of contending views of truth each claiming that it is orthodox and that others are not. Out of this diversity of contending views, we can than ask how followers of Jesus created distinctions between orthodoxy and heterodoxy (inside/outside) and in some cases the institutional structures necessary to maintain and transmit that distinction from one generation to the next.

Teaching this way requires that we include nontraditional texts that reflect the views of critics of a tradition and that we teach students to read texts beloved by traditions critically. So, for example, I pair Irenaeus ("Against the Heresies") on apostolic succession with the "Coptic Apocalypse of Peter," a third-century text that describes bishops and deacons as "dry canals" incapable of understanding the deeper meaning of scripture.[19] With the help of Elaine Pagels, we dig deeply into Irenaeus's text, analyzing the views of his immediate opponents (the followers of Ptolemaeus, including the enigmatic Marcus), who apparently advocated a second initiation (or second baptism) into higher, more perfect knowledge. Reading between the lines, we compare the competing interpretations of the prologue of the Gospel of John offered by Irenaeus and the Ptolemaeans and the implications of their views for their understandings of the crucifixion, the relation between the divine and human Christ, and Christian initiation.

Knowledge of the claims and practices of his immediate opponents brings the text to life as a historical document. Reading it this way not only allows us to consider what they believed to be true (what counted for them as the living tradition) but how they defended their beliefs. Scripture was the first line of defense, but as the text makes clear, this was not enough. While Irenaeus and the Ptolemaeans agreed that scripture had to be read correctly, they did not agree on what that entailed. It is in this context that Irenaeus turned to the "Rule of Truth," a proto-creedal statement,[20] to establish the authority of his reading of scripture. As there were multiple variant proto-creeds, the Rule of Truth was in turn linked to the idea of apostolic succession and the assertion of the preeminent authority of apostolic tradition as preserved by the church at Rome. It is in this context, then, that Irenaeus could argue that the bishops, whom he claimed constituted a line of authority from the apostles down to his own time, "neither taught nor knew of anything like what these [heretics] rave about." Because he was convinced that the apostles committed the churches to bishops and especially to Peter, he could then add the finishing touch to his argument, saying that "if the apostles *had* known hidden mysteries, which they were in the habit of imparting to 'the perfect' apart and secretly from the rest [as his opponents were claiming], they would have delivered them especially to those to whom they were also committing the churches themselves" (III.3.1). If the apostles had had hidden mysteries to impart, in other words, they would have imparted them to *us* and not to *them*!

This kind of analysis allows us to examine the way in which the definitions of orthodoxy (that is, definitions of the "living tradition") that survived went hand in hand with the emergence of the structures needed to defend and maintain them. Though Jesus' immediate followers claimed that he appeared in person to help them interpret the [Hebrew] scriptures in the wake of his crucifixion (e.g., Luke 24:13–35), claims of this sort expanded rather than narrowed the interpretive options. A stable understanding of truth required a stable interpretation of scripture, which in turn required more developed claims regarding how those in the present knew that their understanding of the truth was authentic. It is in this context that we can understand the historical development of lines of succession and the need to extend the idea of bishops all the way back to the apostles. We can see, too, how lines of descent from apostles, like genealogical lines of descent, fan out from the original ancestors to create multiple heirs. So even lines of descent from bishops were not enough. There had to be a way to either prioritize their views (by giving some preeminence over others) or by forcing them to come to agreement (for example, in councils).

The understanding of apostolic succession, of course, is not static within the tradition. It has been interpreted and reinterpreted in order to keep the tradition alive. At the end of the course, we analyze a recent reinterpretation of apostolic succession—one offered in an essay by Cardinal Joseph Ratzinger in 1998 on the place of new ecclesial movements—in more depth. To understand the place of these movements in the church, Ratzinger argues, "the concept of apostolic succession must be given greater breadth and depth,"[21] especially in light of the thirteenth century controversies over the new movements of that era led by (unauthorized) mendicant preachers. Students compare Ratzinger's reading of Irenaeus and the thirteenth-century controversies with the relevant primary texts we have already discussed in order to see how Ratzinger builds his theological argument on a thirteenth-century theological discussion that was parallel in many ways to the situation he was facing.

Positioning Catholic Studies in Religious Studies

This way of positioning Catholic Studies within religious studies differs in significant ways from other understandings of Catholic Studies. Most chairs and programs in Catholic Studies are driven by a concern with Catholic identity. In Catholic colleges and universities and in some non-Catholic institutions as well, Catholic Studies is seen as a means of fostering Catholic identity, as a means of forming Catholics, and a context in which the tradition can be passed on to a new generation.[22] As such, of course, it is a site of intense conflict over what actually counts as authentic Catholic identity, with some viewing it as a potentially liberal site of formation and others hoping for just the reverse. However faculty position themselves in relation to these debates, they are arguing for what counts as Catholic identity and for a vision of what it means for the tradition to be passed on, that is to live. They are engaged, in other words, in a process of forming a new generation of Catholics. This suggests that we can view the difference between teaching Catholic Studies as religious studies in a secular, public university and teaching Catholic Studies in a Catholic college or university in light of the question of who we are forming for what end or, to put it another way, what we are trying to make. When I am teaching Catholic Studies in a religion department, I am not only participating in the making of religious studies, I am also participating in the formation of students in the liberal arts, in the humanities, and in the discipline of religious studies. My aim in that context is not to form Catholics.

To put this more generally, students may pursue the study of religion within programs in secular universities that have no connection to processes of religious or spiritual formation. In doing so, they enter into a process of academic formation under the direction of academic insiders whose insider status is established by academic traditions (degrees, promotions, tenure) rather than through participation in specific religious or spiritual traditions. Conversely, the task of forming persons religiously or spiritually may be taken up by the traditions and reflected on by persons formed within those traditions independent of processes of academic formation. Religiously affiliated colleges and universities, like theological seminaries that aim to combine processes of academic and religious or spiritual formation, occupy a complicated institutional middle ground. Although Catholics tend to agree that Catholic institutions should combine both types of formation, what it means to do so in practice is hotly debated.

Conclusion

In contrast to some who argue for a distinction between doing religious studies and doing theology, I understand doing one or the other as a matter of adopting a role or stance. This means that we are not confined to one role or the other but can decide which role is most appropriate depending on the context or situation. If we understand these roles in relation to defining or not defining the constitutive terms of a discipline or tradition, we can assume either posture relative to disciplines or traditions depending on our aims and circumstances. We can decide situationally whether to define key concepts such as religious studies or Catholic Studies or Catholicism or sit back and track how others are defining them. Either stance has its strengths and liabilities. Each allows us to see some things while obscuring others. The key is to figure out what we want to see under any given circumstances.

I would argue that we can model both roles to some degree in both public and Catholic colleges and universities. Indeed, making a distinction between the two roles makes it possible to model the distinction by signaling when we are switching from one to the other. Modeling the distinction can allow faculty in departments of religion to incorporate methods and viewpoints, which, if pursued exclusively, might threaten to undercut the overarching ideal of refraining from advocating particular religious viewpoints. Conversely, a distinction between the two roles can allow faculty in departments of theology in Catholic institutions to incorporate methods and viewpoints, which, if pursued exclusively, might threaten the school's overall commitment to fostering Catholic identity.

In a public university, issues of religious or spiritual formation do come up. Although the undergraduates I teach come from a variety of religious and secular backgrounds and take Catholic Studies courses for many reasons, some of them are deeply invested, devout, and vocal Catholics. In a class on "Catholicism and Modernity" that attracted a number of such students, we worked at distinguishing between speaking from a position inside the tradition, with presuppositions held only by those within the tradition, and speaking about the different presuppositions held by those who identified with the tradition. They understood the distinction, but sometimes failed to make it, then caught one another and worked together to clarify what they wanted to say. Making the distinction allowed fairly conservative Catholics, Catholics by upbringing, and non-Catholics to engage in a common conversation. Some of the more conservative students wound up in my office, asking the same sort of questions that first-year seminarians ask when grappling for the first time with historical critical methods. I offered what reflections I could, assuring them that others before them had struggled with these issues, but I was also aware that the most religiously invested students were actively involved in the local campus parish. It turned out that our discussions in class spilled over into the parish, where some in the class met to continue to wrestle with texts we were discussing in class in a context specifically devoted to issues of Catholic formation.

6 A Definition of Catholic

Toward a Cosmopolitan Vision

JEANNINE HILL FLETCHER

Catholic Studies emerges in the North American context precisely at a time when the boundaries for identifying "Catholic" are contested. Under conditions of globalization when persons shift in and out of a variety of local and transnational affiliations, the identifier is not as clear as perhaps it once was. In earlier periods, in so-called Catholic countries, the category "Catholic" encompassed the whole of society and the definition was bound up with national and ethnic identities. In non-Catholic Christian contexts, such as in the United States, where identity was constructed "over-against" the dominant ethos, the category "Catholic" was identifiable in contrast to the largely Protestant society. Yet, as one set of researchers conclude regarding the present North American context:

> Today Catholics no longer feel so distinct, and they don't need to defend themselves against the outside. Now they feel freer, more allowed to make their own choices—whether to be a loyal churchgoing Catholic, an ethnic Catholic, a private Catholic, a Catholic in name only, or none at all. Now the boundary between Catholic and non-Catholic is fuzzy, and the social environment provides little "identity from outside."[1]

As the field of Catholic Studies emerges when the lines between Catholic and non-Catholic are blurred, providing a definition of "Catholic" that might guide Catholic Studies is an exercise in self-reflexivity. As feminist theorist Elizabeth Spelman writes, "Since people can be classified and catalogued in any number of ways, overlapping ways, how we catalog them, in particular how we sort out the overlapping distinctions, will depend on our purposes and our sense of what the similarities and differences among them are and how they should be weighed."[2] To what end are the people, events, and ideas of what is "Catholic" selected to fit under the umbrella of "Catholic Studies"? In our globalized, interreligious, and conflict-ridden world, a definition of Catholic that resists tribalism and seeks solidarity is arguably the most fitting.

Institutional Diversity Defies Easy Definition of "Catholic"

One easy way to define "Catholic" (and therefore the scope of Catholic Studies) is through the institutional church. Organizationally distinct, "Catholic" refers to that religious community hierarchically structured under the direction of the pope.[3] Through the work of cardinals and bishops, the magisterium defines the boundaries of "Catholic" and provides the primary resources for Catholic Studies. With this definition in place, the scope of Catholic Studies is, first and foremost, the history of the Catholic Church understood as an organization with its headquarters in Rome. Perusing the course offerings of many Catholic Studies programs in North America, one sees this working definition of "Catholic" implicit, for example, in course titles such as "History of the Papacy," travel programs that make pilgrimages to Rome and course descriptions that identify the primary sources of investigation as papal encyclicals, the texts of Vatican II, and documents prepared by the U.S. Conference of Catholic Bishops.[4] In this approach, secondary materials would include, for example, Thomas Bokenkotter's *A Concise History of the Catholic Church*,[5] in which the primary "Catholics" under discussion are popes and priests. Such a definition of "Catholic" is a reasonable place to begin, since the institutional church centered in Rome forms the most visible symbol of the global institution. Furthermore, the teachings produced out of Rome under the offices of the magisterium do form an identifiable body of material, and a rich one for the investigation of traditions of Catholic teaching and symbolic representation, as well as official responses to contextual social issues such as labor practices, bioethics, and the family.

With this pattern of defining "Catholic" in its close association with the institutional and hierarchical church, the subjects of the discipline are popes and priests, the focus is on teaching, and the definition of "Catholic" centers on the integrity of a coherent tradition. But defining

"Catholic" following representative male leaders along the lines of a single tradition masks a more varied reality available for the investigation of Catholic Studies. As Robert Schreiter remarks, "Traditions are often seen, especially by their guardians, as being more cohesive than they in fact might be. There are elements of indeterminacy in every tradition that make innovation possible."[6] The innovation to which Schreiter refers is importantly inherent even in the "institutional" definition of "Catholic," because even with a narrow construction of "Catholic" around the institutional church, the subjects of study are not limited to the male ordained but extend out into the Church as it is evidenced in the world. Thus, an institutional construction of "Catholic" could be centered not only on the lives of popes and the powerful, but also on everyday people in parishes, including popular expressions.[7] When broadening the scope to include parishes and everyday Catholics, the focus expands to include an array of practices, and the working definition of "Catholic" will necessarily include a sense of diversity. The inclusion of Catholics in all their variety will demonstrate the "difference within" that arises from diverse interpretations of the shared resource of the tradition. Focusing in on the diversity of Catholic practice in a given location, it is evident that the shared repository of symbol, story, and teaching provide for widely divergent interpretations and visions of the collective future. Pro-change and conservative visions, gay and lesbian interpretations and practices, feminist and traditionalist understandings all give evidence that the category "Catholic" is far from homogeneous. It is with this diversity in mind, I believe, that Margaret Steinfels raises the question of competing definitions of "Catholic" when she asks, "Who owns the church? Who says what's Catholic? I don't mean doctrinally; I don't think we have a lot of difficulties there. I mean culturally, sociologically, religiously in the broad sense of the term."[8]

While an institutional approach recognizes that the teaching of the Catholic Church comes out of Rome, the institution itself is made up of diverse social and religious practices. A text that charts some of the ideological diversity and could successfully be employed to help students recognize the diversity in the category "Catholic" is Michele Dillon's *Catholic Identity*.[9] Dillon investigates the very different interpretations of the contemporary Church as they are manifested by groups whose positions stand in contrast to the hierarchically defined positions on abortion, women's ordination, and homosexuality. Yet, in addition to ideological, theological, and experiential differences that intersect with "Catholic" for a community of diversity, the local church also embodies cultural and contextual diversity. The global reality recognizable in the institution further expands and exponentially increases the differences of "Catholic" that must be contained in any definition sufficient to Catholic Studies. That is, when tracing "Catholic" through the institution by means of parishes, those parishes are found in nearly every corner and culture of the globe. Resources that bring this to light include the study from Georgetown University's Center for Applied Research in the Apostolate entitled *Global Catholicism*,[10] as well as the many theological texts that emerge under the heading of Christianity in World Cultures.[11] As these studies demonstrate, it is necessary but not sufficient for Catholic Studies to understand the historical roots of Catholicism and its embeddedness in Western European cultural systems. Clearly, the study of local Catholicisms in Europe and the Americas will widen the offerings of Catholic Studies as details are magnified in particular contexts. Yet, as an international reality, the definition of "Catholic" needs also to encompass worldwide Catholicisms and the cultural diversity they embody. How "Catholic" is defined must include Catholics in Asia, Africa, Latin America, and North America as well as in Europe. Attempting a definition of "Catholic" appropriate to a global reality is a far-reaching task. But many commentators will affirm that it is consistent with the earliest use of the term[12] as in the ideology of many writers who assert that the word "Catholic" itself, "indicates the all-embracing character of the Church around the world."[13] Now "Catholic" refers both to the specific institution under the pope and its universal scope, which necessarily includes a wide-ranging diversity.

Quite appropriately, many programs of Catholic Studies reflect this contextual diversity and define "Catholic" precisely as a global religious tradition that takes a variety of cultural forms in diverse social and historical contexts. The types of courses in this framing of "Catholic" are reflected in offerings such as "Irish Literature," "Society and Community in Korea," "Religion and Politics in the Third World," "Hispanic Spirituality," "Christianity in the Global African World," "Contemporary Indian Reservations" and "Multi-Cultural Psychology: Vietnam and

Vietnamese Americans." The interdisciplinary nature of many Catholic Studies programs positively reinforces the idea that the definition of "Catholic" cannot be reduced to the institutional church in a strict way of its history, theology, and politics, but must be broad enough to hold the diverse experiences of Catholics worldwide.

The definition of "Catholic" employed in relation to the scope of Catholic Studies, however, cannot simply be envisioned as the aggregate of these specific global locations and their differences, since globalization's transnational dynamic brings these differences home. Thus, an inculturationist model of defining "Catholic" as a preexisting reality that meets with diverse cultures around the globe (undergoing a mere external change) is insufficient to capture the dynamic diversity of what "Catholic" is. Here we are guided more fruitfully by the theorist of globalization Roland Robertson and his description of the "glocal," which indicates that there is no "global" that stands apart from the specific incarnation in the local. Applying this term to Catholicism, global Catholic culture "cannot be understood as a static phenomenon, but only as a *contingent* and *dialectical process*."[14] "Catholic" does not preexist as a "global" reality to be transplanted onto the soil of local contexts; "Catholic" exists in reality only in the contingent, dialectical process of the "glocal," that is, what is "Catholic" comes into existence precisely in the local contexts, and thus, "Catholic" is a category of ever-shifting diversities. In America alone, for example, the glocal church includes not only the range of ideological leanings and theological applications, but the dynamic cultural diversity of the Euro-American Catholicisms of national parishes, the distinctive experience of African American Catholics and Hispanic American Catholics, as well as Asian American Catholics and Native American Catholics and the encounters among them.[15] A generational view adds a further dimension to help unpack the shifting quality of what is "Catholic," for the Polish American Church is different today from what it was in the 1890s, and Vietnamese American practices may change under the influence of a new generation of Catholics. The category "Catholic" is further transformed as glocal Catholics are in contact and conversation with people of other faiths, whether in native contexts of missionary Catholicism or affected by the movement of persons through global networks. From the American Catholic context, we begin to see that what is "Catholic" is not only diverse in global perspective, but also that glocal Catholic cultures embody a shifting multiplicity of Catholic identities wherever they are found. The glocal Catholic is impacted by diverse understandings of ethnicity, nationality, and interreligious affiliation that change in response to distinct material, political, and social settings. And this dynamism and shifting understanding of what is "Catholic" repeats in diverse ways around the globe. Thus, the definition of "Catholic" employed in Catholic Studies must be fluid enough to allow for the shifting realities that are "Catholic" in today's conditions of globalization.

Seeking a Center and Defining Boundaries

As evidenced in this briefest of glances at the scope of Catholic Studies, it is clear that an internal multiplicity characterizes the category "Catholic." Yet, there is a tendency among some to seek a "Catholic" something that holds this categorical multiplicity together. Thus, Catholic commentators may assert, "Catholic identity, thus, has a center. It also has boundaries, and to keep identity strong those boundaries need to be maintained."[16] The official boundaries set by the magisterium in canon law and magisterial documents center on the Catholic rite of baptism, as in the words of Daniel Pilarczyk, "everyone who has been baptized a Catholic is a full member of the church even if they never do anything as a result of their membership in the Church."[17] The "Catholics" in Catholic Studies, then, would be all those who have undergone the Catholic rite of baptism. But for many Catholic thinkers there is far more than membership that defines the "Catholic," which ties together the collective. In identifying "the new Catholic identity" in 2001, William D'Antonio, James Davidson, Dean Hoge, and Katherine Meyer insisted, "All religious groups need boundaries. Boundaries strengthen collective identity by showing clearly who are members and who are not, and maintenance of boundaries requires clear rules and markers."[18] Concerned with the identification of "Catholic" in the globalized American context, they write,

> Today American Catholicism has four main boundaries. If any of them become blurry, Catholic identity over and against the outside-the-border region will become confused, and many young Catholics

> will begin to wonder if that boundary makes sense. . . . The first [boundary] is with mainline Protestantism, especially the denominations that most resemble Catholicism, that is, the Lutheran and Episcopalian. . . . The second boundary is with evangelical Protestantism. . . . The third boundary is with non-Christian worldviews. . . . The fourth boundary is in the opposite direction: with popular religion.[19]

D'Antonio and his colleagues assert that the definition of "Catholic" requires a strict division and boundary marker between what is "Catholic" and what is not (specifically, Protestantism, non-Christian worldviews and popular religion). The study continued to assess Catholic identity in the early years of the twenty-first century.[20] For this set of researchers, both boundaries and the shared content within those boundaries constitute the defining points for the category "Catholic." The question of what is "Catholic" is addressed by trying to identify what is central for all within the category and what distinguishes them from persons outside the category. Following this construction, it would be logical to assess that the scope of Catholic Studies coincides with this center-boundary identification of what is "Catholic." Thus, to define "Catholic" by pinpointing the center of the collective as a means by which to establish these boundaries is a pressing task that many Catholic writers and researchers pursue.

Following the definition of "Catholic" as under the direction of Rome, the teaching office of the Church may be put forward as constituting the binding and boundary-defining feature. In this definition, those who are "Catholic" are those who were baptized and continue to be guided by the teaching office of the Church. But, as the most recent polls have shown, the majority of American Catholics did not identify adherence to the teachings of the magisterium as necessary for inclusion in the category "Catholic": 58 percent responded that one could be a good Catholic without following the teaching on abortion, 66 percent that one could be a good Catholic without following the teaching on divorce and remarriage, and 75 percent that one could be a good Catholic without following the teaching on birth control.[21] Thus, the working definition of "Catholic" among American Catholics often encompasses even those persons who self-identify as Catholic but do not necessarily understand themselves to be directed by Rome. In

Andrew Greeley's description, these individuals are identified as "communal Catholics." He writes,

> [The communal Catholic] does not care much what the church as an institution says or does not say, does or does not do. He is committed to Catholicism as a collectivity and as a world view (though he reserves the right to interpret that world view to meet his own needs). . . . He will turn to the church for sacramental ministry when it is needed, and he may deem that ministry to be needed very frequently in his life.[22]

In 1976, Greeley shifted attention from Rome to the average Catholic and to the sacramental life on a parish/lived level as providing a connecting element among the category "Catholic." As D'Antonio's study affirms, even "low-commitment Catholics" agree that the sacraments are an essential part of their relationship with God.[23]

Thus, for some, sacramental practices define "Catholic." For example, Michelle Dillon's study of Catholics on divergent sides of key issues reports that "respondents identified the church's sacramental and liturgical symbol system as personally core."[24] That is, while affiliation with the teachings of Rome varied, persons holding competing views on issues of women's ordination, abortion, and homosexuality nevertheless similarly asserted a lived connection with the sacramental life. The studies of D'Antonio and his colleagues confirmed this finding that sacramental participation is an important feature for the majority of American Catholics (76 percent of those surveyed indicated it served as a strong feature of their "Catholic" identity).[25] These writings are among those that offer a definition of "Catholic" rooted in sacramental practice. But in the same polls, 76 percent of American Catholics also said that one could be a "good Catholic" without going to church every Sunday, and only 55 percent identified attending weekly Mass as essential to their vision of what the Catholic faith is about.[26] As Daniel Pilarczyk writes, "many Catholics don't seem to know what they are supposed to *do* as Catholic Christian believers."[27] Whether it is that Catholics do not know what they are "supposed" to do or whether they choose not to do so is up for interpretation. But it is clear that while sacramental practice may be a feature defining "Catholic," it is not consistently the only one. Further, it is helpful to be reminded that "Greek, Russian, and other Orthodox Christians share . . . the same range of seven sacraments."[28] Identification of sacramental practice as central and boundary marking does not sufficiently encompass or set-apart what is "Catholic."

Recognizing that practices diverge among actual Catholics, other commentators and theologians pursue "belief" as the center that holds together the collective category of "Catholic" and that provides a definition to rein in the boundaries. As D'Antonio's discussion affirms, "*creedal beliefs* are the main boundary markers of the faith: belief in Jesus' resurrection and belief in the Real Presence in the Eucharist. They are more important than all the others. Next comes the obligation to donate time or money to help the poor."[29] Yet, here again, even with polls that indicate shared outlooks among many within the Catholic polling set, the absence of communal agreement means that "belief" is not uniformly held by all Catholics. For every identifiable area of some agreement there is a sizeable portion of the Catholic collective that do not agree and a sizeable portion of persons outside the Catholic collective who do agree. On belief in the resurrection, not only Catholics but also other Christians would be part of this categorical set. While belief in the real presence in the Eucharist seems to set Catholics apart from other Christians, about 20 percent of those polled did not identify it as essential to their vision of the faith, and 36 percent affirmed that one could be a good Catholic without holding this belief.[30] On the third most identifiable "boundary marker of the faith," not only does the obligation to help the poor cross religious and nonreligious boundaries (articulated in the precepts of virtually every religious tradition and shared as a common cause with nonreligious humanists), but 44 percent of those polled also stated that one could be a good Catholic without this concern. Farther down the polling list, even devotion to Mary (cited by some as distinctive for defining "Catholic") would be shared by Orthodox Christians.[31]

The problem with these polls and with this approach to a definition of "Catholic" is twofold: it aims at consensus within the category and masks the connections outside the category. In attempting to define "Catholic" by consensus, it is evident that no category has 100 percent agreement. The collective of "Catholic" cannot be defined by a singular (or even multiple) attribute(s) on which all within the collective agree. Further, many of those features identified as "distinctive" to the category "Catholic" are shared among Christians, humanists, people of other faiths, and persons who claim no religious affiliation, as the example of charitable actions toward the poor demonstrates. Even the term "Catholic" is embraced by more than Roman Catholics, as Robert Schreiter recounts:

> [A] brief sketch shows that catholicity has had many meanings: of fullness and orthodoxy, of extendedness and even identification with Empire, of juridical bond and conformity [with Rome], of partial and visible manifestation of the completeness and to-be-revealed lordship of Christ [invoked by non Roman-Catholics]. . . . Today, members of the Church of Rome still see "catholic" as the most distinctive part of their name. Orthodox claim it too as do some Anglicans and Lutherans in their self-identification. Nearly all Christians would claim to be part of the "Church catholic" (as opposed to the "Catholic Church").[32]

As Gerald O'Collins and Mario Farrugia remark, "What is distinctive about the Catholic Church is not always necessarily unique to Catholicism."[33]

While it may be difficult to pin down a tangible distinctiveness of "Catholic" in sacraments, belief, or name, Catholic commentators continue to want to see Catholics as "individuals embodying definitive and recognizable characterizations—and recognizable over a lifetime."[34] Being Catholic is seen as distinguished by "a set of values"[35] or a way of seeing the world. Here the definition of "Catholic" is guided by an intangible quality diffused among the collective. It is commonplace to see the distinction of the Catholic Imagination (over and against Protestant or secular views) as Catholic Studies programs chase after this elusive feature that defines the category "Catholic." In courses that study "The Catholic Vision" or aim to empower students to recognize "Catholic thinking," this purported intangible distinction is offered as the goal of "Catholic Studies." The boundaries of Catholic studies is perceived to be established by studying the distinctiveness of "over-and-against" Protestantism, non-Christian worldviews, and popular religion.

But, in distinguishing "Catholic" by way of boundaries and distinction from what is not Catholic, there tends to be an elevated sense of "Catholic" that echoes through this approach. For example, in seeking the distinctiveness of Catholic identity, one commentator writes, "The individual believer and, in particular, the lay person who participates in Catholic higher education, is called by baptism to be 'like a leaven' that raises up and empowers what is good in the world and transforms what is evil."[36] And another concludes, "Of course, fundamentally we must find our identity in the way Catholics always have, in an understanding of what Jesus did and what he taught, in grasping what he meant when he said, 'Do this in memory of me.' That is, we find our most profound identity in the Eucharist, in our Sunday worship, and then live as if his teaching made a difference."[37]

These writings reflect the desire to hold up Catholic identity as something that positively sets apart the collective from the broader social and cultural milieu. What is "Catholic" is important because of the leaven it provides to the world or in the way it carries on the tradition of Jesus. While an identification of what is "Catholic" in its ideal form positively serves to motivate the Catholic collective to actually *be* leaven or continue the mission of Jesus, it is premature as a definition to guide Catholic Studies. And yet, it does sometimes function in this manner. For example, two historians construct their history of Catholic Christianity by asserting, "it is by examining the better or even the best features of something, rather than its defects, that we can more truly judge what we are looking at."[38] Such an ideology of the "good" of Catholic identity often pervades Catholic Studies in writings on the Catholic intellectual traditions, Catholic social thought, extraordinary lives of Catholics, and course offerings that elevate Catholicism in art, beauty, ethics, and justice. Defining Catholic over-and-against is often constructed through a rhetoric that focuses on the "good" of what is Catholic.

It is important to note that the desire to construct "Catholic" over and against, when coupled with the construction of "Catholic" with Rome at its center, carries with it the dangerous potential for an ideology of separatism and a theology of superiority. For the center in Rome, "Catholic" is not a neutral, descriptive term; it is a theological one. The catechism of the Catholic Church defines the boundaries of "Catholic" theologically: "The Church is catholic or universal both because she possesses the fullness of Christ's presence and the means of salvation, and because she has been sent out by Christ on a mission to the whole of the human race."[39] Here, "Catholic" functions not only as a feature of group identity, but also as a theological marker of the fullness of "Christ's presence and the means of salvation." When it functions theologically, "Catholic" carries with it the hierarchical ordering of "Catholic" over "not-Catholic."[40]

Yet, the elevation of "Catholic" over other categories simultaneously masks the realities of what also is associated with Catholics, Catholic practice, Catholic thought, and the institution of the Catholic Church. That is, the definition of "Catholic" in its association with "the good" ignores the shadow-side of the tradition. There simply are not many courses that announce their plans to wrestle with the negative ways Catholicism has participated in the broader social currents. A review of Catholic Studies offerings does not surface titles like, "Misogyny and the Catholic Imagination" or "Catholics Supporting Slavery" or "The Dehumanization of Gays in Modern Catholic Thought." The closest offerings are, perhaps, interdisciplinary courses such as "The Crusades in Cross-Cultural Perspectives" that could not possibly fail to address the negative dimensions of Catholic-Christian identity, theology, politics, and history. Yet, given the lack of such courses, there may be ideological and theological resistance to interrogating the underside of Catholic traditions that aligns with an approach that implicitly insists on "Catholic" associated with what is "good." In the statement of one Catholic Studies Program, the goal of Catholic Studies, "is not to proselytize or to defend, but to study, explore, and understand." Such authentic critical engagement, exploration and understanding requires that the definition of "Catholic" include not only multiplicity and diversity but also, importantly, even the shadow-side of the tradition.

In elevating the good, defending difference and defining "Catholic" by way of boundaries, Catholic Studies runs the risk of participating in thought-patterns of tribalization. As Linell Elizabeth Cady writes, "Indeed a major response to the increased pluralism and globalization of life in the late twentieth century has been a reassertion of tightly bounded personal and communal identities, what some have called tribalization."[41] In the interest of education in a globalized world, where integration rather than factionalization is key, maintaining a definition of "Catholic" as constituted by boundaries not only does not serve the aims of education but does not match the experience of many Catholics in the world today.

Cultivating a Cosmopolitan Catholicism in Catholic Studies

In his classic *Orientalism*, postcolonial theorist Edward Said captures the construction of identity as "over-and-against" when he suggests that groups "acquire their identities by developing a notion of "self" based upon some "other" in binary opposition."[42] In describing this production of the "other" that is correlative to producing self-identity, Said writes of "a willed imaginative and geographic division"[43] that is created. Defining the "Catholic" for Catholic Studies as a bounded tradition radiating from Rome seems to participate in the "willed imaginative division" whereby what is "Catholic" is defined to set the collective apart as different from what is not.

Yet, in order to define Catholic identity vis-à-vis other sources of identity, one must isolate the feature that will constitute membership in the category "Catholic." The identification of a "Catholic" feature to be shared among all persons within the category "Catholic" is, on the surface, a truism of the discussion. Tautologically, a Catholic is anyone who exhibits that characteristic feature of the category "Catholic," and "Catholic Studies" studies all things/persons "Catholic." Logically, then, there must be a "Catholic" element that serves as the identifiable feature of Catholic identity. Isolating the "Catholic" element, this dimension can be used to argue for a categorical sameness despite intracategorial diversity. This feature serves to construct boundaries for who is in and who is out of the category "Catholic." The fundamentally defining feature serves to bind Catholics to one another and simultaneously exclude otherness. While a tautological and taxonomic truism, we have thus far seen the difficulty in identifying any one feature shared by the collective. Yet, even if we could, it is a live question whether a feature identifiable across the collective can be isolated from other aspects of persons' identities such that it really is "shared" across the diversity.

Thinking about "Catholic" as something shared among "Catholics" leads one to believe that it does not make any difference if one is male or female, gay or straight, black, white, brown, rich or poor, old or young, American or Asian; what is important is the shared "Catholic" identity. This way of thinking encourages us to think of "Catholic" as an element that can be carved out from the other dimensions of who one is and serve as justification for inclusion in the category of "Catholic Studies." The other features of one's identity and location are incidental to one's being part of the category "Catholic," and are secondary to the discourse. And yet, as the myriad forms of contextual theology have shown, the location from which one experiences one's "Catholic" identity matters very much. Liberation theology, black theology, Asian theologies, mujerista theology, gay theologies, and feminist theology, among others, suggest that one's other aspects of one's location and identity inform one's religious identity.

Identity (including religious identity) is not isolatable as "Catholic" only, but one's very "Catholicness" and the experience of "being Catholic" is informed by the myriad factors such as historical location, race, gender, age, sexual orientation, economics, class, education, ethnicity, nationality, culture and any number of other fundamentally defining features. Thus, each Catholic is formed not by a singular feature of religious identity, but instead, each is constituted by a web of identity. As feminist scholar Morwenna Griffiths describes, the self is "intricate, entangled and interlaced, with each part connected to other parts."[44] Each strand of the web of our identity is interrelated with each other strand and each is also related to communities that help to form that dimension. In a word, Catholics cannot be reduced to their "Catholicism," but bring into the category "Catholic" a multiplicity that is irreducible. And, as Martha Minnow suggests, "No one identity category, sexual orientation, gender, ethnicity, class, family status captures [an individual's] whole world. These very difference afford chances for connection."[45]

An image of pluralistic selves with multiple affiliations encourages a shift away from conceptualizing "Catholic" as a boundary-enclosed grouping and toward "Catholic" as forever blurring and transgressing imagined boundaries. Thus, the very search for a boundary-defined "Catholic" identity is called into question, since the Catholic may be at home in community with other Catholics, but the multiple facets of his or her identity and the web of identity allow each individual to forge innumerable solidarities by virtue of association in multiple communities. Instead of the "Catholic" standing in contrast to social milieu, secular culture, or other religious traditions, Catholics are shaped by them in negotiation with the resources of the Catholic tradition, which always produces a hybrid identity for glocal Catholics. In response to the concerns of D'Antonio and his colleagues, Catholics should wonder whether the boundaries between Catholic and Protestant, Catholic and non-Christian, and Catholic and popular religion make sense, since Catholics themselves are forever crossing these boundaries. By virtue of the individual's pluralistic self, countless possible associations are enacted in complex lives, and the boundaries erected to define "Catholic" are blurred in lived experience. But instead of experiencing these blurred boundaries as a threat to Catholic identity, we might see them as constituting Catholic identities.

Recognizing "Catholic" as always already engaged in the dynamic exchange with that which is outside the boundaries of the institutional church, an even more complicated but potentially cosmopolitan understanding of Catholic Studies comes into view. Contrasting a "tribalistic" response to globalization's transnational dynamic, sociologist Ulrich Beck promotes a "cosmopolitan vision" as one in which persons simultaneously view themselves as part of a narrow, localized collective *and* as part of a wider, global world. In Beck's words, a cosmopolitan outlook is one "in which people view themselves simultaneously as part of a threatened world and as part of their local situations and histories."[46] Cosmopolitan vision does not see oneself as cut off from those who are different in an enclave of distinctiveness, but interwoven with the lives and futures of those whose culture, religion, and outlook are different. For Beck, this interweaving of lives with a view toward the future is undertaken particularly in light of the risks we face as a global interreligious, intercultural, and international community. A cosmopolitan vision requires a concern for nothing less than the future of humanity. Given the traditions of Catholic thinking toward universality, such an outlook seems more than compatible with Catholic Studies; a cosmopolitan vision seems to be required for a Catholic Studies relevant to the future.

By investigating those places where "Catholic" has always been interwoven with other categorical groupings, a Catholic Studies with cosmopolitan vision becomes possible. In the lived religion of Catholic expression in Robert Orsi's *The Madonna of 115th Street*, for example, the definition of "Catholic" may be infused in the institutional church but overflows into the home and spills out into the streets. Once it has done so, it is irrevocably intertwined with what is "other-than" Catholic such that the boundaries are no longer hard and fast, but indeed, hazy.[47] The process is similar when tracing Catholic social thought not in the documents of the magisterium but in the lived practices of persons in the world. Here, again, the definition of "Catholic" by necessity bleeds out into the wider world and purposefully blurs the boundaries. For example, the young leaders of Youth Ministries for Peace and Justice in the South Bronx were motivated by Catholic social thought, but their programs necessarily promote peace and justice across denominational lines through the renovation of green space, campaigns to decrease city-generated pollution and demonstrations against police brutality in the community. In the words of founder Alexie Torres-Fleming,

> There's a principle of Catholic social teaching that says we have a responsibility to family and community, that we see the community as our larger family. Sure it's great that your kids have trees and get to go to good schools, but the problem with that is that all the gifts that God has given you are being used to protect just two or three people. I think the call to family and community is to share and use our gifts to protect other people and to live a life of generosity. This is a different level than wanting only to "take care of your own."[48]

In the abstract, "Catholic" may be defined over-and-against through boundary construction, but in our globalized world, where the encounter with difference repeats locally and globally, and where the principles passed on in the Catholic traditions promote an engagement with the world, the definition of "Catholic" necessarily includes the intertwining with "non-Catholic."

This is precisely the case if we take as our starting point not the institution of the hierarchical church with its tight boundary drawing, but instead start from Catholic institutions such as education, health care, and social services. Herein, the definition of "Catholic" is affected by the shifting sands of encounter and dynamic identity-construction. In Catholic hospitals "the promotion of human dignity, the common good and a preferential option for the poor" necessarily encompasses non-Catholics in its mission and outreach.[49] In Catholic schools, what it means to be "Catholic" is unmistakably intertwined with people of diverse faiths. Although Muslims and Hindus probably do not often join in Sunday celebration of the Mass, they are, in many parts of our globalized world, present in our Catholic institutions of learning—whether in grade schools, high schools, or colleges. By one account, "Tokyo's Sofia University, a Jesuit school, and Nagoia's Nanzan University, a Divine Word school, can assume that between 1 and 5 percent of their student body and faculty, not counting the members of the religious communities, are Christian."[50] In North America, globalization's flow of immigration also creates contexts where Catholic schools are internally interreligious. A definition of "Catholic" in these institutions includes non-Catholics. Seeking a definition for the category "Catholic" with the help of postcolonial theorist Trinh T. Minh-ha, the nature of "Catholic"/"Non-Catholic" or "We"/"They" constantly overlap, and the dividing line is not always clear: "Despite our desperate, eternal attempts to separate, contain and mend, categories always leak."[51] This dynamic of identity-formation happens all the time in our globalized world, and it might be reflected in a dynamic definition of "Catholic." This is why classes such as "Martyrdom in Interreligious Perspective," "Religions of the Silk Road," "Marriage and Family Through an Interdisciplinary Lens," "The Search for the Divine: Hindu, Christian, Muslim, and Buddhist Ways in India," "Yoga and Meditation," "The Politics of Christian Art," and "Feminist Perspectives on Christianity and Judaism" represent a form of Catholic Studies that recognizes the hybridity in all that is "Catholic," as Catholic thought and Catholic persons engage across boundaries in dynamic interaction with the many different cultural, religious, and ideological forms throughout the world. Embracing hybrid notions of identity and multiple communities, Catholic Studies will be complicated with the question of who is in and who is out of the discipline's boundaries, encouraging a consistent reflexivity on the politics of cataloging and defining.

Defining the Future of Catholic Studies

In 1960, in a collection entitled *The Idea of Catholicism: An Introduction to the Thought and Worship of the Church*, Walter J. Burghardt and William F. Lynch describe the book as providing a total image of Catholicism and the "master ideas that unify" it.[52] With a vision of the integrity of the tradition, they could write,

> Once a man recognizes the religious problem in his own life, he is in a position to see Catholicism for what it is: a transcendent act of God in history and an answer to man's religious longings. For, as all our remaining writers will indicate, Catholicism is unique. But it is unique, not in the sense that Christ and the Church are just so many more special interesting developments of the religious sense and religious history. This book wishes to say that these two things, Christ and the Church, *are* religion; they are not parts of it but dominate it and define it as God sees it. They either cancel out every other form or bring it to perfect fruition.[53]

Fifty years later, we can read the transparent ideological and theological elevation of "all things Catholic" expressed in a text aimed at communicating the idea of Catholicism. The definition of "Catholic" employed by Catholic Studies must resist this self-elevating project.

Writing in 2001, William D'Antonio and his colleagues seemed to fear the other extreme: if "Catholic" is not self-evidently elevated or at least distinct, and the boundaries are fluid between Catholic and non-Catholic, there is the problem of relativism and "anything goes": "Any group without subjective boundaries will find that its members are troubled by questions about how they are different from outsiders and whether existence of the group really matters. Catholicism without boundaries would have a problem of 'everything goes' and an indefiniteness about who is a Catholic and what being a Catholic means."[54] But it is precisely that there *is* an indefiniteness about what "Catholic" means, as even this brief survey of the many different definitions or identifiers suggests. Defining "Catholic" for Catholic Studies today comes precisely at a time of instability and change. But, instead of resisting this in a self-enclosed tribalism, we might seek a guiding definition of "Catholic" that allows for the positive insights that emerge when we embrace the fluidity of life, of "Catholic" and the boundaries of Catholic Studies. "Catholic" is itself hybrid; Catholic Studies should reflect that. "Catholic" is itself contested; Catholic Studies should reflect that. If there was one course offering that captured the necessary way forward to Catholic Studies, it might be "Rethinking Catholicism," currently offered in at least one Catholic Studies program. If there were a methodology to be encouraged, it would be "multiperspectival," considering the varied forms of the "Catholic" phenomenon on its many levels: the institutional, ideological/theological, local, translocal, interreligious, and transcultural perspectives.[55] If there were a definition of "Catholic" to be suggested, it would be one with fluid boundaries and an in-built uncertainty so that rather than promoting and preserving a predetermined definition of "Catholic," Catholic Studies might participate in the ongoing exploration not only of what is "Catholic," but also what "Catholic" is.

7 Method and Conversion in Catholic Studies

RICHARD M. LIDDY

A former editor of the prestigious theological journal *Theological Studies* is reported to have remarked that Bernard Lonergan's work was the most frequently cited in that journal. Whether accurate or not, as Lonergan's former student in Rome in the 1960s, and as someone who owes him an immense debt of gratitude, I can testify to the great explanatory power of his work. It is no wonder that the University of Toronto Press is now publishing the many volumes of his *Collected Works*. In this essay I employ Lonergan's work to delineate the methodological issues emerging in the relatively new field of Catholic Studies. In line with Lonergan's fundamental emphases, I highlight the importance of intellectual conversion or epistemological awareness—"knowing what you are doing when you are doing it"—in Catholic Studies.

Catholic Studies represents the emergence of a new specialization within the academy, along with other cultural studies such as Jewish Studies, Women's Studies, and African American studies.[1] For some, Catholic Studies is obviously a branch of historical cultural studies. For others, it is a subspecies of religious studies. For still others, it can be seen as rooted in Catholic theology but prescinding from any practical purpose. For still others it can be seen as having an avowedly practical purpose: that is, as linking the Catholic tradition with all of culture, that is, with the transformation of the disciplines, professions and human society in general. So the question arises: is there any way of both distinguishing and integrating these various approaches? Is there any way of seeing the various methods as complementary? I will begin by highlighting various contemporary issues in Catholic Studies and then employ Lonergan's work on method as especially helpful in sorting out these issues.

Issues in Catholic Studies

In recent years, the Curran Center for American Catholic Studies at Fordham University has sponsored a number of conferences that have brought together people interested in Catholic Studies. At a meeting in December 2005, some of the issues raised about the present situation of Catholic Studies were the following:

The relation of Catholic Studies to religious studies: is Catholic Studies a subsection of religious studies?
Does Catholic Studies imply theology? In what sense?
What is the role of exigent historical study in Catholic Studies and the possible interference of theological concerns in historical research?
The role of spiritual and moral "formation" in Catholic Studies programs: is there a role? Should there be?
Should we emphasize a "triumphalist" or "defensive reading" of Catholic Studies as opposed to a more honest historical presentation?
The "political" dimension of Catholic Studies: Who is sponsoring them? For what reasons?
Whose "Catholicism" are we talking about? that of whites? males? the First World? the marginalized?

In addition to these issues, others were enumerated in *Listening: Journal of Religion and Culture*:

The "public" character of Catholicism and the possible influence of Catholic Studies on public policy, especially with regard to the poor and the marginalized: Should Catholic Studies aim at having such influence?
The role of Catholic theology and Catholic Studies in the human sciences, such as psychology, sociology, and economics: Should it have such a role?
Catholicism and the professions: Is there a role for Catholic Studies in relation to the various professions?

Further questions with regard to Catholic Studies can be highlighted, for example, the relationship between Catholicism and other religious traditions in the contemporary world. What is the church authority saying? What are Catholic theologians saying? What is happening on the ground?

And to all of these issues can be added the one issue symbolized by the recent attack on all religion by prominent figures in contemporary culture, such as Richard Dawkins, Daniel Dennett, Sam Harris, and Christopher Hitchens.[2] Such avowedly secularist attacks raise fundamental methodological issues: for example, can one be a Catholic and nonetheless do exigent historical and scientific work on Catholicism? More broadly, can one be religious and still do scientific work in the field of religious studies? Does commitment to a particular religion interfere with objectivity? Can one be objective about one's own religion, one's own Catholicism, about another's religion? Or, on the opposite side, can one be totally "tone deaf" to religion—even opposed to all religion—and at the same time write meaningfully and objectively on religious concerns?

There are, therefore, all kinds of issues in Catholic Studies and various "sets" of issues: for example, issues having to do with the "objectivity" of research, the intrusion of bias into research, the validity of "the question of God" and religious experience, the role of bias and the relevance of the intellectual, moral, and religious development in the work of researchers, and so on. Here we will approach all of these issues under the rubric of methodology, beginning with a section on method in general, emphasizing Bernard Lonergan's articulation of a general empirical or "transcendental" method that for Lonergan was rooted in what he called "intellectual conversion."[3] We will then apply that method to a dialectical account of history and illustrate the value of distinguishing functional specialties in the doing of human studies that aim at having a practical effect. In that light, we will treat the distinction between religious studies and theology. Finally, we will consider the method of "praxis," the method that specifically takes the development of the researcher into account as she seeks the transformation of the world. Specifically treating Catholic Studies as employing such a method, we will conclude with the observation that Catholic Studies can employ and benefit from all these methods.

General Empirical Method

In order to approach in a fruitful way all the issues listed earlier, it is necessary to have some kind of a systematic or methodical approach. Such a method can be quite general, but at the same time, if valid, it must have a relevance to all the various issues at stake. The most conspicuous example of fruitfulness flowing from the adoption of a correct method is the use of mathematics for treating basic issues in the physical sciences.[4] Similarly, the way for fruitfulness in human studies is to have a method rooted in central notions of the human spirit, that is, notions such as meaning, truth, and value. In the words of Bernard Lonergan:

> What has made natural science successful has been the Galilean proposal to mathematicize nature; what can make human studies no less penetrating seems to be, not the mathematicization of man's world, but the discovery that it is a world mediated by meaning and motivated by value.[5]

Such notions of meaning and value respond to basic levels of the human spirit. Why? Lonergan answers: Because that is the way we are built. We are built to use our minds in a certain way, and the various methods are all expressions of the human mind working in this area or in that. The root of every successful method is the structure of our own minds, an all-purpose "machine tool" that can be adjusted this way or that to handle this set of issues or that in an expeditious and fruitful way.

What, then, is that basic structure of the human mind? According to Lonergan, that basic structure consists of various levels of conscious activities all functionally related to each other. We pay attention to and ask questions of our experiencing in order to understand; we think and we reflect on our understanding in order to come to true judgments; and we evaluate our judgments in order to make good decisions—and ultimately, to love. The innate human drive to know and to love unfolds though this conscious dynamic structure of experiencing, understanding, judging, and deciding.[6] It manifests itself in what Lonergan calls the "transcendental precepts": "Be attentive!" "Be intelligent!" "Be reasonable!" "Be responsible!" These can be extended to "Be loving!" and "If necessary, change!"

Of course, it has taken a long time for the human family to learn how to use the human mind successfully in this area or in that—as is evident in the history of the natural sciences. And the reason for this long delay is that there are substantial obstacles to arriving at fruitful answers. Egoism is one such obstacle: a concern for "what's in it for me?" can get in the way of objective questioning and derail the disinterestedness necessary to arrive at truth. Prejudice can be another obstacle: "my country right or wrong but my country"—my group, my race, my religion, and so on. Such group biases can be powerful deterrents to a fruitful inquiry and are at the root of great historical conflicts. Finally, there can be a basic resistance to questioning itself, to moving beyond "what is obvious" to the reality of things. Philosophies claiming to be "the truth" can actually smother the search for truth. So also, powerful cultural undertows, assisted by popular advertising or an uncritical culture, can interfere with basic questioning.[7]

In all such scientific and scholarly process there can be discerned the basic pattern in which the human mind functions: a pattern of experiencing, understanding, judging, and deciding. The process is sparked by the desire to know, and as the human mind unfolds, such conscious activity is followed by more refined experiencing, deeper understanding, more reflective judging—so that even in an area as complicated as human history the noted historian, Carl Becker, could judge that gradually we can build up a body of substantial historical knowledge.[8] A constant reference to this general method can keep Catholic Studies focused on the underlying drive to authenticity working to heal the biases implied in the issues listed at the beginning of this article: biases such as prejudice, Catholic triumphalism, and so forth.

Historical Knowing

Historical knowledge is another area where this basic process of experiencing, understanding, and judging, sparked by the desire to know, can reap substantial fruit. For what is research but focusing on the first level of consciousness—experience—and attending to the data? And what is the specialization of "interpretation" but trying to understand, on the basis of the data, what so and so in this place at this time actually meant? And what is history but judging what de facto was "going forward"? History is not just biography or the sum of biographies. Rather,

> [T]here is social and cultural process. It is not just a sum of individual words and deeds. There exists a developing and/or deteriorating unity constituted by cooperations, by institutions, by personal relations, by a functioning and/or malfunctioning good of order, by a communal realization of originating and terminal values and disvalues. Within such processes we have out our lives. About them each of us ordinarily is content to learn enough to attend to his own affairs and perform his public duties. To seek a view of the actual functioning of the whole or of a notable part over a significant period of time is the task of the historian.[9]

Lonergan describes this process of historical research as one in which one small insight follows upon another until one reaches the point at which one's initial assumptions begin to be challenged. At that point the researcher might mumble to herself, "How could I have been so stupid as to think *X*?" Elements once assumed to belong in one context fit more securely into another and one gets closer to the historical understanding and judgment one has been seeking. Thus, Pseudo-Dionysius is understood not to have belonged to a first-century context—he quotes Proclus—but to a fifth century one.[10]

Intellectual Conversion

Such transformations of mind were of great interest to Lonergan, because they illustrated the basic dynamic method of the human mind as it operates in scientific and scholarly research. In both areas the questioning of data gives way to insights, both direct and inverse ("How could I have been so stupid as to think *X*") and such insights eventually give way to processes of scientific verification and historical judgment. Both methods spring from the basic method built into the human spirit, the conscious dynamism that moves from data to understanding to judging and eventually to deciding.

There is, then, a specifically human development needed to handle the methodological issues raised by the emerging field of Catholic Studies. Lonergan often used the phrase "intellectual conversion" as shorthand for such a development.[11] Genuine self-appropriation, genuine knowledge of what is going on within us amounts to a conversion, a radical change on the intellectual level: a move from an implicit materialism—reality is attained by "taking a good look"—to a critically realist philosophy of the world. Such a development consists in realizing that reality is attained not just by experience, but also by penetrating understanding and refined judgment. One reaches the world, not by giving in to bias, but by understanding, by making distinctions, by critical judgment. Reality is not "a blob out there" but rather the endlessly varied intelligibility of the world to be known by long chains of reasoning, developed understanding, and true judgment. Augustine's *Confessions* represents a vivid example of someone desiring to get things straight and at least a partial satisfaction of that desire when at the age of thirty-one he read "some books of the Platonists."[12]

Such intellectual conversion inoculates against bias: not just the individual bias called selfishness or egoism, and not just group bias or prejudice, but also the general bias expressed in false philosophies and cultural mindsets that fail to realize the nature of the human mind's drive toward the true. So the phrase "intellectual conversion" highlights the issue of authenticity, especially the authenticity involved in coming to know ourselves. It involves dependence on an inwardly known and appropriated criterion of authentic understanding and judging, an explicit commitment to intelligence and where it leads, unencumbered by bias, which freezes or obscures the operations of intellect. In his historical studies Lonergan highlighted the explicit commitment of the classic writers Augustine and Aquinas to such an orientation.

Dialectic and Foundations

The eighteenth- and nineteenth-century development of historical consciousness is the basic cultural framework within which the discipline of Catholic Studies has arisen. Such consciousness essentially consisted in erudite and detailed studies of ancient societies and cultures, studies reflecting increasing awareness of pluralism, development, and diversity. This was quite a distinct kind of culture from the previous classicist culture, which basically saw itself as normative, the only authentic culture in relation to which all others were considered "barbarians"—the unlettered.[13] On the contrary, modern historians first produced detailed studies of ancient Greece and Rome, then studies of early Christianity. Such studies were threatening to many as they challenged facile interpretations. Eventually, however, they exercised a massive influence. Among Christians, historical studies revealed the vibrancy of the early church and liturgy, eventually contributing to the modern liturgical movement and a greater awareness of the diversity of local churches with their own unique and vibrant histories.[14]

Such, I take it, is the origin of Fordham University's decision to focus its Catholic Studies program on American Catholic history. The vibrancy of such historical studies was represented at the Fordham meeting mentioned earlier by young scholars writing on such topics as "The Knights of Labor and Catholics vis-à-vis the Minimum Wage Movement," "Catholics, Communists and African Americans," "Catholics and the American Literary Canon," "Catholics and the Waterfront: The Unionization of the New York Waterfront," and the like. Similar studies are also being made on Catholic history in other countries and contexts under such topics as "English Catholic Studies," "Filipino Catholic Studies," and so on. Such studies have profoundly changed the face of Catholic theology. Where prior to Vatican II, virtually all Catholic theology in the early twentieth century involved a scholastic framework said to be rooted in the writings of Thomas Aquinas, historical study tended to relativize even the contribution of Aquinas. Since it counsels understanding an author in the context of his times and not according to someone else's polemical aims, such study threatens facile interpretations.[15]

Nevertheless, historical study of itself can be deeply ambiguous. For we can ask: Was "what was going forward" good or bad? Did it represent genuine progress or decline? On such issues historians themselves can disagree in a quite fundamental way. Should I read Bertrand Russell's *History of Philosophy* or the quite opposed reading of that history by Frederick Copleston? Should I read Richard Dawkins's history of Catholicism, or one written by a devout Catholic?

All of which show that there is another series of questions that have to do with major cultural conflicts flowing beneath the surface of historical studies, questions that need to be addressed by a distinct method. Such conflicts have to do with the very meaning of the words "good," "bad," "rational," "irrational," "progress," "decline." Here we are faced with fundamental intellectual, philosophical, ethical, and religious differences, and there is need for another method to clarify and treat these issues. Lonergan calls that methodological specialization "dialectic," that is, "a generalized apologetic conducted in an ecumenical spirit, aiming ultimately at a comprehensive viewpoint, and proceeding towards that goal by acknowledging differences, seeking their grounds real and apparent, and eliminating superfluous oppositions."[16] The method of dialectic, then, deals with such conflicts as expressed in the contemporary secularist view of religion and reality versus religious views of religion and reality. It deals with one's interpretation of "science" and its bearing on the meaning of "religion." It also deals with the differences and similarities among religious people about what it basically means to be religious as well as the differences between people within the same religion with differing theological orientations. These are amply illustrated in the issues raised about Catholic Studies at the beginning of this essay. Lonergan's transcendental method, focused as it is on the invariant dynamisms of the human spirit, provides a criterion for making judgments on the unintelligent, the irrational, the wrong, the evil, the unloving. Ultimately it provides the criterion for making explicit what constitutes historical progress and conversely, human decline; that is, what is rooted in authentic intellectual, moral, and religious conversion and what is not.

So, from a plurality of data, historical scholarship moves toward a dialectical unity, that is, a comprehensive viewpoint that sets out the basic conflicting positions and counterpositions bequeathed to us by the past. Not only will these be between secularist and religious views, but also there will be significant differences of horizon even among religious views between those who would interpret the past in a fundamentalist way and those who, attributing proper value to science and scholarship, would take a more differentiated approach. Even religious people are not exempt from materialist undertows and materialist interpretations of religious realities.[17] It is here that concerns about "the politics of Catholic Studies" come in; or concerns about the inordinate role of "formation," or the reputedly moral or religious to the detriment of the intellectual. On the other hand, there can rightly be concern for a merely sterile intellectual formalism that does not take into account the moral and religious concerns of the heart.

So one reaches what Lonergan calls "the end of the age of innocence," the age that assumed that human authenticity could be taken for granted.[18] All human studies have to cope with the complexity that recognizes both (1) that the data may be a mixed product of authenticity and of inauthenticity and (2) that the very investigation of the data may be affected by the personal or inherited inauthenticity of the investigators. Here we are face to face with "the personal quotient," that is, the role of the development or conversion in the life of the scholar.[19] "It takes one to know one," goes the old expression: what one knows and says and does is influenced by who one is. To say this in another way, there is the underlying influence of our personal and communal "horizon." By a horizon is meant the complexus of experiences, understandings, judgments, and decisions that have brought us to this point. Has my journey to this moment been error-free? Were there moments of inattention in my own personal life or in that of my community? Instances of oversight that have remained? Of fundamental error and moral failure? Of bias and prejudice? Of religious inauthenticity? Am I biased because I am a Western person? White? Male? Does such bias impact my reading of history? Does a certain materialism influence the way I look at things?

Method as Functional Specializations

We have spoken about issues in Catholic Studies and about the need for a transcendental method in arriving at a comprehensive method for approaching its most basic issues. Such a basic method of the human spirit becomes specialized in this area or in that as needed. In his *Method in Theology*, Lonergan distinguishes three types of specialization. First there is "field specialization," the easiest to understand because it divides and subdivides the field of data so that the specialist is the one who knows more and more about less and less.[20] However, anyone who has taken a course in a department knows another type of specialization and that is "subject or department specialization." Here what is divided is no longer the field of data to be investigated, but the results of investigations to be communicated. Here what counts is a conceptual classification that distinguishes departments and the subjects taught in a particular department: for example, physics, Catholic Studies, history, and so on. For example, "Irish Catholics in Early Twentieth-Century Jersey City" would be an example of a field specialization; and Catholic Studies would be a subject or departmental specialization.

Nevertheless, there is a third type of specialization and that is what Lonergan calls "functional specialization." This type of specialization distinguishes and separates the successive stages in the process from the data of field specialization to the conceptual results of subject specialization.

> Thus, textual criticism aims at determining what was written. The interpreter or commentator takes over where the textual critic leaves off; his aim is to determine what was meant. The historian moves in on a third level; he assembles interpreted texts and endeavors to construct a single narrative or view.[21]

Thus, functional specialization allows for various methods to be integrated into a progressive and fruitful set of interlocking methods. According to Lonergan, such a differentiation of specializations begins with historical studies but can also end with human studies aimed at concrete policies and actions. Such a division of specializations is important for any historically rooted set of disciplines that aims at taking a stand in the present with a view to influencing the future. So government think tanks sponsor all kinds of historical and empirical investigations with a view toward planning and policies whose execution will be tested by feedback processes.[22]

In human studies the functional specialties would line up in the following way: parallel to the level of experience there is research; parallel to the level of understanding there is interpretation; parallel to the level of judging there is history; parallel to the level of deciding there is dialectic. In such specializations research employs all the levels of consciousness (experiencing, understanding, judging and deciding) in order to achieve its end of bringing to light the data on a particular question. Similarly, all the levels of consciousness are employed to achieve the level of understanding that is interpretation. Similarly, all levels cooperate to achieve the functional specialization that focuses on historical judgment. Investigations on the basic conflicts involved in history, however, leads you to the functional specialty of dialectic, that is, the specialization that articulates fundamental differences on the level of decision making, differences rooted in different fundamental options on basic philosophical, ethical and religious questions.

It is on this level of dialectical oppositions that foundational convictions enter in: convictions flowing from one's basic personal horizon. That horizon—the basic "space" we are coming from—has been deeply influenced by our historical situation, but it has also been deeply shaped by the basic decisions we ourselves have made. Such decisions are "extra-academic" events; events in the personal lives of researchers, interpreters, historians, theologians, and so on. Lonergan calls the functional specialization that articulates our basic intellectual, moral, and religious convictions "foundations." He writes:

> As conversion is basic to Christian living, so an objectification of conversion provides theology with its foundations. By conversion is understood a transformation of the subject and his world. . . . Inasmuch as conversion itself is made thematic and explicitly objectified, there emerges the fifth functional specialty, foundations.[23]

Works that might well illustrate the objectification of conversion would be Augustine's *Confessions*, Newman's *Apologia pro vita sua*, and Lonergan's own works: *Insight* and *Method in Theology*. Here one enters into the area of fundamental commitments, commitments historically conditioned by the past but also affecting the shape of the future. But now, just as the functional specialties regarding the past can be seen as ascending from research through interpretation and history to dialectic according to the levels of consciousness, so now one can see the remaining four theological specializations as descending in an inverse order to emphasize decision, judgment, understanding, and experience. That is, as foundations objectify the basic level of personal decision, so doctrines articulate basic judgments, systematics the kernel of our understanding, and communications the experiential implementation of our understanding. All four levels of consciousness are involved in each of these specializations, but the emphasis is different in each.

These eight functional specialties are outlined in the following table. From a Catholic theological perspective these functional specializations can be seen as identifying the Word of God coming to us out of the past, calling for conversion in the present and the basis of our communication of that Word to the future.

Hearing the Word	Proclaiming the Word	Conversion
Dialectic	*[deciding]*	Foundations
History	*[judging]*	Doctrines
Interpretation	*[understanding]*	Systematics
Research	*[experiencing]*	Communications

These eight functional specializations reflect Lonergan's general empirical method as it deals with taking a stand in the present on the basis of what has gone on before us. The key levels of the human spirit are at the basis of the eight questions theology asks as it looks toward the past and toward the future. Such functional specializations reflect the way our minds work when they operate well historically and try to bring historical judgments to bear on contemporary issues.

Religious Studies and Theology

Let us now take our bearings to reflect on the distinction between religious studies and theology, two "subject" or "department" specializations. After the textual critics, interpreters, historians, foundational philosophers, and doctrinal and systematic people do their thing, all has to be brought together in an academic department in order to be communicated to students. So, when it comes to the study of religion, the distinction between theology and religious studies is key. Is one comparing the historical unfolding of Catholicism to other religions? Certainly a religious-studies approach is justified.

On the other hand, typically those studying Catholicism do so for reasons rooted in inner commitment. Their interest is neither purely historical nor comparative. They have a sense that their religious symbols, beliefs and practices relate them, not just to others, but also to the beyond.[24] While religious studies primarily concern religious phenomena and symbols wherever they may be found in their thisworldly aspects, theology consists in reflection on particular religious symbols in their otherworldly dimension.

> Religious studies and theology are not identical but distinct. The theologies tend to be as many and diverse as the religious convictions they express and represent. In contrast, religious studies envisage all religions and, so far from endeavoring to arbitrate between opposing religious convictions, commonly prefer to describe and understand their rituals and symbols, their origins and distribution, their history and influence.[25]

It is the singularity of religious symbols that gives rise to the distinction between religious studies and theology.

> For religious studies leave to theology questions concerned with what is believed to be more than man, what is not of this world. They confine their attention, as does the whole of modern science, to what is within this world, to the things man experiences, and even to human experiencing itself. Nor is there any doubt in my opinion, about the general soundness of this restriction.[26]

Theology takes seriously the claim that these religious phenomena purport to deal with what goes beyond this world. "The theologies endeavor to discern whether there is any real fire behind the smoke of symbols employed in this or that religion."[27] This relationship to what purportedly goes beyond this world is often termed "faith."[28] Such faith finds expression in historical beliefs, doctrines and unifying articulations. Theology deals with the validity of such beliefs and their current formulations. With regard to Catholicism, a religion that is rooted in faith and in the belief that God has revealed himself to humanity in Christ, theology asks such questions as:

> Have we got it right? Have we heard God's Word rightly?
> What precisely has God truly revealed to humanity, and how has that self-revelation been received by historical humanity?

What is the role of the church in such reception and in the passing on of divine revelation? The role of the Catholic Church and its sacraments, authoritative structures, and beliefs?

Have we heard God's Word in Christ correctly, or has our historical hearing been contaminated by historically and culturally conditioned biases? Such questions are linked to particular historical studies such as Irish Catholicism, Filipino Catholicism, and so on.

How is such a revelation related to the rest of human living today? What is its essence? Its core?

What questions arising out of human life today impact on our hearing of God's self-revelation?

To the extent that theology takes into account other religions, it can be seen as a species of religious studies. This has become particularly significant for Catholic theology since Vatican II, with its concern to relate Catholicism to other Christian groups, other religions, and even nonbelievers. Such a fact requires the theologian to reflect on his religion, not in isolation from all others, but in conjunction with others.

Religious studies lead to the philosophy of religion, that is, the question of how it is possible that religions commonly purport to deal with what transcends this world. Such philosophy of religion deals with the validity of the question of God and the conditions for the possibility of religious experience, religious commitment and religious belief. Theology, on the other hand, since it expresses an orientation to the transcendent, can have a powerful influence.[29] It is because of this potential power of theology that it is all the more important to be careful in our theologizing and not claim that we know more than we do. If, as someone once said, theology is "truth-claimology," is it not incumbent upon us to at least show how our beliefs are historically grounded and "make sense"?

> Theology and religious studies need each other. Without theology religious studies may indeed discern when and where different religious symbols are equivalent; but they are borrowing the techniques of theologians if they attempt to say what the equivalent symbols literally mean and what they literally imply. Conversely, without religious studies theologians are unacquainted with the religions of mankind; they may as theologians have a good grasp of the history of

> their own religion; but they are borrowing the techniques of the historian of religions, when they attempt to compare and relate other religions with their own.[30]

Religious studies, then, tends to be located on the more historical side of the equation. Theology adds further steps, beginning with the objectification of personal commitment and conversion. Catholic theology in particular attempts to articulate what the Christian religious symbols literally mean. Religious studies can lay out the historical scene: theology reflects on a particular religion's transcendent claims.

As perhaps is obvious from these reflections, this is a shifting field. Religious studies, solidly grounded in historical studies, seems at first sight to be obvious and easily identifiable. Theology, on the other hand, seems much more diffuse. Seemingly diffuse though it may seem, however, it can be powerful; it taps into an orientation to the beyond that can shape one's whole horizon. At times that orientation can be identified with the totally secular. Or it can be identified with a fundamentalist identification with a particular religious expression. Or it can be identified with Teilhard de Chardin's belief in the orientation of the whole natural universe toward the Omega Point that is Christ. The key would be a discernment of these horizons, a rejection of what is unauthentic and a holding on to what is good. The ideal, it would seem, would be a symbiosis of historical religious studies and authentic theology.

Catholic Studies as Praxis

In "The Ongoing Genesis of Methods," Lonergan abbreviates what he has said in *Method in Theology* by stating that after experimental, historical, and dialectical methods, there is the method of "praxis." Such a method asks the question, "What are you going to do about it?" that is, now that you have a refined vision of the human person in history? He locates this question in the context of "the end of innocence"; that is, when belief in the omnicompetence of scientific rationalism has lost its sway. It is only when the issue of a personal authenticity, an issue deeper than scientific rationalism, comes to the fore that praxis can become an academic subject.

Following Paul Ricoeur, he describes the method of praxis as involving a twofold hermeneutic, a hermeneutic of suspicion and a hermeneutic of recovery. It is a distinct method involving a compound of theoretical and practical judgments of value. But it does not just aim at practical results; rather it relates to the very self-constitution of the researcher.

> Now to ask whether theology is a praxis in this second sense, is . . . to ask a general question and a rather technical one. It is to ask whether there are basic theological questions whose solution depends on the personal development of theologians. Again, to use a distinction made by Paul Ricoeur, it is to ask whether issues on which theologians are badly divided call for the employment of both a hermeneutic of suspicion and a hermeneutic of recovery, a hermeneutic of suspicion that diagnoses failures in personal development and a hermeneutic of recovery that generously recognizes the genuine personal development that did occur.[31]

But what about our issue of Catholic Studies? Much of what we have said leads to the conclusion that in one respect Catholic Studies can be considered as simply historical religious studies: that is, as studied by the first three functional specialties of research, interpretation, and history. On the other hand, there are the dialectical and foundational issues and within a specifically Catholic context, such as the context of a Catholic university, Catholic Studies can be seen as obviously theological: that is, as rooted in personal conversion and as finding expression in doctrines and systematic theology.

But in the light of the method of praxis another question can be asked: Can Catholic Studies be seen as something more? That is, can it be seen as not simply the communication of doctrinal judgments and theological understandings, but also as the dynamic transformative interaction of Catholic theology with all the dimensions of modern culture? That is, besides seeing Catholic Studies as religious studies or as doctrinal or systematic theology, can it be understood as involving both theoretical judgments *as well as* practical judgments of discernment as Catholicism comes into interaction with particular disciplines and professions for the transformation of the world?

Such a transformative interaction involves an in-depth understanding of a particular area of contemporary culture, listening to the questions posed by that particular area, as well as perhaps suggesting healing perspectives and concrete implications. From the point of view of Lonergan's *Method in Theology*, such theological communications is absolutely essential for the fruitfulness of Catholic theology.[32] Lonergan describes such communications as the link between the rest of theology on one hand and all other areas of contemporary culture on the other.

On one hand, again, while Catholic Studies as communications is linked to the rest of theology—historical, doctrinal, systematic—on the other hand, it is related externally to the disciplines and areas of culture where it can possibly play a dialectical, purifying and transforming role. That is, it would seem that a major goal of Catholic Studies as it is presently emerging in the academy is to link the Catholic intellectual tradition with all the other disciplines, professions and areas of contemporary culture and in that capacity to allow theology to begin to exercise an integrating and transformative role. This, of course, demands a very capacious way of evaluating what is "Catholic."

Could there then be a role that Catholic theology can play as "yeast" or "leaven" in contemporary culture through Catholic Studies? Thus, in *Method in Theology* Lonergan calls for "integrating studies," that is, interdisciplinary studies between Catholic theology and the human sciences. For theology illuminates only part of the human condition: "Theology illuminates only certain aspects of human reality . . . the church can become a fully conscious process of self-constitution only when theology unites itself with all the other relevant branches of human studies."[33] Lonergan illustrated this himself in his studies of economics. His intense study of that field enabled him to discern "a pure cycle" of economic activity from which moral principles could be drawn. Principles regarding "moral" or "ethical" economic activity should not be "moralisms" preached from afar, but rather rational ethical principles arising from an understanding of the very nature of the economy itself.

Pope John Paul II's apostolic exhortation of 1990, *Ex corde ecclesiae*, encouraged such an interdisciplinary dialogue between the different disciplines and Catholic theology. As with any genuine dialogue, this is not a one-way street in which theology does all the teaching and the other disciplines do all the learning. Rather, "the various disciplines are brought into dialogue for their mutual enhancement."[34] Contemporary science and scholarship, then, tell us some very concrete things about the human person that we could not know from theology alone. As such, they pose questions to Catholic theology. Catholic Studies as theological praxis and communications can act as a bridge feeding back into systematic, doctrinal, foundational, and historical theology new questions arising among people of today that can even bring to light unrealized aspects of the deposit of faith. As the Scriptures put it, "Every scribe who becomes a disciple of the kingdom of heaven is like a householder who brings out from his storeroom things both new and old" (Matthew 13:52).

At the same time, the bridge goes both ways. Catholic Studies can bring all the resources of the Catholic intellectual tradition to bear on what it means to be a human person today. Certainly, one such area where it can make a major contribution would be in the human sciences, which often tend to be materialist or reductionist.

An understanding of the foundational methodology of the human spirit operative in a Catholic theology of the human person could have a healing effect on the human sciences in their practical policy-setting and feedback emphases. In addition, Catholic Studies has something very important to bring to the humanities. For the humanities deal with the human person in the widest sense, and the widest sense includes not only human frailty and sinfulness, but also the healing and elevating love of God. To highlight only one area in Catholic Studies among the many that could be mentioned, there often arises the question of "the Catholic imagination" in literature. It is sometimes claimed that there can be discerned a specific character in the works of Catholic writers, a certain kind of "earthiness," a specific way of using myth and symbol, a certain spirit infusing works of literature, art and even film.[35] Certainly such discernment can be contested, and in a pluralistic culture alternative accounts can be given. Nevertheless, for one steeped in Catholic theology and open to the method of praxis, one can also contend that living Catholic faith brings a particular quality to one's writing. One's personal horizon enters into the very warp and woof of what is written. So also, in the midst of a culture tempted to nihilism, one can perhaps see a work of art, a movie or a play that leads one to say:

"This author is not far from the Kingdom of God." Compassion for the human condition, a sensitivity to suffering, hope against hope—all such qualities in works of art can lend themselves to Catholic Studies. Catholicism should appeal to such catholicity.

So also, the historian of Catholicism, James Fisher, expects that studies of Catholicism should have a practical effect on the larger life of society as he asks:

> Is Catholic Studies well-positioned to address the growing desire for attentiveness to the religious dimension in public as well as academic life? Roman Catholicism offers not only a "holistic" vision" but a deep tradition of engagement with the human person in all dimensions. Catholicism in America has been "different:" can it come to terms with other "differences," such as in the area of sexuality or cognitive/physical disabilities?[36]

As G. K. Chesterton once wrote on the reason for Catholic schools:

> There is a Catholic view of learning the alphabet; for instance it prevents you from thinking that the only thing that matters is learning the alphabet; or from despising better people than yourself, if they do not happen to have learned the alphabet. I am only pointing out that every education teaches a philosophy if not by dogma than by suggestion, by implication, by atmosphere.[37]

Thus, all the various methods can collaborate to influence Catholic Studies as "praxis" in its transformation of the culture. For such transformation is the name of the game, and the game is both personal and cultural. In fact, the two go together: personal conversion opens one out to the transformation of the culture. The more loving, good, and intelligent one is, the more one will see the seeds of renewal already operative in the disciplines and professions and one will be able to cooperate in the transformation of the world. The more transformed one is—religiously, morally, intellectually—the more one will see what needs to be seen and the good that needs to be done.

This vision was articulated in a quasi-poetic way by Teilhard de Chardin, who dreamed of the transformation of the earth through transformed human beings. Basing himself on Saint Paul's teaching on the

Body of Christ, Teilhard saw the cosmic Christ reaching out to the whole universe, including the material world of human work, and radically transforming that world. Through their work in science, technology, government, education, and so on, humans are called to develop this world. "Collaboration in the development of the cosmos," he wrote, "holds an essential and prime position among the duties of the Christian."[38] Such a collaboration is not without its own deaths, its own asceticism, its own denial of egoism. Suffering is not just a penalty for sin, but rather the price each of us must pay to bring the universe to its completion in Christ.[39]

Such a vision needs to be translated into each area of human culture: into all the disciplines of the university, into all the arts and the sciences, the humanities and human studies, and also into the various professions: the law, business, nursing, medicine, education, and so forth. In each area there needs to take place a transformation: a transformation from meaninglessness to meaningfulness, from dryness and boredom to clarity and truth, from drifting to engaged commitment, from hatred and indifference to love. This is the point of Catholic Studies on its theological-pastoral side: to make the bridge from the theoretical judgments of theology and particular disciplines to the practical judgments flowing into every area of culture: especially those practical judgments that spell redemption and progress in the face of decline. To make those theoretical and practical judgments, spiritual discernment is needed: a discernment that is able to distinguish what is genuine from what is false, what is for the good of all from what is only apparently good. Countless other areas could be added to the ambit of Catholic Studies as "praxis," that is, as invoking excellent theology on the one hand and practical spiritual discernment on the other hand for the transformation of the world.

Part III: Pedagogy and Practice

8 Catholic Studies in the Spirit of "Do Whatever He Tells You"

UNA M. CADEGAN

During a celebration of the University of Dayton's sesquicentennial in the year 2000, the singer-songwriter alumnus who headed the university's Center for Social Concern performed a song he had written for the occasion, "Do Whatever He Tells You." At the reception after the celebration, a colleague still fairly new to the university, personally nonreligious but with an evident affinity for the university's mission and commitments, commented that he thought the song was a little odd—hadn't something like "do whatever he tells you" been written over the gates of Soviet labor camps? My first response to the remark, phrased more wittily than I can recall here, was laughter, but I also felt the pull of the teachable moment.

The song's catchy, singable refrain ("Do whatever he tells you/Do whatever he says/Everything will work out fine/Jesus will turn water into wine/Do whatever he tells you") quotes Mary's words to Jesus at the wedding feast of Cana (John 2:1–11), a scene long of importance to members of the Society of Mary (Marianist), the religious congregation that founded UD, because of its meaning for the society's founder, William Joseph Chaminade. Trying to maintain a light touch (we had, after all, reached the wine and hors d'oeuvres portion of the event, and a junior faculty member showing up on a Friday afternoon like a good citizen did not deserve to be rewarded with a sermon from a senior colleague), I noted the story's importance to the Marianists, and I also tried briefly to indicate the line's complexity in the story. Far from a simple, authoritarian directive, it represents a complex moment in which Mary, despite Jesus' somewhat curt rebuff to her hint that the wedding party had run out of wine ("My hour has not yet come"), nonetheless anticipates his intervention by alerting the servants to stand by for imminent instructions. Foreknowledge? Motherly nudging? Prefiguring of thwarted female ecclesial authority? The story's complex valence could and does lead in many directions, and it seemed important in that moment to point this out to my colleague, who had so reflexively, if jokingly, associated the song's refrain with an ethos catastrophically counter to that of a university.

This episode passed quickly into small talk over carrot sticks and mini-quiches, and I doubt my colleague even recalls it. But it has long been emblematic for me of the complexity involved in communicating the university's mission and identity to faculty colleagues. "Do whatever he tells you" (and all it stands for concerning Marianist educational heritage and philosophy) has rich resonance not only for those committed personally and spiritually to Catholic tradition and its Marianist embodiment, but also for a compelling vision of intellectual life and university purpose. Its meaning is far from apparent on the surface, however, and communicating it to those who are fully a part of the university enterprise but distant from the Marianists as a religious community requires time, relationship, study, and luck, all in impeccably precise and perfectly timed proportion.

Instead, of course, what we get is real life. Even for those tolerantly open or actively predisposed to learning about the university's mission, such learning requires, among other things, time. It therefore inevitably competes for the time required by other commitments such as classes and research and meetings and the occasional moment of leisure. Yet if it does not somehow take place the university abandons all hope of being meaningfully Catholic, since if the faculty do not own and embody the mission, there may be some Catholic elements to a university—but it will not be a Catholic university.

This conundrum is (perhaps numbingly) familiar to everyone involved in thinking about how to make and keep Catholic universities Catholic. Over the past couple of decades at the University of Dayton, we have explored a variety of ways to address it, none of them unique, but nonetheless distinctively informed by the university's Marianist heritage and character. In describing Dayton's approach, I hope to do more than make a list of committees and speakers. In the spirit of Jim Fisher's hope that this project reflect explicitly on ways in which American Catholic Studies might serve as an intellectual resource for the Church in passing on the faith to the next generation, I would like to situate Dayton's approach within what I understand to be the contemporary intellectual and institutional context of Catholic higher education. I will not neglect the nuts and bolts entirely, because the mundane building blocks of meetings and minutes and budget requests provide the framework within which intellectual resources can exist and flourish. But I think the nuts and bolts are distinctively configured in ways that reflect the University of Dayton's founding commitments, history, and contemporary location.

This essay is an attempt to articulate the ideas that have both shaped and resulted from the University of Dayton's practices, over the past two decades or so, aimed at enlivening Catholic intellectual tradition on campus in service of sustaining and extending the university's mission as Catholic. I begin by describing why the University of Dayton has chosen its particular approach to Catholic Studies, including some consideration of the benefits and risks. I then describe some of the key strategies and mechanisms by which we have worked to put this approach into practice. On the important question of effectiveness, I fear the true answer is that it is too soon to tell, but that answer is presumably unsatisfactory to readers of this volume, as well as to anyone, including me, who has ever had to submit an assessment report. So I return to the wedding feast at Cana, using it as a means by which to think through how to know when and whether Dayton's approach to Catholic Studies is making the contribution we hope, both to the education of our students and to the vitality of Catholic higher education and Catholic intellectual life.

Catholic Studies Without Catholic Studies

The University of Dayton made a conscious decision some time ago not to do two things that many Catholic universities were doing in the quest to strengthen and highlight Catholic identity. We did not establish a degree program in Catholic Studies, and we did not establish an office or a vice presidency for mission and identity.[1] While there are many good reasons for doing both of these things, the people making the relevant decisions at Dayton saw greater advantage in going about things differently. For the university's identity as a university to be meaningfully Catholic, it needed to be embodied and embedded in the curriculum and in the research of the faculty. And to do that, a much more diffuse effort was required, one that sought to transform the way a significant proportion of the faculty went about their work and thought about it. A good Catholic Studies major can provide a solid degree program for a relatively small number of students, but a general-education curriculum informed by Catholic intellectual tradition and supported by a significant proportion of the faculty can affect the learning of every student who passes through the university. An effective office of mission and identity can enhance understanding of and participation in the mission for faculty, staff, and students, but mission and identity as a central aspect of the job description for every dean and vice president have the potential to transform the university as a workplace and as a university.

The advantages of this wide diffusion of knowledge and responsibility across much of the campus are in some ways also its disadvantages. Achieving it is an amorphous and long-term project, requiring time and sustained attention. Determining ownership and accountability becomes much more difficult when the responsibility is widely distributed. Instead of being the visible primary focus of a designated group on campus, it can become just one task in the portfolio of people with many other things to attend to. Then, instead of being an integral element of the academic and intellectual life of the university, it risks becoming one item among many in a boilerplate checklist, and everybody's goal becomes checking it off as fast and painlessly as possible.

When I lay the risks out this starkly, I wonder why we ever thought this approach was a good idea. One area in which it is possible to see a sustained cultivation of the benefits along with (so far) avoidance of the worst of the risk is in the university's general-education program, in place since the early 1980s, now likely in the midst of significant revision, but one of the most distinctive aspects of the Dayton curriculum, in large part because its requirements apply to students from all units of the university—business, education, and engineering as well as arts and sciences. Dayton is one of the largest universities in the country for which this is the case.

When the University of Dayton last revised its general-education curriculum in the 1980s, it put the humanities at the center of the first-year academic experience. Students were required to take introductory courses in religious studies, philosophy, history and English composition, which were organized as a "Humanities Base" around the question, "What does it mean to be human?" and four corollary subthemes: faith and reason, individual and community, autonomy and responsibility, and humans and nature. The decision to make the humanities central was not uncontroversial, but it was justified and defended (crucially by key academic administrators, but also by faculty) as consistent with Catholic intellectual tradition. The central questions of the humanities, able to be framed in infinitely variable ways, but here in the four subthemes, offer avenues appropriate to a university into the issues at the heart of Catholic intellectual tradition. The integrative approach of the humanities, their sustained insistence that the great human questions are interrelated and that investigation of them must be synthetic and relational, reflect a key insight of Catholic intellectual tradition—the unity of truth (richly and complexly and contextually understood as that insight must be).

Making and sustaining this case has never been a straightforward task (it is an ongoing battle, for example, to keep the themes from being formulated as adversaries—say, faith versus reason in a cosmic grudge match), the difficulty of which illustrates one limitation of Dayton's diffuse approach. Diffusion can be hard to distinguish from dilution—if insufficient numbers of faculty and students know that the Humanities Base looks the way it does not coincidentally but precisely *because* the university understands itself as Catholic, then in precisely whose possession is this understanding? One possible way to sustain a credible answer to this question has been a historic strength of the Marianists and of the university—sheer persistence, or, more graciously, "staying at the table." The program was initiated with a two-week series of all-day faculty workshops, and has been sustained with semiannual workshops ever since. When they have been planned (as they have a remarkable percentage of the time) with an eye toward recharging the intellectual energy that keeps a program like this alive, these workshops have been one of the most effective means by which the program's focus has been maintained, developed, and deepened.

How these elements—diffusion and persistence—combine for some noticeable effect over time is apparent in two other examples. First is what is likely to become the next iteration of the university's general-education program, at this writing still very much in process. The current process began when the dean of the College of Arts and Sciences appointed a working group charged with answering the question: What are the elements of a Marianist education? From one angle, this was an extremely familiar question, with extremely well-worn (if earnest and generally effective) answers. But the familiar elements, such as "collaboration" and "integration between liberal and professional education," all had to do with process. The working group's task was to attempt an answer to the much more vexed question of content, one that has been systematically avoided in discussions of general education nationally for well over a generation. The group was composed of faculty from the four units (fine arts, humanities, natural sciences, social sciences) of the College of Arts and Sciences, as well as from each of the undergraduate professional schools (Business Administration, Education and Allied Professions, and Engineering). Chaired by an associate dean from the College, the group was assembled and charged in consultation with the provost.

The working group pursued its charge, through a widely consultative process, during the academic year 2005–2006, and submitted its report, entitled, "Habits of Inquiry and Reflection" in the spring of 2006.[2] The provost was impressed enough with the result that he requested a vote of the Academic Senate on adopting the report's principles as the basis for initiating a review of the university's "common academic program" (a term used to denote all a student's learning experiences, including those beyond the traditional curriculum). This vote was strenuously opposed by some faculty members, who saw the process as circumventing faculty control of the curriculum, but a majority of the Senate (which includes student and administrator members as well as faculty) voted to adopt the proposal, and appointed a subcommittee to do the even harder work of determining how the report's philosophical principles would be embodied in actual requirements and credits.

I present this long account of bureaucratic process in an essay ostensibly about ideas because it illustrates a number of these ideas most effectively. First, and forgive me if the point is obvious, but cultivating a Catholic Studies ethos—that is, a climate in which a rich, interdisciplinary investigation of Catholic intellectual tradition flourishes in multiple forms in multiple venues throughout the university—is often very mundane work. It involves not just the crafting of stirring documents and inspiring speeches, but also early-morning meetings; counting of committee votes; endless circulation of drafts; patience in the face of disagreement, resentment, and misunderstanding. Faculty members commonly use "bureaucracy" as a term of abuse for things that get in the way of our real work. But if faculty governance is real, and incorporating Catholic intellectual tradition into the curriculum is possible, then the mechanics of meetings and minutes and seemingly endless consultation are no more dispensable to us than a carpenter's tools are to the finished piece of cabinetwork.

Second, staying at the table is not a short-term affair. Even very good curricular structures for integrating Catholic intellectual tradition with general education will not be sustained by inertia, tending once in motion in the direction of ever greater and more meaningful integration. It needs constant tending and renewal of the source of energy, which is provided by a group of faculty interested in and in touch with each other about what excites the enthusiasm of faculty as faculty. Dayton's general-education revisions in the 1980s resulted in a somewhat uneasy but nonetheless fruitful partnership between explorers of the widened intellectual horizons that transformed Catholic higher education from the mid-1960s onward and inhabitants of the broad and deep Catholic intellectual and educational tradition that seemed in danger of being swamped. (Membership in these groups overlapped, of course.) Because the two groups stayed in conversation, however, they were able to attract and help develop an ever-widening circle of faculty committed to the idea that wide intellectual horizons and long and deep intellectual traditions were both essential to whatever a Catholic university was going to be in the third millennium. When the time came for renewed conversation about general education, then, concerns about the role of Catholic intellectual tradition were already a part of the mix, a part of the ongoing concerns of a significant number of faculty, not something that had to be introduced externally by academic administrators or mission officers.

One more curricular example will illustrate these ideas, and add an additional dimension to Dayton's approach to Catholic Studies. Interest persisted on the part of key administrators that the university establish a degree program (in this case, a minor) that would somehow participate in the "Catholic Studies" movement. They were, though, amenable to the idea that such a program should distinctively encompass what Dayton and the Marianists are about. So, in a surprise development, a committee was appointed. Again, its members came from all areas of the university, and took as its task two complicating factors. First, members agreed that the minor should be something students could come to relatively late in their university career—at the end of the sophomore or beginning of the junior year—since many of the students it would be looking to serve discover the Marianist "thing" only after having been at the university for a while. Second, the committee members placed an even higher priority on the minor being available to students in all majors, including the professional schools. Because Marianist education at all levels has always aimed to serve people from all sectors of society, students in business, education, and engineering, as well as the natural sciences, have often been the ones to become most dedicated to the idea of using their professional training in service to society. Making it possible for them to complete an interdisciplinary minor reflecting on Marianist education was integral not just to maximizing the potential constituency for the program, but also to its reason for existing in the first place. The result was a program in "Marianist Social Transformation," emphasizing the connections among Marianist history and charism as a response to changing times, Catholic social teaching as a response to industrialization, and a student's own intellectual and professional training as a response to the needs of the contemporary world.

The minor's requirements, therefore, needed both enough flexibility to adapt to a wide variety of major programs and enough coherence to give it shape and purpose. The details of the solution (a familiar mix of choices among component courses along with a planned capstone) are less relevant here than is the process and the outcome—both their advantages and disadvantages. Advantages include the presence of people in each professional school ready to serve as advocates and resources for the program as it gets underway, because of their involvement on the committee and in consultations. Another advantage is the nature of the program itself—distinctively tailored to help students see just how, in specific times and places, Marianist heritage and commitments embody Catholic tradition. Disadvantages reflect additional drawbacks to the University of Dayton's "diffused" approach. It is relatively easy, at least within a small but well-defined intellectual community, to talk about developing a "Catholic Studies program" at Dayton. It is more difficult, sometimes to the point of self-defeat, to convey clearly what it means to establish a minor in "Marianist Social Transformation." This does not mean it is not worth doing, just that it carries an inescapable disadvantage that must be accounted for in thinking through how to help the program succeed. The task is worth taking up, because at stake is an understanding of what Marianist higher education has to contribute to contemporary Catholic intellectual life and culture.

In what sense can a university that has deliberately decided not to establish something called "Catholic Studies" offer its approach as a potential resource for thinking about what Catholic Studies might have to offer the Church as it passes on the faith to the next generation? In the area of curriculum, even the partial answer sketched here is at least threefold. First, the "Catholic Studies without Catholic Studies" approach can pay off in distinctive ways. An institutional decision to ask faculty from all academic areas to consider the role Catholic intellectual tradition plays in their teaching and research yields over time a multifaceted set of answers that in turn helps to reshape notions of what Catholic Studies can be. Collaborating with the student development division, as Dayton has done, adds an additional, crucial, dimension to the task.

Second, the balance between explicit and implicit efforts, between content and method, is a delicate one, but necessary. That is, the attempt to diffuse investigation of Catholic intellectual tradition throughout the curriculum can result in a kind of conceptual shapelessness. It is a sign of curricular health and institutional confidence to encourage all faculty members at a Catholic university to find ways in which their disciplines and their classroom approaches can enter into the overarching questions of what it means to be human. What can but probably should not follow is that whatever results be considered sufficient as a curricular exploration of Catholic intellectual tradition. Some explicit study of Catholicism as a religious and intellectual tradition is necessary, though where and how and by whom it should be delivered are always going to be questions requiring diplomacy, persuasive skill, and scholarly patience and seriousness.

Which leads to my third and concluding point in this section: while the diffuse approach to Catholic studies can yield transformative benefits, this outcome is not automatic, and neither is the approach particularly efficient. There is a standing joke at Dayton that S.M. (Society of Mary) really stands for "still meeting." The downside of genuine commitment to collaboration and consultation is a slow, cumbersome, often amorphous process. The vision of widespread participation in incorporating Catholic intellectual tradition into the curriculum at all levels is a compelling one. The reality is that differences in interest and expertise will lead significant numbers of faculty to opt out, absent some compelling motivation or incentive. And compulsion is not the most edifying catalyst for curricular vigor. So is the vision anything other than an illusion? Potentially, yes, if faculty development is undertaken in sustained and appropriate ways. The good news is that this part is the most fun.

"What Are Those Meetings Where Everybody's Laughing?"

A colleague asked this question one summer afternoon, having passed the open departmental conference room door that morning and the day before. The meeting in question was a summer seminar in Catholic intellectual tradition, composed of faculty doing what we sometimes have to remind ourselves is what got us into the business in the first place—reading new and interesting work and discussing ideas together. Seminars have been a key means by which Dayton has sought to cultivate a group of faculty with an interest in Catholic intellectual tradition. The seminars have been of three types, all of which have played a significant role.

When the university initially began seeking to enhance Catholic intellectual tradition on campus after a major mission and identity report in the early 1990s, the greatest obstacle was the absence of a community of faculty committed to research in Catholic areas. There were surely faculty doing such research, and committed to it personally, but few opportunities to develop the intellectual community that can give institutional life to such a project. Dayton therefore committed to fund a full-year faculty seminar, involving fifteen people from across the university, each of whom received a one-course reduction each semester. The seminar held biweekly three-hour meetings throughout the academic year. In the first semester the seminar did a kind of overview of Catholic intellectual tradition from thirty thousand feet, as an introduction and review for those with little or long-ago background in the area. In the second semester, the seminar focused on what work in Catholic intellectual tradition looked like in a variety of disciplines.

It is difficult to measure, but probably hard to overestimate, the extent to which this seminar helped to forge an intellectual community around topics in Catholic intellectual tradition. That is, it both helped create a community, and it designated that community primarily as intellectual. The university had sponsored a number of faculty seminars on other topics in the years preceding the CIT seminar; sponsoring one on Catholic intellectual tradition put it on the same footing, as a subject for scholarly study and investigation, and the experience of the seminar members during and after that academic year has borne out that realization. Seminars have played probably the single most important role in overcoming what may be the most intransigent obstacle to a lively intellectual identity as a Catholic university—the suspicion among many faculty members that promoting Catholic intellectual tradition is closer to propaganda and restriction on academic freedom than it is about free inquiry and scholarly seriousness. The best remedy for this suspicion is creating conditions under which faculty encounter work that is indisputably part of Catholic intellectual tradition and indisputably of high scholarly quality. It can be a freeing and energizing thing for faculty to encounter classic texts and examine them as scholars. Many academics may not have dealt with religious materials since before the beginning of their real academic training, and they may be pleasantly surprised to understand that studying history and tradition requires a scholarly sensibility but not an act of faith. The university also agreed to fund and support a second all-university seminar ten years after the first, to make available to a new group of faculty the same opportunity.

A second type of faculty seminar has been equally important. Conducted by the University Professor of Faith and Culture (and, in one case, by the Ferree Professor of Social Justice), these seminars have been more topically focused, aimed at drawing faculty from specific disciplinary and professional areas into discussion of how Catholic intellectual tradition relates to their specific areas. These seminars have been conducted with faculty from the humanities, social sciences, natural sciences, law, education, business, and engineering. Each ran for one semester and offered a one-course reduction for participants. These seminars also offered funding for summer research, and required that participants propose and produce work related to the seminar topic. Some faculty members used the opportunity for initial personal reflection on what was an entirely new area of scholarly study for them, some were launched into new research projects within their own fields, and some began cross-disciplinary collaborations with fellow participants. Perhaps the most distinctive by-product of these seminars was Dayton's 2005 conference on "The Role of Engineering at Catholic Universities."

For all their importance in creating and sustaining intellectual community around issues of Catholic intellectual tradition, the single greatest drawback of such seminars is their expense. While it is possible to make a strong case that the benefits are well worth the investment, in many cases the funds and the release time for such large-scale efforts are simply not available. But many of the benefits of the long-term seminars can be gained with much more modest funds, as our summer "meetings where everybody's laughing" indicate. During a number of summers (ad hoc as organizers were available), we have hosted shorter-term seminars for interested faculty. Some have offered modest stipends; some have not. Some involved a week of daily meetings, some biweekly or monthly meetings over the course of the summer. The most ambitious involved two weeks of two-hour meetings at the beginning of the summer, a six-week interim in which participants worked on and circulated drafts of writing projects, and a final week of daily meetings late in the summer to discuss the works in progress.

These more modest seminar efforts worked because of a combination of elements. First was combining wide invitation with some targeted recruitment. It is important to extend open invitations, in order to identify people with an interest whom others might not know about. Intentional recruitment is also essential, for a variety of reasons—to aim for some balance among disciplines and career stages and among other kinds of diversity, as well as to involve colleagues whose work could benefit the group, or benefit from participation in it. The second key element is food and drink, appropriate to the time of day. It adds immeasurably to the sense of collegiality that makes these seminars successful. And third, the centerpiece of the effort has to be reading and discussing first-rate work in a variety of fields, clearly scholarly but accessible to a wide range of readers. Over time, as a given group of faculty develops a sense of itself, suggestions for possible reading will emerge with more frequency than the meetings can keep up with.

Catholic Studies, the University of Dayton, and the Marianists: Resources for Future Work

In asking what "Catholic Studies" might mean in the absence of an explicit degree program, I have looked at *what* Dayton sees itself to be about in this area; by looking at seminars and other avenues to faculty development through study and research into Catholic intellectual tradition, I have explored one crucial aspect of *how* it is we go about it. I would like in the final section of this essay to spend some time thinking about *why*, but in the specific and localized sense of *why now, and why here*? Why might this approach to Catholic Studies be particularly appropriate to the University of Dayton, at this particular time in the long history of Catholic intellectual tradition and the life of the Catholic university? My aim here is not to document the institutional deliberations that resulted in this approach, but to reflect on it in retrospect and make the case that it offers distinctive answers to the question of what role Catholic universities should play in the twenty-first century.

Two aspects of the University of Dayton's identity are particularly germane to its approach to Catholic Studies: it is a Marianist university, and it is a comprehensive university. Priests and brothers of the Society of Mary founded the university as St. Mary's School for Boys in 1850, but the word "Marianist" had then and has now a wider resonance. It applies not only to the members of the Society of Mary, but also to the women's religious congregation, the Daughters of Mary Immaculate (F.M.I.), and to members of the lay communities, sodalities, that were the first form of Christian community organized and led by Marianist founders Father William Joseph Chaminade, Adèle de Batz de Trenquelleon, and Marie Thérèse de Lamorous. The fact that "Marianist" denoted a layperson before it denoted a priest, brother, or sister reflects a powerful ethos of lay collaboration that still animates Marianist enterprises, and it has had tangible effects on how the university has approached Catholic Studies and its wider commitment to renewing and enhancing Catholic intellectual tradition on campus. Members of the vowed religious congregations have certainly been crucial to Dayton's efforts as leaders and participants. There has been at every stage and every level, at the same time, a conscious and successful attempt to include laity as well as participants and leaders both. This is true at many Catholic colleges and universities, of course, but it has a particular resonance and self-consciousness at Dayton because of the Marianists' historical commitments.

Marianists have been dedicated to the education of all classes since their founding in France in the aftermath of the Revolution. This historical commitment, combined with the situation in which they found themselves upon locating in southwestern Ohio in the middle of the nineteenth century, led to a focus on practical education in the institutions that are the University of Dayton's historical precursors. The city of Dayton's centrality to so much of the technological innovation that shaped the twentieth century, especially aviation and the automobile (but not forgetting the cash register), helped reinforce this emphasis. Revisions of general education and renewed emphasis on Catholic intellectual tradition, initiatives undertaken in the 1980s, were consciously building on a legacy of commitment to technical and professional education. Despite the occasional tendency to disparage this legacy ("Jesus Tech"), on the whole faculty and administrators have confronted the issues of curricular renewal and faculty development by thinking through the ways that liberal and professional education can and must depend on each other, both for the sake of helping students develop highly proficient and marketable skills and for the sake of students' capacity to see themselves as participating in the transformation of society.

An underappreciated aspect of the Marianists' historical commitment to technical and professional education is that so many of the brothers were teachers and scholars of mathematics and the natural sciences. This was not only a powerful witness to generations of students about the consonance between study of all subjects and deep dedication to God—it also, I believe, helped to create a natural pool of interdisciplinary interest and expertise. Regardless of academic field, Marianist brothers, priests and sisters virtually all had some exposure to, and often deep expertise in, theology and church history, even if it was primarily through the liturgy and the celebration of the liturgical year. At the University of Dayton, therefore (and probably at many Catholic colleges and universities to an extent we have yet to consider fully), when the curricular discussions of the postconciliar decades took shape, they were rooted in this distinctive kind of interdisciplinarity. It was largely implicit, and to the extent that it became a subject of explicit consideration it could be and was vehemently contested, but it helped to hold together perspectives that might otherwise have retreated to their separate academic enclaves.

In addition to being a Marianist university, Dayton is also a comprehensive university; that is, it has a strong and central College of Arts and Sciences with Bachelor of Liberal Studies requirements that apply to all students earning degrees in the College, and it also has three undergraduate professional schools (Business Administration, Education and Allied Professions, and Engineering) and a School of Law.[3] This composition from one angle seems like an obstacle to Catholic Studies, since so much of the curriculum, especially for undergraduates, is focused on professional preparation, and since the research focus of faculty in those areas will necessarily be in disciplines not historically associated with Catholic Studies as an interdisciplinary field. The university has made substantial efforts, and had some notable successes, however, in seeing the combination of liberal education, Catholic intellectual tradition and professional preparation as an opportunity to reimagine key elements of the purpose of a Catholic university. This enterprise is frustratingly complicated, exhaustingly long-term, and enormously rewarding. It involves attention to faculty hiring and orientation, but—perhaps more crucially—attention as well to faculty who become convinced of the consonance between their professional passions and the university's enterprise only after they have been here for a while, sometimes a very long while. One concrete and innovative outcome was a 2005 conference on "The Role of Engineering at a Catholic University" (RECU), in which engineers and theologians reflected on how engineering as both a profession and an area of study and research can and should reflect the most fundamental commitments of Catholic higher education.

The RECU conference illustrates the potential scope of what we are attempting: not just safeguarding the faith of undergraduates while they acquire the tools of success, nor foregrounding ethics in professional training, but using Catholic intellectual tradition as a lens through which to view the academy's approach to knowledge and the professions' approach to practice. (The scrutiny is mutual and reciprocal, in case you were wondering.) Catholic higher education has to be about more than fitting (primarily) Catholic undergraduates for success within the status quo. Historically, this made sense as a mission, since the kind of success that allows for stability, security, and some measure of influence was largely unavailable to Catholic immigrants and children of immigrants. There are some institutions of Catholic higher education for which this mission of basic access to the American middle class is still at the heart of their reason for being. But for institutions that are now educating the children and grandchildren of college-educated parents, whose access and identity as members of the middle and upper classes have never been in question, something more is required.

Required by what, or by whom? By, I would argue, the nature of Catholic intellectual life and Catholic intellectual tradition, which themselves, of course, are grounded in the imperatives of the Gospel. A university is not a church, of course, and for good reason. And all people of good will can be compelled by a rich intellectual tradition and vision without espousing the faith that gives rise to it. But a Catholic university needs to be animated by a vision of the good that results from ongoing communal reflection on the gospels, and it needs for all its most basic work to be at the very least consonant with that vision of the good.

High-flown rhetoric, perhaps a little sectarian in tone. What does this look like in practice? And what has it got to do with Catholic Studies? After a little more than twenty years working as a scholar, teacher, occasional administrator, and pretty-near-constant mission-and-identity committee factotum, I am more rather than less convinced that the next era of the history of American Catholic higher education can be the most interesting and influential yet. "Can be" because nothing is certain, and historians get drummed out of the union if they predict the future. But there is what seems to me an unprecedented confluence between the wealth and status of many Catholic colleges and universities and the most pressing and urgent—and interesting—problems of the day. What I am *not* suggesting here is that we "follow the money" (though I think there may often be greater opportunities to do well by doing good than we allow ourselves to believe). What I am suggesting is that the method I described, using Catholic intellectual tradition as a lens through which to view the academy's approach to knowledge and the professions' approach to practice, can lead to some of the richest, most innovative and inviting fields of investigation on the contemporary intellectual landscape, in the service of human flourishing.

Examples abound, and proliferate exponentially upon consideration. For example, it is clear that without significant reform, the current system for health insurance and delivering health care in the United States is unsustainable. At the same time, the issue provokes something like despair from most commentators, because it is so complicated and because the path to change is so crowded with obstacles. Catholic universities could both serve the poorest and most vulnerable populations in the country and, most likely, benefit themselves if they were to identify and develop curricular and research strengths related to the multiple dimensions of this issue. It could produce (and surely is already producing) important work at the intersection of biomedical ethics and social ethics, as theologians and philosophers recognize and explore the influence of political and economic power in limiting access to what almost all other developed nations recognize as a fundamental right. Economics, management, and marketing departments could explore—both as emphases in faculty research interests and in innovative curricula—how a transition to universal access to health care could be accomplished in ways that were the least economically disruptive, and they could help students think about a wide variety of alternative economic models that could serve the basic principles of Catholic social thought more fully and successfully, while contributing to human flourishing at least as effectively as the current one. Political science and history departments could aid students in seeing clearly how systems function in complex societies, making transparent processes and forces that too often remain opaque and intimidating to the citizens whose lives they structure. Public relations and graphic design courses could equip students with the skills necessary for effective communication and the commitment to use the skills in service of accurately and constructively shaping opinion on crucial decisions. Engineering schools could achieve national prominence for a curriculum that not only taught budding engineers how to design and create innovative medical technology, but also helped them know enough about the world to want to influence how and where and by whom it is used when they enter the professional world.

Similarly dense intentional, interdisciplinary collaborations could cluster around a wide variety of other urgent issues. Dealing effectively and rapidly with the challenges of climate change and environmental sustainability requires the same wide spectrum of philosophical and theological clarity, scientific expertise, and political savvy if we have any hope of acting before it is too late. Taking up as intellectual communities (rather than relying solely on the appearance of particularly dedicated individuals) the obligation to help ameliorate the scandalously deepening global inequities in health and wealth, redefining profit to include imagining the possibility that the extension of capitalism to other parts of the world need not replicate its most destructive historical features (in human and environmental costs) could produce innovative and influential thinking in areas ranging from philosophy to finance. History, philosophy, theology, literature, political science, and engineering would all be needed to work effectively at imagining and daring to work toward a future without war, helping students to see clearly the militarization that has been one of the single most prominent features of post–World War II American culture, and the most urgent problem of nuclear proliferation. Constructing the institutions needed for a global civic society, so that multinational corporations and militaries are not the only institutions with real global reach, defining and working to ensure and extend human rights—as I said, the list of intellectually rich, professionally fruitful, humanly urgent areas of inquiry proliferates exponentially.

I would like to emphasize that I am not advocating self-sacrificing altruism here. Not that there is anything wrong with doing so, but it cannot be a prescription for the future of Catholic Studies and the mission of Catholic colleges and universities. Individuals can commit themselves to total self-giving; institutions cannot. In imagining how Catholic Studies, broadly conceived, can serve as a resource for the Church and for the world, we can retain a constructive pragmatism about an institution's need to protect and perpetuate itself, precisely so that it can, to the extent possible, create the conditions under which all of these other things can take place. Universities have more experience doing this than almost any other societal institution in the modern world.

A number of years ago I played a small role in an interdisciplinary research project that sought to apply the principles of Catholic social teaching to the delivery of adolescent health care. The project involved sociologists, theologians, a specialist in medical communication, physicians, nurses, psychologists, and ethicists.[4] The most lasting insight for me personally was realizing that probably three-quarters of all the reforms suggested by reflection on Catholic social teaching would save considerable amounts of money. I wondered when it was all over if what we really should be about at Catholic universities is training lobbyists—only a half-facetious suggestion, since what seemed clear to me about the results of the adolescent health project was that changing people's minds about certain basic political decisions was key to actually implementing all the things that were the right thing to do in multiple senses of the term. Selfless giving in service of the poor is a powerful prophetic witness to which we are probably called in more ways than we know how to listen for. But there is ample room to work for justice between where most Catholic universities are and where the point of real sacrifice might be reached.

Clearly, there are many, many people who are not Catholic and not employed by Catholic universities committed to and actively working on all of these issues. You do not need to be Catholic to be concerned about the future of the planet. But there is a powerful argument to be made that Catholic intellectual tradition offers distinctive, perhaps unmatched, resources for helping us to reimagine intellectual life in ways that can serve these needs more fully. The configuration of the academy looks different today than it did a century ago and it will look different a century from now. We cannot know for sure the exact content of that difference but since it results at least in part from human choices, we may as well try to shape it in accord with our deepest and truest commitments. The expertise of all fields is necessary and interdependent: collaboration between philosophy and natural science, good use of the tools of social science, cultivation of the imagination of students through the humanities—these and other relevant tasks are ideally suited to the integrative vision of Catholic intellectual tradition.

Exhortation by itself does not remove real and persistent obstacles. Interdisciplinary work is and will remain difficult. In particular, sorting out how disciplines other than theology form part of Catholic intellectual tradition is both an interesting intellectual problem and a potential source of neuralgia. To the extent that Catholic Studies as a movement has been motivated by a perceived need to reconnect young people with the traditions of Catholicism, examining its dark side and the dishonorable aspects of its history as an institution raises hackles. Those inclined to debunking and those inclined to defending often have little to do with each other. Instead of working at cross-purposes, however, these two groups might instead explore the possibility that they are both essential. Most immediately, for example, one of the huge hurdles to making any kind of case for Catholic Studies as a resource for addressing urgent contemporary needs is the drastic loss of credibility brought about by the clergy sexual abuse crisis. One suspects that a public proposal offering these resources would be met with a polite "no, thank you," from many of our secular peers (that is, those whose rejection did not consist of "hell, no"). Clarity and honesty about what gave rise to the crisis will take enormous amounts of scholarly energy for at least the next generation. And that is the best-case scenario—absent such honest dealing, the loss of credibility could well be (justifiably) permanent. And all of these obstacles could be terminally daunting well before we even contemplate the inevitable difficulty of swimming against the cultural tide, and against the interests of corrosive understandings of money and power that have had the dominant cultural voice for a very long while.

Which brings us back to the wedding feast at Cana. I used it at the beginning to illustrate the complexity of the culture and intellectual tradition into which Catholic universities invite secular colleagues and colleagues from other religious traditions, along with the delicacy and extent of the acculturation required, should colleagues accept the invitation. But it has also served for me as a symbol of a certain kind of hope. For vowed Marianists, the touchstone for interpreting the story is a letter written by founder William Joseph Chaminade in 1839 instructing priests preparing to preach annual retreats, and celebrating the recently received papal approval of the Society of Mary's constitution. The letter closes by saying, "Ours is a great work, a magnificent work. If it is universal, it is because we are Missionaries of Mary, who has said to us, 'Do whatever he tells you.'"[5] That sense of being sent is vital to the Marianist charism. As a layperson and a faculty member, I hear in the story a number of things that can sustain, perhaps beyond what current circumstances give us reason to expect, a commitment to the potential of Catholic Studies.

Mary's "Do whatever he tells you" places us sometimes in the role of the stewards. What did they think upon receiving this command? Did they think filling the huge wine jars with water—no small physical task—was pointless? Did they complain about being forced to do useless work while there was a wedding celebration going on? Did they laugh at Mary behind her back for giving such an irrational order? If the jars had remained full only of water, they could have complained and jeered justifiably at the embarrassment. But, regardless of what they thought, we know what they did: They filled the jars. We do not have to be entirely confident of the outcome to do our best to hear and respond to the needs around us in ways that we are best suited to. We might feel silly and perhaps resentful laboring away at something that could well be embarrassingly ineffective. But it is also possible that our cooperation, our response, helps to create the conditions for the most unlikely of gifts.

What this story indicates about the relationship between Jesus and Mary also offers material for reflection. Mary is attentive to the needs of the celebration in which she is participating, and confidently assertive both in her approach to Jesus ("They have no more wine") and in her command to the servants, apparently in contradiction to Jesus' answer. It would be easy and dangerous to take this analogy too far, but in attentively discerning the needs of the contemporary world, asking for help to accomplish what is beyond our own capacity, but then taking bold steps to prepare to receive that help even despite its apparent refusal, we would be acting in imitation of the relationship between Jesus and Mary, another absolutely vital Marianist stance. That Mary seems to recognize something about Jesus' "hour" even before he was ready to commit to it publicly suggests that discernment is a deeply communal and relational process in which human and divine collaboration brings about new things in the world.

Finally, one of the most important things about the story is that it takes place at a wedding celebration. Jesus' first miracle is not to heal someone suffering hopelessly or to give food to the poor and hungry, but to ensure the provision of appropriate hospitality in the service of great celebration. It is easy to survey the landscape of the contemporary world, conclude that it is difficult and expensive enough simply to educate competent professionals, and take our primary cues from professional associations and the front pages of the *New York Times* and the *Wall Street Journal*. But if our cues come fundamentally from the gospel, we find there a God who understands that it matters whether wedding guests have wine. A wedding: there is no more ordinary nor more magical sign of hope and assent to the future. Celebration, real festivity, as philosopher Josef Pieper so often made clear, depends on an idea of time in which the Incarnation is always real and always present. Catholic intellectual life as a response to the need for deeper, more genuine, more extended celebration—that is a mission into which I suspect Catholic higher education can invite partners fruitfully for many years to come.

9 Afflicting the Comfortable

The Role of Catholic Social Teaching in Catholic Studies Programs

MARGARET M. McGUINNESS

Faculty members involved in Catholic Studies programs at Catholic colleges and universities throughout the United States (and their deans, provosts, and presidents) should pay careful attention to a recent report released by the Pew Forum on Religion and Public Life detailing the religious landscape of the modern United States. Based on interviews with 35,000 Americans over the age of eighteen, the study found that many of us move from one religion to another with relative ease. More than a quarter of Americans, for instance, no longer practice the religion in which they were raised and have either joined another denomination or disassociated themselves from organized religion altogether; if change in religious affiliation is broadened to include those who have moved among Protestant denominations, the number increases to 44 percent.[1] The section of the report focusing on American Catholicism is particularly telling. As a number of sociological and demographic studies have reported over the years, Catholics in America continue to constitute about 25 percent of the general population—a figure many of us have dutifully repeated in classes—but, as the Pew report's summary notes, Catholicism "has experienced the greatest net losses as a result of affiliation changes." Furthermore, although "nearly one-in-three Americans (31 percent) were raised in the Catholic faith, today fewer than one-in-four (24 percent) describe themselves as Catholic." Overall, "approximately one-third of the survey respondents who say they were raised Catholic no longer describe themselves as Catholic." In other words, about 10 percent of Americans describe themselves as former Catholics, a net loss of 7.5 per cent. "These losses would have been even more pronounced," the report continues, "were it not for the offsetting impact of immigration."

The portrait of American Catholics displayed on the Pew Forum's website demonstrates most American Catholics live comfortably and enjoy educational advantages that were not available to their grandparents. Sixty-nine percent of Catholics earn more than $30,000 per year; 33 percent earn more than $75,000. Only 17 percent of U.S. Catholics do not graduate from high school; this figure may be as high as it is because it reflects the impact immigration is having on the demographics of the Church. Forty-seven percent have attended college. Although charts and statistics cannot tell us everything we need to know about the state of Catholicism in the United States, they do help educators to understand that today's undergraduate students attending Catholic colleges are not always the first in their family to receive a post–secondary school education.[2]

Raw statistics, however, do not reveal the changes in the ways U.S. Catholics, particularly those under the age of thirty-five, view their church. Many millennial Catholics (young adults), who are the children and grandchildren of those who came of age in the aftermath of the Second Vatican Council, not only often disagree with church teachings but also sometimes question the traditional definition of what it means to be a practicing Catholic. Georgetown University professor Chester Gillis describes this generation of Catholics as "less institutionally identified . . . less informed on theological and doctrinal matters, [and] more inclined to favor individual conscience over institutional dictates." They "are a generation," Gillis writes, "raised on religious education programs that stressed Christian behavior rather than doctrinal beliefs."[3] An example proffered by sociologist James Davidson supports Gillis's contention. Speaking at a 2007 forum sponsored by the Woodstock Theological Center entitled "Young Adult Catholics: Believing, Belonging, and Serving," Davidson drew nervous chuckles when he told the audience about an experience he had had during a lecture in Detroit. During the course of his talk, Davidson explained that one way in which sociologists measure religious commitment is by church attendance. A young man from the audience stood up and asked, "Why would you ever use Mass attendance as a measure of religious commitment?"[4] Recent studies have shown the young man who challenged Davidson is not unique. Young adult Catholics view "helping the poor," for instance, as far more important than attending a weekly religious service they may not find spiritually satisfying.[5] Thirty-four percent of Catholics between the ages of eighteen and twenty-nine report that they attend Mass weekly, as opposed to 43 percent of those over thirty.[6] They do not see themselves as members of an exclusive group (that is, members of the one true faith) because they have had much more contact with non-Catholics—and non-Christians—than either their parents or grandparents had had at their age.[7] The challenge for Catholic colleges and universities is to prepare these future church leaders by offering them curricular and co-curricular ways in which they can understand, challenge, and practice their faith.

A number of Catholic colleges and universities have developed Catholic Studies programs in an attempt to engage undergraduates in a study of Catholic culture while preparing them to assume leadership in the twenty-first-century Church; but it is worth considering that students such as the ones described by Gillis—perhaps the very ones our schools hope to reach—may not be sympathetic to a traditional academic approach to the study of Catholicism. The Catholic intellectual tradition, in other words, may not inspire or inform the faith of the majority of the student body. Catholic Studies courses emphasizing other aspects of Catholicism such as Catholic social teaching, however, may appeal to an additional group of undergraduates and provide an added bonus of linking academics to activities that traditionally have taken place outside of the classroom.

The development of Catholic Studies programs in the 1980s and 1990s, according to Fordham University's James Fisher, responded to a question posed by Catholic institutions of higher education that blended "pastoral, political, ecclesiastical, and ideological dimensions: 'How do we preserve the Catholic identity of our colleges and universities?' "[8] Given recent studies such as the Pew Forum's report, this question should perhaps be rephrased to ask: What role should Catholic colleges and universities play in passing down the faith (and the Church) to future generations? In other words, what must Catholic higher education do to ensure that students are adequately prepared to participate actively in the Church of the twenty-first century? The development and implementation of programs offering certificates, concentrations, majors, and minors in Catholic Studies are one response to these questions.

Catholic Studies should be interdisciplinary, and indeed it is. Not only do students need to understand that the study of Catholicism is not limited to required theology courses, but it would be shortsighted for colleges and universities to assign discussions of Catholic identity to a single department or program. Theology and/or religious studies are obviously an important dimension of any program, but courses offered through other departments can help students increase their understanding of the place of Catholicism in modern culture. Philosophy, English, sociology, political science, and economics courses can also engage students in the history, teachings, traditions, and cultures of the Church.

Incorporating the study of Catholicism throughout an undergraduate curriculum, however, is often easier said than done. Creating a list of courses designated as Catholic Studies simply provides students with an opportunity to enroll in a Catholic studies course; it does not guarantee that one will do so. Moreover, students enrolled in a professional course of study (such as business, health sciences, or engineering) often have few electives from which to choose, and even though administrators usually support the idea that those enrolled in these programs should be exposed to a certain amount of Catholic teaching, practical problems related to credit hours and major requirements often complicate the situation. Adding a requirement in Catholic Studies to an already full course of study is easier said than done. The demands of professional programs (which often receive separate accreditation from outside agencies) mean that liberal arts departments, including philosophy and religion, find themselves struggling to keep core courses emphasizing the humanities, natural sciences, and social sciences a significant part of the undergraduate curriculum. Despite their best efforts, deans and provosts often have to reduce (albeit reluctantly) the number of core credits required by professional programs in order to enable students to graduate in four years.

Although there is no easy solution to the curricular dilemmas facing Catholic higher education (or higher education in general), courses centered on the themes of Catholic social teaching (CST) offer one model—among many—to expose students to the church's position on social justice, strengthen the Catholic identity of colleges and universities, and provide a vehicle for passing down the Church and faith to the next generation. For those millennial students who view helping the poor as a badge of Catholic identity, CST is a visible manifestation of the Catholic tradition of "comforting the afflicted and afflicting the comfortable."[9] In addition, courses emphasizing CST allow students to wrestle with current issues facing the Church and American society, such as the role of women, capital punishment, and the ecological crisis, within the framework of an organized body of teaching that demonstrates that the Church is indeed very much a part of the contemporary world.

Catholic Social Teaching

In many ways, the story of Catholicism can be told through the lens of Catholic social teaching. To study the history, life, and culture of Catholics exclusively from the perspective of either doctrine or hierarchical statements does not adequately reflect the possibility that the Catholic Church may be the "largest and most productive nongovernmental organization in the world, accomplishing good works, without strings, around the globe." The theory of Catholic social teaching is not always easy to digest, but when the principles of CST are demonstrated through the stories of "hospitals, schools, universities, social welfare organizations, [and] labor unions," to name just a few, it is easy to see its importance in the life and work of the Church.[10]

The Office for Social Justice of the Archdiocese of St. Paul and Minneapolis offers a concise and accurate definition of the current understanding of Catholic social teaching on its website, explaining it can perhaps be best understood as an "effort to articulate what the broader social tradition means in the era of modern politics, economics, and culture."[11] Although the principles of CST can be found in both the Jewish and Christian scriptures, there is some disagreement as to where it can be located within official Church documents. It is generally agreed that there is "a limited body of literature written in the modern era that is a response of papal and episcopal teachers to the various political, economic and social issues of our time."[12] *Rerum Novarum*, Leo XIII's 1891 encyclical on labor, which addressed the condition of workers in an era when labor unions and socialism were both gaining in popularity, is generally viewed as the starting point of modern Catholic social teaching.[13] Pius XI issued the second major document of CST,

Quadragesimo Anno, in 1931, on the fortieth anniversary of Leo's encyclical. Written during a worldwide economic depression, the document reiterated and expanded upon the ideas expressed in *Rerum Novarum*.

Since the issuance of *Quadragesimo Anno*, nine other papal encyclicals have been added to the CST canon. John XXIII wrote two of them, *Mater et Magistra* and *Pacem in Terris*; two, *Populorum Progressio* and *Octogesima Adveniens*, reflected the social thought of Paul VI; and five, *Laborem Exercens*, *Solicitudo Rei Socialis*, *Centisimus Annos*, *Evangelium Vitae*, and *Fides et Ratio*, were published during the papacy of John Paul II. Many theologians also include *Gaudium et Spes*, *Justice in the World* (the 1971 statement of the Synod of Bishops), and the 1988 pastoral letter of the U.S. Bishops, *Economic Justice for All*, in the body of literature defining CST, and some have suggested that Benedict XVI's 2005 encyclical *Deus Caritas Est* is an important recent addition to the development of the social thought of the Church.

The first and primary principle of CST focuses on the dignity of the human person. This foundational idea is based on the premise that all men and women, because they are created in the image and likeness of God, possess an inherent dignity. Ten other teachings of CST are related to this "first principle":

> all human beings have inalienable political and social rights;
> preferential option for the poor;
> subsidiarity: government functions should be performed at the lowest possible level;
> global solidarity, which teaches that because we are all part of the human family we are called to work for justice on a global level;
> stewardship of the earth;
> our responsibility to work for and contribute to the common good;
> economic justice;
> promotion of peace;
> participation in the life of society;
> the fulfillment of responsibilities to achieve a just society.[14]

All of these ideas may be found in one or more of the papal and episcopal documents that define Catholic social teaching.

At first glance, it appears that the challenge for those working in the area of CST, whether they are employed by campus ministry departments, diocesan peace and justice offices, parishes, or academic departments in high schools and universities, is to transform abstract principles into a concrete way of life that can be embraced by American Catholics (and the faithful throughout the world). In fact, however, this task has been rather successfully accomplished by many churches and schools—elementary, secondary, and institutions of higher education—throughout the United States. Campus offices for peace and justice, as well as local parish communities, have been able to implement the principles of CST through a variety of local, national, and international programs. Some groups have focused on a particular neighborhood or town; a parish, for instance, might reach out to the area's homeless while its members educate themselves and others about the problems faced by those seeking affordable housing. Other local, national, and international organizations are involved with lobbying and educating government officials concerning a specific need of the poor and dispossessed, such as jobs or childcare.

Many teachers, administrators, and campus ministers working in Catholic higher education support the premises of Catholic social teaching and believe it should be an integral component of campus life because it both promotes the university's mission and contributes to the institution's Catholic identity. As a result, it has not been difficult to incorporate CST into the extracurricular life and activities of Catholic universities. Spring-break service trips, neighborhood outreach programs, and student groups advocating for peace and justice abound on Catholic campuses. A dedicated group of students participate in these programs and projects, including those that take place during spring break and summers, and attempt to educate both themselves and others on issues of societal justice. In addition to manifesting CST on their campuses, these students are a very visible presence to faculty and administrators, and even though they do not always constitute a majority of the student body, they—and their mentors—play an important role in the life of Catholic higher education.

Although Catholic universities continue to search for ways that will involve more students in the work of advocating for social justice, it is not an easy task; many students attending our universities hope to make a good deal of money within a few years of graduating and are not sure they want to look too closely at issues of societal injustice. It is also important to ensure there is a connection between the work students do in the classroom and the extracurricular activities in which they are involved, and a variety of approaches have been developed to strengthen the links between class content and student life. Some are long-standing components of a university's academic and extracurricular programs; others have only recently been implemented. Each reflects the character and mission of its institution, and has been designed to reflect issues impacting American society at any given time. Social justice activities during the fall semester of the 2008–2009 academic year, for instance, often reflected issues related to the presidential election.

Incorporating Catholic social teaching into the curriculum—core and major-related—is one way to connect the work students do in the classroom with issues of societal justice affecting those in the "real world." But Catholic undergraduate students also need to acquire the tools necessary to assume leadership in the twenty-first-century American church, and in order for this to happen, colleges and universities need to do more than encourage their participation in service activities. If during the four years (or more) they spend at our institutions they become lifelong advocates and practitioners of Catholic social teaching, they may indeed be the generation that brings new life to a church that has had its share of problems during the past several years. Our students should not only be taught the principles of CST, they should understand how these ideas have shaped and continue to shape the American Catholic Church.

By incorporating CST into appropriate courses, Catholic Studies programs can play an integral role in helping students understand the connection between the classroom and the outside world. It is often left to a few areas, notably religion, American Studies, English, and history, to take responsibility for introducing Catholic Studies and CST in undergraduate courses. Other departments, however, can and should help disseminate the principles and practical applications of CST to undergraduate students, and even the occasional graduate student. A course offered in the economics department, for instance, could include *Economic Justice for All*, providing students with a very different perspective on the letter from what they might find in a theology course. Students enrolled in professional degree programs should be able to focus on principles of CST related to their field of study. Education majors should certainly be familiar with issues of tuition vouchers and the closing of inner-city parish schools, while nursing students can be exposed to the Catholic position on reproductive technologies and physician-assisted suicide.[15]

A specific course on Catholic social teaching offered through the Catholic Studies program (and given a religious studies or theology designation) allows students to make a very explicit connection between the work they do inside and outside of the classroom, while at the same time contributing to the Catholic identity and mission of the university.

Catholic Social Teaching and Catholic Studies

In her preface to *Living the Catholic Social Tradition: Cases and Commentary*, Monika K. Hellwig writes that although there "is no lack of good will about passing on the social teaching of the church at Catholic colleges and universities," faculty members and campus ministers are unsure how to go about it. Hellwig offered five reasons why it has been difficult to incorporate Catholic social teaching into an academic curriculum. First, CST is interdisciplinary in nature; this means scholars from a variety of academic areas must have at least some familiarity with the social teachings of Catholicism. Second, the encyclicals containing the principles of CST are "written in a style quite alien to that to which our students are accustomed." Third, Hellwig noted it is sometimes difficult for students to understand the principles of CST because they do not understand the Scripture and tradition upon which they are based.[16] The fact that most undergraduate curriculums require only six credits in religion and/or theology is the fourth reason colleges and universities have found it difficult to include Catholic social teaching in their curriculums; there simply is not enough room for an additional requirement. Fifth, many professors in fields relevant to CST (such as economics and sociology) possess little knowledge of the social teachings of the Church.[17] These issues may seem daunting to one trying to develop a course specifically focused on the social teachings of the

Church, but examining the subject from the perspective of Catholic Studies may lead to a new way of teaching CST and serve as a way to "pass down the faith" to the current generation of students.

A couple of Hellwig's points merit further emphasis. Her assessment of the style in which theological documents—even those devoted to issues of social justice—as one with which most American undergraduate students are uncomfortable is critical. Papal encyclicals are not "an easy read," and they cannot be quickly skimmed in the hour before class begins. In addition, it is difficult to assess students' knowledge of the documents. How do we begin to test students on material they do not understand? We can require readings that include selections from relevant papal writings, but anyone designing a syllabus around CST will have to include readings written in a style with which undergraduates are comfortable.

Hellwig's observation that most undergraduate core curriculums in Catholic colleges and universities require only six credits in either theology or religion is also important. If students complete two religious studies courses during their four years of undergraduate education, and one is at the introductory level, that leaves room for only one upper-level religion or theology requirement. Does this guarantee adequate preparation of future Church leaders? Incorporating Catholic social teaching into a variety of courses might provide at least a partial solution to this dilemma. Hellwig writes, "it must be admitted that in the ideal Catholic college or university one would expect vigorous and sustained conversation on peace, social justice, and the common good among professors of various disciplines. And one would expect that the cumulative wisdom of the Catholic tradition on such issues would be part of the conversation."[18] This reinforces the idea that although a specific course devoted to CST should be offered at the undergraduate level, the topic, like Catholic Studies programs in general, ought to be interdisciplinary and taught throughout the professional and core curriculums.

Hellwig's essay offers an important realistic assessment of the requirements of undergraduate core curriculums and major courses of study as they relate to a course dedicated to the social teachings of the Church. The reality, she notes, is that courses in Catholic justice do not "constitute career advancement" for most Catholic college students. At the same time, the hope is that courses of this nature will appeal to a broad range of students, not just those involved in campus ministry programs and service projects. One solution, Hellwig argues, is to require a course in Catholic social teaching for students majoring and/or minoring in either Catholic Studies or theology or religious studies. This may not reach as many undergraduate students as those charged with promoting Catholic identity would like, but it at least guarantees that a percentage of students will receive some exposure to Catholic social teaching.

A Course on Catholic Social Teaching

What might a course on Catholic social teaching look like, and how might it examine other aspects of Catholic thought and culture? Before developing a course entitled "Catholic Social Teaching," I taught several courses that touched on CST in a number of ways. The course I teach is based on what I have learned from those related courses ("Faith and Justice," "A Theology of Peace"), as well as my early experiences teaching a course dedicated specifically to the social-justice teachings of the Church.

Courses on the subject of Catholic social teaching can take a variety of forms, but one underlying assumption is essential: it should not assume that students have more than a cursory knowledge of Catholicism. In a discussion of core religion courses with my colleagues at Philadelphia's La Salle University, one faculty member put into words an idea with which a number us of had been wrestling. Not too long ago, she noted, faculty teaching introductory courses in theology or religious studies at Catholic colleges and universities could assume that the great majority of their students were Catholic high school graduates. It was further assumed that these students entered college with some basic knowledge of scripture, church history, and moral theology. This does not appear, she concluded sadly, to be true today. My colleague's recent experiences teaching first-year undergraduates may or may not be normative, but it is true that fewer students entering our colleges and universities attended Catholic high schools, and as a result our students know less about Catholicism than their undergraduate professors might assume.[19]

Topics

Although the principles of CST and the encyclicals upon which they are based constitute an essential component of Catholic teaching, undergraduates will not develop a burning interest in social justice from a series of classroom lectures. As a rule, I spend about two days focusing on the principles themselves and their biblical roots. Although it can be difficult to generate discussion on the aforementioned ten principles until they are connected to specific individuals and movements, especially considering that this is probably happening early in the semester when class dynamics are not yet solidified, the biblical basis of CST can lead to a solid class discussion. Because students' knowledge of scripture will vary, it is helpful to provide them with some background concerning societal injustices during the first century—and earlier if one is using texts from Hebrew Scripture—which will allow them to begin to make some connections between the worlds of Jesus and today and begin to see that the Church has attempted to take seriously (at least at times) the social teachings of the gospels.

Although it is important to take Hellwig's concern about the language and style of the papal encyclicals seriously, it is equally essential that students realize the principles of CST are drawn from theological documents written in response to particular historical eras and problems. Marvin L. Krier Mich's 2001 book *Catholic Social Teaching and Movements* is one example of a text that approaches this subject by juxtaposing documents with either people or issues that manifest particular teachings. The topics Mich chose to include reflect both historical ("'Social Catholics' and *Rerum Novarum*") and contemporary ("The Challenge of Peace and the Catholic Peace Movement") issues. Although the book can be used in undergraduate courses, it was written to reflect the author's experiences teaching graduate classes at St. Bernard's Institute in Rochester, New York. I have used Mich's book with undergraduates and liked it, but at other times I have simply spent a day or two discussing the encyclicals and bishops' letters from a general perspective as a way to explain that Catholic social teaching was not created out of thin air. The drawback to this approach is students do not get a good sense of the story behind each document. They are, however, prepared for the remainder of the semester's work, which will focus on particular people and movements manifesting Catholic social teaching in today's world.

Although papal encyclicals and bishops' letters are an important piece of CST, they are not the only repositories for the Church's teaching on issues related to social justice. My experience teaching classes on CST and related Catholic Studies courses (such as "Faith and Justice," "Heroes of Conscience," and "Modern Catholicism") has convinced me that undergraduate students respond well to learning about "real" people and the work they do. The ten-volume documentary series published by Orbis Books is a good starting point for those looking for the historical roots of CST.[20] When examining CST from a contemporary perspective, I try to choose topics and focus readings on people who will generate enthusiastic class discussions. Figures that routinely evoke a positive response from students include Sister Helen Prejean, Dorothy Day and the Catholic Workers, John Dear (the Jesuit antiwar activist), and Archbishop Oscar Romero.

The benefit of using figures such as the ones noted above to frame a class on CST is that they are relevant to more than one principle of the Church's social teaching. Assigning *Dead Man Walking* by Sister Helen Prejean, for instance, allows the class to wrestle with issues related to the "consistent ethic of life" (war and peace and nonviolence) in addition to the death penalty. Focusing a unit around Dorothy Day and the Catholic Worker movement means discussion about ways in which those residing in houses of hospitality throughout the world live the principles of CST. Either Day's *Loaves and Fishes* or Robert Coles's *Dorothy Day: A Radical Devotion* are appropriate in this context. Readings centered on Church leaders such as El Salvador's Archbishop Oscar Romero are more problematic. James R. Brockman's *Romero: A Life* and Jon Sobrino's *Archbishop Romero: Memories and Reflections* are informative, but students often remark that they did not reflect the work or person of the archbishop in a way they found helpful. As a result, I often either discuss Romero in the context of brief readings about his work and message or assign sources that can be related to his ministry. One can talk about his work in El Salvador, for instance, by asking students to familiarize themselves with the School of the Americas Watch or discussing the four missionaries killed in El Salvador in 1982.

Autobiographies and biographies work well in courses on CST, and the reason for this is very simple: real people personify the principles of Catholic social teaching in a way that students can understand and appreciate. What better way to exemplify the concept of the dignity of the human person than to read about Dorothy Day's life and ministry? The story of her life before converting to Catholicism, including her abortion, is as relevant to a discussion on human dignity as her encounters with the poor of New York City's Lower East Side as a Catholic Worker. *Dead Man Walking* vividly exemplifies the principles of preferential option for the poor, the promotion of peace, and the idea that all human beings possess inalienable political and social rights.

The topics and related readings suggested here—and there are many others—contribute to students' knowledge of Catholicism, and they are therefore relevant to the broader field of Catholic Studies. The opening chapters of *Dead Man Walking*, for example, offer readers insight into the changing lives and ministries of American women religious during the 1960s and 1970s. Oscar Romero's story reminds undergraduates of the diversity of global Catholicism and provides them with some knowledge of both martyrdom and liberation theology. Any discussion of John Dear, S.J., and the antinuclear movement allows for further reflection on Catholic activism in the second half of the twentieth century. If the course is carefully planned, students will come to understand that the principles of Catholic social teaching are an intrinsic part of Catholic history and culture.

Assignments

In addition to reading, exams, and class participation, I have used some specific assignments to help develop students' awareness of CST. Class members are usually required to complete two five-page papers and a larger project. The first paper is designed to help students think about what it means to be a practicing Catholic, and it takes the form of a personal statement by asking them to reflect on the general topic—whether he or she is a practicing Catholic—by responding to five specific related questions. I do not define practicing—as opposed to believing—Catholic for the class, but instead leave it up to the individual student to respond to the question based on his or her own definition. There are many reasons why Catholic college students are not actively involved in the life of the Church; some are simply not making an effort to attend Mass while away at school, but others have deeper and more compelling motives for staying away from the institutional church. By writing this paper, students, I hope, will think more about their reasons for remaining aloof from the church.[21]

The first question is quite general: how do you believe one should practice his or her faith? This allows the writer to decide, for instance, how important it is to attend Mass on a weekly basis as opposed to caring about society's poor and dispossessed. The second question asks them to stretch the first idea and think about how one should *live* his or her faith. If a person regularly attends Mass but is unfaithful to his or her spouse, for example, can one be called a "good" Catholic?

The third question pushes the issue one step further: how much of a religion's teachings should one believe and/or practice? Is one considered a good Catholic if he or she does not agree with all of the Church's teachings on sexuality? Does one have to understand the doctrine of transubstantiation in order to be considered a true member of the church? This question is particularly important in light of those sociological studies claiming that young adult Catholics are not convinced one must subscribe to a standard set of beliefs or attend Mass weekly in order to be considered Catholic. The fourth question asks the class to reflect upon what might cause them to leave the Church. Would a Catholic leave simply because he or she marries someone of another faith and agrees to worship in another religious tradition, or have people reacted to stories about either the sexual abuse crisis or rigidly authoritarian bishops and decided to look for a tradition that is more "user-friendly?" The final question asks students to reflect upon their responses in light of CST: How might these principles fit into one's own faith, and if they do not, why not?

In general, the completed papers are thoughtful and revealing. I learn a good deal about my millennial students, and I hope they learn something about themselves. Allowing students to discuss their papers in class usually means a very fruitful discussion about the Church, its problems, and its future. Reading these essays not only gives me a sense of what my students think about the practices of Catholicism and how important the culture of the Church is in their lives, but it also enables me to see how much knowledge of Catholic theology they are bringing to the class and what I can do to deepen their awareness of a very rich and complex body of doctrine.

The second assignment is more directly related to CST. In order to help students understand the many ways in which Catholic social teaching is being implemented in the twenty-first century, they are required to research an organization that is directly involved in advocating for social justice. I provide them with a list of organizations from which they may choose, trying to make sure that the list is reasonably diverse. Past assignments have allowed students to select from the Catholic Workers, Catholic Relief Services, the Campaign for Human Development, and Catholic Peace Fellowship, but there are many more possibilities. The primary goal of this assignment is for students to understand how the church—and I use this term in a very broad sense—implements CST; by researching the history, work, and mission of a particular organization, students also gain some knowledge of American Catholic history and culture.

The major project students must complete is worth 40 percent of their grade; this is designed to get their attention and push them to think about how they will complete this requirement in a timely manner. The assignment's goal is very simple: to engage undergraduate students in Catholic social teaching by asking them to complete a five-hour service project at an appropriate agency or organization.[22] After receiving very specific guidelines for completing the assignment, students choose from a list of Catholic organizations devoted to outreach and/or working for political and social change. I make the initial contact with the agency to explain students should be given a task that will allow them to reflect upon the actual practice of CST (not stuffing envelopes, for example). In the past, students have provided much-needed assistance at Catholic Social Services, a local Catholic Worker house, and a soup kitchen and shelter sponsored by the Archdiocese of Philadelphia.

After completing their service, students complete a ten-page paper describing the agency and the work they did and evaluating the relationship between their placement and the principles of the Church's social teachings. The paper also encourages undergraduates to reflect on aspects of Catholicism very few of them have experienced. They sometimes ask some hard questions about CST and its place in the institutional church: Do organizations based on these principles truly work to bring about societal change, or are they simply putting a Band-Aid on the problem? What changes could be made to these organizations that would demonstrate an even stronger commitment to the church's teaching on the dignity of the human person? It is my hope that these questions will serve them well as they seek to find their place in the church of the twenty-first century.

Completing a report detailing five hours of service is not necessarily related to Catholic Studies; service learning can certainly take many different forms and be offered through many different venues. A course devoted to CST that includes a service component, however, helps to fulfill the goals of university administrators who hope that Catholic Studies programs will both inform young adult Catholics about their faith and help them discern ways in which they might assume leadership roles in the church.

Not all undergraduates will find themselves enamored with the principles of CST. The largest majors at many Catholic colleges and universities are often professional, including business, nursing and health sciences, and engineering. Students enrolled in these programs—and their parents—are often interested in a lucrative career, an idea far removed from the principles of CST and those who have implemented these teachings in their lives and work. If one goal of a course incorporating Catholic social teaching, however, is to "afflict the comfortable," it is perhaps these students for whom a course of this nature can be most valuable.

Conclusion: Catholic Social Teaching, Catholic Studies, and Passing Down the Faith

Offering courses on Catholic social teaching is clearly one way to begin to pass down the faith to undergraduate students. The problem, of course, is that not every undergraduate will register for a course on CST. Even if Catholic colleges and universities are committed to offering such a course every semester, it still means only a small percentage of undergraduate students will be exposed to the academic *and* practical sides of Catholic social teaching during any given year. How, then, do we ensure that as many students as possible gain some understanding of CST, and, by extension, are exposed to some aspect of Catholicism during their undergraduate years?

One way to incorporate CST into classes outside of religion/theology departments is to require all undergraduates to take a class in "justice issues" as a part of their core requirements. Such courses may certainly be related to students' majors, but they can still include some discussion of Catholic social teaching. Nursing majors, for instance, can register for a course on ethics and health care, while psychology majors can take a course related to ethics and the social sciences. A core requirement of this sort means that virtually all undergraduates will have at least some exposure to the church's social teachings.

Not all colleges and universities will require students to take this sort of course, and Catholic Studies programs will have to devise additional ways in which the faith can be handed down to undergraduate students. CST, however, is one overarching theme under which many courses related to Catholicism can be grouped. This will not only expose a greater number of undergraduates to the principles of Catholic social teaching, but it will also offer some coherence to Catholic Studies programs, which can sometimes be very general and esoteric. If enough Catholic colleges and universities graduate students with some knowledge of Catholic social teaching, we can be assured that at least some members of the next generation of church leaders will be familiar with a body of church doctrine that is vital to national and international struggles for justice in the twenty-first century.

10 Teaching About Women, Gender, and American Catholicism

KATHLEEN SPROWS CUMMINGS

On the first day of my "Women and American Catholicism" class one year, a student announced that she had enrolled in the course simply out of curiosity: "I am dying to know," she said, "how a course on Women and Catholicism can last any longer than two weeks." Given women's exclusion from leadership structures within the Roman Catholic Church, she wondered, what could we possibly find to talk about for an entire semester? These and other similar comments reflect the widespread ambivalence that many contemporary young women have about their membership (or in some cases, their former membership) in a religious tradition that remains unapologetically dominated by men. As such they raise a vital question: How can we "pass on the faith" to the young Catholic women (and men) who are alienated both by women's continued exclusion from the Church's institutional power structures and by Catholic teaching on sexuality?

I cannot and do not claim that this course alone provides an answer to that difficult question. Still, I am convinced that for those of us teaching at the intersection of gender and Catholic Studies, our work in the classroom can have profound pastoral implications. Some of my most disenchanted students have often been astonished to discover, through historical exploration, that American Catholic women have always found sources of power, meaning, and dignity within a male-dominated institution. The student who made the "two weeks" comment, for example, had attended Catholic schools all her life, including a secondary academy run by a prominent order of women religious. Yet she had no resources to comprehend the rich and complicated history of women in the Catholic tradition. I am delighted to report that when the two-week mark passed, this student was still showing up for class, and indeed by the end of the semester she was singing quite a different tune. Learning about the past had given her a new perspective on her own future within the Church.

Studying the history of women in the American Church can also affect the faith lives of students who come from the opposite side of the ideological spectrum. Many students arrive in this course skeptical about if not explicitly hostile to feminism. If they have considered women's ordination at all—and most have not—they are opposed to it. Increasingly, many of them are well versed in and persuaded by the theology of Pope John Paul II, especially the "new feminism," which—in my view, at least—bears an uncanny resemblance to the old antifeminism. Once they are presented with evidence of its historical marginalization of women, though, students in this group often become more sensitive to gender injustice within the Church.

I teach this course at the University of Notre Dame, and institutional context is important. There are not many venues on campus where students can participate in thoughtful discussion about women in the Catholic Church. In fact, I was encouraged to develop "Women and American Catholicism" in 2002 by the director of Notre Dame's Program in Gender Studies in partial response to that problem. There have since been other attempts to foster dialogue about gender issues; most notable in this regard was the recent establishment of a Gender Relations Center. Still, discussions over controversial issues—from finding common ground on the abortion question to ongoing debates over the appropriateness of performing *The Vagina Monologues* on campus—are often characterized by aggressiveness, intransigence, and rancor on both sides of the debate. In my classroom, by contrast, the spirit of scholarly inquiry and an atmosphere of openness and trust combine to stimulate genuine discussion. The results are encouraging and, occasionally, even surprising. In fall 2003, a rumor reached campus that the Vatican was about to announce a ban on female altar servers. After reflecting on what this decision would signal about women's place within the Church, the students united across considerable ideological divides to draft a collective letter of protest that was published in our campus newspaper.

Unit One: What a Catholic Woman Ought to Be and Do

I begin the semester with an examination of Catholic gender ideology, a strategy I find helpful for a number of reasons. First, it allows us to begin working with primary sources right out of the gate. Although many of my students are history majors, most are not, and this exercise helps them learn to interpret primary documents. Second, because I assign a variety of sources from the mid–nineteenth century to the present, students learn quickly how to distinguish themes of both continuity and change. Finally, beginning with Catholic gender ideology is essential because it underscores the crucial distinction between "sex" and "gender." Unless they have taken a course in gender studies or feminist theory, my students use these terms interchangeably. After reading these documents, however, they understand that "sex" refers to the biological differences that exist between men and women, while "gender" denotes the meaning that society attaches to those biological differences. I always emphasize that while ethnicity, race, and social class impact assumptions about what women ought to be and do, few factors are as powerful as religious belief in shaping the meaning Americans have attached to sexual difference. The belief that certain gender roles are divinely ordained, after all, makes them much more impervious to challenge. This is as true for American Protestants and Jews as it is for Catholics, although, historically speaking, gender categories are usually more rigid within traditional denominations.

Students read selections from Rev. Bernard O'Reilly's *The Mirror of True Womanhood*, which appeared in seventeen editions between 1876 and 1892. Along with other prescriptive literature of the period, *The Mirror* presented the Catholic "true woman" as a model. The true woman was by nature more spiritual than her male counterpart, and her highest calling was to motherhood, if not in the physical sense, than at least in the spiritual sense. The home was her "God-appointed" sphere, her domain, and the place where she should remain except for attending church or performing acts of charity. The Catholic true woman was characterized by her generosity, humility, and ready willingness for self-sacrifice. She was defined through her relationship with men, and she was permitted to exercise power only by exerting a benevolent influence over her husband, father or son. "Just as Mary gave the savior to the world," O'Reilly noted, "a true woman in every home is the savior and sanctifier of man."

This idealistic view of womanhood had not been invented by O'Reilly, nor was it original to Catholics in general. The distinction between "public man" and "private woman" had emerged in the United States the early nineteenth century, when the advent of industrialization had separated home and work into separate spheres. This gave rise to the concept of the ideal woman of the Victorian era, who was characterized for her piety, purity, domesticity, and submissiveness. In the second half of the nineteenth century, many middle-class Catholics appropriated this gender ideology.

The Victorian ideology of womanhood has had such enormous staying power in that it affects our understanding of gender to this day. But while Catholic gender ideology resembles and is often intertwined with that of American society at large, there is no question that beliefs about women's traditional roles have proved more intractable within a patriarchal institution such as the Catholic Church. A quick aside: my more conservative Notre Dame students sometimes bristle when I refer to the Church as patriarchal, taking offense at what they assume is a pejorative term. Once I explain that the definition of patriarchy is "an institution whose structure and leadership is dominated by males," they realize that while we can argue all day about whether the Church *should* be patriarchal, there is little room for debate as to whether it *is* patriarchal.

In terms of appreciating continuity and change within Catholic gender ideology, Pope John Paul II's writing on women is particularly helpful. When students read him in tandem with nineteenth-century Church proclamations on womanhood, they come to appreciate how progressive the late pontiff was on certain women's issues. He defined sexism as a sin, after all, and recognized women's achievements as well as their changing roles in the workplace. At the same time, he was also the primary architect of the new feminism, which often blurs the distinction between sex and gender, and he repeatedly affirmed that women's primary vocation is to motherhood, physical or spiritual. Students recognize the extent to which the pope's language of "complementarity" reinforces the traditional Church teaching that women are defined relative to men and through their self-sacrificial role within the family.

By the end of this unit, all students, including the most enthusiastic supporters of the new feminism, have a keen appreciation of the ways gender can be socially constructed, and they understand the role that religion in general and Catholicism in particular play in that process.

Acquiring this knowledge signals a worthwhile academic achievement, to be sure. But it arguably represents a notable pastoral one as well. For many students, it has now become possible to envision a future Church that not only recognizes traditional female contributions but also allows for the possibility of expanded opportunities for women's participation and leadership.

Unit Two: Making Saints

The discussion of gender ideology provides a nice prologue to a discussion of sainthood, a subject ripe for gender analysis. Catholic saints have always fascinated Americans from a variety of religious backgrounds, perhaps never more so than during the unprecedented boom in saint-making that has characterized the last few decades. Pope John Paul II substantially streamlined the requirements for canonization, and named more saints than all of his predecessors combined. This unit relies on saints not only to continue the discussion of Catholic gender ideology, but also to introduce the subjects of American women religious, sexuality, and abortion.

In October 2006, Mother Theodore Guerin, founder of the Sisters of Providence of Saint-Mary-of-the-Woods in Terre Haute, Indiana, became the eighth American to be recognized a saint. Guerin has joined a number of other American Catholic women venerated for their "heroic virtue": Elizabeth Ann Seton, who was canonized in 1975, the first American-born person so honored; Frances Cabrini, an Italian immigrant who became the first American citizen to be canonized in 1946; and Katharine Drexel, who became first U.S.-born saint in 2000 (Seton's birth in 1774 meant that she had technically been born a British subject).

Seton's work in establishing a foundation for Catholic education, Cabrini's work with immigrants, and Drexel's pioneering efforts on behalf of Native Americans and African Americans make these women worthy historical subjects. The most compelling part of their stories, though, has to do with the way they complicate conventional understandings of saintly behavior. All of them struggled with clerical superiors who had no use for women who acted independently. In Guerin's case, we read selections from Guerin's diary and correspondence that documented her long-standing controversy with Celestine de la Hailandière, the bishop of Vincennes and her clerical superior. Hailandière insisted, erroneously, that he was entitled to complete control over the Sisters of Providence. The bishop's repeated challenges to Guerin's authority over community matters culminated in 1847, when he locked Guerin in his house until she acceded to his demands. A day later, he removed her as superior, released her from religious vows, and threatened her and any sisters who followed her with excommunication. Guerin resolved to start over in the diocese of Detroit, where she was assured of a warm welcome. But in what was surely providential timing, word arrived from Rome that Hailandière had been replaced as bishop. The Sisters of Providence stayed and flourished under the new bishop, and today their 465 members work in ten states, the District of Columbia, China, and Taiwan. For the more traditional students, hearing about Guerin's struggle with a clerical superior complicated their understanding of what being a "good Catholic woman" means, and they became a bit less inclined to dismiss feminist arguments. Meanwhile, my more feminist-oriented students interpreted Guerin's resourcefulness and faithfulness as a sign of hope and a model for them to emulate.

I incorporate guest lecturers into the class whenever I can, and Guerin's canonization paved the way for one of the most successful visitors, Sister Marie Kevin Tighe, S.P., the member of Guerin's community charged with overseeing the path to the canonization. The students asked her insightful questions that reflected their reading and our previous discussions of the canonization process, which ties in very well with our unit on Catholic gender ideology. Some of them pressed Sister Marie Kevin on elements of her presentation that appeared to conflict with the primary documents we had read, and this disjuncture subsequently became an occasion for the class to discuss the objectivity question and the study of history.

In addition to these sister-saints, we study two American laywomen whose causes for canonization are still pending. The cause of Blessed Kateri Tekakwitha (she has been beatified, the final step before canonization) was first introduced in 1680 by the Jesuits who worked with her, in part to legitimate their mission work in New France. Her case was renewed again in the late nineteenth century to underscore the "Americanness" of U.S. Catholics. Today, her advocates include Native

American Catholics as well as supporters of conservation, of which she has been declared a "patron saint."

Dorothy Day, the founder of the Catholic Worker movement, presents another interesting example of a pending canonization. Day's cause was introduced in 1983, three years after her death. She herself reportedly scoffed at the prospect of her own canonization, saying, "I don't want to be so easily dismissed." Citing this, some of her supporters oppose making her a saint, saying it would both devalue her significance and diminish the power of her example. There is opposition to her canonization on other grounds. Before her conversion to Catholicism, Day had an abortion. While some of her detractors insist that this alone must bar her from canonization, her supporters object to the way some bishops have appropriated her as patron saint of women who have had—and regret having had—abortions. In this respect, it is interesting to juxtapose Day's cause for sainthood with the 2001 canonization of an Italian laywoman, Gianna Beretta Molla. Diagnosed with a uterine tumor during her fourth pregnancy, Molla chose to forgo a hysterectomy to spare the life of the fetus, and she died a week after giving birth to a healthy baby girl. Like Day's, Molla's canonization has been highly politicized, with critics charging that it was intended to shore up the case against legal abortion. As Michael W. Higgins notes in *Stalking the Holy*, the critique of feminist scholars applies in both cases: the politics of motherhood that surround Day and Molla's cause for canonization repeats the familiar pattern of classifying women saints by their family status rather than by their own achievements. Again, we see Catholic gender ideology at work.

In addition to reading primary and secondary sources about Day, students view *Entertaining Angels*, a 1996 film that dramatizes her sexual relationships with men and her abortion before she converted to Catholicism. We also spend an evening at the Catholic Worker house in South Bend. One of the residents is a professor in Notre Dame's theology department, and she speaks to the class about "Dorothy's" continuing influence over the ministry. On one of these visits, my colleague led us on a tour of the community's new drop-in center, describing the painstaking efforts to raise the additional $10,000 needed to open its doors. She explained that the Catholic Workers had not sought any large grants, but trusted that the funds will accumulate, in Day's words, "by little and by little."

Evening gatherings at the Catholic Worker House convey the witness, spirit, and legacy of Dorothy Day far more effectively than my lectures do. So I continue them for valid pedagogical reasons. But I have often seen this experience shape students' personal faith lives. During one visit, one of my finance majors pressed the Workers on their lack of an efficient business plan, arguing that more resources could help them do more good more quickly. This very student, however, later volunteered to bring dinner to the house on several occasions. I doubt that his exposure to the Catholic Worker led him to abandon his plans for a career in business, but I am certain that his new appreciation and awareness of Catholic social teaching will affect him far beyond his college years.

Unit Three: Women Religious

The discussion of Cabrini, Seton, Drexel, and Guerin provides a transition to the next unit, which begins with the arrival of the Ursulines in New Orleans in 1727. In modifying their rule to allow for apostolic ministry, the Ursulines set important precedent for other communities of women religious. In contrast to Europe, where convents were supported through dowries and benefactors, families who could endow or give alms to a cloistered community were few and far between in colonial America. The Ursulines also prefigured other American communities in their response to local needs: they opened several schools, a hospital, and an orphanage. The Ursulines set precedent for American women's religious life in a third, less commendable way. As part of their contract with the Company of the Indies, they received eight slaves. By 1770, they owned more than seventy people, and they remained slaveholders until emancipation in 1863. While it is true that they admitted children of all races to their day school and were by most accounts very kind mistresses who eschewed the more abhorrent practices of the slaveholding South, the fact that the Ursulines—along with every other religious congregation in the American South—accepted the practice of slaveholding indicates the high levels of Catholic support for the "peculiar institution."

The history of African Americans in Catholic religious life further illustrates the Church's complicity in racial oppression. In Baltimore in 1828, Elizabeth Clarisse Lange organized the Oblate Sisters of Providence, the first permanent sisterhood of African descent in the United States. Lange had been born in the French Caribbean and had immigrated to Baltimore around 1813. In 1820 she opened a school for free black children. Lange and Marie Balas, another teacher, had expressed a desire to consecrate themselves to religious life, but no white sisterhoods would accept them as novices, and they had to wait ten years before they found a priest who would sponsor them in founding their own congregation. As historian Diane Batts Morrow notes in her excellent history of the congregation, the Oblate Sisters of Providence used their status as women religious to help them transcend the inferior social position assigned to them by white society. They immersed themselves in the quest for spiritual perfection within a church that preached spiritual (though not social) equality. They dedicated themselves to the pursuit of virtue in a society that presumed a lack of virtue in black women. They devoted themselves to the education of black children, challenging prevailing social attitudes about the propriety of encouraging literacy among people of color. But though vowed religious life offered the Oblates a number of strategies to resist the culture that routinely denied them their humanity, they experienced a great deal of racism within their own church. Diocesan leaders treated the Oblates shabbily, habitually omitting them from church directories and routinely giving more financial assistance to white religious sisterhoods.

Though Catholics discriminated on the basis of race, they themselves were subject to a great deal of religious prejudice. The most infamous incident of violence against Catholics occurred in 1834, when a mob set fire to an Ursuline convent in Charlestown, Massachusetts, sending the nuns and their students fleeing for their lives. A host of factors had contributed to a volatile situation in Charlestown. During the so-called era of the common man, many Americans questioned whether members of a hierarchical church who pledged allegiance to a "foreign despot" could legitimately participate in a democracy. In nearby Boston, the Rev. Lyman Beecher preached inflammatory sermons to this effect. It did not help matters that the Ursulines spoke French, and the fact that they educated the daughters of the wealthy hardly endeared them to the local brickmakers who formed the mob. But what proved to be absolutely unforgivable was that the nuns defied traditional expectations of female behavior. In a telling statement at his trial, at which he was acquitted of any wrongdoing, the mob's ringleader described Mary Ann Moffat, the Mother Superior of the Charlestown convent, as the "sauciest woman I ever heard talk." As women who lived and worked in all-female environments, who ran institutions in the public domain, who wore mysterious clothes, and who took vows of chastity, nuns' "secret" lives figured prominently in lurid Protestant fantasies. The best-selling version of this fantasy was *Awful Disclosures of the Hotel Dieu Nunnery* by Maria Monk, published in 1836.

Over the nineteenth century, women's religious communities grew in both size and number. In 1840, there were approximately a thousand nuns in the country, disbursed among fifteen orders. Sixty years later, the American population of nuns had multiplied to 46,583 sisters among 170 congregations. This unit explores how these sisters, many of whom were Irish American, developed a variety of creative responses to the needs of the local church, founding and staffing schools, hospitals, homes for working women, homes for the aged, orphanages, employment agencies, and home healthcare organizations.

Recognizing that the ruler-wielding nun has long been a staple of American popular culture, this unit explores in greater depth the complex history of the teaching sister in the history of church and nation. At the Third Plenary Council in Baltimore in 1884, U.S. bishops mandated that every Catholic parish in the nation have a school attached within two years. Though that unrealistic goal was never achieved, the Catholic parochial school system developed into the largest non-public school system in the world. Nuns' willingness to work for low wages substantially lowered the cost of parish education, thus making feasible an otherwise financially impossible undertaking and providing for the education of countless American children.

Our study of teaching sisters offers another opportunity to forge connections between the Catholic Church of the past and that of the future. Many of my students go on to participate in Notre Dame's Alliance for Catholic Education (ACE), a program that sends college graduates to teach in understaffed Catholic schools throughout the United

States. ACE and other similar programs, I tell them, represent the newest chapter in the history of American Catholic education. Many of the students already speak of their desire to teach as a "vocation," and learning about the sacrifice and dedication of Catholic sisters only deepens their admiration for and identification with the women religious who built and staffed the parochial school system.

Unit Four: Family, Ethnicity, and Devotional Life

Shifting the focus from women in religious communities, the next unit explores the history of Catholic laywomen through the twin lenses of family and devotional life. Devotional Catholicism covers a broad range of practices, including the recitation of the rosary, novenas, and other prayers of intercession to patron saints and the Blessed Virgin Mary. Because they are performed outside of the sacred liturgy, devotions do not necessarily require the presence of a priest, and unlike Latin Mass, they are usually performed in the vernacular. Thus they provide an interesting way to access habits of prayer and practice among the laity and particularly, women. Because many devotions were performed in the home, mothers played a central role in structuring the family's worship. In turn, Catholics' understanding of family life, both the real and the idealized versions, shaped women's devotional culture. A key part of this unit is our visit to the University Archives, where one of the archivists leads displays artifacts of Catholic material culture. Although devotions like the rosary are resurging in popularity among younger Catholics, it is likely that most of them have not seen scapulars or other once-ubiquitous elements of Catholic devotional life.

We spend a great deal of time focusing specifically on devotions to Mary. As historian Joseph Chinnici, O.F.M., observes, devotions to Mary often tell us more about the devotees than they do about the mother of Jesus. I have to tread carefully here, since many of my students are very suspicious of what they view as any attempt to tamper with devotions that they find very meaningful. I always am careful to assure them that we will not be calling into question either the efficacy of the devotions themselves or the faithfulness of the people who practice them. Rather, we are simply acknowledging that devotions become popular within specific cultural and political contexts, and that they can be used to serve particular purposes. We begin by examining the complex and fascinating history of devotion to Our Lady of Guadalupe. Since her appearance in 1534, Guadalupe has alternately symbolized colonial resistance, Mexican independence, Texan independence, Latino Catholic identity in the United States, and the multiculturalism of contemporary Catholicism.

Devotions to Mary have often been employed as a defense against enemies of the Church. In the late eighteenth and early nineteenth centuries, the primary enemies were liberal revolutionaries in Europe intent on instituting secular regimes. These challenges to the political authority of the Church often fostered an intensification of devotional practices. It is no accident, for example, that an upsurge in Marian apparitions accompanied the European revolutionary crises of 1789, 1830, 1848, and 1870. Throughout this period, various factions of the Church often deployed Mary to defend the papacy and to condemn the twin threats of republicanism and liberalism.

The most popular celebrated Marian visions of the nineteenth century occurred near the town of Lourdes in southern France. In 1858, a young peasant girl named Bernadette reported the appearance of a lady in white who declared, “I am the Immaculate Conception.” Four years earlier, the Church had made official the traditional Catholic view that Mary was conceived without sin. Though the visions ended abruptly, Catholic pilgrims came from all over the world to Lourdes, seeking miracles from the spring waters that Mary had instructed Bernadette to drink.

Lourdes has a substantial local interest for my Notre Dame students. Edward Sorin, C.S.C., the founder of Notre Dame, played a central role in popularizing American devotion to Our Lady of Lady of Lourdes. In 1865, he founded the journal *Ave Maria*, which quickly became one of the most popular Catholic publications in America. In 1877, a replica at the grotto at Lourdes was constructed on Notre Dame’s campus. Father Sorin also cornered the market on the importation of bottled water from the spring at Lourdes, which became a highly desired commodity among Catholics suffering from a variety of ailments. It still is, and the 2004 visit of the ailing Pope John Paul II to the holy waters of Lourdes attracted worldwide attention to the site. Our discussion of Lourdes dovetails with what many students describe as the highlight of the course: Peter Rocca, C.S.C., the rector of the Basilica of the Sacred Heart on campus, leads the class on a tour of the Basilica and the Grotto. Between his careful explanations and the historical context, even students who have made hundreds of visits to these places learn something new.

While Lourdes was a devotion that proved popular among middle-class American Catholics in the nineteenth century, members of more recently arrived immigrant groups embraced their own devotions to Mary. Beginning in the 1890s, Italian Catholic immigrants in East Harlem devoted an entire week each July to a celebration in honor of Our Lady of Mount Carmel. The devotion, like the statue of Our Lady itself, had traveled to Harlem from Salerno. The highlight of the annual *festa* involved a procession, in which thousands of devotees marched behind *la Madonna* through the streets of Harlem, carrying their intentions with them to lay at her feet. The shrines to Our Lady of Mount Carmel that were set up in the bedrooms of Italian Harlem underscored the sacredness of the home and family.

To tie our discussion of ethnicity and devotional life into the previous one on sainthood, students view Nancy Savoca's *Household Saints*, a film set in a New York Italian neighborhood in the 1960s. It deals not only with devotion to St. Therese, the Little Flower, but also explores the possible sainthood of its protagonist, Teresa. The question of whether Teresa is a saint or insane is at the heart of the film.

Like the Italians, Polish Catholics brought their own religious traditions to the American Church. The period of the greatest migration of Poles occurred between 1870 and 1914. Throughout this period, Poland did not exist as a country, its territory having been divided among Germany, Russia, and Austria in 1795. For ethnic Poles, religious devotion was intertwined with devotion to their dismembered homeland. Devotion to Our Lady of Czestochowa, who had been proclaimed queen of Poland in 1656, was thus infused with political as well as religious significance.

Unlike Italians, Polish American Catholics actively participated in the creation of national parishes and parochial schools. Viewing public schools and non-Polish parish schools with equal suspicion, Polish Americans contributed their meager financial resources to send their children to schools were classes were taught in Polish, English was considered a foreign language, and the curriculum emphasized Polish history as well as religion. Polish congregations of women religious, such as the Felicians, came to the United States to instruct Polish immigrant children at parish school in 1880. By 1953, the Felicians operated 250 elementary schools, twenty-eight high schools, and three junior colleges. These and other Polish Catholic schools helped preserve both religious values and Polish heritage. The primary caretakers of religion and ethnic identity, however, were mothers in Polish American homes, where women created and maintained family shrines to Our Lady of Czestochowa.

Like Poles and Italians, Mexican Americans blended family and devotional life in elaborate domestic shrines. A typical shrine would honor Our Lady of Guadalupe, patron saint of Mexico, and would include several candles to symbolize continual devotion, rosaries, novena cards, and special medals. Pictures of family members and souvenirs from Mexico would also be placed in front of the Virgin. The altar was not a separate religious space, but a place where family and religion were brought together.

Though ethnic religious traditions would remain strong well into second and third generations, devotions to Our Lady of Mount Carmel and Our Lady of Czestochowa have decreased in popularity. Guadalupean devotion, of course, is quite a different story. As the Spanish-speaking Catholic population becomes more vocal and gains more influence, and as non-Latino Catholics increasingly understand the Church in global rather than national terms, one of the oldest and strongest devotions of the New World has been receiving renewed attention. This is certainly true at Notre Dame, where the celebration of the Feast of Guadalupe has grown by leaps and bounds within the last decade. Because I almost always teach this class in the fall, one of the last things our class does together is attend the Guadalupe Mass on December 12. As a professor, I see this experience as an opportunity to generate a final exam question that will require them to synthesize the material we learned throughout the semester. As a practicing Catholic, though, I also recognize that this experience may lead them to new devotion.

No exploration of Mary would be complete without attention to how she has been used to idealize marriage and motherhood. In devotional and advice literature of the late nineteenth century, Mary was often cast as a housewife who tended to the needs of husband and child. According to the *Catholic Girls Guide* (1904), the Blessed Mother made her home inviting and comfortable for Saint Joseph when he came home from work. For his part, Joseph was pleased to see "his evening meal ready and everything as orderly as possible." This unit also explores the wealth of material that enshrines Mary's motherhood, providing a nice segue into our next unit, with begins with contraception.

Unit Five: Catholicism and the Body

This unit provides historical context for the most hotly contested issues in American Catholicism, past and present. We start with contraception, beginning with Pius XI's 1930 encyclical on Christian marriage, *Casti Connubii*, which called for strengthened families and promoted a more positive vision of sexuality in marriage by stressing the unity of spouses as the secondary end of marriage. *Casti Connubii* affirmed procreation as the primary end of marriage, and to that end the encyclical reiterated the Church's condemnation of contraception. This was highly significant because it marked a departure between Catholic teaching on this subject and that of other mainline denominations. Most clerics, Catholic and non-Catholic, had maintained a public silence on this issue until the 1920s, when activist Margaret Sanger began her crusade for birth control. Sanger's crusade combined with concerns about population growth and new information about the reproductive cycle to change the landscape. By 1930, four liberal Protestant denominations had endorsed contraception for married couples, as did the Anglican Lambeth Conference. In *Casti Connubii*, Pope Pius XI left no doubt that Catholics would be held to a higher standard. Technological advances after World War II produced new and more effective means of contraception, culminating in the introduction of birth control pill in 1960. Until the 1960s, large families would increasingly serve as a badge of Catholic distinctiveness.

In this unit we also compare guidebooks written for young Catholic men with those written for Catholic women. Multiple versions of these are available in Notre Dame's library, but on occasions some of my students have even produced advice books handed down from grandparents. Students are often appalled by the "double standard" for men and women that was implicit in these guides, and the discussion is inevitably spirited.

It probably goes without saying that students are often uncomfortable discussing contested issues such as abortion, sexuality, and related issues. Initially, many of them are suspicious and even dismissive of any material that they interpret as dissent from or criticism of the teaching of the Catholic Church. I deal with this challenge by emphasizing the importance of historical perspective, close attention to primary sources, and clear definitions. I also make very clear that we will be seeking to understand how controversial problems and questions have developed over time, not to solve or answer them. By the end of the unit, the ground rules are well established, and we move on to the final weeks of the semester ready to discuss these and other sensitive issues critically and, if not exactly dispassionately, than at least with respect for and willingness to listen to those on the other side of the debate.

Unit Six: Transformations in Church and Society

The decrees of the Second Vatican Council (1962–65) shifted Catholics' understanding of themselves, both as men and women within the Church and in relation to the larger society. In the United States, of course, that society was itself being transformed by the civil rights movement, the reemergence of feminism, and the Vietnam War. In this unit, the longest of the class, we explore how the reforms of Vatican II and broader cultural change shaped the experience of American Catholic women in the 1960s and beyond.

Vatican II itself had not said much specifically about women. Women were not even present at its first two sessions. Thanks to a few progressive bishops, who asked how they could reasonably deliberate the future of the Church when half of it was missing, fifteen women (three of whom were American) were invited to be present at the council's third session. Even then, however, they were assigned the official status of auditors, with neither a voice nor a vote. The experience of Vatican II increased Catholic women's collective awareness of their own subordination within the Church.

In the wake of the Council, religious congregations were urged to seek renewal by examining the original charism (mission) of their founders and by subjecting their life and ministry to prayerful scrutiny. Communities were directed to convoke a special general unit meeting (or legislative assembly) within three years, to engage in designated periods of experimentation, and to rewrite their constitutions to permit them to act on the call of the gospel in the contemporary world. Significantly, all members of the community were to be consulted in preparation for this. The search for renewal prompted most communities to implement a variety of structural changes. The strict rules that governed convent life became much less rigid, and community members were permitted more choice in terms of ministry and assignments. In general, American sisters adopted a less sheltered way of life. The most dramatic symbol of this was represented by the decision of many nuns to abandon the habit, which served as a type of "portable cloister." Of course, these transitions were accompanied by conflict and resistance. Thousands of women left religious life after 1968. Some left because they thought the reforms had gone too far, while others left because they thought they had not gone far enough.

Vatican II exercised its most profound influence on religious life not through its explicit statements on the subject, but through its broader message about the whole Church. In *Lumen Gentium*, the council affirmed the invitation to universal holiness, and undermined the two-tiered spirituality that had placed vowed Catholics a plane above laypeople. The strong social content of *Gaudium et Spes* was even more influential in the sense that it prompted many American sisters to choose new forms of ministry. By 1966, Catholic sisters were working in urban renewal programs, advocacy work, addiction counseling, chaplaincy, and government posts. Obviously, these changing apostolates were also influenced by broader social movements. Within Lyndon B. Johnson's Great Society, for example, American sisters worked with Head Start, Job Corps, and VISTA.

Of all the social movements reshaping American life in the 1960s, it was civil rights that had perhaps the most transformative effect on women's religious communities. Events at Selma, Alabama, in May

1965 provide perhaps the best illustration of this dynamic. Under the leadership of Dr. Martin Luther King, civil rights activists had gathered in Selma to march to the state capitol of Montgomery to protest restrictions on African American voting rights. Selma not only represented the first mass movement of whites into the civil rights movement, but it also marked a major entrance of the Catholic Church into the social arena. Selma's white marchers were disproportionately Catholic, and habited nuns attracted a great deal of media attention. Sr. Mary Peter Traxler (or Margaret Ellen Traxler, as she would be known after she reverted to her birth name in the late 1960s) found the Selma experience to be so powerful that she was compelled to redefine her life as a woman religious. Students read Traxler's article "After Selma, Sister, You Can't Go Home Again," in which she urged Catholic sisters to step outside the classroom and convent and work for justice in the world.

Mary Luke Tobin, a member of the Sisters of Loreto, had been one of the three American women who served as official observers during Vatican II. After the council, Tobin emphasized "the ardent desire on the part of religious everywhere to be where the Church is." What this meant, Tobin argued, was that "the Christian today must vitally concern himself with the world of today. It is no longer permitted to avoid it, to ignore it, or merely to tolerate it." In 1972, Tobin and forty-six other sisters formed Network, an organization of religious women who lobby on Capitol Hill. Tobin was among the many sisters who recognized that "going where the Church was" often meant expanding ministry beyond U.S. borders. She traveled to Saigon on a fact-finding mission in the early 1970s, and she later visited Northern Ireland and El Salvador during times of turmoil. Tobin's international outreach provides just one example of the increasingly global ministry of women religious. Thousands of sisters served as missionaries in Latin America, where they and, in turn, their communities were influenced by liberation theology. Occasionally, sisters' work has cost them their lives. We discuss the circumstances surrounding the four women martyred in El Salvador in 1980 and view the moving documentary *Roses in December*. To dramatize the continuing relevance of mission and martyrdom, we also discuss more recent case of Sister Dorothy Stang, S.N.D., murdered in Brazil in 2005.

Inspired by the spirit of Vatican II, American Catholic women did begin to mobilize in support of ordination in the early 1970s, much later than Protestant women. In 1974, the Leadership Conference of Women Religious passed a resolution to support women's ordination, and the next year, Mary Lynch organized the first meeting on the subject of women's ordination. Twelve hundred Catholics gathered in Detroit for the Women's Ordination Conference (WOC). Even as support for women's ordained ministry gained ground, official statements issued from the Vatican and from American bishops gave advocates little reason for optimism. The most definitive statement on the subject was issued in 1976 by the Vatican's Sacred Congregation for the Doctrine of the Faith. In the Declaration on the Question of the Admission of Women to the Ministerial Priesthood, Vatican theologians articulated the two main arguments against women's ordination. The first invokes the unbroken tradition of apostolic succession, and is based on Jesus' example of choosing only men as apostles. A secondary argument is that the "natural resemblance" between Christ and the celebrant of the Eucharist would be difficult to see if the role were not taken by a man.

While the first Women's Ordination Conference had emphasized unity and hope, the second, which followed on the heels of the Vatican Declaration, revealed the movement's growing diversity and radicalism. Further controversy ensued in 1979 during Pope John Paul II visit to the United States. Theresa Kane, R.S.M., head of the Leadership Conference of Women Religious, delivered a brief welcoming address in which she asked him to open all of the Church's ministries to women. In 1994, Pope John Paul II declared that the subject of women's ordained ministry be officially closed to debate, but it remains a heated topic within the Church.

There is a profound irony in the fact that while Catholic women did not gain access to priesthood or deaconate, they increasingly assumed a variety of other administrative and liturgical roles. In 1983, a new canon responded to growing scarcity of priests by opening the possibility of laypersons to exercise pastoral leadership in parishes. Since the late 1980s, women have outnumbered men studying in Catholic Masters of Divinity programs. Assuming roles previously reserved to men, women are now functioning as pastoral administrators, chaplains, and spiritual directors. In priestless parishes throughout the country—as of

2004, there were 3,157 U.S. parishes without a resident priest—women often carry out the ministries of pastor with two exceptions: they do not celebrate Eucharist or hear confessions. Of the nearly thirty thousand U.S. Catholics engaged in paid parish ministry, 82 percent are women.

Feminist theologian Catherine LaCugna has noted another irony in the Church's refusal to accept women's ordination: many women who would have otherwise entered the priesthood were drawn instead to the academic study of theology. Consequently, the leading feminist theologians, including Mary Daly, Rosemary Radford Ruether, and Diana Hayes, have been Roman Catholics. Elizabeth Johnson, C.S.J., is a contemporary feminist theologian who has recently provided a feminist theological interpretation of Mary of Nazareth. Johnson's views of the mother of Jesus are quite different from the descriptions of Mary that appeared in the nineteenth century. You will not, for example, find Johnson explaining how the Blessed Virgin served Joseph a nice dinner when he came home from work! By proposing "a theologically sound, spiritually empowering and ethically challenging theology of Mary, mother of Jesus the Christ, for the 21st century," Johnson provides a portrait of Mary that, like earlier interpretations, tells us more about modern Catholics than it does about the mother of Jesus.

For many Catholic women, as well as men, the most pressing issue in the years after Vatican II involved the Church's stance on the use of artificial contraception. Vatican II had said nothing explicitly about birth control, although *Gaudium et Spes* emphasized the personal love of the couple and the integrity of their sexual relationship even in the absence of children. In 1963, Pope John XXIII appointed a special commission to examine the Church's teachings on the use of artificial contraception, and Pope Pius VI continued that commission after the death of his predecessor. The commission included theologians, experts on population issues, and married couples. In 1966, the Papal Birth Control Commission voted 52–4 in favor of revoking the Church's ban on artificial contraception. After the findings of the commission were leaked, most Catholics assumed that change in Church teaching was imminent. In July 1968, however, the pope concluded in *Humane Vitae* that "the natural law" requires "that each and every marriage act must remain open to the transmission of life." In other words, the encyclical reaffirmed the Church's ban on the use of artificial means of contraception.

Humane Vitae prompted the gravest crisis of authority the Church had faced in centuries. The day after its publication, a group of American theologians released a signed statement at a press conference objecting to the encyclical on a variety of grounds. Severe criticism appeared in lay journals, and a Gallup poll showed 54 percent in opposition and only 28 percent in favor. In the diocese of Washington, D.C., fifty-one priests were disciplined for openly dissenting from *Humane Vitae*. Others maintained that the pope was not speaking infallibly in this instance and that Catholics were free to challenge this particular teaching. Many Catholics did (and do) exactly that. While dissent in practice seems to be somewhat tolerated, in the sense that it is not emphasized by most confessors, no official acceptance of such dissent has ever been made, and several theological dissenters have been censured.

The debate over birth control exposed a broader crisis of authority at a time when more women and men were choosing to make their own decisions on matters they viewed as private and personal. The debate changed ideas about what it meant to be "a good Catholic" and opened discussion about the proper use of papal authority for the first time in the American church. Like other issues regarding sexuality, such as homosexuality and abortion, contraception continues to spark debate in the American and universal church.

The subject of abortion has been controversial since the passage of *Roe v. Wade*. We also read documents pertaining to the abortion debate, including the controversial *New York Times* advertisement (signed in 1984 by a group of Catholic supporters of legal abortion), testimony from the case of Sister Agnes Mansour, who was forced to choose between her position as director of Michigan's Department of Social Services or her religious community (she eventually petitioned for a release from her vows), and reflections by Geraldine Ferraro on the abortion issue in the 1984 presidential election. Of course, all of these events happened long before my students were born. But they resonate with the contemporary debate over abortion, and historical context provides the space for students to engage in discussions that are more fruitful and less acrimonious than most that take place on campus.

Conclusion

We end the semester with a discussion of Catholicism and its relationship to contemporary feminism and antifeminism. Included among the documents we discuss are many of the same ones we began with in our discussion of Catholic gender ideology. When we revisit the documents pertaining to Pope John Paul II and the "new feminism," it is remarkable to see how much deeper and more thoughtful the conversation is compared to what it was on the first day. Using this and other gauges, I can say with confidence that my students, if they have held up their end of the bargain, finish the semester as better historians.

But do they also finish as better Catholics? I like to think they are more hopeful ones. I often require students to interview a women religious about her reasons for choosing religious life. They always approach this assignment with trepidation, for though it would have been ridiculous to think that a Notre Dame student of a generation ago would show up on campus never having met a nun, this is true for most of the students today. Yet the students almost always enjoy their interviews, and they are often pleasantly surprised by their encounters with faithful and vibrant women living a way of life they had dismissed as outmoded. One young woman put it this way: "Going into the interview I wondered what in the world I could possibly have in common with a nun. After speaking with Sister Mary Ann I realized that the answer, if I was lucky, was 'everything.'" This student had earlier confessed that her growing feminist sensibilities were coming into increasing conflict with what she had been taught during her strict Catholic upbringing. Instead of deepening her alienation, this assignment and the course in general increased her hopefulness about the Catholic Church and her own future within it.

This essay has focused on gender issues, but I think my general approach and argument can be extended to the broader field of Catholic Studies. It is not a stretch to suggest that studying the history of the Church can lead students to become more engaged with their tradition and to feel more of a stake in its future. Thus I am convinced that the conversations that take place in my classroom are an integral part of the Catholic education that Notre Dame provides to its students. As Catholic Studies gains more respect and attention as an academic discipline, our teaching and our research must continue to be evaluated on the basis of scholarly merit. But this does not exclude the very real possibility that Catholic Studies can play a significant role in passing on the faith—a faith that, like the past itself, is vibrant, ever-changing, challenging, and deeply meaningful.

For Further Reading

GENERAL

James T. Fisher, *Communion of Immigrants: A History of Catholics in America* (Oxford, 2002).

Paula Kane, James Kenneally, and Karen Kennelly, C.S.J., *Gender Identities in American Catholicism* (Orbis, 2001).

CATHOLIC GENDER IDEOLOGY

Kathleen Sprows Cummings, "Strongly-Willed Sister and Sorin Ally Named a Saint," *Notre Dame Magazine*, Winter 2006–2007.

Robert Ellsburg, ed., *Dorothy Day: Selected Writings* (Orbis, 2001).

Tracy Fessenden, "Worldly Madonna," in *Catholics in the Movies*, ed. Colleen McDannell, 251–276 (Oxford University Press, 2008).

Michael W. Higgins, *Stalking the Holy: The Pursuit of Saint-Making* (Anasi, 2006).

Linda Kerber and Jane Sherron DeHart, eds., *Women's America: Refocusing the Past* (Oxford University Pres, 2004).

Pope John Paul II, "Letter of Pope John Paul II to Women," 1995, http://www.vatican.va/holy_father/john_paul_ii/letters/documents/hf_j (4/16/2004).

Gerda Lerner, *The Majority Finds Its Past: Placing Women in History* (Oxford University Press, 1979).

Mary of Peace, "Woman: Her Meaning in Surrender," *The Cord* (January 1966): 7–15.

Colleen McDannell, "Catholic Domesticity," in Karen Kennelly, C.S.J., *American Catholic Women: A Historical Exploration* (Macmillan, 1989).

Henry V. Sattler, C.SS.R., "Why Female? Why Did God Create Both Man and Woman?" *Marriage: The Magazine of Catholic Family Living* (January 1965): 6–9.

WOMEN RELIGIOUS

Emily Clark, *Masterless Mistresses: The New Orleans Ursulines and the Development of a New World Society, 1727–1834* (University of North Carolina Press, 2007).

Carol Coburn and Martha Smith, *Spirited Lives: How Nuns Shaped Catholic Culture and American Life* (University of North Carolina Press, 1999).

Diane Batts Morrow, *Persons of Color and Religious at the Same Time: The Oblate Sisters of Providence, 1828–1860* (University of North Carolina Press, 2003).

Siobhan Nelson, *Say Little, Do Much: Nursing, Nuns and Hospitals in the Nineteenth Century* (University of Pennsylvania Press, 2000).

Nancy Lusignan Schultz, *Fire and Roses: The Burning of the Charlestown Convent* (Free Press, 2001).

ETHNICITY AND DEVOTIONAL LIFE

M. Christine Athans, "Mary in the American Catholic Church," *U.S. Catholic Historian* 8 (1989): 103–116.

Paula Kane, "Marian Devotion Since 1940," in Habits of Devotion: Catholic Religious Belief and Practice in Twentieth-Century America (Cornell University Press, 2004).

Timothy Matovina, *Guadalupe and Her Faithful: Latino Catholics in San Antonio from Colonial Origins to the Present* (Johns Hopkins University Press, 2005).

Robert A. Orsi, *The Madonna of 115th Street: Faith and Devotion in Italian Harlem* (Yale University Press, 1985).

Ann Taves, *The Household of Faith: Roman Catholic Devotions in Mid–Nineteenth Century America* (Notre Dame University Press, 1986).

CATHOLICISM AND THE BODY

Leslie Tentler, *Catholics and Contraception: An American History* (Cornell University Press, 2004).

TRANSFORMATIONS IN CHURCH AND SOCIETY

Jeannine Grammick, "From Good Sisters to Prophetic Women," in *Midwives of the Future: American Sisters Tell Their Story*, ed. Ann Patrick Ware, 226–237 (Leaven Press, 1985).

Elizabeth A. Johnson, "Mary of Nazareth: Friend of God and Prophet," *America* (June 17–24, 2000), 7–13.

Catherine Mowry LaCugna, "Catholic Women as Ministers and Theologians," *America* (October 10, 1992), 238–248.

Carmel McEnroy, *Guests in Their Own House: The Women of Vatican II* (Crossroad, 1996).

Peter Steinfels, "Sex and the Female Church," in *A People Adrift: The Crisis of the Roman Catholic Church in America* (Simon & Schuster, 2003).

11 Visual Literacy and Catholic Studies

CATHERINE R. OSBORNE

In the late sixth century, Pope Gregory the Great wrote one of his bishops a letter on the question of iconoclasm that has reverberated down almost to the present day, frequently quoted to justify the use of images in Christian worship and later cited by scholars to explain the role of pictures in the Middle Ages. Gregory argued,

> To adore a picture is one thing, but to learn through the story of a picture what is to be adored is another. For what writing presents to readers, this a picture presents to the unlearned who behold, since in it even the ignorant see what they ought to follow; in it the illiterate read. Hence, and chiefly to the nations, a picture is instead of reading.[1]

In Gregory's understanding, an image is the straightforward, transparent equivalent of a written text, inferior but nevertheless capable of conveying the essentials to the simple and above all to the unconverted barbarians ("the nations").

But just as scholarship has rejected the idea that texts themselves are able to straightforwardly convey true information, insisting instead that they be read "critically," it has rejected the notion that images and objects are simply pendants to texts, visual expressions of ideas that are always rooted in words.[2] Art history, and the broader interdisciplinary approach of "visual culture studies" to which it is related, has used the metaphor of "visual literacy" to suggest that images and objects deserve analysis in their own right and with attention to the specifically visual attributes that make them different from texts.[3]

In this essay, I argue that visual literacy deserves attention in Catholic Studies classrooms alongside the more familiar skills of critical reading, and I briefly outline several techniques for interrogating images, drawn from art history and visual/material culture studies. To suggest the breadth and ubiquity of the kinds of evidence the use of the visual might open up in classrooms and in research, I touch on a wide variety of examples. The visual arts—among them painting, sculpture, architecture, and photography—stand here alongside less exalted media like advertising and consumer design.

Why Visual Literacy?

Catholic Studies, as an interdisciplinary program, seeks to understand an entire Catholic world: how Catholics have negotiated their faith in various ways, and how their Catholicism has informed or failed to inform the multiple dimensions of their lives and practices. Theology, history, literature, sociology, and economics all have much evidence to offer here. But relatively little attention has been paid to music and the visual arts. The lacuna is surprising, given the consistent theological stress on Catholic sacramentality and given that Catholics have tended to announce their arrival in any given location not with a speech, a sermon, or a book, but with a building.

There are three major reasons why the ability to analyze images is especially important for Catholic Studies. The first is that, as Colleen McDannell points out, "Christian material culture does not simply reflect an existing reality. Experiencing the physical dimension of religion helps *bring about* religious values, norms, behaviors, and attitudes."[4] In other words, religious images and objects are not just illustrations of one theology or another; they actually comment on or even create theology, and they can make interventions in theological arguments on all topics: God, Christology, anthropology, eschatology, sacramentology. Scholars of visual culture would agree that both iconoclasts and iconodules from the seventh century to the twenty-first have been correct in their assessment of images as powerful and deeply implicated in the formation of actual Catholic beliefs and practices. Studying Catholic images, in this view, is equivalent to studying Augustine, Aquinas, and Rahner, for they make theological arguments in their own right.

The second reason is that the study of visual culture gives us a particular type of historical access that is otherwise largely unavailable. For most of Christian history, written text, while venerated, was only indirectly accessible to the vast majority of the population, who lived in an oral and visual world. This is what Pope Gregory was pointing out. Even today, while surveys record the steep decline in reading, it is the rare Catholic household that has no pictures, statues, or crucifixes. Our understanding of the worlds of Catholics across history, then, would be greatly enhanced by an understanding of their visual worlds: what they saw every day or every week in church, in the margins of their prayer books if they owned them, in cloister sculptures if they were monks or nuns, in tapestries if they were wealthy or the house-servants of the wealthy, and, for Catholics of the last century, in a plethora of material ranging from holy cards to rosaries to the National Shrine of the Immaculate Conception. Sometimes a visual account of Catholic life supports a general assessment of a way of living, as in Eamon Duffy's evocation of village church furnishings in early modern England; sometimes a single image can be shocking in its dramatic insight into a way of thinking very different from our own.[5] It is one thing to know that Spanish Catholics venerated Santiago Matamoros, Saint James the Moor-Slayer, and another to see the apostle rearing triumphantly over rolling turbaned heads (Figure 11.1).

Finally, we ought to teach visual literacy skills in Catholic Studies classrooms because doing so more accurately reflects the world we live in ourselves. Vachel Lindsay, in an early essay on film, famously noted that we live in a "hieroglyphic civilization," not a textual culture.[6] Students are confronted with visual input, from buildings to advertising to TV to book covers, almost every minute of every day. The substantial amount of practice they already have (whether they know it or not) in interpreting images may mean that for many students, the visual is an easier door than the verbal to unfamiliar habits of thought and practice. But because, as noted earlier, images are no less difficult than texts to interpret critically and substantially, we should be wary of simply using them to illustrate a point. The remainder of this essay is devoted to briefly sketching some of the many ways art historians and visual-culture scholars investigate the visual.

FIGURE 11.1. Santiago Matamoros (Saint James the Moor-Slayer), Iglesia de Santiago el Real, Logroño, Spain, seventeenth century. (Photograph by Catherine Osborne.)

Iconography, Stylistic Analysis, and Formal Analysis

Three basic techniques of art history, still the foundation of many introductory textbooks, are iconography, stylistic analysis, and formal analysis. Iconography, simply, is the identification and analysis of an image's subject matter, generally through reference to texts (such as canonical or apocryphal scriptures, theological writing, poetry, mythology, or even scientific writing). An iconographical study of Masaccio's *The Holy Trinity, with the Virgin and St. John and Donors* (Figure 11.2) would thoroughly identify the subject matter, explaining the theology of the Holy Trinity, who the Virgin and Saint John are, the location of the scene in a chapel, and the theology of intercessory prayer which links the two donors (kneeling outside the arch) and the *memento mori* below to the two saints and the Godhead within. Traditional "high" iconography, sometimes also called iconology, would then go on to link specific features of paintings with texts, theological theories, or historical events to which they might refer beyond the obvious subject matter: a sort of hidden code to be deciphered by the art historian. In Masaccio's case, Rona Goffen has argued that the painting's theology is related to the Letter to the Hebrews.[7]

Stylistic analysis tries to fit an image into a trajectory of visual style. Masaccio's *Trinity* is an important example of Italian Renaissance art that uses the techniques of perspective and *trompe l'oeil*; its figures are naturalistic and three-dimensional; its architectural background suggests a Roman triumphal arch; and so forth. And formal analysis ignores subject matter to examine the play of color, shape, and line within an image: Masaccio chooses a muted palette and an extremely balanced, solid composition with the figures forming a firmly rooted pyramid within the rectangular overall shape and the curve of the arch. Moreover, he applies the rules of perspective so strictly that the viewer's eye is led inexorably to the "vanishing point."

These two types of analysis may initially seem more suited to art criticism than to Catholic Studies, but both can provide interesting insights for how the picture operates within its world. The rhetoric surrounding the introduction of perspective, the use of a Roman civic form (the triumphal arch), and the choice of naturalism all raise interesting questions about the role of art vis-à-vis Christianity and society

FIGURE 11.2. *The Trinity*, by Masaccio (Maso di San Giovanni), Santa Maria Novella, Florence, Italy, ca. 1425. (Source: Scala / Art Resource, New York.)

in fifteenth-century Florence. Meanwhile, formal analysis would point out both the clear linking of the Trinity through the strong central, vertical line and the relative insignificance of the Holy Spirit, a tiny and hazy brush of white, which graphically exemplifies (and perhaps, along with numerous other similar Trinitarian images, even contributes to) the Holy Spirit's underdeveloped role in Western theology.

Finally, the apparently purely aesthetic issues of style and form continue, for many people, to be inextricably entwined with moral and liturgical choices. The very bitterness of disputes over visual style reveals its ideological importance for many Catholics and thus its place in Catholic Studies. Stories of mid-twentieth-century disputes pitting "modernizing" pastors, artists, and parishioners against their more "traditionalist" peers are legion, and while some of these disputes were over the very appropriateness of Catholic use of statuary, many were specifically about the issue of materials and form: welded steel, marble, or plaster? Abstract and streamlined forms, associated with modernistic or futuristic technology, or idealized realism, associated with stability and traditional devotionalism? A very typical post–Vatican II incident illustrates the point: the church staff at St. Joseph's, Greenwich Village, removed a number of original statues from the sanctuary and, apparently believing them to have no aesthetic or spiritual value, put them out for trash collection. A longtime parishioner happened by and was so horrified that he took some of them into his own townhouse—and he never went back to that church. He perceived the decorative revamping of the church as a rejection of a worship style about which he felt strongly, and he switched to a more conservative parish several blocks away.[8]

Rhetorical Analysis: How Does the Visual Function?

Iconography, stylistic analysis, and formal analysis are basic skills of visual literacy because they are directed squarely at the image, asking us to spend time simply looking at what is in front of us before doing anything else. (Willingness to take time to look is an important skill in visual literacy; studies at museums have demonstrated that the average viewer spends only fifteen seconds on a painting, enough to take in broad strokes but not to notice much detail.) But although iconography can initially open a picture, art historians and critics have found it increasingly naïve in recent years, because it assumes the possibility of straightforward access to a picture's meaning through a relatively limited analysis of its explicit content and because it primarily refers to written texts (often texts far removed in space and time from the object's making) rather than to an analysis of the culture for which any object is made. That a picture's subject is a particular saint, or that a building is (say) an office building or a cathedral, is still useful information. But it cannot even come close to conveying the full, multidimensional meaning of the object. Thus, various types of rhetorical analysis investigate the choice of *this* subject, *this* format, *this* stylistic decision, and so on. Their premise is that to understand visual material is not only to understand its content, but also to understand how that content functions in a particular context. What coded messages is an image sending to its intended audience? How have those messages changed over time?

Rhetorical analysis generally understands an object with reference to its maker(s) (production-side analysis), to those who see, use, and/or transform the finished product (consumption-side analysis), or both. Production-side analysis has widely questioned the modernist myth of the solitary maker-genius whose art is a personal expression of his own creativity. Instead, following the British art historian Michael Baxandall, scholars seek to determine "intentionality" in a very broad way, asking what types of social and economic relations, networks, and reasons made it possible for a particular work to be made in the first place. Who could be trained as an artist, and how did that training occur? Who provided the funds? Who chose the subject and the style, and what did these choices mean to them, to the artist(s), to the various audiences for the work? How did groups or individuals produce the work alone or together? How, if at all, was mechanization involved? What economic system drove the visual market, and how did it affect the maker? What did the culture expect of visual work in general and types of visual work in particular? Was art supposed to do something or express something or look a certain way, and how does the work in question conform (or not) to those expectations? If the work is a photograph or a picture, how is the frame used—that is, what is this picture *not* showing the viewer? What happened to the finished product, and how was it (or has it been) used, physically and ideologically?

Examples of clearly rhetorical medieval Catholic art abound, since so much of it was intended as didactic or demonstrative. Some of the earliest of the famous *bibles moralisée* (Bibles that paired illustrations of the text with allegorical or "moralized" illuminations) displayed a deep ambivalence toward the rise of the scientific investigation that was newly making itself felt in France. They may have been part of a campaign to convince the authorities to make scientific investigation formally subject to theology.[9] In the same milieu, Louis IX of France, Saint Louis, was using a massive artistic and building program to position himself publicly as a sort of coregent with Christ, a tenant holding the royal throne until the (shortly anticipated) Second Coming.[10] And in Padua a half-century later, the former usurer Enrico Scrovegni hired Giotto di Bondone to cover a chapel with three registers of frescoes depicting the Life of the Virgin and the Life of Christ, all of which add up to a passionate and sophisticated demonstration of repentance and plea for mediation and redemption.[11] The Arena Chapel frescoes develop the opposing themes of charity, coded as abundantly and naturally fertile, and usury, coded as perversely and diabolically productive; the moneybag Judas clutches to his stomach is directly opposed to the miraculously swelling belly of Elizabeth. The fresco cycle, which begins with the unacceptable offering of Joachim at the Temple, ends with a picture of Scrovegni himself kneeling to offer the chapel itself to the Virgin Mary, who will carry it to Christ on the throne of judgment (Figure 11.3).

All rhetorical analysis includes an understanding of the intended audience of the work; in the wake of the Reformation, a new category of images relevant to Catholic Studies grew up, now directed at non-Catholics. There are many clearly anti-Catholic images produced by Protestants from the sixteenth century on, but more ambiguous cases exist as well, especially as explicit anti-Catholicism faded in the twentieth century. One of the richest potential sources for the study of mid-twentieth-century Catholicism is the massive Farm Security Administration/Office of War Information Collection (FSA/OWI) at the Library of Congress. Actually, there may be many more than we know; but a certain number were specifically identified by the photographers as

FIGURE 11.3. Detail of *The Last Judgment*, by Giotto di Bondone, with Enrico degli Scrovegni offering a model of the Arena Chapel, Padua, Italy, ca. 1305. (Source: Alinari / Art Resource, New York.)

being of Catholic subjects. Many show either church buildings or men, women, or children praying or participating in liturgy or devotions (Figure 11.4). These can be very helpful in illuminating Catholic life prior to Vatican II, but a look at their production raises questions about what, exactly, they were meant to convey.

As historian Michael Lesy has described, these photographs did not appear in a vacuum.[12] They were made for a purpose: at first, the purpose of the FSA photo bureau was to demonstrate that federal FSA funds were being well spent by housing and employing the indigent; but as the project grew, its director, Roy Stryker, became entranced by

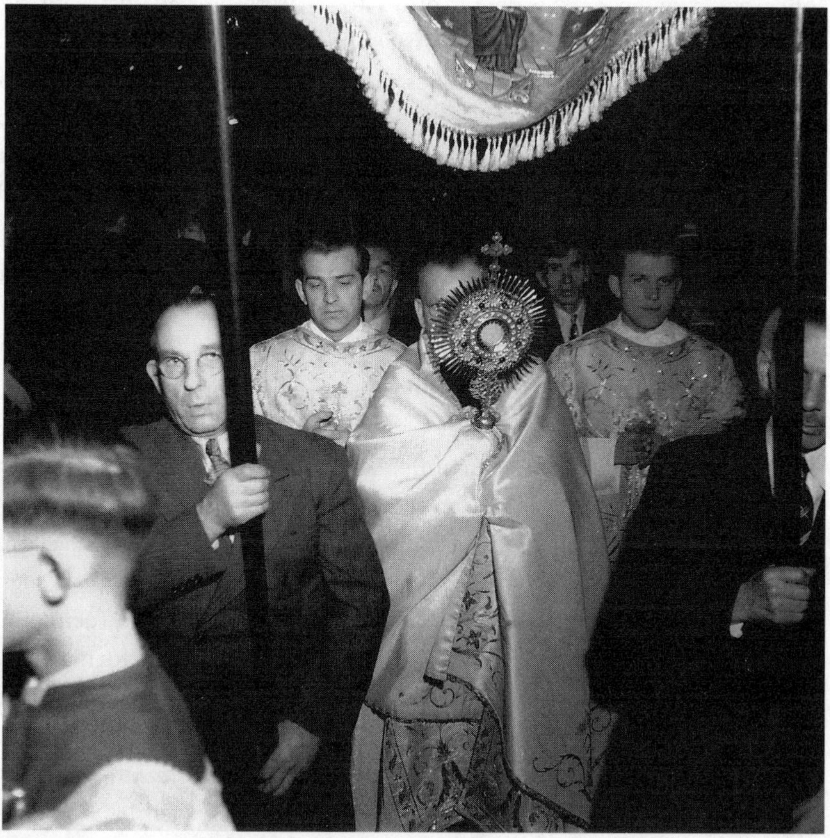

FIGURE 11.4. Procession of the Blessed Sacrament at High Mass on Easter in the Polish Catholic community of Buffalo, New York, April 1943. (Photograph by Marjory Collins; FSA/OWI Photograph Collection, Library of Congress [LC-USW3- 023742-E (P&P)].)

the idea of producing a photographic record of all of American life as he conceived it. He sent photographers on the road with lengthy "shooting scripts" listing all the typically American scenes he wished them to record and went so far as to destroy some negatives he deemed unusable. As with any photograph, they represent a choice of a particular moment or space on the part of the photographer, which does tell a kind of truth but also means the rejection of all the other moments and compositions that might have told a different story. Photographs are not infallible records of truth; they are intentional constructions.

The FSA photographs are thus a record of American life, but also a particular construction of it; they tell a particular story. How do the explicitly labeled "Catholic" photographs relate to that story? Are Catholics constructed as the exotic other to a Protestant mainstream, or does the inclusion of Catholic liturgy and devotion within this record speak to the intimate role Catholics played in building American urban identity? Does the overwhelming mass of liturgical and devotional material obscure the many other aspects of life for Catholics (such as work, public school, and the shared popular culture of movies and radio) at this time? In other words, does it set them apart from the general population *too much*? These are questions Lesy neither raises or answers, but they are germane to the use of these photos in a Catholic Studies classroom.[13]

Production-side analysis concentrates primarily on the forces, ideas, beliefs, and artistic choices that bring visual objects into being. Consumption-side criticism, meanwhile, while it does not always go as far as Roland Barthes in proclaiming that the unity of a text (or in this case an image) "lies not in its origins but in its destination," does accord less importance to why an object was made and more to how it is seen and used by an audience now understood not to be passive recipients of a communication but rather actively and often transformatively involved in reception.[14] This is the type of approach most often used by scholars of contemporary religious visual culture such as Colleen McDannell and David Morgan, who turn to sociological research to point out that "the masses" are not, as was long assumed by well-educated thinkers of varying political and theological persuasions, solely the passive recipients of a culture created and approved by others. Rather, they demonstrate how American Christians typically use and interact with images and objects to create and sustain a religious worldview and practice that refuses to recognize a division between the "sacred" (church) and the "profane" (daily life). They wonder what of importance is missed when scholars concentrate on the intentions of artists rather than on the experiences of viewers.

Taking the Catholic consumer seriously means asking a different set of questions from those generally asked by twentieth-century theologians and educated Catholics, who, as McDannell has shown, adopted a production-side discourse to dismiss popular Catholic aesthetic objects as being in "poor taste"—a condition often associated with the objects' and images' perceived "femininity," from which these critics wished to distance themselves.[15] These objects can be partly understood with reference to such production-side concerns as the nineteenth- and twentieth-century official desire for theological safety and conformity, which led parishes to invest in officially approved (and often artistically negligible by current standards) art and trickled down to the massive production of similar objects on a small scale for personal and domestic devotion. But they are most relevant when studied in the context of these home devotions, with the accent on how ordinary Catholics have understood them: not primarily as aesthetically valuable objects, but as useful tools to be touched, kissed, carried from place to place, or buried, as appropriate. They are also used, as a number of studies have pointed out, to construct and display identity: widely recognizable religious images or clothing both reinforce religious identity and inform others about it. It is the refusal to accept the myth of consumer passivity that sets these studies apart; David Morgan, for example, details how so many Catholic and other viewers "discovered" a chalice (left temple) and host (mid-forehead) "hidden" in Warner Sallman's *Head of Christ* that the artist himself came to believe he had somehow placed them there (Figure 11.5).[16] Morgan's study indicates that Catholics have not been afraid to co-opt a widely recognizable Protestant image when it seems to them to reflect truth. It also demonstrates the intimacy of the relationships that Catholics often form with highly specific portrayals of religious figures. Morgan's respondents comment frequently on how they recognize Christ in Sallman's picture because he painted the eyes correctly. With a different expression or haircut, how might they feel?

FIGURE 11.5. *Head of Christ* (1941) by Warner Sallman. (© 1941 Warner Press, Inc., Anderson, Indiana. Used with permission.)

What are the practical and theological implications of this kind of Catholic attitude toward art?

Finally, the rhetoric of domestic visual culture does not need to be explicitly religious to have bearing on Catholic Studies. It is all too easy to forget what a dramatic visual transformation the suburbanization of

American Catholics would have wrought for many of the migrants. For many Catholics, leaving cramped inner-city apartments or houses would have meant more than racial segregation, long car trips, and material prosperity; it also meant incorporation into the increasingly hegemonic aesthetic of domestic modernity. The Catholic convert and artist Charlton Fortune commented as early as 1936 that "while the future priest is studying in the seminary, his future parishioner is busily concerned with mundane things such as ice-boxes, stream-lined cars and well made furniture, buying excellent things on the installment plan, and learning a considerably amount about beauty in the process."[17] Fortune's point was that, while most religious art remained tied to Victorian ideals, the design of everyday life, from refrigerators to the Eames chair, had become sleek, clean, efficient, and "modern" (qualities she celebrated). She believed that these newly educated Catholics would be reluctant to lead aesthetic double lives, one in the kitchen (or garage) and one at the altar. She was wrong about this—most American Catholics have proven relatively willing to compartmentalize their religious and secular lives, at least on a visual level—but she was correct in pointing out the domestic transformation many Catholic citizens were undergoing. They embraced products regularly marketed as efficient, technological, and futuristic in a way that rendered them, aesthetically speaking, increasingly indistinguishable from their Protestant and Jewish neighbors. More research is needed to determine what effect this change might have had on Catholic self-understanding, communally and individually.

Identity and Environment: Catholic Buildings

While the study of images and objects such as devotional sculptures of the saints focuses attention on individual objects, and while this is perhaps inevitable in a classroom environment where most images will be still photos, this section suggests a further area where visual culture studies bears on Catholic Studies: the built environment. Most images and objects participate in some way in a larger environment: an artistic "program" in a church, a more aesthetically haphazard but no less intentional assembly in a home, and so on. A more three-dimensional analysis of the way in which Catholics experience and participate in liturgical spaces is a major way of using techniques from art history to think about Catholic life.

John McGreevy and Robert Orsi have both pointed out Catholic possessiveness of the urban landscape.[18] Their work should alert us to the importance of the buildings that shape that landscape—not just the fact of their existence, but also the specific aesthetic forms that they take. This kind of consideration begins with location and with the physical experience of arriving. Where is the building located relative to the living space of those who visit it? Does it require an extensive trip, a pilgrimage, or is it around the corner? How, if at all, does it set itself off from contemporary buildings? When a visitor arrives, is there transitional space (such as a courtyard or narthex), or does he or she enter directly from the street? Once inside, where are the eyes likely to be drawn first: to a shop, a font, a particular painting or sculpture, the altar?

The architecture and decoration of a liturgical space is of great importance when considering built environments in a contemporary Catholic Studies context. For many centuries domestic and ecclesiastical architecture developed simultaneously and relatively harmoniously, and a single style tended to dominate all new building in any given location. In the last two hundred years, however, "throwback" styles and eclecticism became, if anything, more popular and usual than what architectural historians would consider the contemporary style. Suddenly choosing the style of a new building was not only possible but also often seemed heavy with moral implications. In an era where multiple choices are possible, the style a patron or congregation or architect chooses often reveals what they think a church building *means*. An exercise a friend uses with beginning religion students asks them to examine interior views of a Quaker meetinghouse, a Gothic cathedral, and a megachurch set in a giant auditorium with a stage and screens, and to speculate about what each space says to visitors about the church's theology. Another basic question for this exercise is how the people in the pictures relate to the space. What is the purpose of the space? If it is to give glory to God and, incidentally, the local bishop; to provide a stage setting for a variety of rituals and processions; and to give a fitting home to important relics, as was generally the case with medieval cathedrals, it is entirely fitting to have an enormous building that dwarfs a small congregation and that soars skyward. If, on the other hand, it is meant to provide a warm and human-scaled setting for intimate group worship, the meetinghouse model might be more appropriate.

Two examples of very different American Catholic churches suggest the openings church buildings might offer to Catholic Studies. Thomas Tweed's assessment of the National Shrine of the Immaculate Conception in Washington, D.C., analyzes its attempt to claim psychic as well as physical space in the heart of the nation, which it does through a visual allusion to the Capitol dome, a Byzanto-Romanesque rejection of the neo-Gothic Episcopalian alternative of the National Cathedral, and an oversized campanile that insistently claims space on the skyline.[19] Tweed's visual analysis considers the intentions and impact of a specific building and proposes that its style was intended to have—and did have—a certain effect on the collective Catholic psyche. Its undeniable panache and kitschy splendor, as horrifying as they were (and still are) to aesthetic purists, successfully state Catholic "arrival" on the national scene, and its corona of chapels dedicated to various ethnicities remain popular draws as pilgrimage sites for the nation's diverse groups of Catholics. But the Shrine's architecture also raises questions about why Catholics in the mid–twentieth century were so reluctant to turn to contemporary art and architecture for their national building, instead insisting on a mishmash of ancient styles.

Whatever artistic judgments may be passed on the National Shrine, its overall plan has not been deemed inappropriate by its custodians, and thus has remained basically unchanged. But sometimes congregations find themselves worshipping in spaces that clash not only with their human needs but also with their theology, either because they have inherited them from previous generations or because their old space has become unusable, perhaps because of fire, and they have been forced into a temporary home. What they do in these situations can be instructive.

St. Joseph of the Holy Family, at the corner of Morningside Avenue and West 125th Street in Harlem, was founded in 1860 to serve a growing German village at a time when northern Manhattan was newly accessible by railroad (Figures 11.6–11.8). Its architectural plan and decoration, much of which remains visible today, were thoroughly typical.

FIGURE 11.6. St. Joseph of the Holy Family, New York. (Photograph by Catherine Osborne.)

The modest brick facade fronted a hall church with a simple nave and shallow sanctuary; a choir loft in the rear of the church completed the facilities. The church had a fairly coherent decorative scheme: stained-glass windows of saints, bishops, and biblical scenes and romantic, softly colored murals of the Crucifixion, the Good Shepherd, and so on. Not unnaturally, all the characters in the murals are fair-skinned, with light hair and eyes. Meanwhile, in the sanctuary, four carved angels hovered, participating in the heavenly liturgy described in the Book of Revelation: one with the book of the gospels, one with a chalice, one with a censer, and one with its hands folded in prayer. The altar, of painted and carved plywood, was initially placed against the far wall of the sanctuary but was moved forward after Vatican II.

Today this church, among the oldest in New York, continues to occupy its original footprint. But the population it serves has shifted dramatically. By the end of the 1990s the parish supported an English-speaking community composed of multiple generations of black Americans as well as immigrants from the Caribbean, Belize, and Africa,

FIGURE 11.7. St. Joseph of the Holy Family, New York. (Photograph by Catherine Osborne.)

along with upwardly mobile second- and third-generation Puerto Ricans and Dominicans, who often easily incorporate African American traditions of prayer and song into their spiritual lives. It also supported a smaller Spanish-speaking community of first-generation Dominicans, Puerto Ricans, and Mexicans with a sprinkling of immigrants from other Central and South American countries. No parishioners claimed German roots; the few regular white communicants were of various ethnicities, and the pastor was Irish American. In 2000–2001, the church's sanctuary underwent a substantial renovation.[20] There was widespread agreement that the decoration was no longer sufficient as a representation of the people and values of the parish. In addition, the sanctuary space itself, along with the altar, needed a redesign in order to comply more fully with the liturgical reforms of the 1960s and to stress the centrality of the Eucharist to the congregation. At the same time, the parish wanted to honor its full history and retain a substantial amount of the original decoration.

FIGURE 11.8. St. Joseph of the Holy Family, New York. (Photograph by Catherine Osborne.)

The architect, Lawrence Hoy, first removed several pews in order to extend the sanctuary out, moving it closer to the congregation and making room for the choir to be located there, reflecting a black church tradition. After substantial debate, Hoy also moved the tabernacle from a side wall of the sanctuary to a slim chapel installed in the location of the old high altar, directly on axis with the celebration of the Eucharist. The chapel is enclosed by gates that the celebrant swings open before the distribution of the Eucharist. Finally, the pastor wanted the flimsy old altar to be replaced by a permanent stone one, in accordance with church directives. The new altar, in granite and wood, was specifically designed to resemble a table, the congregation's "dinner table." It is now located directly underneath the four celebrating angels; this may have been the original intended location of the main altar, and the pastor states that placing the new altar there not only acknowledged the symbolism of the heavenly liturgy but was also a way of honoring the intentions of the original builders.

The German murals remained, but the old altar and all the statuary except for the built-in angels were removed. The new altar, pulpit, and celebrant's chair used New England granite, but woods sourced from West Africa: ebony, bubinga, and anegré. Hoy used the same woods in the gates to the new chapel, the design of which he based on symbols of totality from the Yoruba tribe. The Nigerian artist Samuel Iheme was commissioned to create a statue of the Holy Family, a processional crucifix with an African Christ, and a large Nativity set for the Christmas season. Finally, a New York deacon painted a copy of a large panel of the martyred Ugandans St. Charles Lwanga and his companions, which today, as the Hispanic population of the parish steadily grows, is balanced by a large picture of Our Lady of Guadalupe on the other side of the altar.

The story of St. Joseph's is a local and in many ways a small story. It is unlikely that its renovation will make the art history books of the future. But although these details are clearly the parish's own, continual updating and renovation to fit changing needs, tastes, and desires are very common. One way into any parish's story is through words: its archives, or perhaps oral histories with community members. But with a renovated church, especially one that still makes its earlier face available, we can also enter that history by way of the visual. In the case of St. Joseph's, the history of Harlem itself is written in the layering of styles and images. Some of the liturgical history of the twentieth century is reflected in the shifts in the use of space, and debates about localized, specific, ethnic Catholic identity can be opened, alongside discussions of how a contemporary parish is or should be related to the neighborhood it serves. A careful look at an apparently nondescript church may be able to give insight into how a given parish answers those questions.

Conclusion

I began this essay by referring to one of the oldest, and possibly the most successful, defenses of imagery in the Catholic Church. Although we may be grateful to Pope Gregory for helping to ensure the continued flowering of Christian art, we should not take him too seriously as an assessor of the complexity of the Catholic visual world. Ironically, the iconoclasts—who attributed great potential for harm to images and therefore acknowledged their power—had a better understanding of how seriously we should take visual culture. Because Catholic Studies is deliberately interdisciplinary, images, objects, and buildings would seem to have an important place at the table alongside the texts that theologians and historians more routinely work with. But pictures, buildings, devotional objects, and the everyday surroundings of Catholics, because of their very ubiquity and perhaps because it is still easy for us to assume, like Gregory, that they are little more than a simplified translation for the uninitiated, are often not approached with a critical eye. The point of teaching and practicing visual literacy is to get students to consider critically the astonishing variety and volume of evidence about Catholic life, thought, and practice that is, in a sense, hidden in plain sight.

Part IV: Ethnicity, Race, and Catholic Studies

12 We Have Been Believers

Black Catholic Studies

DIANA L. HAYES AND CECILIA A. MOORE

On a typical sizzling New Orleans afternoon, C. Vanessa White and her classmates were socializing just minutes before their first class in Introduction to Black Theology at the Institute for Black Catholic Studies at Xavier University. Amid the chatter, in stomped an unkempt black man screaming, "Somebody stole all my stuff!"[1] He turned, slammed the door, and repeated, "Somebody stole all my stuff." Angrily he searched the faces of the class and again asserted, "Somebody stole all my stuff!" Completely thrown off guard and frightened, White remembers thinking, "Does he think I took his stuff?" "What stuff is he talking about?" "Where is our teacher?" At that moment, the irate and scary stranger introduced himself to the class as Father Bede Abram, O.F.M. Conv., their instructor. According to White, this dramatic introduction was just the beginning of an unfolding of a Catholic world she and her classmates had never seen or even imagined, even as it also laid bare an experience they knew all too well.

As with the best-executed thefts, one knew something was missing, but just quite what one could not say. In this summer class, Father Abrams's objective was to teach these students to retrieve and restore the record and memory of black Catholic thought, experience, history, and theology, and to redeposit it into the minds of black Catholics—and all Catholics for that matter—for the purpose of transforming the Church and the role Catholicism could play in black communities.

The Birth of Black Catholic Studies

Black Catholic Studies as a formal field came into being in a time of social, political, and religious tumult and transformation. The waning days of the civil rights movement, the waxing days of the Black Power movement, the reforming spirit ushered in by the Second Vatican

Council and its aftermath, and events associated with these movements set the stage for the development of Black Catholic Studies.[2] Nineteen-sixty-eight was a pivotal year. Following the assassination of Dr. Martin Luther King Jr., black Catholic clergy for the first time met together as a body in Detroit during the annual meeting of the Catholic Clergy Conference on the Interracial Apostolate. Father Herman Porter of the Diocese of Rockford, Illinois, urged his fellow black priests to address the violence that was being perpetrated in cities such as Chicago against black youth. In particular, he referred to Mayor Richard J. Daley of Chicago, who called on police to "shoot to kill" rioters in Chicago, many of whom were black youth.[3] In attendance was Father Cyprian Davis, O.S.B., who would later become a primary shaper of Black Catholic Studies in the United States. Davis recalled:

> This meeting, which was held at the Sheraton-Cadillac Hotel, was the first time that black Catholic priests had assembled as a national group. The meeting which began as a planning strategy to face the situation at that time quickly became a concerted effort to share their experiences and their feelings as black men in that institution that was then seen to be a very white organization. They spoke of their disappointments, their hurt, and their bitterness. Not all had had the same experience. Not all were of the same mind, but enough were so that a unity was formed and the decision emerged to challenge the American bishops and to publish a manifesto.[4]

The manifesto was a forthright and fiery declaration that asserted "the Catholic Church in the United States, primarily a white racist institution, has addressed itself primarily to white society and is definitely a part of that society."[5] The clergy followed this statement with a call for greater leadership by black Catholics in the Church, better formation for white clergy and religious serving in black communities, the education of black Catholic laypersons in leadership, and the formation of the National Black Catholic Clergy Caucus.[6] Later Sr. Martin De Porres Grey, a Sister of Mercy of Pittsburgh, who had been present with the priests in Detroit, organized the first ever meeting of black women religious from more than seventy-nine different religious communities from the United States and abroad. The black sisters met at

Carlow College in Pittsburgh and took up similar questions about the role racism played in the Church, the new needs of the black community, and how they as women religious could make a difference. At the end of the meeting they decided to transform their gathering into an organized body, and founded the National Black Sisters' Conference (NBSC). In 1969 the NBSC published a position paper entitled "The Survival of Soul," in which the sisters declared, "We, the members of the National Black Sisters' Conference, pledge ourselves to work unceasingly for the liberation of black people."[7] Of the six objectives the NBSC outlined in the position paper, two were directly related to the creation of the field of Black Catholic Studies. The sisters pledged "to help promote a positive self-image among ourselves, in our black folk, especially our black youth, through knowledge of and appreciation for the beauty of our rich historical and cultural heritage" and "to initiate, organize and/or participate in self-help programs through which we can educate ourselves and our black people, thereby encouraging the utilization of those resources which are useful to black people."[8] Together black Catholic religious brothers, sisters, and clergy along with select laymen and laywomen began to work together to assess the needs and concerns of black Catholics and to find the means by which these needs and concerns could best be met.[9] They determined that reclaiming, reinterpreting, rewriting, and teaching black theology and history were at the heart of answer.

Black Catholic Studies as a field was born of the activist spirit and movement of the late 1960s and early 1970s. It did not begin in academe and its first practitioners and teachers were not people formally trained in Black Catholic Studies. Most of the first teachers and practitioners were black Catholic priests, sisters, and brothers, some of whom were formally trained in theology, biblical studies, English, history, music, education, and psychology, but not in any field directly related to African American studies. Such training would come much later in the development of Black Catholic Studies. The writings of the black clergy, brothers, and sisters, and later the National Office of Black Catholics (NOBC), founded by Brother Joseph M. Davis, S.M., all reflected a strong black consciousness and intention to root all of the elements of what would come under the field of Black Catholic Studies from liturgy to history to theology in black cultural and religious studies. Their work for the first twenty or more years was the intentional work to bring African American Studies and Catholic Studies together in a way that would be authentically black and authentically Catholic. These men and women approached the charge confident they could make this happen.

In "African American Catholics and Black Theology: An Interpretation," black Catholic theologian M. Shawn Copeland outlined how they set about the task. According to Copeland, the Black Catholic Clergy Caucus focused its attention on "confronting ecclesiastical racism at every turn, collectively offering Black Catholics and our activities an offensive and defensive pastorate, and initiating communication with our counterparts in Africa."[10] The caucus pressed the hierarchy to address racism front and center and achieved its goal with the publication of "Brothers and Sisters To Us," the U.S. bishops' 1979 pastoral letter on racism, and then again in 1984 with the publication of "What We Have Seen and Heard: A Pastoral Letter on Evangelization from the Black Bishops of the United States."

The NOBC and the NBSC focused their attention on the education of the laity for leadership. Copeland explained in "What We Have Seen and Heard": "These two organizations carved out space for the development of leadership, for study, for spiritual and psychological formation, for the creative intellectual and pastoral interpretation of the Black Catholic experience in the United States." The liturgy was a primary focus of the "creative intellectual and pastoral interpretation," and throughout the United States, black Catholic religious and laity and white religious who served in black parishes and schools attended workshops, seminars, and conferences designed to educate them on putting into practice the Second Vatican Council's encouragement for inculturated liturgies. The most prominent person leading this liturgical renewal in the black Catholic community was Father Clarence Joseph Rufus Rivers of the Archdiocese of Cincinnati. An early liturgical innovator who cut his teeth in liturgical experimentation at Grailville in the 1950s, Father Rivers traveled the country teaching his *American Mass Program, Mass Dedicated to the Brotherhood of Man*, which brought African American spiritual music together with the Catholic Mass.[11] Later Rivers would be joined in this effort by the famous jazz pianist and convert to Roman Catholicism Mary Lou Williams, who wrote music, hymns, and masses for the Catholic Church using jazz idioms.[12] She too would travel the country teaching this new yet very familiar music to black and white Catholics. Both they and other emerging black Catholic liturgists were aided by the efforts of the NOBC, especially Gertrude Morris, who headed a program that educated and supported the emergence of black Catholic revivals held in dioceses throughout the nation.

In addition to music, black Catholics also sought to incorporate insights of black theology centered on the Sunday worship of the local parish and introduced the nationalist colors of red, green, and black into the vestments and altar linens as well as symbols and fabrics from Africa.[13] Such innovations were deemed wise and healing. Brother Cyprian Rowe explained:

> Catholics of African descent have suffered intensely from the sterility of liturgical rites, because they have somewhere in their bones a tradition of worship in which the sung and spoken words have been fused into celebrations of joy. Afro-Americans are therefore among the first to realize that it is a certain cultural ignorance, and even cultural imperialism that have resulted in their almost total exclusion from worship except as spectators."[14]

Reeducation and formation for ministry in the black Catholic community were among the chief purposes of the creation of the Institute for Black Catholic Studies in 1980 at Xavier University of Louisiana. At the behest of the National Black Catholic Clergy Caucus, Father Thaddeus Posey, O.F.M. Cap.; Dr. Norman Francis, president of Xavier University; Father Edward Branch; Father David Benz; Sister Jamie T. Phelps, O.P.; and Toinette M. Eugene developed a pilot program for the first session of the Institute for Black Catholic Studies for the summer of 1980.[15] The first members of the faculty were Father Cyprian Davis, teaching church history; Father Joseph Nearon, teaching Black Approaches to Theology; and Eugene, teaching Black Approaches to Catechesis. Sixteen students enrolled that summer. In future summers Sister Thea Bowman and Father Bede Abram, both widely regarded as the most influential faculty of the early period, joined the Institute for

Black Catholic Studies and helped to form its distinctly black and Catholic shape and spirit. Today the Institute for Black Catholic Studies draws upon African and African American Catholic religious and lay scholars to teach in its M.Th. program and in its certificate and enrichment programs that include a catechist formation program, a youth ministry program, and a leadership program designed to meet the needs of lay and religious leaders in black Catholic communities. Students come to study at the Institute for Black Catholic Studies from all around the United States and abroad, and they represent the full racial, cultural, gender, educational, economic, and theological diversity that makes up the myriad black Catholic communities of today. The Institute for Black Catholic Studies has become the primary academic, ministerial, and spiritual community of those working in the field of Black Catholic Studies.[16]

Black Catholic Studies Reclaims Its African Heritage

The most influential and significant text in Black Catholic Studies, *The History of Black Catholics in the United States* by Cyprian Davis, was in part a product of the Institute for Black Catholic Studies. Though not the first scholarship on the subject, *The History of Black Catholics in the United States* was and continues to be the only scholarly history to make the case for a vital and influential black Catholicism from the early Christian Church era in Africa through the twentieth century in the United States. A medievalist by training, Davis came to write black Catholic history out of his own need to be able to answer questions that black Catholics had for him when he gave talks at parishes in the 1960s about racial justice and desegregation. Invariably, when he was in a black parish to give a talk, black Catholics wanted to know about their own place in Catholic history. He explained, "Many Black Catholics had been taught that to become a Catholic was to shed one's history, one's culture, one's feelings, and one's mentality. We are to leave all the black stuff at the church door. This was especially the case for those who were entering seminaries and novitiates."[17] Davis was short on answers to give in those days, but he was intent to change that situation. Upon meeting the dean of U.S. Catholic historians, Monsignor John Tracy Ellis, Davis said he asked about black Catholic history, and Ellis told him there was little documentation on blacks and the Catholic Church, so it would not be easy to do any history regarding black Catholics. Davis said he took this as a challenge and not a defeat. He explained, "I had learned at Louvain that there are always documents, although not all were written on parchment or paper, and all are not easily accessible; we must often use ingenuity and even possess a certain flair to dig them up or unlock their existence. But they are there."[18] Thus began Davis's quest to educate himself on the history of black Catholics and ultimately to write a book that would both serve as a text for courses in Black Catholic Studies and extend an invitation to other historians interested in black Catholics and their history to take up the work with him. After many years of research in diocesan, religious, university, local, and Vatican archives, Davis published the award-winning text *The History of Black Catholics in the United States* in 1990.[19]

Davis began with the Bible and the place of Africans in the New Testament, pointing out that the first convert to Christianity recorded in the Acts of the Apostles was an Ethiopian. He presented the theological contributions of Africans such as Origen, Tertullian, Augustine, and Cyril of Alexandria to many fundamental doctrines of the Christian faith and showed the central role African Christians played in establishing the monastic tradition in Christianity, both cenobic and eremitic, and also how Catholic Christianity made inroads in parts of sub-Saharan Africa before the advent of the transatlantic slave trade in the fifteenth century. Davis then took on the history of black Catholics in the New World and the role slavery played in the lives of black Catholics and the wider Catholic Church in the United States, which had been overlooked in most general histories of U.S. Catholicism. Davis's research revealed vibrant black Catholic lay communities in the United States and the work of black Catholic women religious in evangelizing and educating their own communities in the nineteenth century. He carried this history up through the twentieth century, which saw the rapid growth of black Catholics in the 1940s, 1950s and 1960s. Davis's discussion of each period, person, organization, and movement concluded with an invitation for more scholars to take up these questions. Davis started a movement to recover black Catholic history by showing that indeed the sources for understanding, writing, and teaching the history of black Catholics were there.

The Ideas of God Blacks Carried With Them

Although Black Catholic Studies is a relatively new intellectual pursuit, persons of African descent have been a critical part of Christian history and theology since its beginnings, as Davis has ably shown. There has been an African presence in the Christian and especially the Catholic mosaic since the first century. It is only in the latter part of the twentieth and the first part of the twenty-first centuries, however, that these voices have been able to speak from a specifically black as well as Christian theological perspective. Black theology can be said to have begun when the first slave was brought to the shores of the Americas and the Caribbean in chains, but that articulation of faith in a God who knew them and identified with them has very strong African roots.

African peoples have a long and richly textured history of faith. Although each ethnic group has its own particularities, it can be argued that their worldviews and beliefs do overlap in many ways. They reveal a strong belief in a singular God who is the creator of all of reality, living and nonliving. African spirituality revolves around the belief in the presence of aspects of God, however named, in all things—earth and rocks, water, animals, and human beings. African Traditional Religions (ATR) are animistic (spirit-filled) and anthropocentric (human-centered). All of creation is seen as interrelated, and humans, in particular, are responsible for caring for and nurturing all of God's creation.[20] According to African scholar John Mbiti:

> Traditional religions are not primarily for the individual, but for his community of which he is a part. Chapters of African religion are written everywhere in the life of the community. And in traditional society there are no irreligious people. To be human is to belong to the whole community, and to do so involves participating in the beliefs, ceremonies, ritual and festivals of that community. . . . To be without religion amounts to a self-excommunication from the entire life of the society, and African peoples do not know how to exist without religion.[21]

Africans brought to the Americas as indentured servants and then slaves, mostly from West and Central Africa, did not come as empty vessels but as fully articulated human beings. They brought with them a cultural and religious sensibility that enabled them to forge new identities, not only on the slave ships but also in the new lands in which they found themselves.[22] Although often mixed together indiscriminately and deliberately to forestall insurrection, many knew the languages of other ethnic groups or learned them in order to communicate with each other to both foster insurrections and provide a sense of solidarity and security in the face of the unimaginable horror to which they were being exposed.

This knowledge and resilience enabled them to survive the degradation of slavery and its aftermath in the Americas. In the United States, many came already religiously engaged, either as followers of African traditional religions, as Muslims, or as Christians, particularly Roman Catholic.[23] The facts of this religious undergirding are just being revealed and explored today. What scholars are learning about these religions and their place in the African American experience is central to the theological work being done by scholars in Black Catholic Studies.

Most enslaved Africans were not introduced to Christianity formally until the beginning of the nineteenth century. This hesitance was due to the fear of slave owners that Christian instruction would make it impossible for them to hold their fellow Christians as slaves. Others feared the knowledge that would come with teaching the way of Jesus to men, women, and children forced to live as items of personal property. While this reluctance was more evident in Protestant than Catholic circles, many Catholic slaves, often baptized on slave ships, received cursory catechetical education that provided shallow guidance and spiritual solace. Other enslaved Catholics, however, persevered in attaining greater knowledge of their Catholic faith and were attracted by its many resemblances to their own beliefs in traditional religions that Protestant worship and theology dismissed. Historian Albert Raboteau has explained with great insight,

> The nature . . . of Catholic piety with its veneration of saints, use of sacramentals, and organization of religious fraternities among the

> slaves offered a supportive context for the continuity of African religious elements in recognizable form. In contrast, American Evangelical Protestantism, with its emphasis on biblical preaching, inward conversion, and credible accounts of the signs of grace, was not as conducive to syncretism with African theology and ritual.[24]

What is of critical importance for us to understand when considering the significance of African traditional religions to Black Catholic Studies and vice versa is that the faith of the Africans, syncretized with their traditional beliefs, as much of Catholicism has been syncretized over the centuries as different nations and peoples joined the Church, gave them a foundation upon which to build new lives and to protest the treatment they were receiving at the hands of their "masters." A good example of this is Catholic revivalism, a movement that emerged in the late eighteenth and early nineteenth centuries. Much has been written from a Protestant perspective on the two Great Awakenings, but very little from a Catholic view.[25] Catholics, however, participated fully in the Great Awakenings. Such participation led to the founding of the first United States religious order dedicated to the evangelization of Catholics, both white and African American.[26] The Catholic revivals of the nineteenth century were also bolstered by the itinerant work of the Jesuits, Passionists, and Redemptorists who revitalized the faith of many living on the frontier of Kentucky and Ohio who saw a priest and participated in the sacraments only once or twice a year.[27]

Parish revivals, also called parish missions, enabled many Catholics, black and white, to attain a deeper knowledge of their faith and to take fuller ownership of it. Startling events with outbursts of fervent preaching, weeping, and prayer, the Catholic parish mission was every bit a revival of the spirit and faith of Catholics who, because of the shortage of priests, had wandered away from their faith or forgotten the significance of the sacraments, especially the Eucharist. Black Catholics participated fully in these events, often bringing their own styles of music, dance, and spiritual exhortation. Catholic revivalism differed in its emphasis on the sacraments, especially Confession and the Eucharist. African Americans, especially former slaves, flocked to these events as they helped them transition from slavery to freedom, and from rudimentary knowledge of their faith to a stronger identification with and knowledge about Catholicism. Although initially integrated affairs, over time as parishes became more segregated, each ethnic or racial group held their own missions in their individual parishes.[28]

Growth in black Catholicism, however, was significantly restricted by the Church's resistance to the ordination of priests of African descent. Its hesitancy in accepting black men and women in existing religious orders forced them to create their own.[29] The failure of the Bishops at the Second Plenary Conference in Baltimore after the Civil War (1866) to adhere to Rome's request for the appointment of an apostolic vicar for the care of the formerly enslaved Catholics led to the departure of many who moved into Protestant denominations. The majority remained in the Catholic Church, however, and fought to defend the faith that was theirs and their continued presence in it, often in the face of the sustained prejudice of their brother and sister Catholics. Too often, this meant giving up their own culture and taking on that of the white ethnic Catholics with whom they worshipped. Even if allowed their own separate and segregated parish churches, the priests and parochial school teachers were usually, with rare exception in the case of the teachers, white. There was little done to accommodate or inculturate their own cultural and historical knowledge and experience into their faith. Indeed, many black Catholics often attended mass on Sundays and "church" on the same day at Baptist, Methodist, and other Protestant churches where they could celebrate God's action in their lives in more meaningful, culturally relevant ways.[30] In this way, they were able to maintain connections to their spiritual music and forms of worship that they would eventually have the opportunity to bring fully into their practice of Catholicism.

The 1960s brought significant change in the lives of all Catholics, but to black Catholics in particular. The civil rights movement caused blacks in all walks of life to question what they had historically accepted as the status quo. Black Catholics, encouraged as well by Vatican II's openness to the gifts, cultural and other, of Catholics of color, began to retrieve their heritage and proclaim it openly. The Constitution on the Sacred Liturgy (*Sacrosanctum Concilium*) as well as the Constitution on the Church (*Lumen Gentium*) and the Pastoral Constitution on the Church in the Modern World (*Gaudium et Spes*) provided doctrinal support for the movement of inculturation that began to draw Africans and African Americans into searching for innovative ways to incorporate the music they had created (from the spirituals to jazz and gospel songs) as well as their distinctive forms of extemporaneous prayer and fervent preaching styles from the depths of their anguished souls into the rituals that structured their faith, developing a renewed sense of liturgy as participatory and engaged.

Black Catholic Studies and Black Theology

At the same time, African Americans began to explore and claim their history in this country, Africa, and throughout the African Diaspora, recognizing a shared experience of suffering while acknowledging the myriad ways in which that experience had been expressed. Black theology, a theology of liberation that is one of, by, and for persons of African descent, emerged in the midst of these tectonic shifts in self-understanding for blacks and Catholics. It is an articulation of their faith, which had survived slavery, segregation, and second-class citizenship, the expression of their, too often contested, belief in their God-createdness, and a challenge to those who have asserted that theirs was an infantile faith rooted in ignorance.

> Black Theology proposed a critical reading of the US religious, cultural, and social condition in light of God's revelation. In the life and ministry, passion and death, and resurrection of Jesus of Nazareth, Black Theology distinguished Sacred Scripture as the word of God from Sacred Scripture as an ideology wielded for the religious, cultural, and social benefit of white Protestant and Catholic churches and their membership. It directly linked the struggle of black people for freedom and liberation to the message of the gospel.[31]

Black liberation theology is the fruit of African retentions, slave religion and its expression in song, story, prayer, sermon, and ritual, and the centuries' long struggle of persons of African descent in the United States to understand and celebrate the faith that has been both their respite and their burden. It is their response to God acting throughout human history on the side of those on the margins of history, the poor, the oppressed, and the invisible. The emergence of black liberation theology can be seen through the eyes of James H. Cone, a Methodist theologian and the first to articulate a liberating black theology, as the result of several critical catalysts: the nonviolent doctrine of the civil rights movement, the Black Power movement's emphasis on political action, and the influence of Malcolm X on the Black Nationalist movement, as well as the reaction of black scholars to the negative depiction set forth in Joseph Washington's *Black Religion*.[32] It was also influenced by the publication of the Black Power Statement by leading black Protestant ministers, who were members of the National Conference of Negro Churchman, and the founding of the Society for the Study of Black Religion,[33] all of which fostered the development of a theological consciousness that was innovative and praxis-oriented.[34] All of these movements and influences caused a major shift in the theological mindset of persons of African descent from a passive to activist perspective rooted in the Black Church's long history of radically engaging in efforts to affect the lives of their members.

Another leading black theologian, Gayraud Wilmore, describes black theology's development in three stages: first, the move "from the passive disobedience of the Civil Rights Movement to the provocative assertiveness of the Black Power movement"; second, the turn to the academy and the greater involvement of seminary professors as opposed to only radical black ministers; and third, an attempted return to the black community when black theology and its proponents began losing touch with the community and the Black Church.[35] Black theology has now moved into a fourth stage that includes a more global outreach and dialogue, an awareness of the equally critical issues of gender and class, and an ecumenical outlook as black Protestant theologians encountered and critically engaged with persons of African descent in the United States who are Roman Catholic, Muslim, Jewish and Buddhist, among other faith practitioners. These peoples have always been a part of the black community but have historically been overlooked and ignored, leaving the false illusion of a black community that is totally Protestant. These diverse voices are bringing forth the richness of the black religious presence in the United States and contributing significantly to the dialogue of church and state in the public square.

All of these stages, as well as the fuller history of Christianity to be found by including the black historical experience, are of critical importance and need to be included in any program of Catholic Studies. Black Catholic theologians and scholars in other disciplines involved in Black Catholic Studies continue to work to make this happen. They present a broader perspective on Roman Catholicism, revealing its global sweep and makeup, as an amalgam of many peoples, cultures, languages, and worldviews rather than the historically accepted European and Euroamerican one. It is, however, the present stage that is of special interest because it is the narrative of black Catholic theologians and other black Catholic religious scholars who began to articulate a systematic theology from a black Catholic perspective. Black Catholicism has suffered from a peculiar failure, on the one hand, of white Catholic scholars to include black Catholics in any meaningful way in their scholarly research and writings, and on the other, of black Protestant scholars to do the same. Thus, black Catholics find themselves, as all formerly "invisible" people do, as the ones who must defend the faith that is theirs themselves.

The segregation of most Catholic colleges and universities, North and South, during the first half of the twentieth century prohibited black Catholics from obtaining advanced degrees from Catholic institutions. If they went to Protestant or secular institutions of higher learning, they were without access to Catholic mentors and research sources. Fortunately, black Catholics did not allow these obstacles to hinder them. Their response to segregation, discrimination, and racial prejudice within their own Catholic faith, which they saw as truly black and authentically Catholic, was unmarred by the sin of racism. They fought with the hierarchy to gain access to schools and parishes, segregated but built with their own hands and money. They supported and were supported by the black women's religious orders, which despite the resistance of many in the Church developed schools, orphanages, and other programs that enabled free blacks and former slaves to become educated leaders in their parishes.[36]

Fathers Bede Abrams and Joseph Nearon were the first black Catholic theologians to speak and write about a black approach to theology that was inclusive of the historical and cultural experience of persons of African and Catholic descent in the Americas. Nearon, in a 1974 address to the Catholic Theological Society of America, challenged members by asking "to what extent is Roman Catholic theology racist and to what degree can reflection from the black experience enrich Catholic theology?"[37] His response to the first question was: yes, it was, a racism of omission found in its failure to treat the black experience as relevant. Responding to the second question, he critiqued Catholic theology as a product of the Western European cultural tradition, which saw only that culture as capable of transmitting the gospel message.

Following Nearon and Abrams, Sister Jamie Phelps, O.P., Toinette Eugene, M. Shawn Copeland, and Diana L. Hayes were the first of the new wave of black Catholic theologians to engage in theological research from a black Catholic perspective. Their work in ecclesiology, political theology, and liberation and womanist theologies provided the foundation for greater knowledge of the critical role of persons of African descent in Christianity and the Roman Catholic Church. They set forth the foundations for a black Catholic theology of liberation, grounded in the historical experience of black Catholics' centuries-long struggle to remain faithful, that reworked Catholic systematic theology, freeing it from its Western European captivity.[38]

Today, black Catholics are engaged in the development of a theology that truly speaks to and for them, expressing who they are and whose they are for the enlightenment of the entire Church.[39] Black theology in this Catholic context is "a paradigm shift" that cannot be confined to any one confessional, denominational, or ecclesial context. It is a contextual theology that emerges from the diversely rich historical experience of persons of African descent and presents their challenge of the "universal" or white theology that has been the norm. It responds, as do all theologies whatever their origins, to the needs, concerns, and experiences of those developing the theologies, in this instance, African Americans whose eyes have always been watching God.

With the founding of the Black Catholic Theological Symposium in 1978, black Catholic scholars established a forum for critical theological reflection among themselves and with other theologians, particularly Hispanics, as well as a nursery for budding black Catholic scholars. Hosted by the first order of black Catholic women religious, the inaugural meeting of the Black Catholic Theological Symposium was at the motherhouse of the Oblate Sisters of Providence in Baltimore, Maryland. Black Catholic scholars, primarily in the field of theology but joined by historians, liturgists, and canon lawyers, met to share their scholarship, to get to know each other, to establish a scholarly society dedicated to furthering the work and influence of Black Catholic theology, and to engage the scholarship of the colleges, universities, and seminaries with the real day-to-day needs and concerns of black Catholics. One of the most important results of this initial meeting of the Black Catholic Theological Symposium was the publication of *Theology: A Portrait in Black*,[40] which presented the papers given at the first meeting. Topics covered included values, self-concept, liturgy, catechesis, and spirituality. Crucial to the discussion of the first Black Catholic Theological Symposium meeting was "the development of a distinctively Black Catholic theological and pastoral response to the Black condition."[41]

In 1980, the Black Catholic Theological Symposium convened again to work with the theme of the *Nguzo Saba*. The papers from this meeting were never published, and the symposium did not meet again until 1991, when Jamie T. Phelps, one of the original participants, reconvened the group.[42] With only one exception, the Black Catholic Theological Symposium has met every year since 1991. Its membership reflects its commitment to the interdisciplinary nature of Black Catholic Studies and includes theologians, historians, canon and civil lawyers, and scholars in English, classics, psychology, spirituality, sociology, ethics, liturgy, music, Scripture, philosophy, cultural studies, and even pharmacy. It includes established black Catholic scholars, black Catholic graduate students pursuing doctorates in fields related to Black Catholic Studies, and non-black Catholic scholars whose work is concretely engaged in the concerns of Black Catholic Studies. Each fall the BCTS meets at the home institution of one of its members. In 2007 it published the first volume of *The Journal of the Black Catholic Theological Symposium*. The inaugural journal included articles about Catholicism and the color line, the Jesuits and African marriage practices in colonial Zimbabwe, challenges black faculty face when seeking tenure, black Catholics on the social frontier, and economic ethics and health care.

During the symposium, members present their works in progress, sponsor a keynote address by one of the members for the benefit of the host institution, and engage with members of the local black Catholic community of the host city in what it calls "Listening Sessions." The purpose of those sessions is to bring the concerns of the local community to the awareness of the scholars and to invite the local community to make use of the resources black Catholic scholars can provide. The listening-sessions tradition is integral to the field of Black Catholic Studies because the local black Catholic community was and continues to be the primary reason for the field's existence, and the needs and concerns of everyday black Catholic women, men, and children continue to drive the work of black Catholic scholars. The listening sessions also point to the continued influence that black theology has on the field of Black Catholic Studies, in that black theology is a living expression of black faith that continues to expand and develop, enriching itself with the ongoing interaction of persons of faith with their God in good times and bad. With its contemporary focus on race, class, and gender, and the added voices of womanist scholars, it serves as a constant challenge to Christianity and its churches that the message of Jesus has still not been fully practiced and that past sins and omissions will no longer be tolerated.

In 2000, *Theological Studies*, a leading Catholic theological journal, devoted an entire issue to "The Catholic Reception of Black Theology." Black Catholic theologians, who since the 1970s endeavored to engage their fellow Catholic theologians in one of the most revolutionary paths of theology of the late twentieth century, regarded this issue as a significant breakthrough. Not since 1974 had *Theological* Studies published an article on black theology and its relationship to Catholic theology.[43] The journal's focus on black theology in 2000 acknowledged that black Catholic theologians play a significant role in the theology of the Catholic Church. Diana L. Hayes, M. Shawn Copeland, Cyprian Davis, Jamie T. Phelps, and Bryan N. Massingale analyzed the place and role of black theology in Catholic theology from the perspectives of systematic theology, moral theology, and church history. Founding black theologian James H. Cone also contributed to the issue. Instead of responding to each article specifically, Cone engaged, questioned, and positively critiqued "the basic contours of an emergent theology committed to the experience of *being Black and Catholic*."[44] He challenged black Catholic theologians as well as white Catholic theologians to continue to fight against the covert racism of society and academia, recognizing that indeed things have changed but the struggle against racism is not over.[45] This conversation helped to set the agenda for Black Catholic Studies for the next decade.

The Current State of Black Catholics and Black Catholic Studies

What started out as a movement and a ministry to keep Catholicism a vital faith and power in black communities and to prepare black Catholics for leadership in the Church now includes a field of studies that encompasses history, sociology, art, music, education, psychology, literature, spirituality, liturgy, ethics, and of course, at its core, theology. Today aspects of Black Catholic Studies may be found in Catholic colleges and universities, seminaries, parishes, Catholic elementary, middle and secondary schools, and increasingly in secular universities throughout the United States. The most important center of Black Catholic Studies, and the only one that offers a degree in Black Catholic Studies, continues to be the Institute for Black Catholic Studies at Xavier University of Louisiana in New Orleans. Since 1990, the Archdiocese of Chicago has sponsored the Augustus Tolton Program in Ministry at the Catholic Theological Union. The Tolton Program is named for the first recognized African American priest in the United States,[46] dedicated to training black Catholic lay leaders for parishes and ministries in the Archdiocese of Chicago. Students in the Tolton Program earn a master's degree in pastoral theology and receive formation for service in black Catholic communities. Other more modest ministry-oriented programs in Black Catholic Studies can be found at Loyola Marymount University (Los Angeles), the University of Portland (Oregon), and the Sr. Thea Bowman Program sponsored by the Archdiocese of Louisville, to mention a few. In addition, many diocesan Offices of Black Catholics and Multicultural Offices offer continuing education courses that focus on black Catholic topics, but none of these institutes or programs has a full-time faculty. They call on scholars in the various areas represented in Black Catholic Studies to teach courses in African American history, theology, homiletics, Catholic liturgy, and aesthetics.

There are also summer conferences, such as the Lyke Conference and the Unity Explosion, that are sponsored by dioceses and independent black Catholic organizations that offer a multitude of learning opportunities to black Catholics and others working in black Catholic communities. These conferences give black Catholics from around the country the chance to meet, to talk about the challenges they face as black Catholics, and to celebrate the richness of their traditions. In addition, once every five years the National Black Catholic Congress convenes to give black Catholic lay and religious leaders the opportunity to assess the status of blacks in the Roman Catholic Church in the United States, and to plan and implement programs to meet the needs of black Catholics around the country.[47]

Though no Catholic or secular university offers a doctoral program focusing on Black Catholic Studies, it is quite interesting to look at recent dissertations and to see the inroads that Black Catholic Studies have made in departments of history, sociology, music, education, and religious studies. At one of the newest doctoral programs in theology with a focus on the U.S. Catholic experience at the University of Dayton, two of its first seven dissertations have been about black Catholic historical topics, one on the history of black Catholics in Phoenix, Arizona, and the other on Daniel Rudd and the *American Catholic Tribune*, the first black Catholic newspaper, founded in the 1870s in Ohio.

In addition to new scholars taking up topics in Black Catholic Studies, well-established scholars are also taking a new look at their fields and are either identifying new research topics for themselves or expanding on and further developing topics that relate to black Catholics and Black Catholic Studies. Among the most significant of these recent studies is Diane Batts Morrow's award-winning history of the first black Catholic order of women religious, *Persons of Color and Religious at the Same Time: The Oblate Sisters of Providence, 1828–1860*.[48] Others include *Uncommon Faithfulness: The Black Catholic Experience*, edited by M. Shawn Copeland, LaReine-Marie Mosely, S.N.D., and Albert Raboteau (2009); Copeland's *Enfleshing Freedom: Body, Race and Being* (2010); and *Racial Justice and the Catholic Church*, by Bryan N. Massingale (2010). Theologians who are not black and Catholic are also working in the field of Black Catholic Studies. This suggests the broad reach and appeal that its scholarship currently has. Most recently, theologian Jon Nilson of Loyola University in Chicago has written *Hearing Past the Pain*, in which he acknowledges his own racism and makes the case for why Catholic theologians must take black theology seriously. Another seminal work, *Interrupting White Privilege: Catholic Theologians Break the Silence*, edited by Laurie Cassidy and Alex Mikulich, affirms what black Catholics have asserted:

> The silence of white theologians bespeaks the contradiction between our claims for a universal, ontological human equality and the reality of the social, political, and economic privilege white theologians and ethicists consciously and unconsciously accept and assume. . . .
>
> As Roman Catholic theologians we intend [to] signal that silence or neutrality in the face of this evil is no longer acceptable in the theological academy, church, or society.[49]

Scholars in the fields of history, liturgy, and music who are not black and Catholic are also taking up topics in or related to Black Catholic Studies and are adding to the conversation an ever-expanding body of published research.[50]

A Statistical Overview of the State of Black Catholicism

Though the theology and history of black Catholics are the most compelling aspects of the field of Black Catholic Studies, scholars must also pay attention to the contemporary lives and practices of black Catholics today. Studies such as the Pew Forum on Religion and Public Life and its 2008 "U.S. Religious Landscape Survey" are useful in this endeavor. This study is noteworthy because it seems to be among the first to break African American Catholics out of the general Catholic population and out of the general African American Christian population, which is predominately Protestant, to reveal their views and experience. Scholars—or anyone for that matter—interested in who black Catholics in the early twenty-first century are and what is important to them can learn a great deal from this study. This ability to focus on what makes black Catholics similar to but also different from the rest of the American Catholic Church and similar to yet different from the African

American Protestant community is a very critical ongoing aspect of Black Catholic Studies.

According to the Pew study, African American Catholics in 2008 made up 5 percent of the Roman Catholic community in the United States.[51] Surprisingly, the American West has the highest percentage of African American Catholics, with 11 percent, followed by 6 percent in the Northeast, 4 percent in the Midwest, and 4 percent in the South. This particular statistic is quite interesting. Those working in Black Catholic Studies must ask what is happening in the West for it to eclipse the traditional strongholds of black Catholicism in the South, particularly southwestern Louisiana and the Gulf Coast, and Baltimore in the Middle Atlantic region, which do not appear to be growing.

This study also documents that African Americans are more likely than any other group—87 percent—to describe themselves as being a member of a religious group or community, followed by Hispanics at 85 percent, and the general public at 83 percent. This high level of religious affiliation among African Americans is supported by the fact that over 50 percent report weekly attendance at religious services; 76 percent declare that they pray every day; and 88 percent declare absolutely certainty that God exists. Of the religiously unaffiliated African Americans, 48 percent of them said they pray daily and 70 percent say they are absolutely certain that God exists. It is important to note that of the total Catholic population, only 72 percent assert that God absolutely exists, while when broken out from the general Catholic population, 80 percent of African American Catholics surveyed assert that God absolutely exists, an exact eight-point difference on either side of African Americans who are religiously affiliated and the total Catholic population. These statistics particularly support a central observation of Black Catholic Studies: Black Catholics are integrally shaped by and are a part of the black and Catholic communities. Their religious identities and commitments are rooted in both locations. Other statistics from this study bear this reality out as well.

The Pew study's statistics related to political and social perspectives of African Americans reveal even more interesting information about the thinking of black Catholics at the turn of the twenty-first century. Nearly thirty points separate black Catholics from the rest of the Catholic population when it comes to political party affiliation. Seventy-four percent of black Catholics identify as Democrats or say they lean Democratic in their voting, while only 48 percent of the total Catholic population does so. Seventy-nine percent of African American Protestants are Democrats or lean Democratic in voting. Politically, black Catholics are both more liberal than all other Catholics, with 26 percent self-identifying as liberal and with only 18 percent of all Catholics accepting that political perspective. While 45 percent of all Catholics and African American Protestants say that abortion should be illegal in all or most cases, only 35 percent of African American Catholics agree with this. And while only one-third of all Catholics say that homosexuality should be discouraged by society, 37 percent of African American Catholics and nearly half of all African American Protestants agree with that statement. These findings show how influential cultural traditions and values are in shaping the worldview and social commitments of black Catholics. While on one hand black Catholics are markedly more liberal in their politics than their brothers and sisters in the Catholic Church, they exhibit a more conservative bent that is much more in keeping with their African American Protestant sisters and brothers on issues related to homosexuality. How and why this is so is an important line of inquiry that scholars in Black Catholic Studies should explore and develop more fully. However, the most important statistics from the Pew study that Black Catholic Studies scholars should attend to are those related to religious service attendance. These statistics are crucial because without a practicing black Catholic community there is little reason for the continuation of the field of study. Catholicism is first and foremost a religion defined by community and communal worship in the Mass. However, when it comes to Mass attendance, African American Catholics are less likely than the total Catholic population and the religiously affiliated African American population to be in the pews on Sunday. In the 2008 survey, only 36 percent of African American Catholics said they attended religious services weekly, while 42 percent of the total Catholic population reported attending weekly religious services, and 53 percent of religiously affiliated African Americans said they attended weekly religious services.

This seventeen-point difference in weekly religious service attendance of religiously affiliated African Americans and six-point difference between all Catholics and African American Catholics cannot be ignored. It suggests that there must be something that happens or does not happen at Sunday Mass that causes black Catholics to stay away. Why are African American Catholics less inclined to attend weekly Mass than other Catholics? Is the Mass not meeting the cultural and spiritual needs of African American Catholics? Is their absence due to the high rate of closings of predominantly African American parishes, especially in urban areas? Are they disengaged because of the low number of African American Catholic religious leaders, priests, sisters, and brothers? Do they stay away because of the closing of so many black Catholic parochial schools in inner cities? Are some Black Catholics deciding to worship in other Christian communities or in schismatic African American Catholic communities such as Imani Temple? Are they converting to Islam or other religions? Are African American Catholics disappointed by the lack of attention they continue to receive from leaders of the Church? All of these are questions that scholars working in Black Catholic Studies need to raise and insist on responses to from within the Church in order to promote and support viable black Catholic communities in the twenty-first century. These are also questions that those working in the wider field of Catholic Studies need to address.

Black Catholic Studies is an integral part of Catholic Studies, and the voices of black Catholics, in common with Hispanic, Native American, Asian, and African Catholic voices, bring new insights as well as renewed challenges to the Catholic Church. Once thought unworthy of bearing the weight of the gospel message, these cultures are now the cutting edge of the gospel proclamation in the United States and throughout the world.

13 Asian American Catholic Experience and Catholic Studies

LINH HOANG, O.F.M.

A standard narrative of American religious history has relied on the Puritan sense of a common purpose. John Winthrop's famous "City on a Hill" speech to the Pilgrims is emblematic of this. This narrative of election and purpose has shaped the way other religions have been measured. But in doing so it has neglected the voice of religious dissenters and the significance of racial diversity within the ranks of American Christians. Likewise, social science and historical studies of immigrants and refugees tend to gloss over religious affiliation and focus mainly on adaptation or assimilation processes into American culture. Both religious history and immigration studies tend to compartmentalize the full range of experience of immigrants and refugees to the neglect of the importance of religion in their transition to American life.

The eminent scholar of American Catholicism Jay P. Dolan observes that the recent turn in interest to immigration in American religious history has been attributed more to attention paid to social history and other social developments rather than an explicit attention to the religious impact on immigration.[1] Even with this promising turn, there is still rather little attention paid to the study of immigration in American religious history. In discussing the social mobility and acceptance of American Catholics, Sydney Ahlstrom states that individual Catholics adapted better to America but as a "group had been greatly retarded by a constant incoming tide of immigration which actually reached its peak in the early twentieth century."[2] He adds that by the end of War World II, American Catholics were no longer seen as an "immigrant faith."[3] Catholic immigrants blended into the American landscape and were wholeheartedly embraced as "normal" Americans. This complex process of immigration is seen as only a process of a one-sided assimilation to become Americans. The oversight and even antipathy toward immigration needs to be rectified, especially since immigrants and refugees continue to knock at the doors of America's borders, bringing with them a host of religious expressions and practices that are not easily assimilated.

The reality of American history is that immigrants and refugees have contributed not only to the identity of American religions, but also, and especially, to American Catholicism. From the beginning of the foundation of America, down to our own time, the American Catholic Church, first established by English, Irish, German, and Italian immigrants, has been continually reshaped by newcomers down to the most recent arrivals of Vietnamese, Indonesians, and Filipinos. The immigrant presence in the Church, however, has involved many enduring challenges. These challenges include learning to adapt and live within the dominant culture, which at times has required excluding other immigrant groups or even denying one's own cultural background. As these enduring challenges resurface now among Asian immigrants, it is not only a reminder of the immigrant history of religious America but also reemphasizes the continual need of the American Catholic Church to welcome the newcomers.

This essay will describe the present situation of Asian American Catholics in reference to the complicated history of Asians in America, focusing upon the distinctive features of their immigrant experience within the larger Catholic story. First, a description of the presence of Asian Americans within the larger U.S. population will be given. This sets the scene for understanding the specific issues and challenges that will be presented. Connected to this is a brief introduction to the racial factor in Asian American experience, beginning with a discussion of the racially charged label "Asian American." This label perpetuates "Asians" as racially "other" and as ethnically homogenous despite their cultural diversity. Second, an examination of how Asian Americans are considered generally in American religious histories reveals a relative neglect of their experiences. Only recently have these histories included the Asian American religious communities but then only by paying attention mainly to "Asian religions" in a way that effectively intensifies the invisibility of the Asian American Christian expression. Third, a diagnosis of generational identity issues will show how second and subsequent generations oscillate between single ethnic and pan-Asian identities—something that did not happen with European immigrants. Fourth, there will be a discussion of the way different Asian ethnic groups have responded to the American Catholic Church. The focus will be on the efforts of Asian Americans in building ethnic churches, organizing small communities, encouraging vocations, and lobbying for church leaders. Finally, I will hope to show how the distinctive character of the Asian American Catholics will not only diversify American Catholicism but also add an intriguing chapter to Catholic Studies, because of some of the distinctive experiences they bring that were not found in European immigration.

Asian American Presence

Asian people have been present in the United States of America for over two centuries. During this time, they integrated into American life and have contributed widely to the society. According to the 2000 U.S. Census, the Asian population was counted at about 11 million, or 4.3 percent of the 300 million-plus people in the United States (see Tables 13.1 and 13.2). It is projected that by the middle of the twenty-first century, 10 percent of the U.S. population will be Asian.

Within this Asian population, the religious affiliation of the Asian American community is quite diverse with no single religion claiming a majority of followers. Interestingly, however, over 35 percent of this population claims Christianity as their religion. Two-thirds of those Christians (or 21 percent of the total Asian population) are Catholics. They constitute in turn 2 percent of the total American Catholic population (see Table 13.3).[4] Asian Catholics are more numerous in the

Table 13.1. Asian Americans by Ethnic Origin (2000)

Chinese	2,734,841
Filipino	2,364,815
Asian Indian	1,899,599
Korean	1,228,427
Vietnamese	1,223,736
Japanese	1,148,932

Source: U.S. Census Bureau, *Asian American Population 2000*

Table 13.2. States with the Highest Number of Asian Americans

California	4,155,685
New York	1,169,200
Hawaii	703,232
Texas	644,193
New Jersey	524,356
Illinois	473,649
Washington	395,741
Florida	333,013
Virginia	304,559
Massachusetts	264,814

Source: U.S. Census Bureau, *Asian American Population 2000*. These figures include people of mixed ethnicity.

United States than all Asians of the Protestant denominations combined. Moreover, they are more numerous than any Asian religious group. This statistic is noteworthy because the majority of the Asian countries, excluding the Philippines and Korea, shows less than 8 percent Christian affiliation. While the survey did not break down the numbers by specific ethnic group, it did make the assumption that to measure religions within each ethnic group in the United States one needs to look at the proportions for different religions within that particular Asian country. This may not paint a completely accurate picture,

Table 13.3. Dioceses with the Largest Asian American Populations

Los Angeles	1, 317,890
Honolulu	985,899
Brooklyn	650,868
San Jose	474,218
Oakland	473,218
San Francisco	445,347
Orange	440,577
Seattle	407,738
New York	327,491
Chicago	323,865

Source: United States Conference of Catholic Bishops, 2001

but it becomes a rather safe assumption, since the majority of Asians is foreign-born. Regarding Asian Americans, the largest number of Catholics is found among Filipinos, Vietnamese, and Chinese, with growing numbers of Catholics among other Asian and Pacific ethnics.

Even with this presence, the experiences of Asian American Catholics have not been fully recognized in the American Catholic Church. There have been efforts, beginning with the example of Archbishop Joseph Sadoc Alemany of San Francisco, who initiated ministry to Chinese Catholics in California in the late nineteenth century.[5] Laws restricting Asian immigration and citizenship in the late nineteenth and early twentieth centuries thwarted his efforts, however. Efforts to minister to Asian Americans basically came to a halt and would remain in abeyance until late 1975, when the Church responded to the large influx of Vietnamese refugees after the fall of Saigon and withdrawal of U.S. troops from that country. Since that time the Church has grown more attentive to the growing Asian American Catholic community.

With the publication of the 2001 American bishops' statement "Asian and Pacific Presence: Harmony in Faith," efforts have been made to organize Asian and Pacific Catholics on a national level.[6] Currently, the disparate groups of Asian and Pacific Catholics are brought together in the National Asian and Pacific Catholic Organization (NAPCO). The effort to build this organization has been quite formidable as its members confront past obstacles and future challenges that reflect the challenges of the broader Asian American experience. In the fall of 2007, two Asian American bishops gathered a group of consultants to discuss plans to organize the Asian American Catholic community vis-à-vis the newly formed Office for Cultural Diversity at the U.S. Conference of Catholic Bishops (USCCB). This initiative would take into consideration the different ethnic communities efforts to organize as a Catholic community. This is initiative is still in its early stages but has much support from the different communities.

Defining "Asian American"

Terms such as "Mongolian," "Asiatic," and "Oriental" have been part of the racial vocabulary in America for decades. The term "Asian American" originated only during the late 1960s, as part of a progressive effort that built on the black civil rights movement. Ethnic group identification had in the past been the primary label for describing racial difference—early typologies often referred to a particular race such as Filipino or Chinese. "Asian-American" reflected both a nationalist identity—*Asian* to emphasize race, *American* to emphasize "non-foreignness"—as well as an attempt to dispose of the loaded term "Oriental."[7] It should also be noted that the term "Asian" has traditionally referred to identify only three Asian ethnic groups: Chinese, Japanese, and Korean. I have used "Asian" more broadly to include all ethnics who were born and whose ancestors came from the Asian continent and the Pacific Islands.

The "Asian American" label attempts to identify foreign-born and American-born individuals of Asian ancestry. It also incorporates persons of Asian ancestry who were American permanent residents and citizens and to distinguish them from a white majority, while acknowledging commonality with other racial and ethnic groups. Interestingly, "Asian American" was not decreed by governmental or other external authorities, but rather was coined mainly by U.S.-born Chinese, Filipino, and Japanese college students and community-based Asian organizations on the West Coast and in New York.[8] Many were second- and third-generation Asian Americans. For some, this label has worked well to unite disparate ethnics; for others, it has created an uneasy alliance, especially when many of these cultures have been involved in historical conflict with one another and have histories of mutual hatred (such as between Koreans and Japanese).

The United States government—through the apparatus of immigration laws and policies and through the processes of naturalization and citizenship—has attempted to identify who Asians are in America. These laws established racial differences through the construction of ethnic identities.[9] Starting with the first naturalization act of 1790, the right to naturalization was restricted to "free white persons."[10] The exclusionary laws against Chinese in 1882, against South Asians in 1917, against Koreans and Japanese in 1924, and against Filipinos in 1934 were all restrictions placed on Asians based on race. Though Congress never enacted a law that specifically names "Asians" or "Orientals" as an Asiatic racial category, legal theorist Neil Gotanda has argued that the sequence of laws in 1882, 1917, 1924, and 1934 that excluded immigrants from China, Japan, India, and the Philippines, combined with the series of repeal acts overturning these exclusions, construct a common racial categorization for Asians that depended on consistently racializing each national-origin group as "nonwhite."[11] Thus, to become a citizen meant also becoming white because during this period citizenship was restricted to whites and freed blacks (who consequently were "legally" white). In 1924, Congress passed the Johnson-Reed Act (also known as the Immigration Act of 1924), which restricted immigration from many European nations and denied even a token quota to most Asians. The law barred all immigrants who were ineligible for citizenship, and all Asians and Pacific Islanders who had been deemed ineligible on racial grounds by a 1922 Supreme Court decision.[12]

The requirements for citizenship changed with a series of Asian exclusion repeal acts. The first was the Magnuson Act of 1943, which gave permission for a small quota of Chinese immigrants and also allowed the Chinese to become naturalized citizens. By the end of World War II, the Luce-Celler Act of July 2, 1946, allowed Indians and Filipinos to become naturalized citizens and established a small quota for Indian immigration. As a companion to Philippine independence, President Truman signed the Act and provided an immigration quota for the Filipinos. Finally, the Act of August 1, 1950 (also known as the Organic Act), allowed Guamians to become naturalized citizens as part of a legislation that established self-rule for Guam. The succession of these repeal acts dramatically transformed the status of immigrants of all Asian origins from that of "aliens ineligible for citizenship" to that of "naturalized citizen."[13] In 1952, the McCarran-Walter Act made it possible for Asians not born in the United States to become naturalized. Although the act set an immigration quota of one hundred per year for Asian countries, the entire atmosphere of the Asian American community was changed; those who had been in the United States since the turn of the century were now able to make the United States their home country for the first time. Thousands of Asian Americans acquired U.S. citizenship in the 1950s, when the country was recovering from World War II. After that, the major shift for Asian immigrants to the United States came with the Hart-Celler Immigration and

Nationality Act of 1965,[14] which abolished the restrictive national-origin quotas and exclusions. This laid the groundwork of the broadening of the identities of "Asian Americans." The Hart-Celler Act raised the quota to twenty thousand per year for Asian countries—the same as for European countries. Aliens were now classified by country of birth rather than by race, since all named racial barriers were eliminated from the U.S. immigration acts. This new sense of justice and equality for all made it possible for massive numbers of Asians to come to the United States.

The recent expansion of the label to include variations such as "Asian and Pacific Islander" and "Asian Pacific American" reflects the evolution of the racialization process. Pacific Islanders have different origins and experiences from Asians. Pacific Islanders are those who either themselves, or their ancestors, have migrated from various islands comprising Melanesia, Micronesia, and Polynesia. Many of the islands of the Pacific, including American Samoa and Guam, are territories of the United States, and their residents enjoy status as U.S. nationals or as citizens, which allows them to bypass normal immigration restrictions when entering the United States. However, they are regularly included under the Asian American label. We can no longer rely on the original trio of Chinese, Japanese, and Korean immigrants, to which must now be added arrivals since 1965 from Vietnam, Laos, Cambodia, and the Pacific Islands.

Asian American Catholics in American Religious History

Studies in American religious history have neglected the impact of Christianity in the lives of Asian Americans. Recent studies that have begun to examine the religious experiences of Asian immigrants give attention to mainly those non-Christian Asian religious traditions. This attention only supports the idea that Asian Americans are innately foreign, practicing a strange religion that is difficult to understand. The assumption that Asian Americans are predominately adherents of Buddhism or Islam also implies that they cannot be followers of a Western religion such as Christianity. This suggests that even if Asians were to convert to Christianity, they are still suspect—that is, not fully Christian. The few contemporary American religious historians who do give attention to Asian American Christians assume that they are Christian out of a desire for assimilation or else simply find that Asian "non-Christian" religious communities are intriguing to study. Through these interpretations, Asian cultural difference is then either erased beneath the canopy of white Christianity or constructed as the untouchable "other."

In 1993, in an essay reviewing the scholarship in American religious history in the 1980s, Martin E. Marty bemoaned the absence of research into Asian American religious history.[15] In his own recent project on modern American religion, Marty gives significant attention to the history of Asians in the United States as victims of discrimination and purveyors of non-Christian religions. He also briefly discusses Asian American Christianity, but not the contribution that Asian Americans have made to Christianity. Overall though, his treatment of the Asian American religious experience is still limited to secondary sources.[16] This limitation is understandable because so few scholars are examining Asian American religious history. Less clear is why more than ten years after Marty's article appeared, only a few scholars are examining Asian American religious history.

Influenced by the social history and comparative religious studies movements, some recent American religious histories have given greater attention to the growing presence of Eastern religious beliefs and practices in the United States but still refrain from focusing on the Christian-centered and intellectual history-oriented study of Asian American religious history. For example, the latest edition of Catherine Albanese's *America: Religions and Religion* devotes an entire chapter to Eastern religions in the United States while neglecting the participation of Asian Americans in Christian churches. This shows the tendency to favor comparative religions approach in constructing the narrative about Asian Americans rather than studying Asian American Christian practices. Also, sociologist Pyong Gap Min has pointed out that studies of Asian Americans do not in general consider their religious affiliation.[17]

The studies of Asian American religious affiliation have generally followed two major approaches: pluralist and assimilationist. The pluralist histories interpret Asian Americans through the lens of religious difference. The inclusion of Eastern religions implies the still-exotic nature of Asians and also masks the large number of Asian Christians. The assimilationists view the Asian American experience as one leading to inevitable cultural assimilation. Asian Americans will meld into the larger society, effectively erasing any type of recognizable distinctiveness. Another sentiment seems to infer that religious commitment is not even important for Asian Americans. A leading religious historian, Sidney Ahlstrom, claimed that among Chinese and Japanese Americans "ethnic religious commitments have not figured prominently in their self-consciousness as peoples."[18] These, and similar sentiments, provide the researcher license to overlook the religious—specifically the Christian commitments of Asian Americans.

This becomes even more complicated as other historians weigh in on the religious makeup of America. There appears to be among them more comfort with religious diversity rather than racial or ethnic difference. Edwin Gaustad, an American religious historian, illustrates this point of view in a popular survey textbook. He associates Asian immigrants with Asian religions:

> Similarly, (as in the case of Chinese immigrants), the influx of Japanese along the West Coast, even more in Hawaii, led to sharp restrictions of those who would introduce Buddhism and Shinto, even as the Chinese had brought with them Confucianism and Taoism. Nonetheless, despite unmistakable anti-Oriental prejudices and actions, Asian religions established their beach heads all along the Pacific shores, never to be successfully dislodged therefrom.[19]

Gaustad values the religious diversity created by Asian immigrants, but he is less sanguine about racial diversity. He considers racial segregation a failure on the part of American religion: "The nation's religious forces were no more effective in promoting a blindness to race with respect to the Oriental than they had been with respect to the black." The inability of early missionaries and schools to Christianize and Americanize the Asians created "ethnically restricted churches." For Gaustad, ethnic-specific congregations do not have innate value because their existence is primarily a reflection of white American racial consciousness. He concludes that though ethnicity could be "sometimes seen as enriching and brightening the whole fabric of

American society, it could also be regarded as detrimental to social cohesion and religious destiny."[20] As racial minorities, Asian Americans often find they lack full acceptance by members of the dominant society regardless of their level of religious and cultural assimilation and committed participation.

Recent studies of post-1965 immigrant groups, mostly non-European, have neglected to examine the role of race in their religious experiences. For example, neither of two major edited volumes, *Gatherings in Diaspora* and *Religion and the New Immigrants*,[21] on contemporary immigrant groups' religions has treated race as a significant category of analysis, although each has paid enough attention to the role of gender.

Experiences of Asian American Catholics

Since the mid–nineteenth century, individual dioceses and religious orders have extended their mission to help Asian immigrants. A highlight of these ministerial efforts was the successful outreach to the large number of Southeast Asian refugees who came to the United States in the mid-1970s. The American Catholic Church helped resettle many of the refugees through sponsorship, donations, and employment. Efforts prior to that time offer mixed results stemming from the attitudes of some Catholics toward the Asian population. The general feeling against Asians in America likely shaped these attitudes. Asian Americans encountered the same racism in the churches as they had in the larger society. The racism that was endured by Asian Americans with the exclusionary laws did not ease within the Church, as many had hoped.

The first Chinese priest to work in the United States was Fr. Thomas Cian.[22] He was invited by Archbishop Alemany of San Francisco in 1854 to work with the growing number of Chinese in the diocese. Archbishop Alemany believed that with a Chinese-speaking priest, the small group of Chinese Catholic could grow. What Cian encountered was a few Chinese Catholics widely scattered (some fifty or sixty in San Francisco and the mining regions), and a hostile, racist environment (many Catholics on the West Coast had difficulty believing Cian was a priest because he was Chinese). Cian wrote in 1855: "I cannot see much prospect of doing much good here." He petitioned to build a small chapel for Chinese Catholics in San Francisco, having witnessed the inroads being made by Protestant clergymen among the Chinese. No chapel was ever built. At the heart of Cian's difficulty was that he did not speak the same dialect as the majority of the Chinese in San Francisco. Discouraged by his lack of success, Cian returned to China via Italy in 1865. This did not diminish the need for mission to the Chinese immigrant population.

Paulist Father Ignatius Stark initiated the first (and at that time only) Chinese mission in the West Coast in 1902. This began at Old St. Mary's Parish, located in the heart of Chinatown in San Francisco. Sunday school was offered to the children, but the parish's largest draw were the courses in English taught there. The mission became a foundation to help the growing Chinese immigrant population. This work was not appreciated by all in the American Catholic Church. For example, James Bouchard, S.J., questioned the immigration of Chinese into America in a published article in the San Francisco *Catholic Guardian* in 1873. He questioned the sincerity of the Chinese, especially since the efforts to evangelize were not very fruitful. He opined, "They are an inferior race of people and consequently cannot be a safe class . . . of people in our country."[23]

These sentiments, though, did not deter the Japanese and Chinese from converting to Catholicism. The growing number of converts pushed the West Coast American Catholic community to minister to them. As a result, parish life for the Chinese and Japanese developed along American lines. Little that was distinctively Japanese or Chinese penetrated the Japanese or Chinese Catholic parish, at least in terms of devotional practices and parish societies.[24]

Filipinos were another early Asian immigrant group in America. They were the largest Asian Catholic community, and the Catholic Church was concerned about preserving and protecting their faith against the strong influence and powerful reach of the Protestants both in the Hawaiian Islands and on the U.S. mainland. There were no Filipino priests available to work among the growing Filipino immigrants. Writes Jay Dolan, "Protestant missions, sponsored by such groups as the YMCA, attempted to assist the Filipinos, and raised fears in Catholic circles that the Filipino was being lost to the Protestants."[25] These fears were well founded. A Filipino immigrant said that to be accepted, "we thought that being Protestant would help, but it did not really matter much. We were different and different was equated with inferiority. We were treated like dirt by the Americans, regardless of whether we professed to be Catholics or Protestants."[26]

The pervading theme in the history and experience of Filipinos in the United States has been exclusion. This feeling of exclusion is not an exception but seems to be the reality for most of the Asian immigrants. Thus, as a reaction to this form of institutionalized discrimination and exclusion, the Asian immigrants and refugees have established their own ethnic churches and parishes. A singular complaint of many Asian Catholics is that the America Catholic Church forces them to be like everybody else.[27] Asian Catholics have practiced their faith in their own country and believe that in their new country they should be able to maintain their particular cultural expression of Catholicism.

As racial minorities, Asian Americans often find they lack full acceptance by members of the dominant society regardless of their level of cultural assimilation. This becomes more painful when the church that many converted to and embraced in their home country excludes them when they arrive in the United States. The most striking example of this is in parish life today, when Asian Americans encounter parishes that are already set in their ways or maintaining a survival strategy rather than a sense of hope for new membership and development. Thus, the different Asian ethnic groups are not provided with masses in their language, religious education programs, or leadership opportunities.

The encounter of the Asian Americans in parishes is not so different from the way parish life in America of the early and mid–twentieth century reflected the pulse of the larger American society. While the segregation laws were still in effect, Catholic churches did not take a stance against the wider societal practice but also discriminated against their black brothers and sisters.[28] Not all in the hierarchy tolerated this; there were voices such as that of Archbishop Joseph Rummel of New Orleans, who wrote that Catholics "should be mindful that their colored [*sic*] Catholic brethren share the same spiritual life and destiny."[29]

The push for parishes to be inclusive drew American Catholics back to an attitude of hospitality not only to immigrants but also to all racial minorities. As Asian American Catholics participated in the American parishes, their anticipation was that it was not only a place of spiritual nourishment but also a place where they can establish mutual bonds of support and protection. It would also provide social contact and social nurturing. The parish would function to preserve and maintain the cultural heritage and traditional links with the home community. The way that this would develop in the American Church, however, reflects the different Asian ethnicities' approaches to establishing parish life.

Most Asian American personal parishes are both monoracial and monoethnic.[30] There are number of reasons for this ethnic segregation. First, most Asian American churches are immigrant churches; immigrants established them for the purpose of worshiping and socializing in their native tongue. The ethnic churches are most prominent among first generation, with the monoethnic character built into its original design. The monoethnic aspect of the Church is arguably the most significant drawing factor for new members and visitors. Many Asian American churchgoers admit that their initial reason for attending a parish was to meet people of the same ethnicity. In a sense, any subsequent religious conversion stems from the original desire for ethnic fellowship. This also eases the feeling of racial discrimination that many feel from the larger society.

Second, there is a large degree of ethnic separatism among Asian American churches because of the enormous number of internal differences. The "Asian" racial category is a social construct in the United States that encompasses a wide range of cultures and histories. Although East Asian countries such as Korea, Japan, and China do share some cultural similarities based on Confucian ideals (filial piety, strong family bonds, priority given to education), each country has its own distinct culture and language. These ethnic parishes present a paradox: they strengthen intraethnic bonds and a sense of belonging on one hand and create a sense of separation from other groups and the larger society on the other.

Recently, the Church's attitudes toward Asian Catholics have been more positive, especially in the area of inculturation. This appreciation of culture is highlighted in *Ecclesia in Asia* (November 6, 1999), the Apostolic Exhortation promulgated after the Asian Synod by Pope John Paul II. There he offers a snapshot of what he calls the "Asian soul":

> The people of Asia take pride in their religious and cultural values such as love of silence and contemplation, simplicity, harmony, detachment, non-violence, discipline, frugal living, the thirst for learning and philosophical inquiry . . . respect for life, compassion for all beings, closeness to nature, filial piety toward parents, elders and ancestors, and a highly developed sense of community. In particular, they hold the family to be a vital source of strength, a closely knit community with a powerful sense of solidarity. Asian peoples are known for their spirit of religious tolerance and peaceful coexistence. Without denying the existence of bitter tensions and violent conflicts, it can still be said that Asia has often demonstrated a remarkable capacity for accommodation and a natural openness to the mutual enrichment of peoples in the midst of a plurality of religions and cultures. . . . All of this indicates an innate spiritual insight and moral wisdom in the Asian soul and it is the core around which a growing sense of "being Asian" is built.

These characteristics are of course not exclusive to Asians, nor do all Asians practice them equally. We must avoid romanticizing about Asians as if with these qualities they were morally superior to other ethnic groups. These same qualities have become both a virtue and a vice because as second-generation Asian Americans grow up in America, their rootedness in Asia is nonexistent, and even for the 1.5 generation it is diminished.[31] Thus, these characteristics of a shared cultural identity become the source of tension between the generations.

Second and Subsequent Generations

When looking at an immigrant population, it is important to distinguish between the experiences of each generation. First-generation Asian and Pacific Islanders who arrived in the United States as adolescents or adults are more likely to identify themselves by ethnicity or nation rather than with a pan-Asian identity. Their reasons for entry into the United States and their modes of doing so (as migrants or as refugees) will shape their subsequent experience. As either migrants or refugees, the first generation will have strong emotional bonds to their homeland. Maintaining language and culture will be of great importance, especially with regard to what they wish for their children. These experience and attitude are similar to those of the Irish and Italian Catholics who came to America in the nineteenth century. Their need to be recognized by their province or county better reflected their hold ethnic identity and a connection with the home country. But the desire to improve their lives pushed many immigrants to assimilate into American culture, which was more obvious in the second generation.

Second-generation immigrants are those born in the United States or who came here as small children. They find themselves caught in between two cultures. They wish to remain loyal to the culture and values of their parents, but they realize at the same time that the Asian/Pacific Island homeland cannot be exactly replicated in the United States. They find themselves drawn also to become "American." If the Asian cultures from which they come are influenced by the Confucian valuation of education, that drive to education will only send them deeper into the dominant U.S. culture.

At the same time, however, they hit racial barriers—first of all, as not being white, and second, as being "Asian" (and in the case of Pacific Islanders, as being "exotic natives.") White Americans do not distinguish among Asian cultures as they do among European ones. The generalized "Asian" identity that has been thrust upon them has thus been used by the second generation to create for themselves a pan-Asian identity, where common cause can be made with other Asians.

A recent study of religious affiliation in the United States found that Asian adolescents—when compared to whites, blacks, and Latinos—are the most unchurched racial group of teenagers in the nation. According to the survey, more than half of all Asian high school kids in America have either no religious belief or practice a non-Christian religion. Such a high level of religious disaffiliation within a particular racial group in the United States is rare and makes Asian Americans likely candidates for conversion to a religion later in life.[32]

For most American-born second-generation young people, the understanding of "who I am" is not a given. In a pluralistic setting such as the United States, one's identity formation involves both the process of self-ascription and the ascription from others, an ongoing process of labeling and negotiating engaged in by oneself and others. One's identity involves a continual negotiation process between outsiders' designation and one's self-assertion. Always carrying a portfolio of ethnic identities, Asian Americans learn to put on a socially and culturally defined appropriate identity for a given setting. Young Asian Americans shuffle multiple identities depending on the situation. For example, as a Vietnamese refugee myself, I have identified myself as "Asian American" when I did not want to be singled out as "Vietnamese American," especially when I am with other Asians.

The experience of Asian Americans in the second generation is largely shaped by voices from the racialized, dominant society that seeks to label them in a certain way and by various strategies they themselves employ to resist or to negotiate with these forces. Some second-generation young people have internalized racist messages and become victims of racial self-hatred, and they suffer from deep depression. The majority of others, whether consciously or not, try continuously to "fit" into the dominant society by carrying a portfolio of multiple identities and by oscillating between their Asianness and Americanness as they go through the different stages of life.

Besides wrestling with the questions of cultural identity, there is also the added layer of religious identity. Second-generation Asian Americans are seriously questioning why they should stay in the Asian churches that their parents attend. For Asian Americans who are more westernized and assimilated, their experience of Asian churches is often frustrating, irrelevant, and even stifling of their complex identities.

This topic of generational issues and challenges points to the necessity of beginning an intentional discussion regarding the great need to develop a church planning strategy for the growing population of second-generation Asians in the United and Canada. Asians are the most diverse ethnic people group in North America, culturally and linguistically. The children and grandchildren of the first-generation Asians are assimilated into the American society, but not necessarily into American churches.

Youth ministry is not easy in Asian American Catholic communities, since it involves working with the parents of the young people. Many parents' desire for academic and material success for their children sometimes causes friction with the programs in youth ministry. Youth ministry is ineffective not so much from lack of effort or good intentions, but rather results from lack of awareness or cultural understanding or even insensitivity as to how young people are caught between their parents' expectations and their own aspirations.

The absence of adult involvement means that teenagers in many Asian parishes rarely see their leaders outside of formal church programs, and therefore they lack adequate adult role models who show how the Christian life is to be lived outside of the church. For these young people, their Christian faith is typically confined to church and its activities with little or no impact on their lives outside of the church. A serious problem arises when the Asian parishes fail to address the real needs and questions of Asian American youth and instead expect them to act according to the rules of their Asian culture, especially when this may contradict the rest of their experience. One top-down approach promoted by Asian culture for parents and other adults in raising teens may be communicated to Asian American youth such that their thoughts, insights, and gifts are unimportant or unvalued in the Asian Church, even though they may be highly praised for their achievements in their school and community leadership opportunities.

Many second-generation young people experience deep personal struggles as they seek to honor their parents while also desperately trying to work on their own ethnic, vocational, gender, and religious identities. The family may become similar to the workplace, where conflict and tension arise through misunderstanding and different expectations.

In terms of ongoing ministry, church allegiance is often also attenuated in the second generation when these Asians are also more likely to marry outside their ethnic group. They must make decisions about how to educate their children vis-à-vis their own ethnicity, and issues often arise. The bonds of language will also become less a means of maintaining ethnic cohesion. Second-generation Asian American Catholics seriously question why they should stay in the Asian churches that their parents attend. This becomes a significant tension within the different ethnic communities.

Asian American Catholic Communities

In order to appreciate the complexity of the Asian American Catholic experience, it is helpful to see how the national church approaches the different Asian groups, as well as to understand some of the distinctive characteristics of each group.

The following Asian apostolates have national consultants who collaborate with the USCCB: Asian Indian, Cambodian, Chinese, Hmong/Lahu, Indonesian, Japanese, Khmu, Laotian, Samoan, Tongan, and Vietnamese. It is through these consultations that sketches of Asian American groups are collected. Highlighting a few of them here will give a snapshot of the how the different ethnic groups have come and developed in the United States. The USCCB also has appointed official delegates jointly to the Conference of Bishops in the Philippines and Korea.

By 2003, three Asian American bishops were ordained for dioceses in California: Bishop Dominic Dinh Mai Luong (Vietnamese) as auxiliary of the Diocese of Orange County, Bishop Oscar Solis (Filipino) as auxiliary of the Archdiocese of Los Angeles, and Bishop Ignatius Wang (Chinese) as auxiliary of the Archdiocese of San Francisco. While it is noteworthy that these men have risen to the episcopacy and have been named auxiliary bishops, greater progress will be made when Asian Americans become diocesan bishops themselves. These bishops also represent the presence of Asian Americans in the Catholic Church.

Filipinos

In the Philippines, approximately 85 percent of Filipinos are Catholics, with a significant number of Protestants and Muslims making up the rest of the population. Similar to the Chinese, Filipinos are not accustomed to registering in a parish or contributing through Sunday envelopes. The Filipino parishes are usually very large, with little personal interaction between priest and people. The focus of the Filipino Catholics is on rites and ceremonies. These take shape through fiestas, processions, pilgrimages, novenas, and innumerable devotional practices. What most Filipinos learn about doctrinal and moral values comes through these devotional practices.

Filipinos have begun to take an active role in the life of the American Catholic Church. There are an estimated 1.6 million Filipino Catholics in the United States, with approximately three hundred Filipino priests, brothers, and deacons and more than two hundred religious sisters in the United States. Starting in 1990, Filipino Catholic leaders gathered at four large national "Sandiwa" conferences to proclaim their identity and establish their place in the American Church. A dedication of the

Shrine of Our Lady of Peace and Good Voyage of Antipolo at the national Basilica of the Immaculate Conception in Washington, D.C., secured recognition of presence for the Filipino Catholics.

Filipino faith is embedded in a folk Catholicism. Filipino-Americans express this integrated Catholicism as well. They freely supplement their "official" faith with cultural celebrations and social practices contributed to and validated by various communities. Some of these observances are the penitential devotions during Lent and the rich religious and cultural celebrations of fiestas throughout the year, including elaborate town processions during the feasts of saints and the Virgin Mary.

Vietnamese

Catholicism came to Vietnam during the sixteenth century. Before Christianity was introduced, Vietnamese worship centered on several religions—animism, Buddhism, Taoism, and Confucianism—and existed in a synthesis for centuries before Christianity arrived in Vietnam. With the Communist takeover of South Vietnam in 1975, a large number of Vietnamese Catholics became refugees.

In the United States, the Vietnamese Community of Clergy and Religious was formed in 1968, and then at the first convention of Vietnamese Catholics in 1980, the Vietnamese Catholic Federation was formed, bringing the clergy and religious under the federation. The first president elected was Reverend Joseph Tinh. The National Pastoral Center for Vietnamese Apostolate, with Bishop Dominic Luong as the first director, was established in 1989.

There are approximately 350,000 Vietnamese American Catholics, with about seven hundred priests serving the community. Many dioceses have responded to the pastoral needs of the Vietnamese by creating personal parishes, of which there are now thirty-four in the United States. These parishes are in states such as Virginia, Louisiana, Texas, California, Illinois, Georgia, South Carolina, Kansas, and Minnesota. The first personal parish was established in Fairfax, Virginia, in 1978, only three years after the refugee flight out of Vietnam. Also in 1978, the Congregation of the Co-Redemptrix of Mary (CMC) in Carthage, Missouri, hosted the first Marian Days. This drew about two hundred Vietnamese families from across the United States. This has become an annual Vietnamese Catholic gathering that attracts Vietnamese from all over the United States and from several other countries. It has grown to an annual gathering of more than fifty thousand people.

Chinese

In the nineteenth and twentieth centuries, Chinese immigrants came mainly from Taiwan and Hong Kong. Now most come from mainland China, especially Fujian Province. A large number are Catholics. The Catholic population of Chinese in the United States is estimated at about 340,000, according to Church registration records; however, the number could be higher because Chinese do not have the practice of registering in parishes in China, and many continue that practice after arriving in the United States. As a result, it is hard to estimate the actual number of Chinese American Catholics. A conservative estimate puts the number of Chinese Catholics in America at two million. A large concentration of Chinese Catholics is in California, New York, Illinois, Washington State, and the Washington, D.C., area.

As of 2010, there were approximately thirty-five Chinese priests in America, with a growing number of seminarians. This number of priests included those who have come from mainland China and Taiwan. The number of religious sisters was about seventy, with thirteen religious brothers and seven deacons. The conflict between the so-called Chinese Patriotic Church (recognized by the Chinese government) and the underground Church in China (recognized by the Vatican) is a very painful reality for all Chinese Catholics and those who minister among them. One of Pope John Paul II's and now Pope Benedict XVI's goals is to overcome this division.

Koreans

Most Koreans came to the United States from South Korea. There are approximately one million Koreans in the United States, of which an estimated 7 percent to 8 percent are Catholics. An estimated 140 Korean American communities are spread out over thirty states, mainly in California, New York, New Jersey, Illinois, and North Carolina and along the Baltimore–Washington corridor. There are approximately

75,000 Korean American Catholics in a hundred communities with resident Korean-speaking priests, with the remaining forty communities served through mobile pastoral care of nearby Korean priests. Korean American Catholic communities have been established mostly by laypeople, a practice that resembles the historical establishment of the Catholic Church in Korea.[33] This has influenced how Korean Americans are actively participating in their parishes. They feel like the laity has a major role in the organization of the parish, which also means that some Korean parishes have become active in requesting their pastors.

There were more than one hundred exchange priests from Korea, with an increasing number of U.S.-ordained priests and permanent deacons. There was also a substantial increase in the number of Korean seminarians in the major seminaries. More than eighty Korean religious sisters came from Korea to work in the Korean American parishes and communities. The Korean American Catholics also have a national organization that hosts an annual conference. This is to meet the demand of the growing Korean Catholic population both from Korea and among Korean Americans in the United States.

South Asians: India

According to the U.S. Census Bureau, Asian Indians constituted approximately 12 percent of the Asian population in the United States in 1990. No formal survey has been conducted to report the number of Catholics in 2010, but conservative estimates from local Catholic associations project the population at 290,000 and growing. The majority belongs to the Latin rite, but there are a growing number of Syro-Malabar and Syro-Malankara Catholics in the major cities of the United States and Canada. Since most South Asians coming to America already have English-language skills, they quickly adapt to the American Catholic culture. However, a growing number of recent immigrants do not have English-language skills and need worship opportunities provided to them in their own language. Within various dioceses with large number of South Asian Catholics, there are associations that maintain and provide programs for South Asians. These associations hold annual gatherings to deepen their faith and celebrate their cultural and linguistic traditions, especially Tamil and Malayalam.

An important and highly visible contribution of the South Asian Catholics is the establishment of the Vailankanni Oratory to Our Lady of Good Health in the Basilica of the National Shrine of the Immaculate Conception in Washington, D.C. A dedication ceremony was held on August 15, 1997. This project was spearheaded by the Indian American Catholic Association of Washington, D.C., with donations pouring in from both Catholic and other Indian immigrants from across the United States and Canada. During the month of August, an annual pilgrimage to the Basilica draws a few thousand South Asian pilgrims from across the nation.

Indonesians

Indonesia has long been the largest Muslim country in the world. The number of Christians in Indonesia is very small compared with the number of Muslims, but Christianity has a long history in Indonesia. It was introduced by Portuguese Jesuits and Dominicans in the sixteenth century. When the Dutch defeated Portugal in 1605, the Calvinist Dutch Reformed Church expelled Catholic missionaries and became the only Christian influence in the islands for three hundred years. Because Calvinism was a strict, austere, and intellectually uncompromising variety of Christianity that demanded a thorough understanding of scripture, Christianity gained few converts in Indonesia until the nineteenth century, when German Lutherans introduced evangelical freedom and Jesuits established successful missions, schools, and hospitals on some of the islands, including Timor and Flores.

There are now thirty-six Indonesian Catholic Communities (ICC) in the United States, mostly along both coasts. The number of ICCs fluctuates with the nature of its transience of their members. There are approximately seven Indonesian priests recruited and trained in America with two permanent deacons, and there are now a handful of men in training.

The Challenge of Asian Catholicism

The Asian American Catholic community makes for a complex picture, and Asian American Catholics present serious challenges to the American Catholic Church. These challenges are in part not different from those confronting the Catholic immigrants of the previous centuries, such as the Irish, Germans, Italians, and Eastern Europeans. Like them, the Asian/Pacific immigrants and refugees have to cross the sociopolitical and economic divide separating them from the American mainstream. But unlike previous immigrants, these recent—and at times illegal—immigrants are ecclesiastically powerless, and they have to overcome the gap within the Church itself, which marginalizes them from the power centers that now occupied by the European immigrants. They face racial barriers within the Church that their European antecedents did not have to negotiate. And they face the formidable challenges of ministry to the second generation that have been outlined earlier in this essay.

But these newcomers bring opportunities to the Church as well by increasing substantially membership and the number of religious and priestly vocations. They also bring with them rich and diverse cultural as well as devotional practices with which the American Catholic Church can be renewed and strengthened. Through the more recent various initiatives and organizational structures of the USCCB, the Church has begun to do a better job of welcoming these strangers.

Hopes for the Future

The National Asian Pacific Catholic Organization (NAPCO) stemmed from the efforts of Church leaders from the various Asian and Pacific communities, who first discussed its formation in 1986 in Washington, D.C.

Other efforts to bring together Asian Catholic communities occurred in 1990 at the National Catholic Educational Association (NCEA) in Washington. Leaders of the different Asian Catholic communities in the United States—primarily Chinese, Filipinos, Hmong, Japanese, Khmu, Korean, Laotian, and Vietnamese—discussed their experience of the American Catholic Church, their homelands, and their expectations and recommendations. Some of the major concerns that surfaced during the NCEA gathering were as follows: the need for a national convocation, the ordination of Asian bishops for dioceses in America, and a national pastoral letter addressing the presence of Asian and Pacific Catholics.

NAPCO is a response to the recommendations of the USCCB's pastoral letter "Asian and Pacific Presence: Harmony in Faith." It called for Asian and Pacific church leaders to explore together with the USCCB a national structure that would give recognition, active voice, and liaison with the USCCB. These efforts would yield the promotion of coalitions between different Asian and Pacific communities and organizations in order to build strong advocacy networks.

These different organizations have encouraged and continue to support the formation of young men and women into a religious vocation. In 1993, the Center for Applied Research in the Apostolate first collected data on the ethnic/racial makeup of men training for the priesthood. Of them, 8 percent were Asian and Pacific Islander by 2009 it had jumped to 12 percent.[34] The religious formation of women was also relatively high for Asian and Pacific Islanders at 11 percent out of all young women in formation.[35] The increase in vocations among Asian and Pacific American young adult reflects the encouragement of the parish community, as well as the support of families in which religious vocations are held in high regard.

Currently, the USCCB, through the Secretariat of Cultural Diversity in the Church, gathered Asian and Pacific American leaders from across the nation for a networking convocation in May 2010. This effort was to help these leaders find common ground to work together and to share what they have learned within their communities, and it marked the first of a projected series of gatherings.

Asian American Religious Experience and Catholic Studies

The interpretative lenses that represent Asian Americans as exotic religious "others" or as "model minority" Christians have given little room for alternative perspectives. By not giving enough attention to the social and historical experiences of religious Asian Americans, these lenses risk essentializing Asian American subjects or rendering them invisible.

Catholic Studies can both serve the cause of Asian American Catholic and be served by them. As Catholic Studies attends to the experience and growth of Asian American Catholics, it will enhance a community that will be contributing extensively to the Church in the future.

The challenges raised by the experience of Asian Americans can in turn prompt Catholic Studies to take up issues thematized in recent work in history and the social sciences. The need of Catholic Studies and histories to retrieve the religious Asian American subject will require many things. It will require first of all that Catholic Studies view Asian American religious communities and individuals as creative sites and agents of cultural synthesis. Asian American Catholics have incorporated their language, symbols, and dances into the liturgies. These should not be viewed as merely symbolic gestures during special occasions, but rather as something to be incorporated into the weekly or daily experiences of the people. They should become a common practice, and not something to be rolled out as exotic entertainment.

Second, Catholic historians need to utilize themes of transnationalism and diaspora in their studies of Asian American Catholics. The establishment of ethnic parishes has not only supported the community in the United States but also has created a place where Asian Americans maintain a connection with what is going on in their home countries. All immigrants and refugees carry with them a concern for their countries of origin; this is especially the case for Asian immigrants, since it is only recently that Asians were accepted for U.S. citizenship. The linkage to the home country points to a related issue about how migration and religion inform the notion of the nation-state itself. Churches were always a mix of missionary and native influence, and Christian missionaries in the home country still influence the way Asian Americans understand and practice Catholicism.

Catholic parishes have offered psychic and physical space within which individuals and communities can affirm traditions and customs from the home country, even while wrestling with the changes and conflict that can be engendered by new settings. As a source of faith and meaning as a locus of ritual and spiritual practice, religion is a powerful and enduring influence in the lives of the diversity that is Asian America.

Third, Catholic Studies has to reveal and examine the implicit and explicit racialization patterns that shape attitudes toward Asian American Catholics, both within the general Catholic population and in Catholic Studies programs themselves. Failure to do so marginalizes important groups in contemporary Catholicism.

The Asian and Pacific American presence in the Catholic Church will continue to grow. The different Asian and Pacific communities will need to work together to better relationships across historical and ethnic conflicts in order to better serve the Catholic Church and the larger society. The ongoing efforts of the individual communities to promote leaders for the American Catholic Church will also contribute to the way the Asian and Pacific Presence will be experienced. It is not just the numbers that are important to the growth of the Asian and Pacific presence, but also the commitment to the Church. Asian and Pacific Americans Catholics have shown strength in their faith by bringing to America a Catholicism that was strange and new, and that was an integral part of their lives.

14 Working Toward an Inclusive Narrative

A Call for Interdisciplinarity and Ethnographic Reflexivity in Catholic Studies

KRISTY NABHAN-WARREN

I am a non-Catholic anthropologist of religion who, until recently, has worked primarily within Mexican American Catholic communities in the Southwest, West, and Midwest. In this essay, I raise some questions and concerns that have come up for me as an ethnographer who focuses on lived Christianities in the United States. I continue to work with Mexican American Catholics and have broadened out my scope of inquiry to include Anglo American Catholics and Protestants of a variety of traditions, and I am convinced that the field of Catholic Studies can learn much from histories and ethnographies of Spanish-speaking U.S. Catholics. I am also convinced that studies of U.S. Hispanics must be interwoven with the histories of U.S. Catholicism and U.S. Christianity more broadly. It is possible to reflect the uniqueness and richness of Hispanic lived religion, but it must be interwoven with others' histories in order to reflect common humanity and experience. U.S. Hispanic Catholic history is part of U.S. Catholic history as well as American Christian history. The risk of separating out U.S. Hispanic Catholic history from the larger narratives is that we exoticize and romanticize it, making it seem other and foreign to what other U.S. Catholics have experienced. We also risk trivializing U.S. Hispanic Catholics if we relegate their experiences to a separate chapter, thus denying universalism of experience.

Since the 1980s, the American Catholic landscape has been changing in unprecedented ways as a result of influx of Spanish-speaking immigrants from Mexico, the Dominican Republic, Guatemala, and El Salvador. The field of Catholic Studies needs to figure out how to incorporate these new and not-so-new migrants and their stories and voices into the broader narratives of American Christian history and life so that they are not relegated to the margins. A growing body of literature attests to the level of importance scholars are attaching to Spanish-speaking Catholics and their place in the American Catholic and larger American landscape.[1] But sometimes these studies can romanticize U.S. Hispanic Catholics and make their concerns and realities seem somehow distinct—falsely—from those of other American Catholics.

As scholars of religion, whether we are historians, theologians, or ethnographers, we enter the religious worlds of those we study. Ever since I began conducting fieldwork in South Phoenix, Arizona, in the fall of 1992 for my master's thesis I have wondered what are we doing, or what are we attempting to do, when we study religious peoples and their worlds, particularly when we are encountering these communities of faith as "outsiders." What are our goals as scholars who focus on American Catholicism but who must attend to the larger context of American religious history? As individuals who gain trust and levels of intimacy with those we are "studying" for a thesis, dissertation or book, what are our obligations to community members? These are some of the methodological, existential, and moral concerns I have had. I continue to have them as I work within U.S. Hispanic Catholic communities and branch my inquiry outward, working toward bringing a variety of religious narratives together. In order for our scholarship in the subfield of Catholic Studies to speak to the moods and motivations of our interlocutors and to gain a more global relevance, we must attend to these broader issues. My overarching argument in this essay is that Catholic Studies must embrace interdisciplinarity in order to reflect the lived realities of U.S. Catholics. We must familiarize ourselves with a variety of subdisciplines and disciplines, including American Studies, anthropology, history, Latino Studies, political science, and Religious Studies, and we must incorporate multiple perspectives in our work. We must seek to contextualize our interlocutors' voices and experiences (whether strictly historical or ethnographic) with other Christians. The challenges that Catholic Studies scholars face are also opportunities that will make our work richer, more textured. Some of these dual challenges and opportunities include highlighting the uniqueness of U.S. Catholicism while attending to larger issues on the American religious landscape; noting the special contributions Hispanics are making to U.S. Catholicism as well as how these men and women mirror larger trends in American Christianity; and entering deeply into the religious worlds that we study in order to understand the lived religious realities and worlds our interlocutors inhabit.

I began to formulate these overlapping concerns and questions when I was a young graduate student in Religious Studies at Arizona State. I had become intrigued by the world of Mexican American Catholicism. I was fascinated with Latino gang culture and the appropriation of tattoos of the Mexican Virgin of Guadalupe on young men's and women's bodies—their backs, forearms, and biceps. I was initially drawn in by what seemed exciting and exotic—I was an outsider to this intriguing, titillating religious world which was quite "other" to me—and I wanted to understand this religious phenomenon and how they negotiated their Catholic "religious" and gang identities. So here I was, little miss *gringa*, who at the time I began my research knew no Spanish, had lived outside Indiana for a grand total of three months, and who grew up in a middle-class Lutheran home. I was a curiosity to the young men and women I encountered as much as they were a curiosity to me—they wondered why this "*loca gringa*" was driving around South Phoenix wanting to talk to them about their experiences as young Latinos. It was not common for hardcore *cholos* and *cholas* from the South Side to sit down and talk with a white female graduate student about their cultural and religious experiences; they couldn't quite figure me out, but they kept meeting with me because I took them seriously and wanted to learn from them and their experiences. I was attracted to Mexican American Catholic culture in South Phoenix because it was so different from my own background. I wanted to learn more about the ubiquitous image of the Virgin of Guadalupe, who seemed to be all around me, tattooed on bodies, emblazoned on car windows and bumpers, displayed in yard shrines, and painted on building murals, yet who remains exotic and unfamiliar to millions of U.S. Catholics. This vibrant, living culture beckoned, and it drew me in.

I gained access to local gang members because of a local Catholic priest's helpfulness. Father Doug Nohava was supportive of my interests and told me that he was impressed with my "passion," so he introduced me to Arturo, an "OG," or original gangster, in South Phoenix, who picked up on my interest in the Virgin of Guadalupe, the "patroness of Mexico," saying, "You know, you are interested in the Virgin de Guadalupe—let me introduce you to a special woman I know, *hija*."

What motivated Arturo, a man who was known for being a "bad ass," a "locomania," a man with deep scars on his neck and face, who was no stranger to gang violence in the streets of South Phoenix, to help me, a then-inexperienced, naïve graduate student? He overcame his deep cultural, religious embeddedness and saw where we connected: we shared a reverence for the Virgin Mary. As a devout Catholic, he wanted me to understand the beauty and power of his faith and his lived experience as a middle-aged lower-middle-class Latino who turned to the Virgin Mary for guidance and help. He sensed my openness and engagement and led me to a woman, Estela Ruiz, who became my teacher, confidante, and mentor for the next several years. There is much talk these days about the "risks" that we take as anthropologists of religion: we enter into unfamiliar territory, we expose ourselves to our interlocutors, but there has been no discussion of the risks our interlocutors take when they decide to bring us into their world and to teach us. They risk being abandoned by us, as many anthropologists have done once their projects are "over"; they risk being betrayed when we write about them for our own academic careers and advancement; they risk being shunned by members of their own community because they betrayed certain members. We risk much less than do our interlocutors.

The spiritual oracle of the community, Estela Ruiz, had been having visions and locutions of the Virgin Mary since 1988. I met her on a warm fall day in Phoenix, in Arturo's company. The three of us sat in her backyard, and she told me about her experiences with the Virgin Mary. She talked about how she was saved by the Virgin, empowered by her, and given hope and love.

For the next year and a half I drove from my Tempe apartment to Estela's home twice a week and asked her hundreds of questions about her life, her family, her relationship with the Virgin Mary, and her status as a visionary. My thesis was the culmination of countless hours spent with Estela in her home and in her backyard shrine and focused on the empowering relationship this middle-aged Mexican American woman had forged with a liberating Virgin. Though I met with her husband, Reyes, and members of her immediate and extended family and talked with pilgrims to the backyard shrine to the Virgin, my work was primarily with Estela, and I was deeply moved by her narrative.

After I moved back to Indiana to pursue my doctorate, I kept in touch, visited the shrine for the annual December celebration of the apparitions, and pondered writing my dissertation on Mary's Ministries, the community of Catholic evangelizers that had grown out of Estela's apparitions and that was dedicated to spreading Mary's messages. I called Estela on the phone and asking her what she thought of my returning to write about Mary's Ministries. It was important to me that I ask permission—I did not want to be parasitic—and would only go if I were welcome. Estela said she would call me back. She did a few days later, and much to my surprise and delight, she said that her son Reyes Junior, "Little Rey," and his wife, Norma (and their teacup poodle, Basia), would have me as a houseguest.

By this time I had grown a little older and had a growing sense of responsibility and commitment to Estela and her community. I had taken Spanish courses as part of my doctoral work, could read and translate Spanish fairly well, and was comfortable conducting interviews in Spanish. During my fieldwork in South Phoenix in the fall/winter of 1998, I was asking Mexican American women and men fairly specific questions about their beliefs in the Virgin Mary and about why they came to Estela's backyard shrine space. I wanted to understand more deeply what making a pilgrimage there meant to them. During the course of my research, I became enmeshed in their devotional lives, experienced the faith and trust in the Virgin Mary, their commitment to family, their love of the Catholic faith, and their outreach to their community. Despite my not being Catholic, I was brought in as a member of this community. I was asked to lead rosary prayer sessions at the shrine, help cook meals for the December celebration of the apparitions, and take on other tasks that bound me in innumerable ways to the community. And I was asked questions that prompted me to examine my own religious and moral inventories. What did *I* think about the apparitions? What were my beliefs and values? What drew me to the Virgin as a non-Catholic? I have notebooks full of these questions.

There were few, if any, Religious Studies or Catholic Studies models I could follow at the time, since my work was primarily ethnographic. My interlocutors were anything but "safely historical"—they asked questions back at me, they challenged me, and pushed my intellectual, cultural, and religious boundaries. They were very much unlike the men and women I had encountered in books in graduate school, and the many theories of religion I had learned seemed largely unhelpful once I was in the field. Most scholars who have studied apparitions are historians and attempt to understand them in their social and political contexts.[2] These studies are exemplary scholarship in that they seek to understand the moods and motivations of believers, and they offer a critical commentary, but at some level I couldn't relate to them, removed as they were from the lived religious and moral worlds of their historical interlocutors. Other studies of apparitions have taken a different route by aiming to undermine the believers, and because I was engaged in a deep ethnography and had grown to respect and admire my interlocutors, I could not relate to one-sided theories that attempted to explain away religious belief and praxis. In these studies it is argued that apparitions are manifestations of delusional thoughts, unhealthy fixations on a mother figure, or outright fakery.[3] I have long thought these latter "explanations" were unhelpful, arrogant, and unnuanced, and it was clear that these scholars did not work closely with the believers they studied. For my part, I was not able to exercise an historical imagination in a living community I encountered in intimate ways. I was hearing and seeing how my interlocutors truly believed in these Marian apparitions and how they were deeply moved by what they wholeheartedly believed to be Mary's messages to them. How could I make them safely historical when they were all around me, beckoning me to listen and understand?

An "intimate outsider," I was being transformed by these men, women and children who shared their faith lives with me and who prompted me to explain where my own commitments lay.[4] I was forced to understand my "moods and motivations" for being in South Phoenix in the first place. Yet as appealing as the language and meanings of "intimate outsider" may be, I want to resist invoking any vestige of the binary categories of insider and outsider that have long plagued the academy. Ethnographers have long blurred boundaries between insider and outsider, creating new spaces of intimacy and discourse and non-Catholics working in Catholic communities are among those who push the boundaries of identity. As the anthropologist of religion Karen McCarthy Brown has now famously noted, "when the lines long drawn in anthropology between participant-observer and informant break down, then the only truth is the one in between; and anthropology becomes something closer to a social art form, open to both aesthetic and moral judgment. This situation is riskier, but it does bring intellectual labor and life into closer relation."[5]

I have realized that in being asked the questions by my interlocutors, I have gained a much more complex insight and understanding into why people believe in apparitions of the Virgin Mary, why they pray to *la* Virgin, why they value family and *comunidad* over individual achievements. Living with family members and gaining close access, sharing my own religious and moral history with the Ruizes and other interlocutors, taking a week-long faith course at the shrine, and making and serving food to pilgrims who come to the annual December retreat at the shrine not only connected me to those I was "studying" in lasting and deep ways but also helped me produce scholarship that stems from a wellspring of experiences that thrust me into the heart of this community.

I think that many students, like my twenty-one-year-old self, who want to do ethnographic research do so partially because they think it is "cool" and much more fun than hanging out in dusty, quiet archives. It is. Having lunch with my interlocutors at Ponchos restaurant, sipping cups of sweet *horchata* and eating tacos while discussing matters of faith is heady, exciting stuff indeed, and it is in these spaces of human relationships that we are entrusted with intimate knowledge. This is religion as it is lived and experienced in everyday life, and as anthropologists we are now a part of it. We cannot just sit back and observe—we are drawn in, whether we like it or not. Sitting in Estela Ruiz's backyard shrine and watching hundreds of devotees to the Virgin Mary, smelling candle wax mingled with the pungent scents of cacti and mesquite trees, helped me enter the religious and cultural world of my interlocutors. I was deeply immersed in this world, and it was only because I smelled, tasted, felt, and touched this Catholicism that I was able to understand it. I lived it: I, too, knelt in front of the statue of Guadalupe, carried a statue of Santo Niño de Atocha in the candlelight vigil, made the sign of the cross, and drank water said to be blessed by the Virgin Mary.

Of course, my "truth" was and is a partial one, as the anthropologists George Marcus and James Clifford argued in their landmark book *Writing Culture*.[6] I was writing from what I knew and experienced in the field. I have found that the hardest part of doing research like the kind I was conducting in South Phoenix was when I moved from the field to interpreting my fieldnotes and started writing about the men and women I had grown to know so well. It was then that the moral questions arising out of the ethnographic method could not be avoided. How would I portray this woman and her family? What details would I include? Not include? By this time I was considered a family member: Estela and Reyes called me their "spiritual daughter," and I was an honorary member of their religious, ethnic, cultural world. The best guidance I received when I was in angst, wondering how I could write about these men and women I grown to care deeply about and respect, was from my thesis advisor, Tod Swanson, a gifted anthropologist who has a long commitment to Quechuan men and women in the Andes. Swanson believes that we must grapple with issues of accountability, and he gives this advice in his article "Through Family Eyes": "Imagine them [informants] as being in the audience. Imagine their jokes, their laughter, their anger. Then when we speak we are not talking about Indians in general but about specific people to whom we hold ourselves accountable. Do they recognize themselves in our descriptions?"[7] Swanson raises the issue of morality here as well: we must hold ourselves to a higher standard because we are working with living, breathing men and women who can be hurt by what we write. Sometimes we need to leave out information that, while it may help our career, may hurt those who have entrusted their stories to us.

It is this accountability that I want to now turn to. As anthropologists of religion, we are privileged to be a part of the innermost hopes, dreams, and beliefs of our interlocutors, and we need to take seriously what we are doing when we are in the field and what our obligations are to those we study. Like most anthropologists, I am not a member, culturally or religiously, of the worlds I study. As an ethnographer of American Catholicism, I study the lived religious worlds of my interlocutors and attempt to offer a nuanced interpretation that I hope will lead to a greater understanding of American Catholicism and American Christianity as it is lived today. I am not alone in this quest; we have seen more "outsider" accounts of Catholicism in the past five years, many of which have an ethnographic focus.

The in-between, liminal identity of the non-Catholic scholar who works within Catholic communities is increasingly becoming the topic of conversation among those who "do" Catholic Studies. A few years ago I was part of a panel, "The Ethnographic Turn in the Study of American Catholicism," at the American Academy of Religion's annual meeting. The panel was chaired by Timothy Matovina, director of the Cushwa Center for the Study of American Catholicism at the University of Notre Dame. The panelists, all non-Catholic apart from Matovina, spoke about our research and how our non-Catholic status affected our course of study. We spoke openly and honestly about the challenges we encountered as non-Catholics as well as the particular insights we brought to our studies because of our liminality, as neither "outsiders" nor "insiders," but some kind of combination of the two. As we spoke, we were all firm in our stance that our historic and ethnographic methodologies could benefit the discipline of Religious Studies and our subfield of Catholic Studies because we were challenging categories of insider and outsider/emic and etic and because our Catholic interlocutors did not fit neatly in a "Catholic" category—and in most cases had no desire to do so.

Susan Ridgely Bales (*When I Was a Child*) spoke about the rewards of being a non-Catholic and working closely with Catholic children. She noted that her status as a young woman and non-Catholic placed her on the same level as the children preparing for their First Communion and endeared her to them. They considered her a child, like them, and saw that she was learning along with them. Sue noted that if she had been Catholic, her study would have turned out very differently; she emphasized that she would not have had the same insights into the lived Catholic culture of children. Amy Koehlinger (*The New Nuns*) spoke about her role as a historian and ethnographer who interviewed Catholic sisters who had been deeply involved in the civil rights movement of the 1960s. As with Sue, Amy's non-Catholic identity was not seen as a deterrent by her interlocutors, but rather as an opportunity for the sisters to relate to her on a human level and to recount their days of activism. Her identity as a woman and a committed, empathetic scholar made it possible for these women to open up to her and to share their stories with her.

My comments dovetailed with Sue's and Amy's; I focused on how my identity as a non-Catholic was a crucial factor in the success of my research and relationship to the Ruiz family.[8] They had emphasized to me time and again that if I had been Catholic they would have been less inclined to work with me because they believed that those reading my book would perceive me as a biased insider. My "outsider" status as a non-Catholic was my entrée into this community, and I became deeply enmeshed in their world along the way, becoming an "insider" while I remained on the "outside." Sarah McFarland Taylor (*Green Sisters*) also spoke of how her identity as a woman was the most important factor in her intimate relationships with the ecologically oriented nuns she was working with. She emphasized the friendships she formed with many of the sisters and the kinship she felt and experienced during her research and beyond. At one point during his response to the varied comments, Tim shared his enthusiasm for these newly published works and the growing interest in American Catholicism by non-Catholics to the tradition. He reflected on the state of the subfield of Catholic Studies, noting that the field is greatly enriched by these studies. He remarked that ten years ago he would have never imagined that there would be a growing interest in U.S. Catholic cultures by non-Catholics and a rise in ethnographic studies. What was also striking was that all of the panelists were scholars of American Christianities, and this larger focus was emphasized in our individual works; our books were about some facet of American Catholicism, but we worked to connect the Catholics we studied to other American Christians, both Catholic and Protestant.

Ethnographers studying traditions that are not our own can add an important layer to the current focus on "lived religion" that has resonated among scholars who study religious people and their worlds. We bring an interdisciplinary, broader focus to Catholic Studies and can help make the history of U.S. Catholicism more textured as a result. In our aim to study lived Catholicisms, we hope to capture how the faithful "organize their daily lives and actively put beliefs into practice," as David Hall's edited volume *Lived Religion in America: Toward a History of Practice* puts it. In recent years, scholars have been focusing intently on lived religion and have produced microstudies: localized ethnographies and histories that in addition to providing thick descriptions of religious worlds offer commentaries on religious life, gender, and religious practice that focus on religion as embodied and experienced.

The concept of lived religion, as the sociologist of religion Meredith McGuire has recently written, "is useful for distinguishing the actual experience of religious persons from the prescribed religion of institutionally defined beliefs and practices."[9] Scholars who study American Catholicism (from both outsider as well as insider perspectives) are among those who recognize the rewards of this methodological as well as epistemological take on the study of religion, and they are producing monographs and articles that are reaching audiences outside of Catholic Studies, drawing greater awareness to the subfield and giving it relevance to other disciplines.[10] Attending to lived religion, these scholars tap into a growing body of literature and make the subfield of Catholic Studies more interdisciplinarity.

By attending to the lived religion of their interlocutors, ethnographers of American Catholicisms will also have to address the *intense emotional work* of doing fieldwork and, in turn, the heart of what it means to be living and working among people and focusing on their religious beliefs and practices. As I have found in the course of my ethnographic research, religion is deeply emotional for its practitioners, and ethnographers, because of the nature of ethnographic work, are well poised to address the emotional aspects of faith and community. It is out of this kind of praxis that an understanding of lived religion arises, and without such intense engagement in the field—living it ourselves and working through the emotional quagmire of religion—that we lack understanding. Ethnographic work is emotional work, and ethnographers who study religion can make connections with our interlocutors and gain a deeper understanding of their lived religious worlds. The anthropologist Lynn Davidman has written, "Ethnographers are emotion workers. By acknowledging our own emotions, ethnographers find new ways to cross the bridges to others. Working in this way affords us new insights into the intersecting realms of self, subject matter, and sociological methods; our reflection on each helps us to interrogate and enliven our knowledge of the others."[11] Indeed, doing ethnographic work and focusing on religion involves sharing our own concerns, our own orientations, and making connections with those about whom we will be writing. In letting down our guard and sharing what matters to us, we gain a deeper understanding of "lived religion."

We in turn open ourselves to transformation, and our "subjects" become our guides and teachers.

Our knowledge of the lived religious worlds of those we study is based on our ability to connect emotionally with our interlocutors, and when we move from the field to the writing stage, we must reexamine the inner spaces of our fieldwork. Ethnographers who study the religious lives of others must reflect on the ways in which the communities they study are shaped in part by their presence and how they in turn are shaped by the community. A focus on dialectical relationship between them and us is crucial for responsible, honest scholarship, and we must attend to the new possibilities for discourse and relationships we create. We must take into account the moral dilemma of doing fieldwork, to analyze the power relationships that exist between "us" and "them" in the field, and to justify why we are writing. The Appalachian community organizers and scholars Helen Lewis, Mary Ann Hinsdale, and Maxine Waller offer an important perspective in their collaborative work that scholars (both emic and etic) studying lived religious worlds can learn from. As part of their wide audience, they address academics, whom they hope will find "viable ways of understanding and working with communities and who are looking for authentic ways of giving support to community-based research and reflection processes."[12]

As an ethnographer, I continue to be moved by the stories that women and men share with me about their faith journeys. Since 2005, I have collected oral histories for my current book project on the "Fourth Day" *cursillo* movements, weekend-long Christian encounters that include the Catholic *Cursillo de Cristianidad* movement ("little course in Christianity") among U.S. Hispanic Catholics.[13] I have also worked closely with Protestant *cursillistas* who base their weekend courses directly on the Catholic weekend retreat and who offer a variety of weekend encounters akin to Catholic *cursillos*. During one of these ethnographic encounters, I sat at a small conference table with a group of six *cursillistas*, first-generation Mexican American men and women who had gone through the intensive weekend course. Over the course of several hours these men and women unstintingly shared their stories of suffering, conversion, and triumph with me. They talked about "making" and "living" the *cursillo*, a three-day weekend retreat they had experienced, and invited me in to their lived religious world. Rosita, in a voice that was barely audible, told me why she made her *cursillo* more than thirty years before. Looking down and twisting her wedding ring around her finger, Rosita talked about her daughter, who was killed in a car accident when she was in her twenties. "When she died, I lost it, I mean, I *really* lost it," she said softly. "I lost my faith in God, the Church—everything. God led me to *cursillo* so that I could get through the terrible pain and so that the hole that was left in my heart could heal. After my daughter died I wanted to die, too. I was a dead woman when I made *cursillo* and it made me alive again. I owe my life to *cursillo*."[14]

After she told her story of faith, suffering and perseverance, I, along with several others in the room, found myself wiping away the tears from my face. I was moved deeply by what Rosita had said. She later told me that she trusted me because she saw how much I cared about her and her community and that I was affected by the stories that were being shared. Rosita said she knew that God had sent me to meet her and the other *cursillistas* to hear their stories. She was led to the *cursillo* by God, she said, to help her get through this terrible time in her life and to make her whole again. The *cursillo* healed her and restored her faith, not only in God and the Catholic Church but also in her fellow man. It was during the three-day course that she became part of a community that would help to sustain her in all times—the good and the bad. Today, Rosita is active in the movement and is one of the key organizers of *cursillos* in greater San Diego. Rosita and her husband Enrique devote countless hours to the movement and to creating an environment where their fellow Mexicanos can find themselves and Jesus.

Like Rosita, Carmen has shared her story that was full of suffering, pain, and trusting God. Carmen was eager to talk with me about her experience. She said, "Unlike Rosita, I did not want to make a *cursillo*—I resisted it, I did! I saw the changes in my husband, who had made his, I mean, his face was long and calm, he was a different man! I was frustrated with him—he was like, too good to be true! . . . Me, I loved money too much. I worked in a factory and as a waitress—I loved the feel of money in my apron—in fact, I can still feel it now. How I loved to feel the bulge of money in my pockets! God really worked on me—it took two years—I made my *cursillo* two years after my husband made his. . . . Now I don't want to say that my life has been easy since making the *cursillo*, in fact it has been very, very hard and I don't understand everything that has happened in my life. I have had two hip replacements and shoulder surgery. I have lost my husband and my children. I have gone through many, many tragedies. But it is God and the *cursillo* that have enabled me to cope with everything, even though I don't understand why it has all happened. I need *cursillo*. It is my life." At this point, Carmen began to cry and said, "This isn't fair, I am not supposed to cry right now." Carmen added, "Everyone is changed after making the *cursillo*—everyone. Everything is different. And we see Christ in every one of us."[15]

Because of their experiences in the three-day *cursillo* retreat, Rosita and Carmen were both able to regain a sense of what mattered to them and a sense of centeredness. Family tragedies and circumstances had led them to loss and despair, and they were at a deep and profound loss. Arthur Kleinman has written, "Ordinary experience frequently thrusts people into troubling circumstances and confounding conditions that threaten to undo our thin mastery over those deeper things that matter most, such as our self-esteem, intimate relations, or family values. . . . These common calamities can break our grip on what we hold dear and destroy our sense that we are in control of our fate."[16] Experiencing the three-day course, entering into a supportive, Hispanic Catholic community, and attending weekly group reunion meetings helped ease the pain and helped them rebuild their lives and to live on hope. The challenge as an ethnographer working with people of faith is to take seriously these narratives of pain, suffering and anguish and to take care not to explain them away. We must engage the emotion and even experience it for ourselves to have empathy and to understand our interlocutors' perspectives. Our interlocutors open up to us and trust us with their stories, powerful testimonies of faith. Our job, as scholars of religion, is to treat their stories with respect, whether we agree with them or not.

Engaging in ethnographic work is a privileged enterprise in which one hears stories such as Rosita's and Carmen's and is left wondering how to interpret them and how to honor them. Renato Rosaldo has noted that fieldwork is "deep hanging out."[17] It is much more than that.

Fieldwork is consuming, exhausting, and pushes us to our physical and existential limits because if we are doing our job right, we are working intimately with others and are forced to examine our own selves and our own moral agendas. We are forced to clarify what it is that *we* believe and why it is that we are in the field to being with. Our interlocutors ask us hard questions, and we must answer them. There have been times that I have envied historian friends of mine who do not have to open themselves up to their interlocutors. I agree with Ann Taves that historians' aim is "neither to seek to keep traditions alive not to 'kill' them, but rather to observe and analyze the processes that those who identify with them employ to maintain and transform them." I also think that for ethnographers, if we are doing our job right, we cannot help but be drawn in to the lived religious world in ways that add another layer to our etic/outsider observations and analyses.[18] Yes, we observe and analyze, but we are drawn into the complex worlds of our interlocutors in ways that are impossible to avoid, given the work of ethnography. We observe, analyze, and learn from our own engagement in the religious and moral worlds we are studying.

In other words, because of the emotional work of fieldwork and the intensity of the relationships we have with our interlocutors, ethnographers are observers and analyzers but are more than that, too. We occupy another space of inquiry that pushes boundaries that have been set before us. We are somewhere in between those who "treat the tradition or discipline as a set of human beliefs and practices that can be understood historically" and "those who actively seek to keep a tradition or discipline alive in the present by defining what it means to live in the present."[19] Ethnographers tend to be outsiders to the traditions they are studying and often study the particular culture/tradition because it moves them in powerful ways. We end our ethnographic work as changed individuals, neither outsiders nor insiders but somewhere else. We have crafted a new space for ourselves, and we have been shaped by those we set out to study.

Most scholars within the subdiscipline of Catholic Studies are or were "insiders" to the tradition. At the very least, those who write about American Catholicism were, at some point in their lives, "Catholic" and their scholarship often emerges out of these deeply intimate familial intimate ties. Robert Orsi best exemplifies this genre of writing, and his scholarship is deeply informed by his childhood memories and experiences of Italian American Catholicism. In *Between Heaven and Earth*, a movingly written account of Catholic faith, belief, and praxis as experienced by his Italian American kin, Orsi excavates the hidden and not so hidden moral worlds of his grandparents, uncles, and parents. Orsi's love of family and faith is evident in his writing, and his scholarship is always mindful of those about whom he is writing.[20] Like Orsi, the sociologist of religion Michael Carroll was also raised Catholic, and his scholarship is directly informed by his Catholic childhood and culture. Though he claims to write as a "scholar and not a practitioner," all of his scholarship is inspired by the Catholic imagination instilled in him at a young age in San Francisco's North Beach. The back chapels of statues at his parish church, those that depicted bloodied and wounded saints in graphic ways, intrigued him at an early age and spurred what later became his research.[21]

Orsi and Carroll's scholarly imaginations are directly informed by the Catholicism of their youth. They are not alone as even a quick perusal of Catholic Studies literature will show that the vast majority of scholars who research and write about American Catholicism have ties to the faith, and many have a particular kind of investment in what they write. The editors and most of the contributors to this volume are themselves insiders to the tradition they study. They speak a certain language and know Catholic cultural codes that an outsider to the tradition, no matter how informed and empathetic, cannot quite grasp. I have been to many Catholic Studies conferences and seminars over the years, and while my hosts are always kind and welcoming, because I lack the historic and familial grounding in the tradition, I often feel like an outsider.

I think that it is precisely because of my non-Catholic status that I have been able to raise the issues that I have raised so far, which include seeking to write more inclusive Catholic histories that reflect the experiences and histories of U.S. Catholics as well as other American Christians, and working to create an inclusive Catholic narrative that addresses U.S. Latinos concerns and realities as an intrinsic part of American Catholicism. If we truly want to write about lived religions, in this case lived Catholicism, then we must attend to what Catholics share with Protestants. I have found in the course of my research for my current book project on Catholic and Protestant *cursillos* that millions of U.S. Catholics and Protestants are seeking the same thing: a deeper relationship with Christ and a vibrant community of believers who can challenge them to live their faith each day. It has been the methodology of ethnography that has helped me see that those Catholics with whom I have worked share similar concerns and hopes of their Protestant brothers and sisters. I began my academic journey as a scholar of U.S. Hispanic Catholicism, and today I work to integrate Catholic and Protestant, Hispanic and Anglo narratives into one history precisely because I see and hear how they share similar hopes and dreams.

As an ethnographer of contemporary lived Christianities, I am repeatedly asked questions such as, "Well, what do *you* believe?" "Do you think Mary is appearing?" "What do you think about what I have just told you, *hija*?" As ethnographers, we are dealing with living people, we gain their trust—even when history tells them they should not trust us, they do. And, to be sure, many academics have betrayed the trust of the communities in which they worked. Why did Arturo trust me and introduce me to Estela, a spiritual matriarch of South Phoenix? Why did he take a risk and drive me to her home? Why did Estela and her family take me in, open their hearts and homes to me over a period of several years? Why have Rosita and Carmen, among others, shared their heart-wrenching stories with me? The Mexican Americans with whom I have worked have been among the most generous people I have ever met and placed their trust in me, a young, inexperienced scholar when they first met me, and trusted that my motives were good and that I would represent them and would help their community by spreading the news of what they were accomplishing. As ethnographers of religion, we must honor this trust by excavating our own agendas, by exposing ourselves to our interlocutors. If we do this, we will produce scholarship that matters because it comes out of a caring commitment to those we study.

We must respect those about whom we write, whose who take us in, who tolerate our questions, who place their trust in us because they believe in what we are doing—sometimes more than we do. We are part of our interlocutor's world, what Pierre Bourdieu has called *habitus*. According to Bourdieu, *habitus* is "how the micropractices of everyday life are interconnected in webs of significance that govern our experiential engagements with the world."[22] As I was sorting through my fieldnotes and writing my first book, reading Bourdieu was helpful to me in understanding the Mexican American Catholic beliefs and practices in South Phoenix because it acknowledged that individual and collective practices are the product of history. Moreover, what Bourdieu is getting at here is the dialectical relationship between the scholar and her interlocutors: we are enmeshed in the very webs we are studying.

I remember drinking hot chocolate in December of 1998, listening to several men and women share their experiences with the Virgin and I, unprompted and willingly, talked about being "touched" by the Virgin and feeling a sense of peace there—this was true. I talked about how I had goose bumps when I heard a song that was sung to the Virgin Mary—this was also true. I talked about missing my husband, who was far away in Indiana, while I was living in South Phoenix. I spoke of our desire to have children, my goal of securing an academic job, and my then-state of spiritual wandering. In setting out to study a religious phenomenon in South Phoenix—gang members and their devotions to Mary and apparitions of the Virgin Mary—I unwittingly was being pushed to clarify my own beliefs, my own views on community and what matters in life. It was only fair, right? If we expect others to take our questions seriously then we need to take theirs, too. Why, exactly, had I fallen away from the Lutheran faith? How did I define and live my faith? I was asked these questions and was forced to deal with them. Yes, sometimes I felt really uncomfortable, but this is the part of the work of doing ethnography, and in the process of exposing my own religious and moral world I gained a greater understanding to the Mexican American Catholic world I was studying.

In my current research on Catholic and Protestant *cursillos*, I am being told by my interlocutors in California, Indiana, Florida, South Carolina, and Illinois that I should make my *cursillo* in order to truly understand what they are telling me. For all of the *cursillistas* I have met over the past five years, while their weekend retreat was instrumental to their new lives as Christians, what they chose to emphasize to me in the course of our conversations is that the most important thing is to "live the fourth day." The *cursillo* retreat itself is three days, and the fourth day is "the rest of your life," according to *cursillistas*.

Soon after the *cursillo* is over, the participant is to join a small group (called a reunion group) and work on living his or her renewed Christian faith each day. Over the past five years I have been privileged to listen to Catholic men and women such as Rosita and Carmen share personal testimonies of how they have been healed, transformed, and saved by Jesus and the Holy Spirit during a *cursillo* weekend and how they receive love and support from the men and women in their weekly group reunion meetings. I have listened to witness talks at a Lutheran Via de Cristo *ultreya* (reunion of group reunions) and can see what links these Lutherans to their Catholic counterparts in San Diego. These Anglo and Hispanic Lutherans in Orlando, Florida, are concerned with living their fourth day just as their Hispanic Catholic counterparts are in San Diego. And just as these Catholics and Lutherans work on "living their fourth," so do the variety of Protestants I met at a Tres Dias ultreya in Rockford, Illinois. Presbyterian, Lutheran, nondenominational Christian, and Catholic Christians met at a Presbyterian church to talk about their love for Christ and how they work on "living for Him."[23] First- through fourth-generation Mexican Americans and Anglo American Catholics and Protestants have spoken passionately about their group reunion meetings that help sustain them in their daily lives once the *cursillo* weekend is over. I have spoken with scores of U.S. Catholics and Protestants who say that those weekends changed their lives and made them better, more faithful Christians. I have talked with men in Rock Island, Illinois, who have been meeting each week since they made their *cursillo* together twenty-seven years earlier and who count on their weekly gathering for sustenance and strength. I have talked with women from a variety of Protestant traditions, and they all emphasize the importance of meeting regularly with other women in their group reunions. My ethnographic focus has helped me realize that the widespread phenomenon of Christian small groups includes Catholics and Protestants, and they are saying essentially the same thing. The Catholic and Protestant men and women I have encountered in the course of research for my current book all downplay denominational differences in favor of what connects them: a desire to know and experience Christ and to be Christians who live their faith each day.

What it means to do Catholic Studies as a non-Catholic ethnographer of religion is to have certain challenges. U.S. Catholic and Protestant histories are deeply connected, and in order for it to achieve and maintain a deep kind of relevance in academia, Catholic Studies needs to be part of Religious Studies more broadly. Ethnographies are one way to contextualize Catholics with the larger American religious and social landscape in which they live. I have come to see it as my job to connect American Christian religious narratives and histories precisely because I am an ethnographer who listens and hears common themes from her Catholic and Protestant interlocutors. Moreover, if we as Catholic Studies scholars attend to the larger methodological and moral concerns of our interlocutors, whether historical or living, we will ensure that the subdiscipline remains an active contributor and participant in Religious Studies, sociology, and anthropology. Catholic Studies matters as a discipline, and non-Catholics can offer insights, coaxing us to new areas of inquiry and linking Catholic and Protestant concerns. We must always be careful to listen closely to our interlocutors and strive toward understanding. If we do our job right, we will be led to see, as I have found in the course of my own historical and ethnographic research, that what U.S. Hispanic Catholics are doing and saying reflects broader themes and issues that affect Anglo Catholics and Protestants alike.

Part V: The Catholic Imagination

15 Seeing Catholicly

Poetry and the Catholic Imagination

ANGELA ALAIMO O'DONNELL

In her poem "The Robin's My Criterion for Tune," Emily Dickinson attempts to describe the peculiar vision that powers her imagination and informs her poetry. With typical deftness, she states simply, "I see—New Englandly." Anyone who has read even a few of Dickinson's poems—each sparse and spare, yet offering up food for the soul even the angels might savor—recognizes exactly what she means by this. Dickinson's geographic home, an accident of her birth, has located her in the universe, given her a vantage point from which to see the world and a language to engage it. The rhythm of New England seasons lends to her poems their sense of temporality, the slant sun a light to her landscapes. Also embedded in Dickinson's remark is the looming presence of the dark, Puritan God, who is a permanent part of her consciousness. Although she rebelled against her family's Calvinist faith, which took the form of Orthodox Congregationalism, Dickinson could never quite shake the gloom of her religion, and it casts its long shadow even in her sunniest poems.

Apparently with no surprise
To any happy Flower
The Frost beheads it at its play—
In accidental power—
The blind Assassin passes on—
The Sun remains unmoved
To measure off another Day
For an Approving God.[1]

God's indifference to the world and the suffering of its creatures portrayed in this poem is typical of the Puritan vision, famously expounded by Jonathan Edwards in his sermons as well as in the writings of his Puritan predecessors. Dickinson inherited this New England theology along with the local air and accent, all of which contributed to the evolution of her vision and her poetic practice. To "see—New Englandly" is to see the world in a necessarily circumscribed way, but it is also to see it clearly. Dickinson lays claim to her identity as an artist with this simple description, yet rather than flattening out her body of work and rendering it typical or generic, the defining phrase sharpens our sense of its uniqueness, throws into high relief the special qualities that give it heft and texture, a presence in the physical world.

I want to borrow Dickinson's poetic formulation, making a slight adjustment, to identify another very particular way of seeing the world, one less informed by physical geography than by a spiritual one. Writers whose minds, hearts, and spirits have been shaped to some extent by the Catholic Church might be said to "see Catholicly." Anyone who has been brought up in a Catholic household, undergone the process of formation in preparation to receive the sacraments, or been educated in Catholic schools has been initiated into the unique configuration of reality afforded by Christian theology as communicated through scripture and church tradition. The world according to the Catholic writer is distinctive, different from the one seen by Dickinson, for example, and the God who oversees it is different as well. This distinctiveness, evident in the work of any number of Catholic writers, is nowhere more present than in the poems of Dickinson's contemporary, the English Jesuit poet Gerard Manley Hopkins.

As with Dickinson's, many of Hopkins's poems focus on the landscape native to him, the shimmering green world of the British Isles. He, too, has a keen eye for telling detail and feels a kinship with the things and creatures of earth. Taking his cue from his spiritual mentor, Saint Ignatius of Loyola, Hopkins recognizes and celebrates the presence of "God in All Things." For Hopkins, every aspect of creation bears the imprint of its Creator—expresses God's singularity, energy, and sheer delight in the fact of existence. The most seemingly ordinary creatures and objects are suffused by the transforming medium of light enabling him to see the "inscape" of each thing, its *haecceitas* (a term Hopkins borrows from another spiritual mentor, Duns Scotus) or thisness. Every thing is important and worthy of such attention for its own sake, but it takes on even greater significance when seen as a means through which God communicates boundless goodness to us. In his sonnet "As Kingfishers Catch Fire," Hopkins articulates this principle of uniqueness in the highly condensed language and fractured syntax characteristic of his work as he attempts to say the unsayable:

> Each mortal thing does one thing and the same:
> Deals out that being indoors each one dwells;
> Selves—goes its self; *myself*, it speaks and spells,
> Crying *What I do is me: For that I came!*"

The physical world is informed and animated by the divine principle of self-emptying love, and this principle is most evident, the poem reminds us, in human beings, who are made in the image of God:

> For Christ plays in ten thousand places,
> Lovely in limbs, and lovely in eyes not his
> To the Father through the features of men's faces.[2]

Hopkins's perception and understanding of the world is mediated by Christ and colored by the Incarnation, its history and consequences. For him, the truth of the imagination is inseparable from the vision accorded him by his faith. In short, as a priest, as a poet, and as a human being, he sees the world Catholicly. And he is far from alone in this.

In his classic study, *The Analogical Imagination,* David Tracy has developed a critical vocabulary to describe the characteristically Catholic vision evident in Hopkins's poems and in the work of other Catholic writers. Tracy's terminology has served subsequent readers, writers, and critics well in the ongoing attempt to map the rich and varied geography of the Catholic imagination. At the heart of Tracy's argument is the distinction between the analogical (or Catholic) and dialectical (or Protestant" imagination. Sociologist and novelist Andrew Greeley summarizes succinctly some of the differences between these two ways of seeing the world in his own book *The Catholic Imagination*:

> Tracy noted that the classic works of Catholic theologians and artists tend to emphasize the presence of God in the world, while the classic works of Protestant theologians tend to emphasize the absence of

> God from the world. The Catholic writers stress the nearness of God to His creation, the Protestant writers the distance between God and His creation; the Protestants emphasize the risk of superstition and idolatry, the Catholics the dangers of a creation in which God is only marginally present. Or, to put the matter in different terms, Catholics tend to accentuate the immanence of God, Protestants the transcendence of God.[3]

These generalizations summarize accurately some of the key differences in voice and vision evident in the poems of Catholic Hopkins and Protestant Dickinson discussed earlier, and the passage also suggests their universality, though the latter point is accompanied by some important caveats.

In the present consideration of the Catholic imagination, I would like to examine the phenomenon as a disposition that defines itself not only in contrast to other religious visions (Protestant, or, for that matter, Judaic, Muslim, Hindu, or Buddhist), but as a counterpoint to the predominantly secular worldview that asserts itself in most aspects of the current culture, including the art it produces and the critical methods typically employed to critique it. The essay will attempt to describe the various forms the ordinary world takes when seen Catholicly—thorough the eyes of poets, novelists, filmmakers, and artists—and to provide answers to some questions one might raise in connection with this issue: What are some hallmarks of Catholic vision that might allow readers to identify a Catholic imagination at work when they encounter one? Is it possible to identify lines of continuity among writers whose work is original and entirely unique to that person? And, finally, in what way can seeing—and representing—the world Catholicly bear the stamp of truth for non-Catholics as well as Catholics?

I would like to delineate, at the outset, the limits of this essay. In mapping the Catholic imagination, one encounters some difficult terrain, and I make no pretense of making the rough ways smooth. Authors of more ambitious studies than this, including Paul Giles in *American Catholic Arts and Fictions* and Paula M. Kane in "American Catholic Culture in the Twentieth Century," have demonstrated the impossibility of identifying a singular and unified Catholic imagination that cuts across time and circumstance. Indeed, Kane notes the "hybrid identity"[4] of Catholic writers in all times and all places, shaped as they are by forces large and small, including geography, ethnicity, historical moment, politics, and local and family practice of the faith. From age to age, Catholic writers struggle to align an ancient faith with a modern culture, the former attempting to hold to tradition and the latter in a constant state of flux, and their art is a direct result of this tension. Accordingly, this essay acknowledges the various and changing nature of the Catholic imagination. Rather than constructing a narrow gate through which only the most conservative and traditional Catholic writers may pass, I am proposing a broad (though, hopefully, not easy) path, one wide enough to accommodate the enormous range of people that the Church itself (in the tradition of "H.C.E."—that is, "Here Comes Everybody") encompasses. Such a range includes the pious priest (Hopkins), the faithful cradle Catholic (Flannery O'Connor), the naughty convert (Mary Karr), and the near-apostate (Czeslaw Milosz), along with many others.

In addition, rather than offer a triumphalist account that celebrates select Catholic writers in attempt to create a strict canon and thus "revive an imaginary Catholic Golden Age,"[5] as some studies have done, this essay seeks to explore the work produced by recent and current authors, each writing from within his or her own particular milieu, and discover the ways in which they redefine the Catholic Imagination even as they engage and exercise it. My goal in conducting this exploration is not to assert, in the end, that Catholic writers are better than writers of other faiths and backgrounds—but to suggest that they are "different," to use Garry Wills's wonderfully vague but telling term, and that oftentimes their "difference" takes similar forms.

Grace Is Everywhere

At the conclusion of his novel *The Diary of a Country Priest*, which tells the story of a young, newly ordained priest trying to live out his faith amid a parish of spiritually impoverished rural Catholics in mid-twentieth-century France, George Bernanos depicts an epiphany the young man experiences as he dies an agonizing death from untreated stomach cancer: "*Grace is everywhere*."[6] These are words of wisdom or of lunacy—there is no middle ground here. He is either led by what he would call the Holy Spirit to a vision of the true nature of reality—one that is suffused, transformed, and redeemed by the presence of the Divine—or he is suffering the final throes of delusion at the conclusion of a deluded life, his mind addled by pain so horrific it warps what he sees and understands about the world he has been living, and is now dying, in.

This same either-or proposition—lunacy or wisdom—has also been provocatively applied to the sayings of Christ by Christian apologist and Anglo-Catholic writer C. S. Lewis. When Jesus tells his followers in John's Gospel that they must eat his flesh and drink his blood in order to gain salvation, most of them are so utterly appalled at the proposition that they leave. Only Peter and the disciples remain—though they are deeply troubled by what their Master has said—offering only this poignant explanation for their continued allegiance: "Lord, to whom shall we go? You have the words of eternal life" (John 6:68). Only God or a madman, Lewis proposes, would dare to make such outrageous claims. And it is, in fact, the extravagance of Christ's claims that convince his followers that he speaks the truth: the institution of the Eucharist both attracts and repels them, entices and disgusts, and somehow precisely this combination of the ordinary and the seemingly absurd—articulated through the agency of word and metaphor—wins their loyalty and their admiration, though not their understanding. In his justly famous statement about the mystery entailed in the Eucharist, Lewis emphasizes the fact that Jesus knew that what he was calling his followers to was the exercise of radical faith: "The command, after all, was Take, eat: not Take, understand."[7]

The vision of salvation offered by Christ in the gospels and by George Bernanos's little priest is the same one: beauty, truth, and, ultimately, love lurk in the lineaments of the world and are embodied in the least likely forms. This is the revelation that Hopkins articulates in the sonnet quoted earlier and in many of his other poems as well. "The World is Charged with the Grandeur of God" the poet assures himself and us—even the bare soil and the bleared-smeared, charred-scarred landscape of the postindustrial twenty-first century—even, I would argue, the horrific postnuclear earth described so chillingly in Catholic novelist Cormac McCarthy's novel *The Road*. In one of that book's rare luminous moments, the dying father glances down the road that is their only possible means to salvation and sees his son "glowing in that waste like a tabernacle."[8] For the child, inexplicably, to the father's mind, instinctively loves his fellow creatures, horribly corrupt and misshapen as they are. He does not realize the love he sees radiating from the boy is a reflection of his own absolute, unconditional, self-emptying love—the kind of perfect love ascribed to God and enacted by Christ.

The landscape of grace pervades the work of these two Catholic novelists—Bernanos and McCarthy—and the Catholic poet Hopkins. As Flannery O'Connor has observed, the role of the Catholic, and of the Catholic writer in particular, is to "cherish the world at the same time you struggle to endure it."[9] Each of these writers asserts a vision that is grounded, first, in the Gospels—and second, in the sacramental theology of the Catholic Church, most notably that of the Eucharist. Because of this grounding in scripture and tradition most Catholics experience from the time when they are very small children, the Catholic imagination is characteristically attentive to words and things simultaneously. In his brilliant study *Christ and Apollo*, William Lynch examines the complex nexus between theological concept and aesthetic practice, or more specifically, the Incarnation and art. Lynch asserts the primacy of the premise that it is through finitude and concrete being in the world—flesh and bone, blood and breath, bread and wine—that the infinite God makes Himself known to us over and over again, and demonstrates the ways in which the artist uses this same concrete finiteness—the object, the image, the word—to body forth in his or her art this implicit reality.[10] This devotion to "the definite" is especially pronounced and identifiable in the work of Catholic writers. What defines a Catholic poet and Catholic poetry cannot be readily summed up in terms of content or technique; instead, Catholic poetry reflects and embodies a particular disposition towards the world. It is corporeal, perhaps even bloody-minded, in its insistence upon an embodied, incarnate faith; it is grim in its acknowledgment of the presence and power of real evil in the world; and it is ultimately hopeful in its assertion of the meaning of suffering and in its persistent search for God even when God seems to be absent.

We might describe this disposition as an Incarnational awareness, and it takes many forms. Catholic art depicts transcendent truth made manifest in the material reality of the world, especially through the body—so much so, that even the vision of heaven and hell offered by that most Catholic of poets, Dante, is a three-dimensional flesh-and-blood depiction of the spirit world as physically present to us as any scene from a film by Martin Scorsese (another Catholic artist who shares this bloody disposition). Consider, for example, Dante's depiction of Count Ugolino gnawing inexorably on the brains of Archbishop Ruggieri in the lowest circle of Hell—the punishment for Ruggieri's imprisonment and starvation of Ugolino and his children and for Ugolino's possible cannibalism and quenchless appetite for revenge. Aside from its gruesomeness and relentlessness, what is striking about the scenario is its poetic justice: the punishment they endure is a horrific perversion of Eucharist, wherein Ruggieri becomes the body and blood the perpetually starved Ugolino devours instead of Christ, and the ritual becomes one that tends toward their mutual destruction rather than eternal life. A Catholic poet writing for readers who share a devotion to the Eucharist, Dante can depend upon his audience to understand this scenario to be an infernal version of the sacrament that saves. This is the Catholic poetic imagination at work, habitually and instinctively returning to the reality and symbol of flesh and blood to express meaning.

God in All Things

Catholics take a lot of abuse for their tendency to invest particular material entities with supernatural significance, to see in ordinary objects a bodying forth of the Divine, which pervades All. They have been portrayed in literature and film as idol-worshipping pagans, credulous fools who delight in apparitions and miracles, and death-obsessed, relic-loving ghouls. And, in all honesty, there is some small truth in these caricatures. Witness the Catholic affection for graven images—ranging from quaint carvings of Saint Francis preaching to the birds to Bernini's sublime depiction of Saint Theresa in ecstasy—their passionate pilgrimages to holy places such as Lourdes, Medjugorje, and Mount Tepeyac—their love of artifacts and paraphernalia, rosary beads and scapulars, pix and monstrance, extends even to the words that describe them. I once heard a genial monk explaining to a group of people touring his monastery's relic collection that the Catholic practice of revering the bones and teeth of dead saints was a lot like keeping hand-me-downs or heirlooms left to us by members of our families. Catholics love *stuff*—treasure the this-ness of things—material reality made sacred by its association with the human and the holy. Incorruptible saints' bodies, pieces of the true cross, and stigmata in the hands and feet of real people fill them with wonder.

Of course, these things are sometimes as appalling as they are appealing precisely because they point towards a supernatural world we cannot comprehend. I confess to having been frightened, as a child, by the fierce, pagan-influenced Catholicism of my immigrant grandparents. My siblings and I were terrified of the enormous Infant of Prague statue that stood in the darkness of my grandparents' bedroom. It was surrounded by perpetually lit votive candles, and there was a worn wooden kneeler in front of it, attesting to my grandmother's terrific piety. As kids we would dare one another to spend thirty seconds in the room with the door firmly closed. None of us could ever stay for the duration—not with that Infant staring at us from across the room. Somehow He knew we were up to no good, and there was no telling what He might do.

This fear has long been a characteristic quality of the Catholic imagination. Unfortunately, post–Vatican II Catholics have become afraid of fear—afraid of acknowledging it as a key element of faith. When I studied for Confirmation as a twelve-year-old many years ago, we learned by heart the Seven Gifts of the Holy Spirit. The list contained Wisdom, Understanding, Right Judgment, Courage, Knowledge, and Reverence and concluded with the Fear of the Lord. When my own children were going through the process of catechesis some years ago, I was surprised to find that this spiritual gift had been renamed "Wonder and Awe." Granted, these terms capture more accurately the attitude one ought to cultivate as one develops a mature relationship with the Divine, and they describe feelings the Friends of God might harbor, as opposed to those experienced by those estranged from God. Yet, still, I must confess some disappointment in this—it is almost as if the revisionists believed we could deny the element of fear that is inevitably present when any mortal creature faces the prospect of eternity. Even Jesus felt fear—and famously so—in Gethsemane—so why should *we* be exempt?

Sin

Poetry written by Catholics bears witness to fear in all kinds of ways—the fear of death, of course, but also the fear of ourselves—of what we are capable of—the destructive power of our words and actions—of the inevitability of sin, despite our best efforts. As Ruggieri and Ugolino discover, what one does in the present life has consequences for eternity, both in literal and metaphoric ways. Belief in sin posits great power in human action. It acknowledges the consequential nature of each and every human being's life, both for good and for ill. If "*Grace is everywhere*" it is because "*Sin is everywhere*"—you cannot have one without the other—and most poetry written by Catholics incorporates, in ways hidden and overt, this unresolvable paradox.

This paradox is most visibly embodied by God's broken body upon the cross, an image displayed prominently in every Catholic Church, kept in most Catholic homes, and present, at some level of consciousness, in nearly every Catholic psyche. This is not an empty cross, one from which the body has been decently removed and disposed of. It is a wounded, bloody corpse, fully present to the viewer in its suffering, its humiliation, and its apparent weakness. And it is this same body that is celebrated at communion, broken up into its components of flesh and blood, consumed in the form of bread and wine that simultaneously is food both ordinary and supernatural, a sacramental understanding that embraces and includes ourselves, so that our own bodies, processing up to the altar, become recognizable as eternal souls as well as weak mean and women who will die someday.

An ancient devotional practice—one traceable, ultimately, to Calvary—is to place oneself at the foot of the cross and enter into Christ's suffering. This is something Catholics are encouraged to do, even as children, in order to appreciate the significance of the Incarnation in human terms. To do so is not only to partake in Christ's pain, but also to be absorbed, inevitably, as a participant in the crime of the crucifixion. Theologically speaking, human sin (our common inheritance) is both the cause and justifying purpose of Christ's death, making the latter a lamentable but absolutely necessary eschatological event. Thus, the watcher at the cross must hold in suspension twin realities: the shame of sin and the grandeur of God's grace that turns even our evil to good. It is this double-mindedness that I have tried to express in "The First Art," one of several crucifixion poems I wrote some years ago while engaged in the Spiritual Exercises of St. Ignatius Loyola:

> The rough wood splits and yaws
> worn smooth in places
> where hands, heads, buttocks, feet
> of the crucified before Christ
> rubbed and writhed and rested.
> A well-used cross,
> borrowed, not bought.
> Nothing new,
> not even the nails.
> The ropes rented,
> the spear in the side plagiarized.
> All rehearsed ten thousand times,
> revised ten thousand places,
> until we got it right.

The poem's initial focus on the cross, rather than the corpus, attempts to suggest imagistically that even the instruments of Christ's death are embodiments of divine grace, part and parcel of the ritual execution long-awaited and prepared for (as scripture indicates) in the fullness of time. And though the poem may part company with literal and historical fact, the idea of a secondhand cross leads the reader to the contemplation of the Body that hangs upon it as the universal corpse—of Christ's death as one that has occurred over and over again—thus representing each and all of ours.

The Catholic response to the central event of Christianity and to the sacraments that commemorate it is a complex mingling of fear and pity, guilt and gratitude, happiness and horror—all implied, perhaps, by "Wonder and Awe." Considering the magnitude of meaning inherent in these events, any ordinary assemblage of words seems inadequate. It seems all but inevitable that the Catholic sensibility would resort to poetry as a means of conveying this complex of ideas.

Words and Things

Catholic sacramental practice is heady stuff, indeed, and we learn all of this when we are seven—sometimes younger. As Garry Wills states, with characteristic succinctness, in the opening words of his memoir about his Catholic boyhood, *Bare Ruined Choirs*, "We grew up different."[11] It is activity of body and soul that imprints itself on the consciousness of the cradle-Catholic, in particular, at the most impressionable time of his or her life. In her memoir *Virgin Time*, the poet Patricia Hampl describes the indelible imprint it leaves:

> Mine was a Catholic girlhood spent gorging on metaphor—Mystical Body, transubstantiation, dark night of the soul, the little martyrdom of everyday life. And remember, girls, life is a journey. Your own life is a pilgrimage. Maybe we had too much learning too early. It was like having too much money. The quirkiness of life was betrayed, given inflated significance by our inflated symbology. We powered around our ordinary lives in the Cadillac language of Catholic spirituality, looking on with pity as the Protestants pedaled their stripped down bicycles.[12]

This routine access to the language of mystery Hampl speaks of resonates loudly with most Catholics. Each of us has our own story of learning to live with this extraordinary legacy, myself included. I grew up in a bookless single-parent household, one of five children raised by a dear but undereducated mother who, if not the Mistress of Malaprop, was at least a very good apprentice. We grew up believing that the word for green pepper was "mango." Our mother is a woman who habitually misnamed the shampoo my sister used as "Herbal Adolescence," and who announced loudly in an intersection in Philadelphia one summer afternoon just after she caused a fender-bender that we needed to call "A.A." right away, despite our *sotto voce* suggestions that she supply the third and crucial "A." From this linguistically challenged household setting, we would venture into the rarified word-world of Our Lady of Sorrows Church, where we would learn the distinction between "mortal" and "venial" sins, master the definitions of the Imminent and the Economic Trinity, where we would memorize the exact formula for a perfect Act of Contrition. In short, we learned a respect and a reverence for words that conjured God. We learned that language had precision and power—that when arranged in particular sequences of sound, when recited in community according to a cadence decided upon and obeyed by all, it could call down the miraculous, it could heal mortal illness, it could exorcise demons, it could resurrect the dead. Prayer was poetry, and we all practiced it regularly, faithfully, thoughtlessly. It was as effortless as breath.

Such language and such richness of symbol made it hard for us to know where the sacred stopped and the profane began. The Church taught us that the world had meaning and that it meant intensely. It also taught us that the method of communication between the two realms was an issue of great concern: how you say a thing can be a matter of life or death. And though contemporary philosophers, such as Charles Taylor in his recent book *A Secular Age*, argue persuasively that the modern self is no longer capable of wholly dwelling in the "enchanted world" inhabited by the medieval Catholic, the Church of my childhood was the only institution that offered us even the possibility of such a world. Such teaching has long been particularly compelling for those in possession of a lively imagination, and even those whose imaginations might be more sluggish could depend upon plenty of stimulation from good (and bad) church art, stories of saints' lives, and urgent sermons focused on the pleasures of heaven and the pains of hell.

Given all of this, it is not surprising that so many fine poets are Catholic. Earlier I suggested that Catholic writers seek out poetry as a congenial means of expression, but the opposite also seems to be true as well—that poetry seeks out—or, more precisely, appeals to—Catholics, and powerfully so. This is true of Catholic artists who are born in the Church, those who come to it later in life as converts, and those who have, ostensibly, left the Church. One such "recovering Catholic," Martin Scorsese, once said, "My whole life has been movies and religion. That's it. Nothing else."[13] Clearly in his mind, his art and his faith have everything to do with one another; they coexist in equal measure in his imagination as shaping, formative influences.

Art as Sacrament

David Jones, the Welsh poet and artist who converted to Catholicism just after the First World War, writes lucidly in his essay "Art and Sacrament" about the link between the artistic and the religious impulse, the awareness of the sacramental quality of creation and the defining identity of human beings as makers or artists. Grounded in natural-law theory as articulated by Thomas Aquinas and Jacques Maritain, Jones asserts the basic identity of man as rational creature who differs from animals in his possession of reason, volition, and the ability to engage in creating things that are both beautiful and gratuitous. In the course of his essay, Jones expands the definition of "art" until it includes not only the poem and the painting, but also any object that is created with "significant intent"—that is, designed to say something beyond itself and to communicate with another being outside the self. The signmaking activity of artistic creation is of a piece with the signmaking that we typically think of when we hear the word "sacrament." Sacramental activity engages the transcendent through the use of mundane materials: the priest may use water, bread, and wine, while the artist may use paint, stone, wood, glass, film, ink, and paper. Moreover, based upon this similarity, Jones enables the reader to see celebration of the sacraments as a kind of artistic making: the ritual of transubstantiation becomes an artistic act, as God transmutes wine into blood and bread into flesh through the agency of the priest. All signmaking becomes art, according to Jones's theory, and all artists the agents of the Divine, leading him to make the surprising statement, at last: "Calvary itself . . . involves *poesis*."[14] This depiction of the crucifixion as art, an essential action whose commission has significance both inside and outside of time—gives us a clear sense of the comprehensive nature of Jones's definitions of the sacramental, of *poesis*, and of the sacred quality of both. Artistic and religious endeavor become one, and all of it manifests the reality of grace.

Many, if not all, Catholic writers are *conscious* of the artist's role as a signmaking sacramentalist. They perceive the connection between their art and their religion—even though they often struggle with that relationship—and they call the reader's attention to it, both within the context of their art and beyond. In James Joyce's *Portrait of the Artist as a Young Man*, young Stephen Daedalus ultimately rejects the church he was raised in, but he cannot undo or erase the traces of the Catholic formation he has undergone. In a famous passage wherein he asserts his independence from the Catholic Church and chooses his vocation as poet over the priesthood, he uses the language of the Eucharist, stating his implicit belief that the role of the artist is equally sacramental and that it is, indeed, a higher calling to serve as "a priest of the eternal imagination, transmuting the daily bread of experience into the radiant body of everliving life."[15]

Contemporary Catholic Poets

So who are the Catholic writers among us now? As a reader, writer, and teacher of poetry, I began about ten years ago to seek out recent and contemporary poets who write from this Catholic perspective and demonstrate this disposition. I did this, in part, because I wanted to connect with other poets who were engaged in the same enterprise I was—trying to write from the standpoint of faith as a given condition of my being. I also wanted to offer to my students an additional lens through which to view poetry—one that uses a language of word and symbol that would be familiar to them (as students attending a Catholic university) and one that might speak to their own experience of being Catholic. This approach, incidentally, has proven to be a useful one in engaging students who might otherwise not enjoy poetry. I was also pleased to find that my non-Catholic students enjoyed learning about some of the aspects of Catholicism that had previously been mysterious to them through reading poems written by Catholics.

The timing of my growing interest in Catholic poetry has proven to be propitious in a number of ways. Writers and critics across various disciplines have observed a sea change in recent years in terms of artists' willingness to discuss the connection between faith and art, or, at the very least, to characterize one of the dimensions of their creative activity as spiritual. Conferences and journals devoted to faith and writing have been founded and continue to proliferate, attracting first-rank writers as presenters and contributors, and even secular writers' conferences, including the yearly gathering of the Association of Writers and Writing Programs (AWP), have begun to devote sessions to the topic.

This change in attitude has been attributed to a number of possible causes: the reaction against postmodernism, generally, and more specifically, 9/11 and subsequent horrific events, leading to the collapse of state institutions and secular ideologies. Such catastrophic events have supposedly led to a reevaluation of religion and its role in peoples' lives, both on the small and grand scale. The election (and reelection) of an evangelical Christian president, George W. Bush, brought religion into the realm of political, and therefore social, intellectual, and artistic, discourse in the United States, and the increasing awareness of religion and its importance in cultures around the globe has brought matters of faith to international attention on a daily basis.

Whatever the cause, or causes, there is little doubt that it has become acceptable for the first time in decades to regard faith as a subject worthy of consideration in an academic context. This has been a great boon for poetry in general and for Catholic poetry in particular. It also promises a further awakening of interest in Catholic Studies methodology as a viable approach to criticism and the teaching of literature, certainly at Catholic colleges and universities, where Catholic literature courses are now being offered on a regular basis, and, perhaps, at non-Catholic and secular universities as well.

The roll call of Catholic poets is a long and varied one and includes the likes of Thomas Merton, William Everson, Czeslaw Milosz, Seamus Heaney, Adam Zagajewski, Denise Levertov, David Craig, David Citino, Madeleine DeFrees, Louise Erdrich, Les Murray, Michael Dennis Brown, Josephine Jacobsen, Kate Daniels, Franz Wright, Mary Karr, Paul Mariani, and Dana Gioia, among others. Moreover, this list is steadily growing. I regularly teach courses in Contemporary Catholic Poetry and Literature—am always on the lookout for new voices—and, truly, it seems I "discover" and/or meet a new Catholic poet every month. Assembling such a list, however, is an activity fraught with complication.

The variety of voices and visions represented by the work of these writers is a testimonial to the enormous possibilities and permutations of Catholic poetry. The sampling of writers above embraces Catholics of every stamp—including lay and religious, cradle-Catholic and convert, liberal and conservative, and sacramental and communitarian—and includes poets of every stamp, as well—among them devotional and nondevotional and formalist and nonformalist writers. Clearly, there is not *one* Catholic way of writing but many, and any definition of Catholic poetry—and of the Catholic imagination—needs to be capacious enough to contain this variety. Given these complexities, how does one decide (and who decides) which writers belong on the list and which do not?

There is also the essential question of literary quality to consider: presumably, any list of Catholic poets would include only those who are competent practitioners of their craft. It is not their religion but their art that interests readers. Flannery O'Connor's dictum on fiction in her essay, "Catholic Novelists and Their Readers" is surely applicable to poets as well: "what is good in itself glorifies God because it reflects God. The Catholic artist has his hands full and does his duty if he attends to his art. He can safely leave evangelizing to the evangelists."[16] The first responsibility of the Catholic poet is to be a good poet, and the primary responsibility of the critic (Catholic or otherwise) is to read and evaluate the work carefully and well.

Finally, we have the poets' preferences to consider: who would want to be on the list, and who would object? Who might bristle at the term "Catholic poet" as reductive, divisive, and dismissive—an excuse some might use to ghettoize a writer—and who might embrace it as a part of his or her identity and an accurate description of his or her particular way of being in the world? There are certainly incentives for poets not to lay claim to their Catholic identity. Chief among these is the generally dismissive attitude of American culture toward Catholicism. Catholics are often mistrusted by other religious groups (including many Protestants, despite the fact of the Christian beliefs they hold in common) as well as by the (still) largely areligious American intelligentsia. Though sensitivity to religious identity and practice is encouraged, it is not considered intellectually respectable to be a practicing Catholic in most academic and in many creative-writing circles. In her celebrated essay that appeared in *Poetry* magazine, "Facing Altars: Poetry and Prayer," poet Mary Karr tells the amusing yet troubling story of receiving a postcard from a longtime friend in response to her conversion to Catholicism on which he had written, "Not you on the Pope's team. Say it ain't so!"—as if her newly pledged allegiance to the Church somehow meant she would of necessity become a lesser thinker, a lesser writer, and, even, perhaps, a lesser friend. Anti-Catholicism has been termed "the last acceptable prejudice."

Given this bias, there is little wonder many Catholic artists feel ambivalent about this fact of their biography and background, but embracing or denying one's formation as a Catholic does not alter the fact of it. As Patricia Hampl suggests, the experience of being in the Church—its language, its symbols, its sacraments, its artifacts, its saints and its sinners, and its art—profoundly affects the imagination. And regardless of how the individual writer feels about that experience, he has become the writer he is, or she has become the writer she is, at least in part, because of it. Irish Catholic novelist John McGahern acknowledges in his *Memoir*, written shortly before his death as he was battling cancer, that despite the fact that as an adult he came to regard the Church and his Catholic upbringing as a burden and a source of sorrow, it was the Church that introduced beauty into the grim, impoverished life he and his siblings knew. As a child attending Mass with his devout mother, as an altar boy, and later as young man aspiring to the priesthood, he learned to love the grace and beauty of religious observance and conceived the desire to create beauty himself through his writing as a result of his formation as a Catholic. For many Catholic writers, it is often in our poems and novels, perhaps more so than in any other area of our lives, that one's Catholic identity makes itself evident, both to our selves and to our readers. The act of making gestures toward the transcendent, a universe whose language is the language of the eschaton, that speaks a vocabulary of signs signifying *sin*, *grace*, and *redemption*.

Seeing Catholicly

"In the Crevice of Time," a poem by Josephine Jacobsen, conveys a characteristically Catholic vision, one that incorporates many of the concepts entertained in this essay and focuses, in particular, on the deeply Catholic sense of the sacramentality of art. Unlike the work of more overtly Catholic writers—the ebulliently Incarnational poems of Hopkins, or the devotional poems of Thomas Merton or William Everson, or even the biblically informed poems of Denise Levertov and Mary Karr inspired by the experience of praying the Spiritual Exercises of St. Ignatius—Jacobsen's poems contain quiet, more indirect manifestations of her Catholicism. In fact, it is quite possible that even careful readers of her work might remain unaware of her identity as a Catholic. Jacobsen once asserted in an interview with poet A. V. Christie, "My religion, like my work, is very private."[17] There are many possible explanations for her relative reticence, including the anti-Catholic sentiment discussed earlier. In addition, an interesting condition of Jacobsen's faith that sets her apart from the poets just mentioned is the fact that she is a lifelong Catholic, brought up in the Church by a devout mother who converted to Catholicism when the poet was a young child. Since she has not come to the Church from another faith or from a state of unbelief, being Catholic is something she takes for granted as a condition of her being. She, quite literally, does not know how to be anything else. As a result, her work lacks the self-consciousness evident in many Catholic writers who have converted and who explore in their poetry the new condition of life they find themselves in. In addition, Jacobsen has always, throughout a writing career that spans nearly nine decades and most of the twentieth century, understood herself to be a Catholic writing for a broad audience of readers, most of whom are not Catholic. Like Dickinson, who surely hoped her poetry would be read and appreciated by non–New Englanders as well as locals, Jacobsen wants her poems to reach all potential readers. Thus, Jacobsen's work serves as exemplar of a Catholic poetry informed by faith and yet consciously universal in its appeal and in the truths it communicates.

The title piece of her collected poems, "In the Crevice of Time," is characteristic of Jacobsen in that it moves by indirection, engaging theological and aesthetic concepts as grounded in earthy reality. The poem depicts a prehistoric hunter-priest struggling to comprehend the death of one of his fellows:

> The thick gross early form that made a grave
> said in one gesture, "neither bird nor leaf."
> The news no animal need bear was out:
> The knowledge of death, and time the wicked thief,
> and the prompt monster of foreseeable grief.
> It was the tentative gesture that he gave.

The human response to knowledge of the ultimate is to make something—a word, a poem, a picture, a song—a work of art, primitive though it may be, created in attempt to embody and communicate this fresh-felt truth. Thus, the prehistoric man in the cave becomes one with the reader as he enacts our own grief:

in the abyss of time how he is close,
his art an act of faith, his grave
an act of art: for all,
for all, a celebration and a burial.[18]

The grave he makes, the paintings on the cave wall, are all "tentative" gestures made here, in the crevice of time—attempts to express the timeless and the eternal through forms and substances that cannot last. The rhythmic repetition of "for all, for all" brings us inexorably into the poem, into the strange light of that ancient cave, invites us to become participants in the ritual making that acknowledges and insists upon the significance of the individual life even in the face of the overwhelming fact of death. Art manifests our intuitive longing for and deep knowledge of immortality and bodies forth, all at once, human sorrow, human wonder, and human joy. It is both celebration and burial—words that also describe the Catholic liturgy and its central sacrament, which commemorates both death and life, human sin redeemed by the agency of divine grace. It also reminds us of the practice common among Catholics of eating, drinking, singing, and storytelling at wakes and funeral suppers—a tradition still very much alive among even the most Jansenistic (one might say Calvinistic) branch of the Catholic family tree, the Irish. Death and mirth may seem strange bedfellows, but bedfellows they are in the Catholic imagination.

The terrible joy associated with death is yet one final element of Catholic art that marks it as such. No matter how dark the vision presented in the poem, the film, or the novel—no matter how close to despair Bernanos's dying priest may come, or how desolate Hopkins finds himself in his "Terrible Sonnets," or how hopeless the father in Cormac McCarthy's novel feels about his only son's future in the ruined world—the work of art asserts faith in the words it employs and the significance of the things they name. Toward the end of his long life,

Catholic poet Czeslaw Milosz, who had always pursued his art as a means of discerning ultimate truth, devoted himself with even greater urgency to this task. His poem, "Meaning," poses the questions we all ask, and answers them poignantly, as only a poet who has dedicated himself wholly to his art can:

—When I die, I will see the lining of the world.
The other side, beyond bird, mountain, sunset.
The true meaning, ready to be decoded.
What never added up will add up.
What was incomprehensible will be comprehended.

—And if there is no lining to the world?
If a thrush on a branch is not a sign,
But just a thrush on the branch? If night and day
Make no sense following each other?
And on this earth there is nothing except this earth?

—Even if that is so, there will remain
A word wakened by lips that perish,
A tireless messenger who runs and runs
Through interstellar fields, through the revolving galaxies,
And calls out, protests, screams.[19]

The word continues to sound, long after the poem ends and after the poet has died, insisting that there is meaning in human life and human death, beyond what we can readily perceive and understand, and we know this instinctively, intuitively, particularly in the breath-and-blood experience of it. This is, in part, what it means to see Catholicly. Far from being a limitation, such seeing fixes on the concrete and the finite as a means of discovering the reality of infinitude. Be it wisdom or lunacy, the Catholic artist hopes and affirms in the very act of Making that "*Grace is*," indeed, "*everywhere*," and sets out to find it.

16 Cultural Studies Between Heaven and Earth

Beyond the Puritan Pedagogy of The Scarlet Letter

THOMAS J. FERRARO

American literature is distinguished by the number of dangerous and disturbing books in its canon—and American scholarship by its ability to conceal this fact.

Leslie A. Fiedler

When the North American Studies section of the American Academy of Religion asked me to respond, in November 2005, to Robert A. Orsi's book *Between Heaven and Earth: The Religious Worlds People Make and the Scholars Who Study Them*, I cast about for a way of revealing, in concentrated but also prismatic form, what is at issue in Orsi's work for American Studies at large.[1] Surely, Orsi has succeeded in mainstreaming Italian American social history, ethnicizing American Catholic historiography, and challenging the Protestant-centeredness of U.S. religious history, and just as surely the religious-studies wing of our profession does not need me—a literature-and-arts guy—to tell them that. On the other hand, U.S. cultural studies came of age in the 1990s confident not only of the basic irrelevance of religious phenomena—there was not a single panel on religion at the 1994 American Studies Association (ASA) convention in Nashville, where Routledge editor Bill Germano told me to "forget about it, they are just not interested"—but also of the secular inviolability of its methods and commitments, certain stirrings of the spirit in Native American, Latino/a, and Black Atlantic studies notwithstanding. But we now are most definitely thinking otherwise—evidence the recent ASA formation of the Working Group in American Religion and its widely acclaimed special issue of *American Quarterly*.[2] As neglected issues and scholarship are brought to the common table under rubrics such as "religion and politics," what difference will they make not only to our scope of inquiry but also to our disciplinary assumptions and methods? How, in particular, might the work of Orsi—a seminal figure in the new religious history, a recent president of the American Academy of Religion, and a writer of theoretically knowing, formally experimental ethnography par excellence—unsettle cultural studies?

I have neither the space nor the expertise to do Orsi's scholarship or its potential use-value for cultural criticism full justice. What follows is a brief exegesis—part imaginative leap and part polemical gambit—designed to take one measure of Orsi in, I hope, illuminating, strangely old-fashioned because mythopoetic, interdisciplinary terms. It comes from my suspicion that what is old news in religious studies is new news in cultural studies, and vice versa; more importantly, it comes from the conviction that we should never underestimate the residual influence of either religion or literature in the intellectual practices of Americanists, particularly those schooled in the United States—where Protestant sensibility, as filtered through Protestant and post-Protestant understandings of predominantly Protestant writers, still speaks, however sotto voce.

Robert Anthony Orsi, our greatest scholar of urban working-class devotionalism, of the uses of Saint Jude, Saint Gemma, and Blessed Margaret of Castello, of Marian apparitions and first communions and maternal sacrifice, is also our greatest reader of America's most hallowed novel—and I bet he doesn't even know it. To link by fiat a contemporary work of religious history and a hoary, indeed encrusted New England antebellum novel, as I propose to do here, sounds foolhardy at best, an act of decontextualizing academic violence. It is certainly not the sort of thing scholars do these days—especially given the now longstanding repudiation of classic American literature (indeed, of the assumed use-value of literary analysis itself) and the renewed calls to multicultural, transnational, and postcolonial ethnography. Still, I will stand on the heuristic value of this juxtaposition, as well as the overt stylization of my rendering of it—which is a mode both of access and address, of evidence and enactment. At stake in the tactical cross-identification and interrogation I am about to pursue briefly here is nothing less, I think, than the long, complex, utterly vexed interaction of fiction, faith, and intellect in the United States: our received understandings of who and why we are, how we have gotten where we are and what we are doing to imagine otherwise.

From the start, Robert Orsi has been drawn to the *margins* of mid-twentieth-century U.S. religious historiography—to those immigrant working-class devotions that have long been marginal to our top-down, parish-centered accounts of American Catholicism, to those Catholic women and children and the aged and the disabled and the incarcerated who have long been marginal to our focus on American congregationalist Christianity, and to those ethnographies of divine presence that have long been marginal to our otherwise pluralist debunking of essential Americanness and American exceptionalism. In *Between Heaven and Earth*, Orsi takes these recovery operations to new depths of insight and empathetic imagination, but he also mounts with oracular acuity from the specifics of immigrant Marian Catholicism to the observational plane of scholarship writ large, urging us to suspend our postmodern rites of suspicion and disavowal in order to register the divinity felt by others, to look less at official forms of the sacred (doctrine, sanctuary, sacrament) and more to the sacred encounters of home, hills, and street, and to reconceive religion not as hypostatic meaning-in-the-abstract (good *or* bad) but as the situated making-of-meanings (good *and* bad).[3]

"Of all aspects of religion," Orsi reminds us, "the one that has been clearly most out of place in the modernizing world—the one that has proven least tolerable to modern societies—has been the radical presence of the gods to practitioners."[4] Now, if you think felt presence causes problems for those committed professionally to the study of religion, for thirty years now we literary critics have worked assiduously to erase all traces of such radiance not only from our accounts of the interactions between characters in literature (who are ideologically deluded) but also from our responses as readers to literature and from our understanding of literature's social impact (the deconstruction of hegemony, the politics of subversion). "Always historicize! always demystify! never incant!"[5] Nonetheless, for all the semblance of consensual attitudes and practices, I do not believe that the literary-critical turn away from religion over the last quarter-century has been as successful as planned or advertised, and I believe that Orsi holds a key to recognizing and reinflecting the blessings disguised within cultural studies.

In a jeremiad more than now fifteen years old, yet still indicative of how American studies continues to miss its main chance, the courageous late Jenny Franchot castigated Americanists for having neglected real religion—"the interior life of the person," "the ethical and the mystical," "individual . . . obligations to invisible spirit"—in favor of what she saw as our parochial and even prurient obsession with "the colors and copulation habits of our bodies."[6] And yet Franchot's hauntingly Pauline insistence on severing the soul (as mind, as conscience) from the body, which operates in lock step with her startlingly familiar, Protestant-focused definition of what is to count as "true religion" and its scholarship, is just exactly wrong if it is the variety of experienced radiance ("mystery," as Franchot herself puts it) we are really after—which is what, after all, Orsi demonstrates on every page of *Between Heaven and Earth*.[7]

Orsi has learned, the hard way, the rigorous way—from Italian immigrant women and their varied fellow travelers—that human beings are in relation to the divine through each other and in relation to each other through the divine; that the body (kneeling or eating or touching, whole or broken or beside-itself) is as fundamental to the experience of holy presence as scripture or doctrine; and that violence (physical, psychological, social) is even more constitutive of the gods' continuing earthly dominion than of their storied heavens or mythic pasts. "The materialization of religious worlds," Orsi writes, "includes a process that might be called the corporalization of the sacred. I mean by this the practice of rendering the invisible visible by constituting it as an experience in a body—in one's own body or in someone else's body—so that the experiencing body itself becomes the bearer of presence for oneself and for others."[8]

What does acknowledging and interrogating the corporalization of the sacred hold in store for those of us whose field of study—I want to say, whose equipment for living—is literature? It means thinking about literature in a way that goes against the shibboleths of professed secularity, of course; but it also means thinking about religion-in-literature in a way that goes against the individually focused, ideal-essenced, thing-rejecting, body-fearful, ethically obsessed Protestant modeling of true religion; and it even means thinking about the Protestant experience *in* literature and the Protestant experience *of* literature in ways that confess that model's own (at least partial) *undoing*. This is, I believe, the Orsian mandate for American literary studies, and I know no more promising place to begin—being a student, myself, of overdetermination—than with the most canonical, and thus canonically "Puritan," text of them all, *The Scarlet Letter*.

The Scarlet Letter we know all too well is *The Scarlet Letter* of the American classroom—in the high schools especially, but by no means only there—and it is this hoary *Scarlet Letter* that illustrates almost to a tee the Protestant understanding of religion that remains stubbornly at the center of U.S. pedagogy and scholarship—our supposed agnosticism and secularity and objectivity notwithstanding. This is no coincidence. For *The Scarlet Letter* is the first, the one and only uninterrupted, and still most pointedly religious, canonical novel in American history.[9] *The Scarlet Letter* was used from the beginning to instill and has served ever since to maintain, revitalize, and modify a very particular—only residually Calvinist, but strongly middle-of-the-road Protestant—understanding of religious experience: that religion is a matter of right conviction, righteous behavior, and just community, rooted in overdrawn distinctions between public and private (the anxiety of hypocrisy, the lightening bolt of epiphanic conversion, the triumph of enlightened self-discipline), and transcendentally figural in type and allegory. Its canonization—our word, taken from the sacred texts of the Christian Mass—began only a couple of years after it was published in 1850, and it began not so much in the nascent community of letters, though Melville and the transcendentalists were thrilled, as it did in the seventh- and eighth-grade classrooms of the Know Nothing/Fugitive Slave law eras, when the bachelor teacher and spinster schoolmistress were called upon to rally the new immigrants (including the German and Irish Catholics), the new city dwellers, and indeed the rebellious white Southerners to a shared sense of the United States of America grounded not only in Republican citizenship but also in the ethos and ethics of Protestant sentimentality. Do spare the rod; internalize individualism, Pauline morality, and the guilty pleasures of self-incrimination—which are of course so much more effective.[10]

The Scarlet Letter remains integral to U.S. literary pedagogy, where its reigning interpretation is used at the very least to discipline the scholastic reading habits of not only the most recalcitrant but also the most pliant—AP English policing corridors of college admissions. But it also continues to serve as a reference text for American literary scholarship—especially for the new cultural studies, which gained traction when Jane Tompkins took Hawthorne (a.k.a. Ann Douglas) to task for authorizing critical condescension to Protestant sentimentalism, when Sacvan Bercovitch characterized *The Scarlet Letter* in particular as a template for the modern rites of American consensus, and when Lauren Berlant delineated the novel's self-installation at the epicenter of the multilayered, oppressive, and invidious operations of "the National Symbolic."[11] *The Scarlet Letter* remains, in short, either the whip or the whipping boy, depending on where you stand—the second because of the first, and the first, I am suggesting, because of the second. Orsian-inspired reinterpretation is therefore not just another wrangling over the meaning of a much-used, much-abused novel: tutoring a shift in the religiousness of our relationship to the novel, it instigates an alternative mode of dissent from the legacy of American theocracy than that of the republican liberal subject or the freethinking isolate; it allows us to pursue a different usable past from that of Puritan conscience and Emersonian self-reliance, to make of the novel a different form of equipment for living than that of either Protestant renewal or protofeminist individualism, and to feel the novel's registering of the divine and thus our registering of the divinity of the novel in a way different from that of the reformed sinner or the courageous modern, the allegorical parable or the transcendent symbol.

Belief is, of course, as Orsi counsels us to expect, the crux of the canonical version of *The Scarlet Letter*: Hester Prynne the adulterer is understood as a potential antinomian and protofeminist, who can not however go all the way; what is foregrounded as the religious issue in the novel is the evolving state of Hester's consciousness—spirituality is located in conscience, whether as theological correctness or formulated heresy: is Hester a rebel in her mind, or does she ultimately capitulate to the Puritan within? In the meantime, Dimmesdale the minister-lover is wracked by guilt—he understands himself to be a secret embarrassment to the cloth; he is unable to rid himself of the sense of damnable sin; and he drives himself into a crazed, increasingly hallucinogenic fit of self-immolation, with not a little help from his supposed friends. Hester survives as the good mother, as an artist of the needle, and as the town social worker.

Well, what else is there? The canonical version of *The Scarlet Letter* is not so much wrong as self-limiting. Protestant Christianity, as practiced on and by our established version of *The Scarlet Letter*, relies upon and hence puts into effect a hermeneutics of the pure (saint/sinner, insider/outsider, before/after) that effaces its own multiplicity—conflict, fracture, and drift. What Robert Orsi has to teach us is to have, instead, the strength of history's ambiguous juxtapositions and literature's untoward contradictions. Let Orsi's Hawthorne lead us, then, into a renegade Italian Catholic sense of divinity and a proto-Catholic mode of inquiry already at work within the Protestant American reflexive imagination.

When Hester emerges from the prison house door and strides to the town stocks—the Mediterranean *passeggiata* transformed into a Massachusetts Bay gauntlet—she is positively, shockingly, inexplicably radiant: "Those who had before known her, and had expected to behold her dimmed and obscured by a disastrous cloud, were astonished, and even startled, to perceive how her beauty shone out, and made a halo of the misfortune and ignominy in which she was enveloped."[12] Body transfixing eyes, mysteriously incarnate, not despite but because of the punishing context, with God as witness and at issue. The crowd goes immediately into denial; but must we readers go, too?

It is an American critical reflex to chalk Hester's radiance up to the spirit of rebellious individualism—fair enough—but Hawthorne floats another kind of meaning making by us: "Had there been a Papist among the crowd of Puritans, he might have seen in this beautiful woman, so picturesque in her attire and mien, and with the infant at her bosom, an object to remind him of the image of Divine Maternity, which so many illustrious painters have vied with one another to represent."[13] Of course Hawthorne immediately takes this analogy back—"but only by contrast"—insisting that because of Hester's "deepest sin" the force of her maternal presence is strictly and doubly damning ("the world was only the darker for this woman's beauty, and the more lost for the infant that she had borne"). And yet it seems to me that Hawthorne protests a bit too much here. What he has explicitly proposed, what his novel works surreptitiously to envision, and what remains metaphysically frightening, is the specter of female desire and maternal eros as salvific, as graced and potentially redemptive, at once transgressive, reproductive, *and* transfigurative: "What we did had a consecration of its own."[14]

I wonder to what degree our culture's obsession with *The Scarlet Letter* reflects both its guilty need to scapegoat sexual wanderlust and its contrary emerging desire to worship female sexuality or by means of female sexuality, so that Hester's transfigurative and reproductive transgression can be read as an inkling of Protestant America's Mediterranean Catholic underside, making Pearl—girl-child not boy-child, all selfish desire, the unbridled energy of feminine supernature—the dangerously pagan progeny of an unsanctioned marriage of Protestant sentimentality to sacramental fertility. Yet this somewhat Catholicized, somewhat paganized Protestant Mariolatry, however devoutly to be wished, is not the end-all and be-all of *The Scarlet Letter* as written. The secret of what Orsi has to teach us about *The Scarlet Letter* and thus to its tellingly sanctioned place in national culture is in regard to a very different kind of ratcheting up of Protestant bodies, Protestant selves.

Where goeth the body in *The Scarlet Letter*? It is almost impossible to believe that Dimmesdale ever got around to knowing Hester carnally; at the very least she clearly took him, no doubt about that. But the guilt that ensues for Dimmesdale—I am a sinner, I am a hypocrite, I am a bloody coward—entails disciplinary entanglements—autoerotic, homoerotic, and hetero-titillating—that, Hawthorne is suggesting, lie at the heart of Puritan male self-knowing: a prism onto the religious situatedness of gendered violence that rivals Orsi's own tour-de-force narrative exposé of the Marian-structured disciplines of Saint Gemma and Grandma Guila. Literally whipping himself into a frenzy, Dimmesdale is drawn compulsively to the aggrieved cuckold and stalking avenger, Roger Chillingworth. What ensues is a sadomasochistic dance of escalating extravagance and stunning explicitness, culminating in the most charged scene in the novel, when Chillingworth violates Dimmesdale's multiple sanctities—his study, his sleep, his clothing—to expose the A branded onto Dimmesdale's chest. It is there, in that study, with those men, that Hawthorne discovers the overdetermined—aestheticized because eroticized because sacralized—violence of the Christian God's impress on everyday lives.

At such moments, possessed by readerly awe, I wonder, is Orsi our best Hawthornian; or is Hawthorne, prophetically, our best Orsian? It must appear, on first reading of this essay, that I have taken considerable liberty in translating Orsi's insights from one century to another to a third, from one form of Christianity to another, from ethnographies of actual lives to the exegesis of imagined lives, and from his mode of judicious, patient, carefully historicized, and deeply empathetic narrative analysis to my own extravagances of nominalization and provocation—to the point where Orsi himself might not even recognize them.

But consider this: Orsi tells us to watch out for religious investments in children, and there we have Pearl, herself radiant and in full rebellion from what her Puritan fathers and their sentimental co-conspirators would make of her; Orsi tells us to suspect American Christianity's iconization of the cripple, and there we have Chillingworth, corporeally disfigured as well as sexually wronged, back from the woods having cavorted with those "damned Indians," pursuing by means of their shamanistic arts his pound of arch-Puritan flesh. And Orsi tells us to beware, most of all, of what transpires between clerics and laity, and there we have the blazingly erotic spell of Dimmesdale over his female congregants, especially the young ones, who like to think they are protected from their verboten feelings by the very "sacred office" that is, in fact, responsible for generating such feelings—while we, like Hester, look on in voyeuristic wonder, variously complicit yet sinfully tongue-tied, in full knowledge that relations such as these, between heaven and earth, are only too easily, and all too tragically, effected.

Jenny Franchot, working herself out of Protestant temptations to Catholicism, bequeathed the title, "Hawthornian confessional," to characterize the imp of the Catholic in *The Scarlet Letter*, illuminating the famously evasive posture of Hawthorne's narrative voice.[15] But, as regards the plottings of cuckoldry and *omertà*, it is the social orchestration of the ritual of absolution—which directs God's interest in relations between individuals in one particular way rather than in others—that is the very thing denied to Dimmesdale. The only forms of professing sin available in the novel are radically private, face-to-face with Chillingworth, or radically public, on the scaffold with Pearl and

Hester before all of Boston. The special intercession of the priest-mediated confession is literally unimaginable: unimaginable to Dimmesdale, unimaginable to seventeenth-century Calvinist New England, by and large unimaginable to Know-Nothing mid-nineteenth-century America, and even unimaginable to high-tech critic after high-tech critic committed to putting *The Scarlet Letter* in its New England Protestant place. For what makes *The Scarlet Letter* ultimately a Puritan tale after all, despite its wildly Catholic, seductively pagan syncretism, is Hawthorne's refusal to countenance (in his fiction at least) the *social* efficacy of the Roman Catholic sacrament of confession: a form of absolution-gaining contrition and penance that insists upon a renewal of right conduct—God forgives you, go forth and sin no more—that in addition, when working properly, absolutely forbids what we now understand as the sadomasochistic self-indulgence of extraconfessional self-revelation, for the priest is obligated and the confessant commanded to keep their mouths shut.

In the end, then, Nathaniel Hawthorne that "blue-eyed darling" is still somewhat too blue-eyed and not quite darling enough. So in the final analysis, my grand gestures to the contrary, what I have tried to effect is less a revolution than an evolution in taking *The Scarlet Letter* for what it always was, a Protestant temptation to Marian Catholicism with a perversely American revenge twist.

I realize that what I have done in this essay is not likely to win me many friends. On one hand, instead of a closely nuanced weighing and evocation of Robert Orsi's painstaking work, which instructs me on every page and in every turn of phrase, I have worked to move back across the disciplinary divide—to recruit Orsi to the reintegrative advance of renewed culture wars, assuming an alliance of method and an iconicity of religious difference that I suspect will give him pause, and certainly is not what a good reviewer would be doing. On the other hand, I have pushed religion onto the American literary agenda before ascertaining "good" or "bad," deploying Robert Orsi's analytic apparatus not to demystify the novel's Protestant hegemony but to remystify—to identify, play with, and reanimate—its Protestant/Catholic/pagan fissures and fusions, which from an English disciplinary point of view is not the hermeneutics of suspicion I am supposed to be practicing either. Melville called this no-man's land of discursive liminality "the deadly space between," and it is just like Orsi to reassure folks like us—"it is the path in between that causes such dismay and that seems to some impossible"—that we are not alone in our ethnological and professional suspensions.[16] Are we?

The Scarlet Letter is a notoriously fractured text, even slipperier than I have made it out to be—and my real close reading has only just begun. But within the novel there is a trajectory of image and insinuation, of character and plot that anticipates Orsi in the ways I have outlined. By teasing out that trajectory, I seek to reinflect what we—general readers, the cultural studies academy at large, and literary Americanists—understand as the religion issues in the themes not just of *The Scarlet Letter* but of any given text, what we understand as the religious operations of these texts on their own terms but also in relation to each other, and the religiousness of our relation as readers and even as writers not only to *The Scarlet Letter* and those texts deliberately mindful of it but also to the mainstream tradition as a whole, especially that of the long twentieth century, and not in literature only. This is what I am flagging as the great Orsian potential of canonical revision—or more materially, in Orsi's sense of relation between human and spirit—as canonical *revisiting*, which is in turn, I believe, the larger (more catholic, with the little "c") work of Catholic Studies, literature-and-media-arts division.

What Catholic Studies has to offer the arts, first and foremost, is a recommitment to critical decency in general—a renewal of close reading and close viewing and close listening (eschewing habits of condescension and preemptive dismissal)—an investigatory form of bearing witness in which we analyze the textual work of astonishment to the point where the text, less destroyed than revitalized by the act of interrogation, analyzes us back. The challenge is to meditate then mediate, inhabiting an imagined world so fully that it comes to live in us in return, at least for the duration of critical writing, classroom praxis, and scholarly exchange, working to induce in readers, students, and colleagues something akin to the experiences of grace and capture.

In writing this essay, I have come to conceptualize canonical revision more and more in Orsian terms as a textual revisiting—that is, an ongoing ever-returning visit to texts that matter, that matter because they hail us and because we accept being hailed, however affirming or dissenting, a relationship in effect with texts that are in relation to other texts through us and that put us into relation to each other through texts, with God and His rebels at issue within, between, among. We tend to think of reading in Victorian terms, as a private enterprise of word-consumption undertaken alone in library or den, which is the first and recurrent step in the process. Orsi counsels us to look for the relatedness between the soul and its special personae, in this case between a reader and those beings called forth by imaginative literature, happily devolving into a relay of spirit from reader to reader.

Of course, critics of Catholic persuasion and their fellow travelers are not alone in renewing empathetic and transformative engagement, no monopoly there. Concomitantly, since the early 1990s, scholars and thinkers have been working out how to identify, interrogate, and honor literature and the arts in ways that are not only vaguely Christian or religious (or "just humanist") but quite specifically—if waywardly and brokenly and combinatorially—Roman Catholic.

In *Roads to Rome: The Antebellum Protestant Encounter with Catholicism* (1994), Franchot insists that we take the nineteenth-century Protestant temptations to Catholicism seriously, as with Hawthorne here, interpreting the Protestant representation of Catholicism as something more complex than prejudice (an iconography of the Catholic, perhaps), not only as a scapegoating of Catholics (now to be understood in terms of their exclusion from liberal subjectivity) but also as a legitimate sign of spiritual wanderlust and wonderment; thus, *Roads to Rome* builds to a religious climax, ending with the converts. So too, Paul Giles's *American Catholic Arts and Fictions* (1992) demonstrates how we do not have to rely on valorizing Protestant impulses to conversion if it is twentieth-century cultural production we have in view; we can consider instead—he does so capaciously—the significance of Catholic backgrounds and orthodox commitments for so many of the moderns, especially the (Anglo-) Catholic poets, the immigrant as well as the Thomistic novelists, and the moviemakers. More recently, Tracy Fessenden's *Culture and Redemption: Religion, the Secular, and American Literature* (2007) clarifies the difficulties faced by scholars working in the tradition of American literature and historiography attempting to build on Franchot and Giles. In demonstrating how over a very long nineteenth century, Protestant notions of sectarianness, purity, and religious-cultural difference took refuge under the flag of secularism, she provides not only a history of institutionalized U.S. representation writ large—"the consolidation of a Protestant ideology that has grown more entrenched and controlling even as its manifestations have often become less visibly religious"—but an implicit challenge to our own critical thinking and scholarly practices: how to address the force of Catholicism without treating it according to the Protestant typologies of U.S. multiculturalism, that is, without treating it as a minority discourse of authenticity, purity, and policed difference.[17]

Given the puritanizing force of American-style multiculturalism, it should come of no surprise that the scholars of the new U.S. Catholic Studies, including if not especially its arts-and-letters branch, possess a larger than normative tolerance of and often attraction to wayward Catholic energies. By wayward Catholic energies, I mean forms of recognized popular devotionalism or presumed secularity or even intended heresy, often understood as "lapsed" or "ex-", necessarily syncretic with the dominant Protestantism and its myriad often idiosyncratic rivals in faith, that nonetheless take their logic from and often reinduce (at times profoundly) Catholic forms of lived spirituality, for better and for worse. And this reemergence of not-just-cultural Catholicism entails the intuitions, methods, and goals of the scholars—not just their subjects. Recall Orsi's *The Madonna of 115th Street* as an act of filial homage that reveals the terrible conflicting pressures of immigrant motherhood so movingly only by taking to heart, formalizing (no Italian ever used the term "domos"), and making emphatic the street theology in which She is held. Indeed, I first thought of Orsi as a founding member of a cohort of religious historians and cultural critics—raised after Vatican II and trained outside of the American Catholic Academy—who not only had begun to deploy the hermeneutics of suspicion (Marx, Freud, and Nietzsche in their newer guises) to interrogate reigning accounts of how Catholicism works in the United States, and for whom, but who also had begun, whether self-consciously or not, to leverage Catholic ways of being and knowing and doing—informing scholarly curiosity, address, and value—against the underlying assumptions of the poststructuralist and social-constructionist academy, particularly its anxieties of presence, power, and materiality.[18]

One of the thorny issues plaguing cultural studies in general that has emerged in clearer perspective among theologians and scholars of American religion is the sectarian logic underlying the ethnicity paradigm: isn't thinking of Catholicism in the United States as a minority religion or promoting the cultural distinctiveness of minorities within U.S. Catholicism theologically if not pastorally counterproductive? A contradiction-in-terms or at least in norms, drawing upon and giving succor to sectarian divisiveness? Since the early 1990s, scholars of Catholic backgrounds have worked to think outside the binaries of ghetto/mainstream, private/public, and sacred/secular, parsing out in unprecedented ways the dialectical complexities of consent and descent, self and other, freedom and fate. For me, it was not only Orsi but also his peers and their respondents, especially James T. Fisher, Paula Kane, Colleen McDannell, and Julie Byrne, who showed what could be accomplished—the religious paradoxes of culture revealed, the cultural paradoxes of religion transfigured—by applying theological acumen to ethnic specificities and seeing ethnic interactions play out in theological terms.[19] And it was the maverick literary critics—Richard Rodriguez, but also Mary Gordon, Frank Lentricchia, and Camille Paglia, as well as quieter agitators such as Leo Braudy, Peter Gardella, John Gatta, Ellis Hanson, and Edward J. Ingebretsen—who insisted, against the grain, each in his or her own way, that we consider both the Catholicizing fractures within the Protestant canon and the seductive force (or shall I say, universalizing communion?) of Catholic religious-aesthetic difference.[20]

What we art critics have most learned from the cultural historians is to be on the look out for the sanctification of the Mediterranean dinner table (the Eucharistic celebration, domestically developed), old-neighborhood Irish-tinged bars (monastic brotherhoods of the officially discarded), and the collegiate women's basketball court (womanist sisterhoods of bodily achievement); for the self-reflecting hagiography of cult movies such as *The Pope of Greenwich Village* or *The Song of Bernadette* and the other-directed *Corpus Christi* of jazz or rock performance; even for the material sacramentality of texture, sound, and image. As McDannell and her colleagues have most recently shown us, in their collection *Catholics in the Movies*, it is possible to pursue both sides of such syncretizing dialectics—between the sacred and the profane of what we study, between the senses of insiderdom and outsiderdom among those whom we study, and between the insinuating of suspicion and the courting of reverence in how we convey what we study.[21] It is even possible—McDannell leading the way, Carlo Rotella too—to do so in a common idiom, without theoretical fanfare, working for a general readership.[22]

Back to the future of *The Scarlet Letter*, one final time.

Revisiting *The Scarlet Letter* is foundational for the new Catholic criticism not just because the novel has been used as a scene of instruction in what constitutes true religion—right conviction, righteous behavior, social justice—but because it makes the bodily experience of spirit—a felt consecration of sexuality, including its violence—the litmus test for such matters. The sanctification of erotic passion, derived ultimately from the Italians, nonetheless turns out to be an especially American way of imagining trouble, as Leslie A. Fiedler insisted some time ago; and an especially effective way of inducing self-subversion, as D. H. Lawrence observed longer ago still. Therefore I am by no means the first reader to think that the dead-white-guy masterworks of U.S. literature are neither as Anglo-Saxon nor as Protestant as we have supposed them to be, and for the very reason that they pursue, to the point ultimately of obsession, the problematic so central to *The Scarlet Letter*—transgression or redemption?—doing so, with vary degrees of explicitness, within an Orsian iconography of the Pagan and the Catholic.[23]

Whatever the tautological risks of hypothesizing the existence of a Catholic imagination apart from the beliefs of real-live practitioners, there is no doubt that where goeth adultery in the modern American novel there goeth the Catholics and the iconography of the Roman Church, too. More than two decades ago, Werner Sollors traced the embrace of romantic love back to the Puritan encounter with Native peoples, as fundamental to what he suggestively termed the American dialectic of consent and descent: desiring the difference they demonized, embodied in an Other as Lover, the Puritans conjured social and cultural transformation, including Indian dissent.[24] In the ensuing years, we have become especially attuned to the racial and homosocial dimensions of forbidden romance, particularly star-crossed versions of crossover love (often hidden in regimes of passing, the closet, and genuine Americanism), but we seem increasingly to have lost track of the central casting of the Catholic in the role of other, which dates at least to the antebellum nineteenth century and reaches full force among the moderns. Even when we recognize that it is a Protestant and a Catholic who are cavorting (warrant enough, perhaps, to bring the tradition under the purview of Catholic Studies), it has scarcely occurred to us that there might be something actually religious at stake, the specter of an "adulterous" fusion of rival Christianities.

The task of reading for the religious syncretism begins, for me, with a simple recollection. The trope of transgressive love, including the high romance of requited (even consummated) but socially impossible love, however useful as an American countermeasure against inherited European customs of arranged marriage, was not aboriginally Protestant: the adultery novel, with its concern for the morality and practicalities of middle-class marriage, which arose in the Protestant nation-states of northwestern Europe as capitalism emerged in the eighteenth century, yes, but not the romance plot more broadly, which in its balder, more audacious and extravagant forms—as poetry and folktale, puppet show and opera, ultimately Hollywood and Tin Pan Alley—is the product of an earlier time and warmer climes. How have we forgotten Denis de Rougement's *Love in the Western World* (1940), which demonstrated, beyond a shadow of a doubt, for all its otherwise debatable details, that the Western obsession with forbidden-romance began not in post-Reformation Protestant Europe proper but in late medieval Provence and its neighboring principalities, and, above all, in never-to-be-reformed southern Italy, where the narrative of adultery was and to a large extent remains a matter not of class and gender negotiations but of the cosmic interplay of sex, violence, and sanctity? [25] At the very least, recalling the georeligious origins of romantic eros returns us to the Hawthorne of *The Scarlet Letter*, whose flirtation with Mediterranean Catholicism runs yet deeper than his Orsian affinities. In good gothic style, *The Scarlet Letter* subverts the very tradition of Protestant self-understanding that it constellates and canonizes, but it does so not only and not wholly in the Protestant way, which is why its literary and critical legacies entail, if not authorize and instigate, the Catholicizing of American Studies.

One more instantiation of my approach: Reputedly the most Puritan-besotted writer of America's Puritan-obsessed canon, Hawthorne makes an appearance—at least his words do—in, of all things, a terrific episode of our late Mafia melodrama, *The Sopranos*. The Hawthorne we encounter in *The Sopranos* would seem to be that specialist in the consummately Calvinist terrors of masquerade and self-division, an explicit acknowledgement, from a moment late in *The Scarlet Letter*, of the ongoing authority of the Protestant imagination and an open invitation, it would seem, to therapeutic moralism: "No man can wear one face to himself and another to the multitude without finally getting bewildered as to which may be true." But the episode in question, when chief mobster Tony takes his daughter on a New England college tour, draws upon Hawthorne in more substantive ways and in so doing draws attention to our more disturbing, interpretively dangerous Hawthorne. The "College" episode of *The Sopranos* features a sexually wandering priest, a communally sanctioned revenge plot, female complicity in male-on-male violence, and the metaphysics of Evil's daughterly issue. Now, where have we seen those narrative conceits before? The stunning truth is not the contemporary deployment of Hawthorne in Mafia television—after all, David Chase and his cowriters are students of the American mythic tradition (Todd Kessler studied with Werner Sollors at Harvard)—but Hawthorne's original borrowing from the treasure-trove of southern Italian storytelling: town adulteress, predator parson, cuckold's vendetta, cross-gender *omertà*, and bedeviled children at risk. Once again, what we have here, in *The Scarlet Letter*, is not the classic European novel of adultery per se, not just a Puritan morality play and not just a protofeminist tale of would-be Emersonian self-determination, but the greatest sexual revenge narrative of the American nineteenth century, wherein the felt holiness of the body in relation to other bodies is what matters ultimately, even perhaps to God. As I read it, the effort to comprehend the American interplay between cuckoldry and Catholicism is part and parcel of what scholars like to call the project of the U.S. novel itself, to my mind always already autoethnographic in uncanny ways.

The dramatic staging of the Protestant/Catholic borderline through the illicit courtship between Protestant and Catholic is so ubiquitous and, at points, so overdetermined in the U.S. cultural and aesthetic imagination—in the modern American novel especially—that the tradition itself can be said to call forth Catholic Studies, practically from the very beginning, and at times quite literally. Consider, for instance, a novel that since the second world war has been intermittently hailed as one of the great neglected American texts, only to fall immediately back into neglect and then of course out of print: Harold Frederic's gently sardonic, shockingly prescient *The Damnation of Theron Ware* (1896). Not only does Frederic restage *The Scarlet Letter* from Dimmesdale's point of view, but he also dramatizes marital drift as an explicit encounter between theological worldviews, devotional practices, and institutional structures. What seduces the novel's eponymous hero, that wayward Methodist minister Theron Ware, is not the brilliant redheaded Celia Madden alone, though she ranks among the most radiant of American sexual personae, but rather the trinity of Catholic-saturated intellectuals—aristocratic priest, fin-de-siècle new woman, bachelor-scientist—in which she is held, as One-in-a-Charismatic-Three. And what Frederic puts explicitly on the table, in this the second most aggressively intellectual novel of the American nineteenth century (after, I better aver, *Moby-Dick*) are the very terms—ethnosociological, religious-historical, and theological—that begin to account not only for the allure to Protestants of Catholic difference, and not only with 20/20 hindsight certain of Hawthorne's temptations too, but also for the preponderance of the sacred mythic bodily romances that lie at the absolute epicenter of the tradition to come.[26]

It is a simple observation—why has it been so long since anyone has made it?—that the warhorses of the modern American canon—F. Scott Fitzgerald's *The Great Gatsby* (1925), Ernest Hemingway's *The Sun Also Rises* (1926), and William Faulkner's *Absalom, Absalom!* (1936), now updated with antiracist, antichauvinistic, antihomophobic, and even anti-Christo-centric insight to include Kate Chopin's *The Awakening* (1899), Willa Cather's *The Professor's House* (1926), Nella Larsen's *Passing* (1929), Zora Neale Hurston's *Their Eyes Were Watching God* (1938), and Nathanael West's *The Day of the Locust* (1939)—are passion plays of overdetermined transgressive desire, foregrounding in no uncertain terms the holy danger of sexual charisma and the moral dilemmas of seemingly sanctified infidelity: simply put, these are adultery narratives, de jure or de facto, hetero and not, of a most beguiling order.

Nearly a generation ago, Nina Baym famously challenged the postwar consensus-era critical establishment for constructing a sexist male-belly-button-staring "melodrama of beset manhood."[27] It is a splendidly resonant phrase, not least because the canonical modern novels are each and everyone of them, *melodramas of beset sexuality*, focalized in many but not all instances over men (thus big boy romances) but by no means limited to men's issues (masculinity suffering in them as much from suspicion as from homage, and female sexuality being what men want to own or succumb to): the primary issue, male or female, that of aberrant yet graced desire. And that means that the novels are, like so many others of the American twentieth century, the direct offspring—courageous daughters and prodigal sons—of the mother of all U.S. adultery narratives, *The Scarlet Letter*.

The Scarlet Letter is my first step, then, in an Italian pagan-Catholic rereading of the American literary and aesthetic center, a reclamation of our tradition's always already, increasingly determinative Marian energies. I want in particular to revise and redeploy Fiedler's thesis that the Protestant vs. Catholic war dividing Europe for centuries morphed in the nineteenth-century United States to an internecine Protestant battle between the moralistic sentimentality of desexualized middle-class romance and the putative innocence of male-male camaraderie in domestic flight. I am especially emboldened by Fiedler's sense that from time to time the fundamentally Protestant U.S. imagination suffers the return of the pagan Catholic repressed, often in the form of the (re)sexualized Virgin. It is my suspicion that the Protestant victory stateside was less thorough and more pyrrhic than Fiedler knew what to do with, particularly after the massive arrival of Southern and Eastern Europeans; that Mary the Refulgent was in profound ways there even from the very beginning, especially where we should most expect her; and that what she has given to the American Mythos is a combination of dark sexual knowing and unlooked-for grace: transgression as redemption, incarnate.

My concluding Orsian-Hawthorne call-to-arms goes like this, then: there is a fabulous tradition (call it mainstream, though it includes many of the rediscovered or revalued texts of the neo-canon) of American narratives, novels especially but movies and songs, too, that puts self-determining souls in violative, even violent sexual motion (as it was in the beginning, with Hester), under the sign of incommensurable love (in all varieties of recognition, reciprocation, and consummation), with damnation at risk from the start and more experience of grace if not salvation than received codes or even rebellious conscience can prepare us for. In this tangle of love and death are to be found—Catholic signs abounding—the martyrs of twentieth-century U.S. literature and nearly all of its storied saints.

17 Catholic Studies and the Sacramental Imaginary

New Directions in Catholic Humanism

MAUREEN H. O'CONNELL

Coming of age as a Catholic in metropolitan Philadelphia in the 1980s and 1990s, I was desensitized to the unjust reality of urban poverty at an early age. I simply assumed that trash and graffiti, abandoned cars, blocks of blighted row homes, schools that looked more like prisons, and massive stone churches that used to be Catholic were as natural to the urban landscape as homes with manicured lawns and driveways, parks for soccer and baseball, and church bells that rang at noon were to my suburban one. Even as a young adult, I assumed that both environments were simply givens, with little connection to my own family's history on both sides of the city line or with any hope for meaningful change.

Acts of charity and works of mercy in my Catholic education in the Archdiocese of Philadelphia, from first grade through my senior year of college, did little to challenge this false assumption or to reconstruct the unjust dichotomies of city and suburb. I simply associated loving my inner-city neighbor with seemingly endless canned good drives, Catholic Charities Appeals, hot meals delivered to homebound folks living with HIV/AIDS, and spring break "urban plunges." While personally transformative, these acts of charity trapped those of us from the affluent suburbs in a good-intentioned but unreflective cycle of charity that treated the symptoms of social injustice, but never its root causes. They precluded me from perceiving the real humanity of the neighbor, as well as from acknowledging my family's complicity in causes of urban injustice. Charity and mercy did not necessarily cultivate the imagination either. We spent little time conjuring different futures for Philadelphia or dreaming up alternate ways of "brotherly love." In short, my Catholic education also gradually desensitized me to the hard intellectual, spiritual, political, and physical work that the real solutions to urban poverty demand.

One might call the double desensitization I experienced in my formative years as a Catholic—against the reality of poverty and the ethical demands of my faith tradition—a failure of the imagination; or more specifically, a failure of the Catholic *sacramental* imagination. Andrew Greeley defines the Catholic sacramental imagination as "the way Catholics picture the world and God's relationship to it" that stems from the central beliefs of Catholicism: God is incarnate or present in the world, not mysteriously withdrawn from it; ordinary physical objects can mediate or disclose to us God's extraordinary grace or loving presence; and we can best understand God metaphorically and in the context of stories and narrative images.[1] Imagination provides the primary means to encounter and be in relationship with a God who cannot be understood or experienced logically but rather in the context of mystery that invites ever-deeper interior reflection and ever-expansive external engagement in the created world.[2] By ignoring the uncomfortable reality of dehumanizing injustice just miles from my home and in ignoring the uncomfortable imperative of social justice in my faith tradition, I and others in my faith and learning communities simply failed to perceive, to encounter, and to participate in the grace of God incarnate in the inner city.

This lapse in one of Roman Catholics' distinctive capabilities for social change presents a significant challenge to those of us with a vested interest in the socially transformative content and processes of the Catholic tradition, or in the viability for Catholic higher education to humanize its faculty and students in order to respond to injustices such as urban poverty. As my experiences as a suburban Catholic indicate, while our religious imagination is deeply personal and highly transcendent, we do not necessarily rely on it to make our communities more just.

In this essay, I attempt to resuscitate the Catholic capability for the imagination. I propose a *Catholic sacramental imaginary* that arises from new "sites" and methods for theology. In my case, that new site comprises community murals in inner city neighborhoods in Philadelphia (Figures 17.1 and 17.2), and the new method is the constructive practices of imagination and creativity. I suggest that the sacramental imaginary helps Catholics, particularly educators, to stand at intersection of

FIGURES 17.1 AND 17.2 *(above and opposite).* "The Families Are Victims Too." (© The Philadelphia Mural Arts Program / Barbara Smollen.)

the sacramental imagination and the social imaginary, to cultivate new elements of Catholic humanism needed to resist the desensitization of millennial Catholics, and to illuminate new ways of understanding justice that can complement the charity that suburban Catholicism does so well.

From Sacramental Imagination to Sacramental Imaginary

Central to my notion of the "Catholic sacramental imaginary" is famed political philosopher Charles Taylor's concept of the "social imaginary." Taylor describes this as "the ways in which people imagine their social existence, how they fit together with others, how things go on between them and their fellows, the expectations which are normally met, and the deeper normative notions and images which underlies these expectations."[3] In other words, the social imaginary is the collection of beliefs, values and myths that we deliberately incarnate through reflective corporate practices. It is at once our social capital as well as the

strategies we use to increase its yield and to invest it in the community. The social imaginary consists of multicultural and religiously plural communities imagining together alternative visions for ourselves and then working together to bring those visions to fruition. Taylor asserts that Catholicism has influenced the social imaginary throughout Western history, often in countercultural and imaginative ways. For example, practical piety guided family living, lavish festivals bolstered civic pride with religious fervor, environmentally conscious mystics cultivated an ecological awareness, and pacifism continues to resist the military and prison industrial complexes.[4]

Even Taylor would have to agree, however, that Catholicism's capability to grow and invest our social capital in contemporary American has been widely undermined by a variety of factors in addition to the emotional effects of our millennial and global age: the decline in priestly vocations, sexual abuse scandals, tension between doctrinal orthodoxy and intellectual freedom, ecclesial statements on women, homosexuals, and contraception, single-issue politics and communion-rail controversies threaten the moral integrity and social efficaciousness of Catholicism. I am concerned about the vitality of the Catholic contribution to our social imaginary, to the extent that we have become desensitized to our responsibility to attend to the social injustices of our modern times as well as to resources in our tradition that might assist us in doing so.

Integrating the worldview of the Catholic sacramental imagination with the disposition and practices of Taylor's social imaginary makes the mandate to participate in God's ongoing justice in the world more explicit. The *Catholic sacramental imaginary* provides a way to respond. By Catholic sacramental imaginary I mean the dialogical, creative, and relational processes through which unexpected religious experiences, encounters, stories, images, or practices serve not only as a conduit for individuals to better understand and participate in the Divine (the sacramental imagination) but also as a collaborative process for otherwise disparate individuals to intentionally participate in creating a more just world (the social imaginary). The "sacramental imaginary" offers an imaginative and collective way of perceiving the many facets of reality, including the transcendent dimension. It creatively engages these facets with a shared concern for how we ought to live together. The Catholic sacramental imaginary attempts to perceive more clearly God's call to live in life-giving relationships—an imperative that is constitutive of God's presence in all sacramental things and experiences—and then attempts to more effectively respond to that call as a community of believers.

In other words, if we integrate the Catholic sacramental imagination into the content and process of the wider cultural social imaginary we might re-sensitize those who participate in the Catholic tradition—as scholars, students, parishioners, and social ministers—to the demands of our social reality and to the resources in the tradition to meet them. In addition, we might attune the focus of the wider social imaginary to the demands of social justice that are so easily lost in our contemporary consciousness. Said differently, with the help of the Catholic sacramental imaginary we might rekindle our collective Catholic moral imagination to think creatively about what a more just social order might look like and to partner collaboratively with those beyond the Catholic tradition creating it.

As such, the Catholic sacramental imaginary provides a way to attend to what systematic theologian James Bacik identifies as a tension in contemporary Christian spirituality "between prayerful reflection and involvement in the world."[5] The sacramental imaginary encourages a personal and public relationship with a God who is concerned both with personal salvation and collective liberation. Moreover, the sacramental imaginary calls attention to the ethical implications of personal encounters with Divine and suggests ways of acting imaginatively with the mind of Christ. If the imagination "awakens, and discloses the ordinarily unseen, unheard, and unexpected,"[6] then the sacramental imaginary provides spiritual practices that actively engage those otherwise invisible insights in the context of our relationship with God and others. Through it we are better able to imagine God, what it means to be human, and how we ought to live, and to do so with an attention to the ethical implications of these imaginative ruminations.

The Catholic sacramental imaginary brings three new things to American Catholic studies: elements of educational humanism, a theological site and method, and approaches to social justice.

An Imaginative Catholic Humanism

The tradition of Catholic humanism has long espoused the importance of imagination in making its practitioners and students more fully human by inviting them to discover the depths of the human mind and heart, the things that distinguish human beings from each other and the rest of the created world, and those things which bind us together as one of many species on this planet.[7] In fact, Catholic humanism boldly asserts "whatever humanizes" or "whatever expands the mind, opens the imagination, frees the will, enlarges our capacities as human beings makes us more like God."[8] Said differently, what humanizes also divinizes.[9] Catholic humanism has historically contributed to the wider social imaginary in a number of ways:[10]

The traditions of a humanist education, however, are increasingly dissected and discarded by the bottom-line pressures of the competitive market of higher education. Moreover, Michael Buckley suggests that given the many distinctive aspects of our contemporary context, which I described in terms of my own experience of double desensitization,

Catholic humanism cannot simply be concerned with making teachers and learners more human. We must also ask ourselves whether this education makes us more *humane*.[11] Catholic humanism, therefore, has a particularly urgent responsibility to "awaken both a sensibility to the suffering of human beings—both nationally and internationally—and an educated commitment to address this suffering if the university is to educate the students into a humanism adequate for our times."[12]

The Catholic sacramental imaginary assists Catholic humanism in making students more human and more humane by attuning their ability to experience God's vision of a more just society and cultivating collective practices that make that vision a reality. It identifies three underdeveloped themes in Catholic humanism, it unpacks their transformative potential, and then it integrates these Catholic insights into to the wider social imaginary.

Humanism of the Cross

By privileging the narrative images, memories, and experiences of those on the margins, the Catholic sacramental imaginary resists the tendency in the humanist tradition to celebrate the many human achievements, accomplishments, and capabilities to know and to do the good at the expense of interrogating the equally pervasive human atrocities, catastrophes, and capabilities for destruction that challenge the viability of the humanist building blocks for social morality. The Catholic sacramental imaginary supports what David Hollenbach, S.J., calls "ethics under the sign of the cross" because it places experiences of unjust suffering at the heart of the Incarnation, or what it means to be God and to be human. In other words, by taking seriously experiences of suffering, the Catholic sacramental imagination can help "[bare] witness to the distortion and destruction that human beings are capable of inflicting on themselves, each other, and the whole of creation.

The Catholic sacramental imagination breaks through the prevailing logic that denies these ugly aspects of our humanity by lifting up what systematic theologian Edward Schillebeeckx calls "negative contrast experiences."[13] These experiences undeniably reveal to us that things are not right with the world and they provocatively compel us to do something about this not-rightness. By inviting us to participate in aesthetic reflections on the experiences of human suffering that in turn deepen our understanding of what it means to be human, the Catholic sacramental imaginary reminds us of our connections to others in complex webs of social injustice, as well as ways that authentic relationships with others can address this suffering.

Humanism of Accountability

The Catholic sacramental imaginary not only situates humanism under the sign of the cross, but, with the help of negative contrast experiences, it also cultivates an ethic of accountability that acknowledges the pervasiveness of white privilege in our self-understandings, worldviews, and commitments to social justice. Sociologist Peggy McIntosh defines white privilege as an invisible knapsack of special provisions that consciously and unconsciously protect the social advantages of some people while ensuring the disadvantage of others.[14] These privileges might include social and professional mobility, relative assurance of being heard by persons in positions of power and influence, never having to speak for one's race, finding beauty products or even bandages that compliment one's skin tone, experiencing one's race as the cultural norm in the media, receiving credibility for one's opinions or civic contributions as a result of one's race, and so on.

To the extent that the tradition of humanism continues implicitly and explicitly to identify whiteness as culturally, intellectually, spiritually, and economically normative it fails to fully humanize and "humane-ize" students. For example, Mary Elizabeth Hobgood suggests that white privilege dehumanizes those who carry these invisible knapsacks of privilege as well as those who do not. It puts forward a series of values—about work, embodiment, relationality, emotional expression, and sexual intimacy—that "serve the vested interests of the few while they limit everyone's choices and impoverish the quality of all relationships."[15] Moreover, a humanism that denies the subtle pervasiveness of white privilege only perpetuates the deeply entrenched social injustices it seeks to redress through the very process of humanization. The problem is not the marginalized do not have a vision or a voice, but rather that our privileges make us unable or unwilling to see it and hear them. The problem rests with us.

The Catholic sacramental imaginary corrects our ignorance of our blindness and deafness to white privilege in several ways. First, it invites us to critically reflect on our respective "epistemological standpoints"[16]—where we evaluate ourselves, our reality, our notions of God, and our commitments to others—by transplanting us in different "sites" or standpoints. In these different sites, such as among the community murals in inner-city neighborhoods, we see ourselves and our connections to others from different perspectives. Our vulnerabilities, our complicities in social injustices, and our capabilities to set the world right are prophetically revealed to us. We are encouraged to reflect on the limits of prevailing logic, preferred language, or dominate images that we employ to make sense of reality. The sacramental imaginary reveals a new logic, a new language and new images that might open up new ways of understanding and responding to situations.

In addition, the sacramental imaginary invites us to experience deeply God's alternative vision in the context of creative relationships with others that we find in these new standpoints. Part of this experience of God in these relationships includes the cultivation of our emotional intelligence. This "EQ" makes us aware of the depths of ourselves, the depths of our dependence on others, and the many dimensions of what living justly together might look, taste, smell and feel like. Bruce Springsteen captures this idea in reflecting on his own songwriting: "I wanted the songs to have a kind of intimacy that took you inside yourself and then back into the world."[17] In this movement we learn from and with others how to deeply mourn and grieve, how to express gratitude and outrage, how to embody hope and resistance, how to dream and develop. The increased capacity for these deeply evocative relationships resists the logic of "ignorance, arrogance, and isolation"[18] that keeps us trapped in lifeless and meaningless cycles of apathy at worst and charity at best. We come to realize that being accountable to others begins with a willingness to empty our knapsacks of privilege to become vulnerable in, with, and through them.

Catholic Secular Humanism

Finally, given its incarnational impulse, the Catholic sacramental imaginary encourages us to experience, evaluate, and participate more fully in the created world rather than to withdraw suspiciously from it. This desire enables us to more accurately understand secularism as Charles Taylor does, namely in terms of constantly changing patterns and practices of belief and unbelief that can potentially enrich the social imaginary, rather than as threatening phenomenon that subtracts God from reality and likewise the social imaginary.[19] A few aspects of the sacramental imaginary make this constructive stance possible.

First, the Catholic sacramental imaginary moves the religious contribution to the public square beyond the confines of language and doctrine. It does so by recognizing that "religion—at the pre-reflective level—is closely correlated with creativity because both are metaphor-making, meaning-bestowing processes."[20] Therefore, the sacramental imaginary encourages creative aesthetic expressions of God and God's vision for the world that compel affective and emotive engagement that words alone often cannot generate. These nonverbal expressions complement rather than compete with other creative expressions of our ultimate concern, or the ground of our being, or our relationship to the cosmos. They offer another way of believing that thickens the secular social imaginary with images and symbols that metaphorically convey our deepest and most commonly shared sensibilities. In addition, the sacramental imaginary connects these expressions with practices that reinforce the centrality of the vision for the community, or that assist the community in achieving it.

In addition, the sacramental imaginary fosters an understanding unity in terms of *communio* or Trinitarian community. By this I do not mean unity through physical likeness or ideological similarity but rather a relational contribution of different gifts to a vision that is commonly shared and actively sought. Therefore, the Catholic sacramental imaginary does not simply tolerate or politely dismiss the differences among persons for fear of conflict, tension, or vulnerability. Rather, it embraces this difference as invaluable for experiential wisdom, for alternative perceptions of the contemporary reality, or for creative visions of a different future. In fact, the sacramental imaginary seeks the marginalized of society precisely because they do not participate in cultural, ethical, and social norms that perpetuate the status quo. As such, their wisdom might best challenge cultural norms that need to be challenged.

In many ways, this aspect of the sacramental imaginary reflects the life and ministry of Christ who deliberately encountered persons outside of his own socioeconomic and religious enclave. Their experiences shaped Christ's own understanding of God, his approach to discipleship, and his ideas of the Kingdom of God. John Haughey, S.J., provocatively asks, "Look at the Beatitudes and ask yourself whether the insights they convey might have originated in conversations with those who hungered and thirsted for justice"[21] The sacramental imaginary ensures that urban planning, school-district restructuring, or healthcare reform originate in conversations with those who hunger and thirst for justice in our contemporary public square.

Finally, the Catholic sacramental imaginary challenges Taylor's notion of the "buffered self" in the contemporary secular age. Here Taylor refers to the gradual historical evolution of human self-understanding from that of a "porous" or fearful, superstitious, reactionary, and powerless self moving through an unpredictable world that could not be controlled to a "buffered" or confident, reasonable, proactive, and empowered self who harnesses an ordered and intelligible world. The Catholic sacramental imaginary refuses to relinquish aspects of the porous self that we might identify as necessary meaningful interaction and relationships with others in a pluralistic civic square. For example, it insists that well-being or human flourishing is a collective experience that requires the ability to become vulnerable, or porous, in relationships with others. Being porous in this way is particularly necessary for those wrestling with the moral challenges of white privilege. In addition, the sacramental imaginary reminds us that emotions, which we often cannot control, sharpen our rationality or deepen our cognitive experiences of the world. To only know the world cognitively perpetuates ignorance that fuels social injustices that stem from broken relationships among persons.

New Sites and Method for Catholic Studies

Despite these insights about the pivotal role of the imagination in Catholic humanism, many theologians in my post–Vatican II generation, those born between the years of 1966 and 1975,[22] continue to wonder about Catholicism's contribution to the social imaginary. Any number of factors suggests that we live in particularly unimaginative times. Taylor observes that our current "secular age" is marked by a shift from an "enchanted" to a "disenchanted" worldview where imaginative sacramentality takes a back seat to scientific materialism.[23] Globalization exacts an emotional toll and weakens our capabilities to relate authentically to others: we experience compassion fatigue that we treat with retail therapy; we feel increasingly powerless despite our near total control over all aspects of our lives; we connect with people in virtual reality rather than physically relate with them in actual time and space; and we lose ourselves in insulating and isolating "i" devices that cater to our already hyperindividualism.[24]

Robert Wuthnow notes that when Americans do employ our imaginations, more than 80 percent of us ponder other worldly things such as the nature of God or heaven, and not necessarily solutions to deeply entrenched problems of social justice in this world.[25] Moreover, the millennial generation is steeped in "moral therapeutic deism," a particularly unimaginative belief that "God wants people to be good, nice and fair to each other" and that "the central goal of life is to be happy and to feel good about oneself."[26]

Moreover, unlike our predecessors in the tradition and the academy, theologians of the post–Vatican II generation are "Catholic by choice, not by blood" and have come of age in a world increasingly shaped by a "multiplicity of ways of believing and unbelieving."[27] We are aware that the American Catholic theology of the previous generation now operates in a very different context: in an America in an age of empire and a Catholicism in crisis. As a result, many of us choose to explore our faith commitment and these multiplicities of belief and unbelief in relatively uncharted academic territory.[28] We rely on a curiosity about the practical implications or relevance of "faith seeking understanding" or "God talk," two classic definitions of theology, in order to resist the double desensitization I described at the beginning of this essay.

We bring this curiosity to nontraditional "sites" of theology—particular contexts or phenomena in a particular location that raise particular concerns and require particular tools for evaluation. For example, we explore the presuppositions of faith in popular and visual culture, critical race theory, immigration policy, the psychology of trauma, the physical and spiritual meditations of yoga, economics of human development, community organizing, and the prison industrial complex. These sites cultivate a new *constructivist* theological method that reflects the distinctive praxis of the Catholic sacramental imaginary.[29] Whereas the correlationist method translates the tradition into the language of the contemporary context and the positivist method adapts the contemporary context back into the language of the tradition, the constructivist model creates something new out of the tradition and the contemporary contexts. Rather than focus only on the *content* of tradition—the "stuff" that gets carried forward through the generations—the constructivist method also considers the *process* of tradition or the practices that carry the content forward and bolster its relevance in the lived experiences of the community. In other words, *how* we practice our faith, or our active faith commitments, is as important as *what* we believe, or the content of our faith convictions.

This creative impulse in the constructivist method reflects the impulse of the Catholic sacramental imaginary that I believe is necessary to enter fully into and respond to the injustices that define our social realities. The constructivist method is one of discovery. We unearth new insights about the tradition, as well as new perspectives on our current reality in the process of lifting up new faith claims and new ways of examining them. This method underscores the active nature of Catholic faith and theology—these are not self-contained units of knowledge that we passively receive but rather dynamic ways of making meaning that we actively construct anew in ever-changing contexts and circumstances. New sites of theological reflection and the constructivist method remind us of the moral imperative to be creatively engaged in the world where God is at work and to participate in the ongoing work of the tradition. It illuminates the rich practices of faith that help to incarnate the doctrines of faith from generation to generation.

With attention to these new sites and method of theology, I have discovered a Catholic sacramental imaginary that enables the Catholic tradition to be relevant, intellectually responsible, and socially transformative. First, the Catholic sacramental imaginary enables us to know justice and injustice as more than cognitive categories or abstract concepts, a frequent epistemological privilege for those who do not regularly experience unjust suffering. Rather, we come to know quite viscerally these things through experiencing them with others in a creative process that involves a multiplicity of ways of knowing our reality. Second, it cultivates an imagination that interrupts the cognitive logic of the way things are with countercultural alternatives that can be realized through collaborative relationships with others. Finally, it encourages that we move beyond language as the primary medium for articulating faith convictions. As a result, doctrines that frequently separate persons give way to nonverbal faith commitments: practices of deep listening, love of neighbor, compassion, and joy, which unite persons and enrich the public square.

Community Muralism and the Catholic Sacramental Imaginary

Imagine my surprise when my scholarship unexpectedly drew me into the Philadelphia neighborhoods to which I previously had been so desensitized. Here, writ large on more than 2,900 walls, I continue to discover an unexpected site of theology that resensitizes me both to the reality of urban poverty and to the difficult demands of the Catholic tradition in the area of social justice. I literally find theology or "God talk" in the larger-than-life narrative images of the city's community murals, a significant number of which are created by faith communities or incorporate religious imagery. In short, they continue to spark my Catholic sacramental imaginary.

Community murals offer extraordinary perspectives on ordinary experiences, invite deep reflection on the relationship among the various meanings of the narrative images portrayed, and potentially spark conversions or changes in values, desires, and ways of knowing. The murals invite viewers to transcend the material world by entering into an imaginative reverie where all are empowered to participate in the murals' many symbolic meanings. These murals have become the physical and visual space where marginalized communities explore the practical application of the presuppositions of faith.

The content of the murals cannot be separated from the socioeconomic context out of which they arise or the dialogical process that creates them. Many of the pieces in one of the world's largest public galleries are displayed in neighborhoods of concentrated poverty where, according to the U.S. Census Bureau, more than 40 percent of residents live below the poverty line of roughly $20,000 per year for a family of four. They are exhibited on streets where gun violence claims lives at one of the highest rates in the nation each year. And they are displayed on the walls of racially segregated public elementary and high schools whose resources pale in comparison to their suburban counterparts. As products of their inner-city environment, Philadelphia's community murals draw our attention to the concrete details of the neighborhoods in which they reside; and yet as products of the human imagination, they provocatively point to something much greater than themselves and invite us to participate in that vision.

Throughout my pilgrimage among the murals of Philadelphia, I encounter a palpable sense of the Divine's vision of justice as well as a visceral desire to participate with others in making God's vision for us a reality. They have cultivated several critical elements of a Catholic sacramental imaginary.

Attuned Perception

The Catholic sacramental imaginary attunes our perception to others' perceptions of God at work in the world and increases our capacity to see things we either are not able to see or would rather not see given our social location. Like the prophets of Israel, Philadelphia's community murals do not foretell the future, but rather use narrative images to illuminate overlooked dimensions of the injustices of the present and to demand social responsibility.[30] In other words, they provocatively call our attention to aspects of our present circumstances that we ignore or would prefer not to see: the relationship between voluntary and involuntary segregation, or between white flight and apartheid housing or public education, or between opening new suburban parishes and closing historic urban parishes. This is information is absolutely crucial for devising effective strategies for urban development. In addition, just as the narrative images in the medieval cathedral attempted to educate a largely illiterate populace, these murals educate a culturally illiterate suburban and white populace that is largely ignorant about the culture, spirituality, and civic-mindedness in inner-city communities. These insights are absolutely invaluable for deconstructing the attitudes and stereotypes that polarize people along economic and racial lines, that make the poor the scapegoats for their own poverty, or that trap well-intentioned people in comfortable cycles of charity rather than disruptive relationships of social justice.

Increased Capability for Relationship

The Catholic sacramental imaginary encourages us to listen deeply to the stories of others—shared in the context of narrative images—whose memories of the past and visions of the future are often ignored in public debates about the good life. This deep listening transforms storytellers and listeners alike.

In addition, every step in the process of creating a community mural creates community. In many ways, this process is more important than the final narrative image. For example, neighbors impacted by gun violence in one southwest Philadelphia neighborhood submitted an application to the city's Mural Arts Program, a nonprofit organization that straddles city government and the private sector and facilitates the mural making process. This community's application, which required the signatures of at least fifty neighbors, proposed a mural that would remember their loved ones and reinforce the mission of a fledgling support group for family survivors called "The Families Are Victims Too." Once accepted, the neighbors met over the course of six weeks with muralist Barbara Smollen in several publicized community meetings to brainstorm possible images for their mural collectively. They shared the stories and memories of their loved ones, as well as their visions of what healing and remembrance ought to look like. The process of mural making gradually integrated their individual stories and memories into a collectively shared, vibrant narrative image that now nourishes the social imaginary of the entire neighborhood and integrates the neighborhood into a more vibrant civil society.

Aesthetic Option for the Poor

This painstaking dialogical process, often riddled with disagreement and conflict, distinguishes community muralism from other expressions of public art that often privilege the perspective of outsiders with little connection to the physical space where the art is displayed. Community muralism, on the other hand, privileges the perspectives and wisdom of those on the margins in the city of Philadelphia: neighbors in some of its poorest communities, truant and delinquent students in the school system, and prisoners in the criminal justice system. In privileging the neighbors' sense of the beautiful, this aesthetic option for the poor rejects the idea that the marginalized are voiceless or visionless. Rather, it offers them a means to express themselves in narrative images that, unlike their verbally spoken words, are not easily ignored by the wider society.

For example, only when the neighbors connected to The Families Are Victims Too reached consensus among themselves did Smollen begin to draft the mural's design. And only when the neighbors were completely satisfied with her design did she even pick up a brush. This willingness to privilege another's perspective in the creative suggests that the principle of the preferential option for the poor is integral to the Catholic sacramental imagination. In other words, it empowers the marginalized to reclaim their identities, to articulate a vision of the future, and to demand a collective responsibility for bringing those visions to fruition. The aesthetic option for the poor demands that we see, listen, and respond to these narrative images.

A Visible, not Verbal, Religion

Finally, Philadelphia's community murals introduce religious imagery into the increasingly secular public square with the hope of sparking the civic imagination. As such, they offer examples of what Rowan Williams calls "*visible* religion" that "defends the right of a society to have access to meaning" and reminds us that a lack meaning is a dangerous type of impoverishment.[31] This kind of public religiosity reminds us of our shared values as human beings: care and concern for the poor and vulnerable, recognition of the dignity of persons, or commitments to nonviolence. Moreover, it relies on narrative images and symbols that affectively stimulate the whole person—the five senses, emotions, memory—not just the rational intellect. "An artist relates to his environment," said Ras Malik, a Philadelphia community muralist. "Trees, water, sky, sunsets, sunrises. . . . There are so many heavenly things you can almost hear music. An artist needs to *make that feeling* and that is creativity which takes you into spirituality."[32]

These images can also engage people beyond the boundaries of any one faith tradition. They emphasize common human experience, not doctrinal particularity, and invite a variety of interpretations, which opens up much needed emotional and intellectual space for ambiguity and suspension of judgment. Nonverbal religious contributions to the public square increase our collective capacity to envision alternatives and to seek after them together.

The Catholic Sacramental Imaginary and Social Justice

Ultimately, my intentionally Catholic engagement with Philadelphia's community murals suggests that a sacramental awareness of God's presence cannot be separated from an active commitment to live in right relationships with others. This is the basic definition of justice that God offers in the covenant with the people of Israel, in Christ's social ministry, and God's continuing revelation in our sacramental reality. This notion of justice binds the sacramental imagination to the social imaginary. When intentionally integrated as the Catholic sacramental imaginary, the sacramental imaginary suggests new ways of thinking about justice itself.

Justice as Vision

The Catholic sacramental imaginary resists the latent tendency in the rich tradition of Catholic social teaching to consider justice primarily as an abstract concept, an ethical principle, or even an instrumental building block of social relationships that is rationally worked out, diplomatically deliberated, or strategically applied. Rather, it suggests that justice is first and foremost an evocative musing of the human imagination that is free of the constraints of rational logic, language, religious doctrine, or even sacred texts.[33] Justice is narrative image, a vision, a symbol, a dream that surfaces in our individual and collective consciousness as a result of sacramental encounters with God in others and the created world. Perhaps no one in recent understood this idea better than Martin Luther King. A vision of the promised land from the metaphorical mountaintop shaped his dream of racial integration and economic justice. That vision motivated him and so many others to risk everything they had for the sake of a dream that defied the prevailing logic of the 1960s.

The sacramental imaginary proposes that justice is more than an idea—it is a passionate vision that literally and figuratively compels us to create ways of living well together. As a vision, justice is an endless cache of meanings that continue to be revealed as more and more people perceive it. For example, in Philadelphia's community murals, justice appears as a neighborhood drum corps marching resolutely toward an unknown future, as an elderly woman sitting among the sunflowers in her garden, as the embrace of a mother and child silhouetted against an African sunset, as a Haitian inspired landscape, or as neighbors portrayed as winged angels grieving over the city. In addition, justice is not metaphorically represented in these images, but is actualized in the process that creates them, in the capacity to enter into relationships with others and dream with them.

Because it arises from the depth of ourselves, this imaginative musing or vision of justice provokes us to seek after justice in ways that mere rational conceptualizing or doctrinal catechesis cannot inspire or sustain. For example, evangelical pastor and public intellectual Jim Wallis frequently invokes the prophet Amos when he insists that religion offers politics a simple but necessary reminder: Without a vision, the people perish.[34] The Catholic sacramental imaginary illuminates examples of figures within the Catholic tradition, from Augustine to Tim Russert, whose lives were animated by a vision rather than a theory of justice. It points to their creative discipleship as a witness to what it means to be a person of faith as well as what it means to dream after justice.

Justice as Experiential

Mary Elizabeth Hobgood suggests that in order "to act justly in the world, we need to know how the world works."[35] Just as the sacramental imaginary reminds us that justice is not only a theory but also a vision, it also suggests that justice cannot only be known cognitively but is also known experientially. In addition to transplanting us into different standpoints, the sacramental imaginary also invites us to tactilely explore the world with all five senses. In other words, it helps us to better know the world by inviting us to fully experience it not only as thinking people, but as seeing, smelling, hearing, tasting, and touching people. We do not fully know justice until we know what it looks like, what it tastes like, what it feels like. And we need authentic engagement with others and the natural world to stimulate sensual experiences of justice.

In addition, it reminds us that we come to understand the world through participation in practices, rituals, and activities that generate knowledge rather than passive reception of knowledge. Likewise, justice is not a promise that we wait to be fulfilled, but an experience that we constantly seek to create in new contexts. In the context of Philadelphia's murals, justice can be experienced in the conversations of the neighborhood association meetings, in the physical contact with others while rolling tiles or painting on parachute paper, the music, dancing and food that accompany many dedication ceremonies, the sounds of the neighborhood that reverberate off the finished wall and connect its image with the context of its creators. In all of these experiences, we come to know justice more deeply. Michael Himes puts it well: "The entirety of Catholic liturgical life—indeed, of Catholic spiritual, intellectual, and ethical life—is geared toward producing sacramental beholders, people who see what is there in its full depth.[36]

Justice as Beautiful

Finally, the sacramental imaginary reveals to us the beauty of living in right relationship with others. Because it reminds us of God's creative presence in and through all things, the sacramental imaginary reinforces the sense that justice is not only a good thing, it is a beautiful thing. Its beauty reflects that of a relational God who deeply desires to be in communion with us, and who desires that we live in communion with each other. The beauty of justice reflects the beauty of a creative God who transformed chaos with works of grandeur and who desires that we continue the work of creation by participating in social transformation. The beauty of justice reflects the beauty of a compassionate God who was emotionally moved by unjust suffering and resisted it through acts of liberation, and who desires that we become vulnerable in others suffering in order to resist it.

Therefore, beauty is not something that we gaze upon, but rather something in which we actively participate: through a willingness to become vulnerable in others' suffering, through deep listening to others' perspectives, through loving care of neighbor whose well-being is wrapped up in my own, through simple acts of social transformation such as organizing a community meeting or planting a community garden. These beautiful ways of being are also just because they enfold us in the mystery of the interconnectedness of all life. For example, in reflecting on the life of Mother Teresa, Richard Viladesau notes that "a life of self-giving service to others can have power and poetry; that love, and particularly love of the most needy—of those who suffer the ugliness of deprivation and death—is deeply beautiful."[37] Similarly, the beauty of the community murals in Philadelphia is amplified by the goodness of the relationships they create, the civic virtues they cultivate, and the social change they bring to the city.

Conclusion

In this essay I have attempted to reintegrate the Catholic sacramental imagination with the Catholic commitment to social justice. This relationship faces a myriad of obstacles in our contemporary context, most notably what I identify as a double desensitization that keeps us from accurately seeing the social reality that God permeates and that keeps us from participating in God's ongoing creation of a just world. The sacramental imaginary overcomes many of these obstacles by awakening the senses, by sparking the moral imagination, and by illuminating practices that cultivate a sense of the sacred or mysterious. All of these capabilities deepen our understanding of and commitment to abstract ideas such as justice or human development. The sacramental imaginary bridges the distance between the two worlds of my Catholic childhood by prophetically revealing God's justice in unexpected places and inviting each of us to be co-creators of justice in this one world. Empowered by the sacramental imaginary, we reverence the creative and relational impulses in persons, we practice public piety around narrative images or sites where we experience something greater than ourselves, and we participate in the sacramentality of each other. Jane Golden, executive director of the Mural Arts Program in Philadelphia, implicitly captures it well: "When you look at a mural I urge you think about it as a medium for discussion and connection. This kind of art can become the common ground from which we challenge the cycle of crime, poverty and violence and overcome the fear and alienation they cause."[38]

Notes

1. "The Story Is What Saves Us": American Catholic Memoirs

DEBRA CAMPBELL

1. For the epigraph, see Saint Augustine, *The Confessions of Augustine, Books I–X*, trans. Frank Sheed (New York: Sheed and Ward, 1942), 180. For reflections on the connection between this quotation and Catholic Studies, see Philip Gleason, "Becoming (and Being) a Catholic Historian," in *Faith and the Historian: Catholic Perspectives*, ed. Nick Salvatore (Urbana: University of Illinois Press, 2007), 26.

2. In this chapter, the terms "memoir," "life-writing," and "personal narrative" will be used interchangeably, except where the distinction between terms is important for clarity or accuracy.

3. Jay Parini, ed., *The Norton Book of American Biography* (New York: Norton, 1999), 11–12.

4. Ibid., 12–13.

5. Cabeza de Vaca, *Adventures in the Unknown Interior of America*, trans. Cyclone Covey (Albuquerque: University of New Mexico Press, 1983), 87.

6. Mathew Carey, *Autobiography* (New York: Eugene L. Schwab, 1942), 10, 24, 87–88, 115.

7. Sister Blandina Segale, *At the End of the Santa Fe Trail* (Albuquerque: University of New Mexico Press, 1999), xvi.

8. Ibid., 293.

9. Orestes Augustus Brownson, *The Convert, or, Leaves from My Experience* (New York: E. Dunigan & Brother, 1857), v, vii, 420.

10. John LaFarge, S.J., *The Manner Is Ordinary* (Garden City, N.Y.: Image Books/Doubleday, 1957), 246, 318.

11. Phyllis McGinley, "Mary Was an Orphan," *Saturday Review* 40 (June 1957), 31.

12. Mary McCarthy, *Memories of a Catholic Girlhood* (San Diego: Harvest Books, 1985), 13, 50, 19, 24–27.

13. Dorothy Day, *The Long Loneliness* (New York: Harper & Row, 1981), 9–11, 139–140, 148–149, 164–165.

14. Dale Vree, “A Radical Holiness,” *Commonweal* 110 (May 6, 1983), 266.

15. Helen Caldwell Day, *Color Ebony* (New York: Sheed and Ward, 1952), 175–176, and *Not Without Tears* (New York: Sheed and Ward, 1954).

16. Thomas Merton, *The Seven Storey Mountain* (San Diego: Harvest Books, 1998), 416.

17. Michael Mott, *The Seven Mountains of Thomas Merton* (Boston: Houghton Mifflin, 1984), xxii–xxiii.

18. Mark S. Massa, *Catholics and American Culture: Fulton Sheen, Dorothy Day, and the Notre Dame Football Team* (New York: Crossroad, 1999), 50.

19. Garry Wills, *Bare Ruined Choirs: Doubt, Prophecy, and Radical Religion* (Garden City, N.Y.: Doubleday), 1, 7, 15–16, 18, 272.

20. Abigail McCarthy, *Private Faces/Public Places* (Garden City, N.Y.: Doubleday, 1972), 109, 177, 100, 81–82.

21. Robert Hoyt, quoted in Peter Occhiogrosso, *Once a Catholic* (Boston: Houghton Mifflin, 1987), xiii.

22. Gregory Baum, *Journeys: The Impact of Personal Experience on Religious Thought* (New York: Paulist Press, 1975), 2–3.

23. Salvatore, *Faith and the Historian*, 1.

24. Wilfrid Sheed, *Frank and Maisie: A Memoir with Parents* (New York: Simon & Schuster, 1985), 12; Richard Rodriguez, *Days of Obligation: An Argument with My Mexican Father* (New York: Penguin Books, 1993), 48–79, 40; James Carroll, *An American Requiem: God, My Father, and the War That Came Between Us* (Boston: Houghton Mifflin, 1966), 2, 8–9, 103–104.

25. Patricia Hampl, *I Could Tell You Stories: Sojourns in the Land of Memory* (New York: Norton, 1999), 48, 39–41; Patricia Hampl, *Virgin Time.* (New York: Ballantine Books, 1992).

26. Mary Gordon, *The Shadow Man: A Daughter's Search for Her Father* (New York: Random House, 1996), 268–269.

27. For one example of the new forms of life-writing that address the silences, see Peter Phan and Jung Young Lee, eds., *Journeys at the Margin: Toward an Autobiographical Theology in American-Asian Perspective* (Collegeville, Minn.: Liturgical Press, 1999).

28. Carroll, *An American Requiem*, 15.

2. The Catholic Intellectual Tradition: A Classification and a Calling

MARY ELLEN O'DONNELL

1. Sr. Jerome Corcoran, *The Catholic Elementary School Principal* (Milwaukee: Bruce, 1961), 12.

2. Thomas Landy, "Introduction: Yeast and Three Measures of Flour," in *As Leaven in the World: Catholic Perspectives on Faith, Vocation and the Intellectual Life*, ed. Thomas Landy (Franklin, Wis.: Sheed & Ward, 2001), xi.

3. See Louis K. Dupre, *The Enlightenment and the Intellectual Foundations of Modern Culture* (New Haven: Yale University Press, 2004); Peter Gay, *The Enlightenment: Science of Freedom* (New York: Norton, 1996); Peter Hulme and Ludmilla Jordanova, ed., *The Enlightenment and Its Shadows* (London: Routledge, 1990); Dorinda Outram, *The Enlightenment* (Cambridge: Cambridge University Press, 1995); R. Scott Appleby, C.S.J., Patricia Byrne, and William L. Portier, ed., *Creative Fidelity: American Catholic Intellectual Traditions, American Catholic Identities—A Documentary History* (Maryknoll, N.Y.: Orbis Books, 2004).

4. Margaret Mary Reher, *Catholic Intellectual Life in America* (New York: Macmillan, 1989), 1–2.

5. James Turner, *Language, Religion, Knowledge: Past and Present* (Notre Dame, Ind.: University of Notre Dame Press, 2003), 61.

6. Margaret C. Jacob, *The Enlightenment: A Brief History with Documents* (Boston: Bedford/St. Martin's, 2001), 18.

7. See S. J. Barnett, *The Enlightenment and Religion: The Myths of Modernity* (Manchester: Manchester University Press, 2003); James M. Byrne, *Religion and the Enlightenment: From Descartes to Kant* (Louisville: Westminster John Knox Press, 1997).

8. James Heft, "Preface," in *Faith and the Intellectual Life: Marianist Award Lectures*, ed. James Heft (Notre Dame, Ind.: University of Notre Dame Press, 1996), 10.

9. Richard M. Liddy, "The Catholic Intellectual Tradition: Achievement and Challenge," in Landy, *As Leaven in the World*, 7.

10. Ibid., 6.

11. Monica K. Hellwig, "The Catholic Intellectual Tradition in the Catholic University," in *Examining the Catholic Intellectual Tradition*, ed. Anthony J. Cernera and Oliver J. Morgan (Fairfield, Conn.: Sacred Heart University Press, 2000).

12. Liddy, "The Catholic Intellectual Tradition," 6.

13. Hellwig, "The Catholic Intellectual Tradition in the Catholic University," 3.

14. In Pope John Paul II's 1998 encyclical *Fides et Ratio*, Catholics find a papal statement on these distinct but complementary sources for truth.

15. William A. Herr, *Catholic Thinkers in the Clear: Giants of Catholic Thought from Augustine to Rahner* (Chicago: Thomas More Press, 1985), 37.

16. See Catherine Conybeare, *The Irrational Augustine* (Oxford: Oxford University Press, 2006); Benedict J. Groeschel, *Augustine: Major Writings* (New

York: Crossroad, 1995); Eleonore Stump and Norman Kretzmann, ed., *The Cambridge Companion to Augustine* (Cambridge: Cambridge University Press, 2001); Gareth B. Matthews, *Augustine* (Malden, Mass.: Blackwell, 2005).

17. See Saint Anselm, *Basic Writings: Saint Anselm*, trans. S. N. Deane (La Salle, Ill.: Open Court, 1968); Coloman Viola and Frederick van Fleteren, ed., *Saint Anselm: A Thinker for Yesterday and Today—Proceedings from the Anselm Conference Paris 1990* (Lewiston, Maine: E. Mellen, 2002); John R. Fortin, ed., *Saint Anselm: His Origins and Influence* (Lewiston, Maine: E. Mellen Press, 2001).

18. See John Baldwin, *The Scholastic Culture of the Middle Ages, 1000–1300* (Prospect Heights, Ill.: Waveland Press, 1997); Edward Grant, *God and Reason in the Middle Ages* (Cambridge: Cambridge University Press, 2001); Jacques Verger, *Men of Learning in Europe at the End of the Middle Ages*, trans. Lisa Neal and Steven Rendall (Notre Dame, Ind.: University of Notre Dame Press, 2000).

19. See Saint Thomas Aquinas, *Summa Theologiae: Questions on God*, ed. Brian Davies and Brian L. Leftow (Cambridge: Cambridge University Press, 2006); Brian Davies, ed., *Aquinas's Summa Theologiae: Critical Essays* (Lanham, Md.: Rowman & Littlefield, 2006).

20. For more on Aquinas, see Alexander W. Hall, *Thomas Aquinas and John Duns Scotus: Natural Theology in the High Middle Ages* (London: Continuum, 2007); Mark S. Latkovic, John Goyette, and Richard S. Myers, ed., *St. Thomas Aquinas and the Natural Law Tradition* (Washington, D.C.: Catholic University of America Press, 2004); Rik Van Nieuwenhove and Joseph Wawrykow, ed., *The Theology of Thomas Aquinas* (Notre Dame, Ind.: University of Notre Dame Press, 2005).

21. Jude P. Dougherty, "Christian Philosophy: Sociological Category or Oxymoron?" in *Faith and the Life of the Intellect*, ed. Curtis L. Hancock and Brendan Sweetman (Washington, D.C.: Catholic University of America Press, 2003), 172.

22. See Constance M. Furey, *Erasmus, Contarini and the Religious Republic of Letters* (Cambridge: Cambridge University Press, 2006).

23. Ibid., 45.

24. See Fergus Kerr, *After Aquinas: Versions of Thomism* (Boston: Blackwell, 2002); Craig Paterson and Matthew S. Pugh, ed., *Analytical Thomism: Traditions in Dialogue* (Burlington, Vt.: Ashgate, 2006).

25. Interestingly, Catholics are barely mentioned in contemporary discussions of an American intellectual tradition. See David A. Hollinger and Charles Capper, ed., *The American Intellectual Tradition* (New York: Oxford University Press, 2006).

26. Jay P. Dolan, *The American Catholic Experience: A History from Colonial Times to the Present* (Garden City, N.Y.: Doubleday, 1985).

27. See Michael Buckley, *The Catholic University as Promise and Project* (Washington, D.C.: Georgetown University Press, 1999); Robert Emmett Curran, *The Bicentennial History of Georgetown University* (Washington, D.C.: Georgetown University, 1993).

28. Appleby et al., *Creative Fidelity*, 29.

29. William A. Herr, *Catholic Thinkers in the Clear: Giants of Catholic Thought from Augustine to Rahner*, ed. Todd Brennan, vol. 2, *Basics of Christian Thought* (Chicago: Thomas More Press, 1985).

30. Appleby et al., *Creative Fidelity*, 32.

31. Patrick Allit, *Catholic Converts: British and American Intellectuals Turn to Rome* (Ithaca, N.Y.: Cornell University Press, 1997), ix.

32. Jay P. Corrin, *Catholic Intellectuals and the Challenge of Democracy* (Notre Dame, Ind.: University of Notre Dame Press, 2002), 1.

33. Monica Hellwig, "Foreword," in *Enhancing Religious Identity: Best Practices from Catholic Campuses*, ed. John R. Wilcox, Monica Hellwig, and Irene King (Washington, D.C.: Georgetown University Press, 2000), xi.

34. Theodore M. Hesburgh, "Afterword," in *The Challenge and Promise of a Catholic University*, ed. Theodore M. Hesburgh (Notre Dame, Ind.: University of Notre Dame Press, 1994), 372.

35. Anthony J. Cernera and Oliver J. Morgan, "The Catholic Intellectual Tradition: Some Characteristics, Implications and Future Directions," in *Examining the Catholic Intellectual Tradition*, ed. Anthony J. Cernera and Oliver J. Morgan (Fairfield, N.J.: Sacred Heart University Press, 2000), vii.

36. Lawrence S. Cunningham, "Teaching Theology as a Vocation," in Hesburgh, *The Challenge and Promise of a Catholic University*, 69.

37. Ibid., 70.

38. *Collegium: About the Program*, available from http://s188393811.onlinehome.us/about.htm.

39. Ursula King, "The Catholic Intellectual Tradition: A Gloriously Rich but Difficult Inheritance," in Cernera and Morgan, *Examining the Catholic Intellectual Tradition*, 134.

40. See Angela Bonavoglia, "New Foundations: Catholic Women Reshape Theology," in *Good Catholic Girls: How Women Are Leading the Fight to Change the Church* (New York: HarperCollins, 2005); Catherine Mowry LaCugna, "Catholic Women as Ministers and Theologians," *America* 167, no. 10 (1992).

41. See Gemma Cruz, "Asian Women Theologians Make Voices Heard," *National Catholic Reporter*, December 27, 2002; Patrick Marrin, "Coloring Outside the Patriarchal Lines," *National Catholic Reporter*, May 12, 2000; "Theologians Want More Women Appointed to Church Boards," *National Catholic Reporter*, May 14, 2004.

42. Bonavoglia, "New Foundations," 178.

43. See Mary Jo Weaver, "Enlarging the Discipline: Roman Catholic Feminist Theologians," in *New Catholic Women: A Contemporary Challenge to Traditional Religious Authority* (San Francisco: Harper & Row, 1985).

44. Bonavoglia, "New Foundations," 179.

45. King, "The Catholic Intellectual Tradition," 153.

46. Bill Moyers, "Interview with Mary Gordon," *On Faith and Reason*, PBS telecast (2006).

47. Ibid.

3. Passing on the Faith: Training the Next Generation of American Practicing Catholics

SANDRA YOCUM

1. Nicholas Lash, *Believing Three Ways in One God: A Reading of the Apostles' Creed* (Notre Dame, Ind.: Notre Dame University Press, 1993), 8, 9, 16.

2. John Montgomery Cooper, "The Moral Content of the Advanced Religion Course," *The Catholic Educational Review* 21 (January 1923): 1.

3. John Montgomery Cooper, "The Apologetic Content of the Advanced Religion Course," ibid., 207, 210.

4. John Montgomery Cooper, "Historical Content of Advanced Religion Course," ibid., 154, 155, 156, 158.

5. Cooper, "Moral Content," 2, 9, 5.

6. John Montgomery Cooper, "The Ascetic Content of the Advanced Religion Course," ibid., 349, 350.

7. *Man and Modern Secularism: Essays on the Conflict of the Two Cultures* (New York: National Catholic Alumni Federation, 1940), 131.

8. Ibid., 135.

9. Ibid., 131.

10. Ibid., 144–145.

11. Francis Connell, C.Ss.R, "Special Features and Uses for the Revised Baltimore Catechism in Religious Instruction," *Journal of Religious Instruction* 12 (1942): 298, 299.

12. *Man and Modern Secularism*, 118.

13. Ibid., 119.

14. Ibid., 111–112.

15. Ibid., 152, 154.

16. Ibid., 155.

17. Ibid., 157.

18. Dorothy Day, *On Pilgrimage* (Grand Rapids, Mich.: Eerdmans, 1999), 171.

19. In *Conversations with Cassandra* (New York: Macmillan, 1961), 21, 22.

20. Day, *On Pilgrimage*, 122.

21. Madeleva Wolff, C.S.C., *Christmas Eve and Other Poems* (Paterson, N.J.: St. Anthony Guild Press, 1938), 11.

22. Madeleva Wolff, C.S.C., *American Twelfth Night and Other Poems* (New York: Macmillan, 1955), xliv–xlv.

23. Day, *On Pilgrimage*, 197.

24. Harold Bloom, *The American Religion: The Experience of the Post-Christian Nation* (New York: Simon & Schuster, 1992). Bloom is perhaps the best-known proponent of this view of religion in America.

25. Thomas Merton, *Conjectures of a Guilty Bystander* (Garden City, N.Y.: Image Books, 1968), 127–128.

26. Quoted in *Benedictine Daily Prayer: Short Breviary*, ed. Maxwell E. Johnson, Oblate of Saint John's Abbey and the Monks of Saint John's Abbey (Collegeville, Minn.: Liturgical Press, 2005), 2221.

4. The (Catholic) Politics of Catholic Studies

DAVID O'BRIEN

1. Nathan Hatch, "Strengthening Protestant Evangelical Scholarship: Developing a Comprehensive Strategy," report to the Pew Charitable Trust, October 1988. I thank Hatch for making the text available.

2. See David O'Brien, *From the Heart of the American Church: Catholic Higher Education and American Culture* (Maryknoll, N.Y.: Orbis Books, 1994), Chapter 1.

3. I have tried to make this case over the years. See David O'Brien, "Dialogue: How Has American Catholic Intellectual Life Changed Over the Past Thirty Years," *United States Catholic Historian* 4 (1985): 182–187; "The Summons to Responsibility," *Commonweal* (June 6, 1986), 332–337; and "Continuing the Conversation," *Commonweal* (May 21, 1999), 11–12.

4. David O'Brien, "Conversations on Jesuit (and Catholic?) Higher Education: Jesuit Si, Catholic Not So Sure," *Conversations on Jesuit Higher Education* (Fall 1994): 4–12.

5. For information about the Institute and its history and publications, see www.ifacs.com. For a strong statement of the intellectual content of this initiative, see Michael Lacey, "The Backwardness of American Catholic Theology," *Proceedings of the Catholic Theological Society of America* (1991): 1–15.

6. On the most recent developments in Catholic Studies, see the following articles in a special section of the journal *Catholic Education* 12 (March 2009): *Anthony J. Dosen, C.M.*, "The Development of Catholic Studies Programs in American Catholic Universities," 360–367; and James Heft, S.M., "Almost No Generalizations: Reflections on Catholic Studies," 368–383. This judgment is

based largely on my personal experience. I have visited a great number of Catholic colleges and universities, including all twenty-eight Jesuit institutions, and have attempted to keep in touch with Catholic Studies initiatives. There are other signs of the decline of institutional support for Catholic intellectual life, such as the demise of the Catholic journal *Cross Currents* and the refusal of Catholic institutions to provide it a home, the disappearance of the Catholic Committee on Intellectual and Cultural Affairs, the end of a short-lived effort to establish a joint committee of Catholic learned societies, another effort to build collaboration among Catholic Studies centers, and the failure of the ACCU to adopt any significant projects despite the member institutions' vested interest in Catholic intelligence. All these developments suggest modesty when approaching the politics of Catholic Studies. All were influenced by divisions in the church, divisions sharpened by the development of conservative networks, and publications well connected with the church hierarchy and highly critical of Catholic higher education and of many Catholic theologians and academics. While Catholic colleges and universities enjoy widespread popular support, organized support for Catholic scholarship generally and for Catholic Studies in particular remains very limited.

7. See my review of Peter Steinfels, *A People Adrift* (New York: Simon & Schuster, 2003), in *National Catholic Reporter*, August 29, 2003.

8. Inaugural Lecture, Catholic Studies Program, DePaul University, Chicago, October 21, 1996.

9. William Shea, "Theologians and Their Catholic Authorities," *Horizon* 13 (Fall 1986): 350.

10. On the revolution of separate incorporation, see Alice Gallin, O.S.U., *Independence and a New Partnership in Catholic Higher Education* (Notre Dame, Ind.: University of Notre Dame Press, 1996).

11. The recent history of American Catholic higher education is traced in a series of texts collected in Alice Gallin, O.S.U., ed., *American Catholic Higher Education: Essential Documents* (Notre Dame, Ind.: University of Notre Dame Press, 1992), and in her history of Catholic higher education since Vatican II, *Negotiating Identity: Catholic Higher Education Since 1960* (Notre Dame, Ind.: University of Notre Dame Press, 2000).

12. I emphasized Americanization in *From the Heart of the American Church*.

13. Philip Gleason, *Contending with Modernity: American Catholic Higher Education in the Twentieth Century* (New York: Oxford University Press, 1995).

14. Many commentators were greatly influenced by George Marsden's widely read history of Protestant church-related higher education, *The Soul of the American University: From Protestant Establishment to Established Nonbelief* (New York: Oxford University Press, 1996). See, for example, the influential work of James Burtchaell, *The Dying of the Light: The Disengagement of Colleges*

and Universities from Their Christian Churches (Grand Rapids, Mich.: Eerdmans, 1998). Even friends of Catholic higher education started using this secularization argument, despite the efforts of Alice Gallin and myself to challenge them. This development came at great cost, weakening resistance to conservative efforts to restore ecclesiastical control over Catholic theology amid charges that Catholic institutions were "no longer Catholic." While colleges and universities fought for their independence, a great chill fell over their efforts to strengthen Catholic organizational and popular intelligence.

15. The quote is from a report on a speech by Philip Gleason in the *National Catholic Reporter*, October 15, 2005. Italics in the original.

16. Gleason made this suggestion among other places in the ACCU newsletter *Update*, June 30, 1981. In a later essay he blamed the failure of this approach on association with "general intellectual leftism" and an "activism" that was "too far removed from the properly academic realm to be a satisfactory center for the university's distinctiveness." See Philip Gleason, "The American Background of *Ex Corde Ecclessiae*: An Historical Perspective," in *Catholic Universities in Church and Society: A Dialogue on Ex Corde*, ed. John Langan, S.J., and Leo O'Donovan, S.J. (Washington, D.C.: Georgetown University Press, 1984).

17. "The Pastoral Constitution on the Church and the Modern World," paragraph 1, in *Renewing the Earth: Catholic Documents on Peace, Justice and Liberation*, ed. David J. O'Brien and Thomas A. Shannon (Garden City, N.Y.: Doubleday, 1977), 178.

18. The St. Thomas program can be examined at www.stthomas.edu. On that site, a 1995 essay, "Catholic Studies Programs in the Contemporary Catholic University," by theologian and Catholic Studies director Don Briel, sets forth the St. Thomas approach. Briel updates that essay in "Catholic Studies at the University of St. Thomas," *Catholic Education* 12 (March 2009): 384–398.

19. See Thomas Landy, ed., *As Leaven in the World: Catholic Perspectives on Faith, Vocation and the Intellectual Life* (Franklin, Wis.: Sheed & Ward, 2001).

20. I discussed the theology-religious studies problem in *From the Heart of the American Church*, 165–173. See also D. G. Hart, *The University Gets Religion: Religious Studies in American Higher Education* (Baltimore: Johns Hopkins University Press, 1999), and Ann Taves's essay in this volume.

21. Thomas Landy, "Catholic Studies at Catholic Colleges and Universities," *America*, January 3, 1998, 12–16.

22. Hollenbach argues that Pope John Paul II's virtue of solidarity: "a firm, persevering determination to commit oneself to the common good, that is to say to the good of all and of each individual" allows "neither the strategy of avoiding substantive differences" or a strategy of soft toleration. David Hollenbach, "The Catholic University Under the Sign of the Cross: Christian Humanism in a Broken World," unpublished paper.

23. James Turner, "The Catholic University in Modern Academe: Challenge and Dilemma," paper presented at the conference "Storm Over the University," University of Notre Dame, October 13, 1992.

5. Catholic Studies and Religious Studies: Reflections on the Concept of Tradition

ANN TAVES

1. There has been some work on the concept by scholars of religion. See, for example, N. Ross Reat, "Insiders and Outsiders in the Study of Religious Traditions," *Journal of the American Academy of Religion* 51, no. 3 (Summer 1983): 459–476; Armin W. Geertz and Jeppe Sinding Jensen, *Religion, Tradition, and Renewal* (Aarhus, Denmark: Aarhus University Press, 1991); Paul Heelas, Scott Lash, and Paul Morris, *Detraditionalization: Critical Reflections on Authority and Identity in a Time of Uncertainty* (Malden, Mass.: Blackwell, 1996); Steven Engler and Gregory P. Grieve, eds., *Historicizing "Tradition" in the Study of Religion* (Berlin: Walter de Gruyter, 2005); Thorsten Larbig and Siegfried Wiedenhofer, eds., *Tradition and Tradition Theories: An International Discussion* (Berlin: Lit Verlag, 2006); Gavin D. Flood, "Reflections on Tradition and Inquiry in the Study of Religions," *Journal of the American Academy of Religion* 74, no. 1 (2006): 47–58; and C. W. Huntington Jr., "History, Tradition, and Truth," *History of Religions* 46, no. 3 (2007): 187–227. It is not included as a "critical term" in Mark C. Taylor, ed., *Critical Terms for Religious Studies* (Chicago: University of Chicago Press, 1998), Willi Braun and Russell T. McCutcheon, eds., *Guide to the Study of Religion* (New York: Cassell, 2000), or Donald S. Lopez Jr., *Critical Terms for the Study of Buddhism* (Chicago: University of Chicago Press, 2005).

Among historians and social scientists, Edward Shils's *Tradition* (Chicago: University of Chicago Press, 1981) and Eric Hobsbawm and Terence Ranger's *The Invention of Tradition* (Cambridge: Cambridge University Press, 1983) are the most widely cited. Marcel Sarot, "Counterfactuals and the Invention of Religious Traditions," in *Religious Identity and the Invention of Tradition*, ed. Jan Willem van Henten and Anton Houtepen (Assen, The Netherlands: Royal Van Gorcum, 1999), compares Hobsbawm's concept of the "invention of tradition" with the earlier, less well known understanding articulated by Karl Popper, "Towards a Rational Theory of Tradition," *Rational Annual* 66 (1949): 36–55, and considers the value of "the invention of tradition" concept for the study of religious traditions.

Though much has been written about the Catholic tradition, there are fewer significant works on the Catholic understanding of the concept of tradition. Among them, Yves Congar's *Tradition and Traditions* (New York: Simon &

Schuster, 1966) is a landmark work, while John E. Thiel, *Senses of Tradition: Continuity and Development in Catholic Faith* (New York: Oxford University Press, 2000), and Terrence W. Tilley, *Inventing Catholic Tradition* (Maryknoll, N.Y.: Orbis Books, 2000), provide more recent theological considerations of the concept from two different perspectives.

2. Engler and Grieve, *Historicizing Tradition*, 360–361.

3. Shils, *Tradition*, 12–13.

4. See, for example, José Ignacio Cabezón, "The Discipline and Its Other: The Dialectic Alterity in the Study of Religion," *Journal of the American Academy of Religion* 74, no. 1 (2006): 21–38; and Tylor Roberts, "Exposure and Explanation: On the New Protectionism in the Study of Religion," *Journal of the American Academy of Religion* 72, no. 1 (2004): 143–172.

5. The analogy here is to the movement between player in a game and referee or between committee member and chair. Obviously some individuals are less skilled at switching roles than others and some games or institutions may discourage or preclude switching roles. See Peter Donovan, "Neutrality in Religious Studies," in *The Insider/Outsider Problem in the Study of Religion*, ed. Russell T. McCutcheon (New York: Cassell, 1999); David Hufford, "Reflexivity in Belief Studies," in ibid.; Ann Taves, "Detachment and Engagement in the Study of 'Lived Experience,'" *Spiritus* 3 (2003): 186–208; Taves, "Negotiating the Boundaries in Theological and Religious Studies," Convocation Address, Graduate Theological Union, September 21, 2005, available at http://www.gtu.edu/news-events/events/lectures-and-addresses/gtu-convocational-address/negotiating-the-boundaries-in-theological-and-religious-studies.

6. Thomas A. Tweed, *Crossing and Dwelling: A Theory of Religion* (Cambridge, Mass.: Harvard University Press, 2006), 30–33.

7. See Hobsbawm and Ranger, *The Invention of Tradition*; Delwin Brown, "Limitation and Ingenuity: Radical Historicism and the Nature of Tradition," in Larbig and Wiedenhofer, *Tradition and Tradition Theories*.

8. See, for example, Thiel, *Senses of Tradition*; Tilley, *Inventing Catholic Tradition*; Orlando Espin and Gary Macy, *Futuring Our Past: Explorations in the Theology of Tradition* (Maryknoll, N.Y.: Orbis, 2006).

9. See, for example, Eamon Duffy, *Saints and Sinners: A History of the Popes*, 2nd ed. (New Haven: Yale University Press, 2001), 1–19; Peter Lampe, *From Paul to Valentinus: Christians at Rome in the First Two Centuries*, trans. Michael Steinhauser (Minneapolis: Fortress Press, 2003), 397–408.

10. John B. Henderson, *The Construction of Orthodoxy and Heresy: Neo-Confucian, Islamic, Jewish and Early Christian Patterns* (Albany: SUNY Press, 1998), 89–95.

11. Joseph Ratzinger (Pope Benedict XVI), *Jesus of Nazareth* (New York: Doubleday, 2007), xvi–xvii.

12. Ibid., xix.

13. Congar, *Tradition and Traditions*, 307.

14. Gerald O'Collins, *Fundamental Theology* (Mahwah, N.J.: Paulist Press, 1981), 193, 195.

15. Ibid., 195.

16. See John G. Gunnell, *The Orders of Discourse* (Lanham, Md.: Rowman & Littlefield, 1998).

17. Jonathan Z. Smith, "Religion, Religions, Religious," in *Critical Terms for Religious Studies*, ed. Mark C. Taylor (Chicago: University of Chicago Press, 1998), 269.

18. Flood, "Reflections on Tradition," 55–56.

19. Bart D. Ehrman, *After the New Testament: A Reader in Early Christianity* (New York: Oxford University Press, 1999), 196–211, 227–230.

20. Frances Young, *The Making of the Creeds* (London: SCM Press, 1991), 10–11.

21. Joseph Ratzinger, "The Theological Locus of Ecclesial Movements," *Communio* 25 (1998): 480–500, at 495.

22. James T. Fisher, "The (Longed for) Varieties of Catholic Studies," *Listening: Journal of Religion and Culture* 42, no. 1 (2007): 54–67.

6. A Definition of Catholic: Toward a Cosmopolitan Vision

JEANNINE HILL FLETCHER

1. William V. D'Antonio, James D. Davidson, Dean R. Hoge, and Katherine Meyer, *American Catholics: Gender, Generation, and Commitment* (Walnut Creek, Calif.: Altamira Press, 2001), 31.

2. Elizabeth V. Spelman, *Inessential Woman: Problems of Exclusion in Feminist Thought* (Boston: Beacon Press, 1988), 173.

3. This defining characteristic is identified by many who attempt to construct a description of Catholicism or the Catholic Church. It is not an unhelpful place to start since, as Michele Dillon's study suggests, even pro-change Catholics contesting the hierarchical ordering of the Catholic Church in favor of a more egalitarian community often identify the pope as a key figure and symbol of the collective of "Catholicism." See Dillon, *Catholic Identity: Balancing Reason, Faith, and Power* (Cambridge: Cambridge University Press, 1999), 204–205.

4. The titles of course offerings were taken from a survey of current websites providing an overview of Catholic Studies at a variety of institutions. Websites were accessed on May 14, 2007. They are meant to be illustrative of Catholic Studies in general, rather than identifying particular programs working under the outlined definitions of "Catholic" in this essay. I have chosen,

therefore, not to include the institution of origin for any of the courses or self-descriptions of "Catholic Studies" by a given program.

5. Thomas Bokenkotter, *A Concise History of the Catholic Church*, rev. ed. (New York: Doubleday, 2004).

6. Robert J. Schreiter, *The New Catholicity: Theology Between the Global and the Local* (Maryknoll, N.Y.: Orbis, 1997), 76.

7. For example, one collection of essays on the Catholic community identifies the following categories: Parish Life, Vocations, Youth Ministry, Catholic Schools, Higher Education, Evangelization, and International. See *American Catholic Identity: Essays in an Age of Change*, ed. Francis J. Butler (Kansas City, Mo.: Sheed & Ward, 1994).

8. Margaret O'Brien Steinfels, "Are Catholics Active Enough in Their Church? A Reflection on Membership and Catholic Identity," in ibid., 36.

9. Dillon, *Catholic Identity*.

10. Bryan T. Froehle and Mary L. Gautier, *Global Catholicism: Portrait of a World Church* (Maryknoll, N.Y.: Orbis, 2003).

11. For example, R. S. Sugirtharajah, ed., *Asian Faces of Jesus* (Maryknoll, N.Y.: Orbis, 1993); Robert Schreiter, *Faces of Jesus in Africa* (Maryknoll, N.Y.: Orbis, 1991); Ignacio Ellacuria and Jon Sobrino, *Mysterium Liberationis: Fundamental Concepts of Liberation Theology* (Maryknoll, N.Y.: Orbis, 1993).

12. Robert Schreiter writes, "The term first appears with Ignatius of Antioch around the year 110: "Wherever the bishop appears, there let the people be; as wherever Jesus Christ is, there is the catholic church' (*Smr* 8,2)." Schreiter, *The New Catholicity*, 120–121.

13. Gerald O'Collins and Mario Garrugia, *Catholicism: The Story of Catholic Christianity* (Oxford: Oxford University Press, 2003), 333.

14. Here Ulrich Beck is describing Rolandson's description of glocalization and "global culture." I am applying this description to global Catholic culture. See Beck, *What Is Globalization?* (Cambridge: Polity Press, 2000), 49.

15. See, e.g., *Many Faces, One Church: Cultural Diversity and the American Catholic Experience*, ed. Peter C. Phan and Diana Hayes (Lantham, Md.: Rowman & Littlefield, 2005).

16. Dean R. Hoge, "Center of Catholic Identity," *National Catholic Reporter*, September 30, 2005.

17. Archbishop Daniel E. Pilarczyk, *Practicing Catholic* (Cincinnati: St. Anthony Messenger Press, 1999), v.

18. D'Antonio et al., *American Catholics*, 38.

19. Ibid., 41.

20. William V. D'Antonio, James D. Davidson, Dean R. Hoge, and Mary L. Gautier, *American Catholics Today: New Realities of Their Faith and Their Church* (Lantham, Md.: Rowman & Littlefield, 2007). Continuing the studies of 1987,

1993, and 1999, the researchers studied Catholic identity through a series of polls in 2005. The 2007 volume includes overviews and descriptions of the earlier studies. Initial findings were also published in Hoge, "Center of Catholic Identity."

21. D'Antonio et al., *American Catholics Today*, 27.

22. Andrew Greeley, *The Communal Catholic* (New York: Seabury, 1976), quoted in Peter Phan, "To Be Catholic or Not to Be: Is It Still the Question? Catholic Identity and Religious Education Today," *Horizons*, 25, no. 2 (1998): 166.

23. D'Antonio et al., *American Catholics Today*, 42–43.

24. Dillon, *Catholic Identity*, 203.

25. D'Antonio et al., *American Catholics Today*, 24.

26. Ibid., 24, 27.

27. Pilarczyk, *Practicing Catholic*, v.

28. Gerald O'Collins and Mario Farrugia, *Catholicism: The Story of Catholic Christianity* (Oxford: Oxford University Press, 2003), v.

29. D'Antonio et al., *American Catholics Today*, 28.

30. Ibid., 26–27.

31. See, for example, the collection *Mary, Mother of God*, ed. Carl E. Braaten and Robert W. Jenson (Grand Rapids, Mich.: Eerdmans, 2004), for an argument of what is shared across Christian denominations on the person of Mary.

32. Schreiter, *The New Catholicity*, 121–122.

33. O'Collins and Farrugia, *Catholicism*, 367.

34. Steinfels, "Are Catholics Active Enough in Their Church?" 33.

35. Edward Malloy, "The Religious Impact of Catholic Higher Education: Is There a Gap Between What Catholic Universities Proclaim and What They Practice?" in Butler, *American Catholic Identity*, 14.

36. James W. Malone, "Catholic Higher Education and Its Religious Impact," in ibid., 22–23.

37. Steinfels, "Are Catholics Active Enough in Their Church?" 36–37.

38. O'Collins and Farrugia, *Catholicism*, 367.

39. "Catholic," from the glossary of the *Catechism of the Catholic Church*, 2nd ed. (United States Catholic Conference, 2000), 870.

40. This hierarchical ordering rooted in a theological understanding of "Catholic" is evidenced in recent magisterial documents such as *Dominus Iesus* (2000) and "Responses to Some Questions Regarding Certain Aspects of the Doctrine on the Church," issued by the Congregation for the Doctrine of the Faith, June 29, 2007.

41. Linell Elizabeth Cady, "Identity, Feminist Theory and Theology," in *Horizons in Feminist Theology: Identity, Tradition and Norms*, ed. Rebecca S. Chopp and Sheila Greeve Davaney (Minneapolis: Fortress Press, 1997), 26.

42. Glunar Francis-Dehqani, "The Gendering of Missionary Imperialism," in *Gender, Religion and Diversity: Cross Cultural Perspectives*, ed. Ursula King and Tina Beattie (New York: Continuum, 2004), 133.

43. Edward Said, *Orientalism* (New York: Vintage Books, 1979), 201.

44. Morwenna Griffiths, *Feminisms and the Self: The Web of Identity* (New York: Routledge, 1995), 2.

45. Martha Minnow, *Not Only for Myself* (New York: New Press, 1997), 40.

46. Ulrich Beck, *Cosmopolitan Vision*, trans. Ciaran Cronin (Cambridge: Polity Press, 2006), 48.

47. Robert Orsi, *The Madonna of 115th Street: Faith and Community in Italian Harlem, 1880–1950* (New Haven: Yale University Press, 1985).

48. Alexie Torres-Fleming, cofounder of Youth Ministries for Peace and Justice (YMPJ), Bronx, New York, as quoted in *Living the Catholic Social Tradition: Cases and Commentary*, ed. Kathleen Maas Weigert and Alexia K. Kelley (Lantham, Md.: Rowman & Littlefield, 2005), 97.

49. See William E. Stempsey, "Institutional Identity and Roman Catholic Hospitals," *Christian Bioethics* 7, no. 1 (2001): 10. Stempsey cites Gerard Magill, "Organizational Ethics in Catholic Health Care: Honoring Stewardship and the Work Environment," ibid., 67–93.

50. Malloy, "The Religious Impact of Catholic Higher Education," 3–4.

51. Trinh T. Minh-ha, *Woman-Native-Other* (Bloomington: Indiana University Press, 1989), 93–94.

52. Walter J. Burghardt and William F. Lynch, *The Idea of Catholicism: An Introduction to the Thought and Worship of the Church* (New York: Greenwich Editions/Meridian Books, 1960), 7.

53. Ibid., 8.

54. D'Antonio et al., *American Catholics*, 38–39.

55. The idea of a multiperspectival methodology is taken from Beck, *Cosmopolitan Vision*, 82.

7. Method and Conversion in Catholic Studies

RICHARD M. LIDDY

1. See *Listening: Journal of Religion and Culture* 42, no. 1 (Winter 2007), dedicated to articles on Catholic Studies.

2. See Richard Dawkins, *The God Illusion* (New York: Houghton Mifflin, 2006); Daniel Dennett, *Breaking the Spell* (New York: Viking, 2006); Christopher Hitchens, *God Is Not Great* (New York: Hachette, 2007); Sam Harris, *The End of Faith: Religion, Terror and the Future of Reason* (New York: Norton, 2004), and *Letter to a Christian Nation* (New York: Knopf, 2007).

3. These two terms are equivalent. "Transcendental" will often be used within a European philosophical context, while Lonergan, writing within a North American context, will emphasize the "empirical" dimension of this general methodological structure.

4. See Herbert Butterfield, *The Origins of Modern Science, 1300–1800* (New York: Free Press, 1957; 2nd. ed., 1965), 25–26: "nothing could have been more important than the growing tendency to geometrise or mathematise a problem. Nothing is more effective, after people have long been debating and wrangling and churning the air, than the appearance of a person who draws a line on the blackboard, which with the help of a little geometry solves the whole problem in an instant."

5. Bernard Lonergan, "The Ongoing Genesis of Methods," in *A Third Collection: Papers by Bernard Lonergan, S.J.*, ed. Frederick E. Crowe, S.J. (New York: Paulist Press, 1985), 215.

6. The celebrated program of Canon Cardijin's Young Christian Workers, "See! Judge! Act!" conspicuously left out "Understand!"

7. On the biases to understanding, see Bernard Lonergan, *Insight: A Study of Human Understanding*, vol. 3 of *Collected Works of Bernard Lonergan* (Toronto: University of Toronto Press, 1993), 214–227 and 232–269.

8. See *Method in Theology* (London: Darton, Longman & Todd, 1972; reprint, Toronto: University of Toronto Press, 1990), 195–196.

9. Ibid., 184.

10. Ibid., 188.

11. Ibid., 238–242.

12. See Richard Liddy, "Augustine's Intellectual Conversion," in *Core Texts, Community, and Culture*, ed. R. Weber et al. (Lanham, Md.: University Press of America, 2010), 25–30.

13. "Revolution in Catholic Theology," *A Second Collection* (London: Darton, Longman & Todd, 1974; reprint, University of Toronto Press, 1996), 232. Such classical consciousness "was the fruit of being brought up in a good home, of studying Latin and Greek in school, of admiring the immortal works of literature and art of the classical period, of adhering to the perennial philosophy, and of finding in one's laws and institutions the deposit of the prudence and the wisdom of mankind."

14. In his writings Lonergan pays tribute to John Henry Newman for introducing historical consciousness into Catholic circles; thus, the new age in Catholic theology "dates not from 1965 when the Second Vatican Council closed, but rather from 1845 when Newman completed his *Essay on the Development of Christian Doctrine*." See "A New Pastoral Theology," *Philosophical and Theological Papers 1965–1980*, vol. 17 of *Collected Works of Bernard Lonergan*, ed. Robert Doran and Robert Croken (Toronto: University of Toronto Press, 2004), 238.

15. Bernard Lonergan, "The Scope of Renewal," in *Philosophical and Theological Papers 1965–1980*, 283. So also, in his *Method in Theology*, Lonergan warns against the premature influence of contemporary theological issues on historical research, to the detriment of the latter. See *Method in Theology*, 143.

16. Lonergan, *Method in Theology*, 130.

17. A book Lonergan cited in the early 1940s spoke of the implicit materialism of many Catholics: see E. I. Watkin, *The Catholic Centre* (New York: Sheed & Ward, 1939).

18. *A Third Collection*, 156: "I do not mean that human wickedness was denied. But it was felt it could be evaded. Truth was supposed to consist in the necessary conclusions deduced from self-evident principles. Or it was that reality was already out there now, and that objectivity was the simple matter of taking a good look, seeing all that was there and not seeing what was not there."

19. Ibid., 157: "The objective aspect of the problem has come to light in Paul Ricoeur's distinction between a hermeneutic of recovery, that brings to light what is true and good, and a hermeneutic of suspicion, that joins Marx in impugning the rich, or Nietzsche in reviling the humble, or Freud in finding consciousness itself an unreliable witness to our motives."

20. Lonergan, *Method in Theology*, 125.

21. Ibid., 126.

22. See Lonergan's remark on his functional specializations in *A Second Collection*, 210: "Karl Rahner, in his paper, remarked he thought it could be applied to any human science that was fully conscious of itself as depending on the past and looking towards the future. I think that's true."

23. Lonergan, *Method in Theology*, 130–132.

24. Lonergan, *A Third Collection*, 163.

25. Ibid., 113–114.

26. Ibid., 115–116.

27. Ibid., 161.

28. Lonergan often refers to the work of Wilfred Cantwell Smith on the notion of "inner commitment" or faith beneath the beliefs of the various religions. See ibid., 122–123.

29. See Arnold Toynbee, *A Study of History*, 10:69, where he captures the power of theology: "There is, indeed, no limit to the commitment incurred by the inquirer who ventures to be a student of human affairs, for, whether he has foreseen this or not, he has committed himself, in the act, to becoming a theologian too. In consternation he may try to beat a retreat from this perilously exposed position into the dead ground of 'comparative religion,' in the hope that he can escape from theology under the scientific camouflage of anthropological research. But theology is an incubus that a humanist can never

shake off. He may seek refuge from theism in atheism or from animism in materialism. But after each desperate twist and turn he will find himself committed to some theological position or other. Theology is inescapable, and it is dynamite. It will betray its identity through the camouflage by exploding in the end."

30. Lonergan, *A Third Collection*, 164.

31. Ibid., 185.

32. See Lonergan, *Method in Theology*, 355: "[Communications] is a major concern, for it is in this final stage that theological reflection bears fruit. Without the first seven stages, of course, there is no fruit to be borne. But without the last the first seven are in vain, for they fail to mature."

33. Ibid., 364.

34. John Paul II, Apostolic constitution, *Ex corde ecclesiae* (Washington, D.C.: USCCB, 1990), n. 15. See also n. 19: "Theology . . . serves all other disciplines in their search for meaning, not only by helping them to investigate how their discoveries will affect individuals and society but also by bringing a perspective and an orientation not contained within their own methodologies. In turn, interaction with these other disciplines and their discoveries enriches theology, offering it a better understanding of the world today, and making theological research more relevant to current needs."

35. Similar expressions are "the sacramental imagination" or "the analogical imagination." See the various works by Andrew Greeley, such as *The Catholic Imagination* (Berkeley: University of California Press, 2000), or Paul Giles, *American Catholic Arts and Fictions: Culture, Ideology, Aesthetics* (New York: Cambridge University Press, 1992). See also Paul Giles, "American Catholic Arts and Fictions and the New Catholic Scholarship," *U.S. Catholic Historian* 17 (Summer 1999): 1–8.

36. See James T. Fisher, "The (Longed For) Varieties of Catholic Studies," *Listening: Journal of Religion and Culture* 42, no. 1 (Winter 2007): 54–67.

37. G. K. Chesterton, *The Common Man*, available at http://www.gkc.org.uk/gkc/books/Common_Man.txt.

38. Quoted in Thomas King, "A Holy Man and a Lover of the World," *America*, March 28, 2005.

39. Writing to a businessman, Teilhard said: "Since everything in the world follows the road to unification, the spiritual success of the universe is bound up with the correct functioning of every zone of that universe, and particularly with the release of every possible energy in it. Because your enterprise . . . is going well, a little more health is being spread in the human mass, and in consequence a little more liberty to act, to think, and to love."

8. Catholic Studies in the Spirit of "Do Whatever He Tells You"

UNA M. CADEGAN

1. For the sake of clarity, I should note that the office of the university rector, formerly concerned primarily with vowed Marianists working on campus, has taken on a larger and more explicit role in mission and identity work since the university changed the requirement that the president of the university must be a vowed Marianist. But the decision to retain the original title and not explicitly establish an office of mission and identity illustrates my point here.

2. The report is available at http://artssciences.udayton.edu/cmeducation/resources.asp.

3. The University of Dayton has recently been reclassified as a doctoral-intensive university, which may in the long run have some significant effect on some of the issues I am describing here. In the meantime, though, its historical focus as a comprehensive university on undergraduate education and the connection between liberal and professional education still most immediately affects the approach to Catholic Studies I am describing here.

4. It also resulted in the publication of a volume by Brenda W. Donnelly et al., *The Challenge of Adolescent Health: Views from Catholic Social Teaching and the Social and Medical Sciences* (Lanham, Md.: University Press of America, 1999).

5. William Joseph Chaminade, *Letter to the Retreatmasters of 1839, or Circular on the Vow of Stability*, trans. Carl Dreisoerner, S.M. (Kirkwood, Mo.: Maryhurst Press, 1937); quoted in John M. Samaha, S.M., "Mary's Apostolic Mission: Chaminade's Contribution to Mariology," http://campus.udayton.edu/mary/meditations/chaminade/mariology.html.

9. Afflicting the Comfortable: The Role of Catholic Social Teaching in Catholic Studies Programs

MARGARET M. McGUINNESS

1. The Pew Forum's full report can be found at www.religions.pewforum.org.

2. Statistics, however, do not reflect the situation at every college and university. Forty percent of the students in the class of 2013 at Philadelphia's La Salle University are the first in their families to attend college.

3. Chester Gillis, *Roman Catholicism in America* (New York: Columbia University Press, 1999), 20.

4. William Bole, "Listening to the Millennials," *Woodstock Report* 88 (June 2007).

5. Examples of studies involving the faith life and practice of young adult Catholics include Dean Hoge, William D. Dinges, Mary Johnson, S.N.D. de N., and Juan L. Gonzales Jr., *Young Adult Catholics: Religion in a Culture of Choice* (Notre Dame, Ind.: University of Notre Dame Press, 2001); and Tim Muldoon, *Seeds of Hope: Young Adults and the Catholic Church in the United States* (Mahwah, N.J.: Paulist Press, 2008).

6. See the Pew Forum's *Religion Among the Millennials*, February 17, 2010, http://pewforum.org/docs/?DocID=510#affiliation (accessed April 19, 2010). This figure is interesting when compared to the figures for mainline Protestantism; the corresponding figures are 33 and 35 percent.

7. It is certain the sexual abuse scandal has also affected the ways in which millennial Catholics relate to the church, but how this has happened has not yet been determined.

8. James T. Fisher, "The (Longed for) Varieties of Catholic Studies," *Listening: Journal of Religion and Culture* 42, no. 1 (2007): 54–67.

9. The phrase "To comfort the afflicted and afflict the comfortable" is often attributed to Dorothy Day, but the sentiment was first expressed by Finley Peter Dunne (1867–1936), an Irish American journalist and creator of the fictional "Mr. Dooley," who expressed opinions on political, economic, and social topics from his Irish bar on the south side of Chicago. It is important to remember that many of today's Catholic college students are from a part of our society considered "comfortable"; however, other students come from backgrounds that might best be described as "afflicted."

10. The quotations are from James Carroll, *Practicing Catholic* (Boston: Houghton, Mifflin, Harcourt, 2009), 9.

11. Ibid.

12. See www.osjspm.org/answers_to_questions_1_5.aspx#1. This is the first response to twenty-five frequently asked questions concerning CST.

13. See Marvin L. Krier Mich, *Catholic Social Teaching and Movements* (Mystic, Conn.: Twenty-Third Publications, 2001), 20.

14. See Peter J. Henriot, *Catholic Social Teaching: Our Best Kept Secret* (Maryknoll, N.Y.: Orbis Press, 1988), 20–22. The website for the Office of Social Justice of the Archdiocese of St. Paul Minneapolis also lists a total of ten principles.

15. See Una Cadegan's essay in this volume for ways to involve departments and colleges throughout a university in issues relating to identity and mission. These methods could certainly be adapted to disseminate Catholic Studies across the curriculum.

16. The idea that undergraduate students do not have a clear understanding of the place of scripture and tradition in Catholic teaching is one with which

colleges and universities must wrestle. The introductory course in theology/religious studies is a particularly important component in this discussion.

17. Monika K. Hellwig, "Curricular Contexts and Challenges for Catholic Social Thinking," in *Living the Catholic Social Tradition: Cases and Commentary*, ed. Kathleen Maas Weigert and Alexia K. Kelley (Lanham, Md.: Rowman & Littlefield, 2005), xi.

18. Ibid., xiii.

19. As the number of Catholic secondary schools continues to decrease, the number of Catholic undergraduates who have attended Catholic schools from kindergarten through twelfth grade will also continue to decline.

20. The series American Catholic Identities, published by Orbis Books and under the general editorship of Christopher J. Kauffman, includes volumes on Latino Catholics, women, and public Catholicism.

21. Non-Catholic students may be enrolled in a course on Catholic social teaching. I simply ask them to complete the assignment based on their own faith tradition and experiences.

22. It would be very easy to offer a course in Catholic social teaching as a service learning course. Students would engage in weekly service and then reflect on their experience through journals and class discussion.

11. Visual Literacy and Catholic Studies

CATHERINE R. OSBORNE

1. Gregory the Great, "Letter to Serenus," reprinted in *Theological Aesthetics: A Reader*, ed. Gesa Elsbeth Thiessen (Grand Rapids, Mich.: Eerdmans, 2005), 47.

2. As a number of medieval art historians have pointed out, images never did, and never could have, functioned simply as "bibles of the poor" or "books of the illiterate." For an early example, see Madeleine Caviness, "Biblical Stories in Windows: Were They Bibles for the Poor?" in *The Bible in the Middle Ages*, ed. B. S. Levy (Binghamton, N.Y.: Medieval & Renaissance Texts & Studies, 1992), 103–147.

3. "Visual culture studies" and "material culture studies" are both attempts to expand the academic domain of the visual beyond the disciplinary boundary of art history, which, although it has greatly expanded in scope in the last forty years to include such items as crafts, ceramics, quilts, posters, industrial design, and so forth, still concentrates on images and objects that are understood to have aesthetic value—however that is defined. Visual and material culture studies draw on methodology from art history, sociology, and other disciplines and try to consider the implications of entire visual and material worlds, including not only what might be called "art" but also a much wider

range of intentional and unintentional culture: greeting cards, kitchen appliances, home videos, mass-produced statuary, and advertising. See Matthew Rampley, ed., *Exploring Visual Culture: Definitions, Concepts, Contexts* (Edinburgh: Edinburgh University Press, 2005); Tony Schirato and Jen Webb, *Understanding the Visual* (London: Sage, 2004); David Morgan, *Visual Piety: A History and Theory of Popular Religious Images* (Berkeley: University of California Press, 1998); David Morgan and Sally M. Promey, eds., *The Visual Culture of American Religions* (Berkeley: University of California Press, 2001); and Michael Lesy, "Visual Literacy," *Journal of American History* 94, no. 1 (June 2007): 143–153.

4. Colleen McDannell, *Material Christianity: Religion and Popular Culture in America* (New Haven: Yale University Press, 1995), 2.

5. Eamon Duffy, *The Stripping of the Altars: Traditional Religion in England, c. 1400–c. 1580* (New Haven: Yale University Press, 2005).

6. Vachel Lindsay, *The Art of the Moving Picture* (New York: Norton, 1970), 22.

7. Rona Goffen, "Masaccio's *Trinity* and the Letter to the Hebrews," in *Masaccio's Trinity*, ed. Rona Goffen (Cambridge: Cambridge University Press, 1998).

8. Margaret Borden, "Fixer-Upper," *The New Yorker* (June 11, 2007).

9. Katherine H. Tachau, "God's Compass and *Vana Curiositas*: Scientific Study in the Old French *Bible Moralisée*," *Art Bulletin* 80, no. 1 (March 1998): 7–33.

10. Donna Sadler, "The King as Subject, the King as Author: Art and Politics of Louis IX," in *European Monarchy: Its Evolution and Practice from Roman Antiquity to Modern Times*, ed. Heinz Duchhardt et al. (Stuttgart: Franz Steiner Verlag, 1992), 61.

11. Anne Derbes and Mark Sandona, "Barren Metal and the Fruitful Womb: The Program of Giotto's Arena Chapel in Padua," *Art Bulletin* 80, no. 2 (June 1998): 274–291.

12. Michael Lesy, *Long Time Coming: A Photographic Portrait of America, 1935–43* (New York: Norton, 2002).

13. Although the greatest mass of "Catholic" material shows devotional activity, at least one group of FSA/OWI photos goes in precisely the opposite direction. As Colleen McDannell demonstrates, John Collier Jr.'s photographs of Catholics in Taos County, New Mexico, in 1943 are designed precisely to convey an image of Catholics as "good Americans essential to the war effort," not divisive "foreign" elements, and thus show an all-American range of activities for priests: leading Boy Scouts, giving agricultural advice, directing school meetings, and the like. Like all the FSA/OWI images, these must be understood partly in their capacity as propaganda. Colleen McDannell, *Picturing*

Faith: Photography and the Great Depression (New Haven: Yale University Press, 2004), 149–164.

14. Roland Barthes, "The Death of the Author," in *Image-Music-Text* (New York: Hill & Wang, 1977), 148.

15. McDannell, *Material Christianity*, 163–197.

16. David Morgan, *Visual Piety: A History and Theory of Popular Religious Images* (Berkeley: University of California Press, 1998).

17. Charlton Fortune, "Correspondence," *Liturgical Arts* 5, no. 2 (1936): 71.

18. John McGreevy, *Parish Boundaries: The Catholic Encounter with Race in the Twentieth-Century Urban North* (Chicago: University of Chicago Press, 1996); Robert A. Orsi, *The Madonna of 115th St: Faith and Community in Italian Harlem, 1880–1950* (New Haven: Yale University Press, 2002).

19. Thomas A. Tweed, "America's Church: Roman Catholicism and Civic Space in the Nation's Capital," in *The Visual Culture of American Religions*, ed. David Morgan and Sally M. Promey (Berkeley: University of California Press, 2001).

20. I am grateful to Fr. Phil Kelly and to Lawrence Hoy for sharing information on the renovation project with me.

12. We Have Been Believers: Black Catholic Studies

DIANA L. HAYES AND CECILIA A. MOORE

1. C. Vanessa White interview, March 18, 2008. Fr. Abram's claim, "somebody stole all my stuff," is evocative of the Lady in Green's in Ntozake Shange's play *For Colored Girls Who Have Considered Suicide When the Rainbow is Enuf* and her soliloquy, in which she asserts "somebody almost walked off wid alla my stuff." The significant difference is the absence of the word "almost" in Abram's declaration. While the Lady in Green perseveres over her would be thief and holds onto her poems, dance, tacky skirts, silver nose ring, laugh, rhythm, voice, scars, favorite foods, and memories, Abrams did not, and was on a quest to reclaim all that was stolen from him.

2. M. Shawn Copeland, "African American Catholic and Black Theology: An Interpretation" in *African American Religious Studies: An Interdisciplinary Anthology*, ed. Gayraud S. Wilmore (Durham, N.C.: Duke University Press, 1989), 230.

3. Cyprian Davis, "To Be Both Black and Catholic," Marianist Award Lecture, University of Dayton, 2006, 15.

4. Ibid.

5. Cyprian Davis, *The History of Black Catholics in the United States* (New York: Crossroads, 1990), 258.

6. Ibid.

7. "The Survival of Soul: National Black Sisters' Conference Position Paper, 1969," in *"Stamped with the Image of God": African Americans as God's Image in Black*, ed. Cyprian Davis, O.S.B., and Jamie T. Phelps, O.P. (Maryknoll, N.Y.: Orbis Books, 2003), 114.

8. Ibid., 114–115.

9. M. Shawn Copeland, "A Cadre of Women Religious Committed to Black Liberation: The National Black Sisters Conference," *U.S. Catholic Historian* 14 (Winter 1996): 123–144.

10. Copeland, "African American Catholics and Black Theology," 232.

11. Thea Bowman, *Shooting Star: Selected Writings and Speeches of Sister Thea Bowman*, ed. Celestine Cepress (La Crosse, Wis.: Franciscan Sisters of Perpetual Adoration, 1999), 61.

12. See Tammy Kernodle, *Soul on Soul: The Life and Music of Mary Lou Williams* (Boston: Northeastern University Press, 2004).

13. Copeland, "African American Catholics and Black Theology," 233–234.

14. Ibid., 234.

15. The Institute for Black Catholic Studies 1999 Handbook of Policies, Procedures, and Information for the Th.M. Degree, 1–2.

16. The Institute for Black Catholic Studies has published a journal called *The Sacred Rock*, which features the current work in Black Catholic Studies that its faculty and graduates are producing.

17. Davis, "To Be Both Black and Catholic," 12.

18. Ibid., 13.

19. Students of the Institute for Black Catholic Studies from the 1980s fondly recall Father Davis using chapters and drafts of *The History of Black Catholics in the United States* in his black Catholic history course. Davis won the John Gilmary Shea Award for *The History of Black Catholics in the United States* from the American Catholic Historical Association. At this writing, Davis was working on a new edition of *The History of Black Catholics in the United States.*

20. See for example, Benjamin C. Ray, *African Religions: Symbol, Ritual, and Community* (New York: Prentice-Hall, 1999), and Jacob Olupona, ed., *African Traditional Religion in Contemporary Society* (St. Paul, Minn.: Paragon House, 1991).

21. John S. Mbiti, *African Religions and Philosophy* (Garden City, N.Y.: Doubleday Anchor Books, 1970), 3.

22. See Albert J. Raboteau, *Slave Religion: The "Invisible Institution" in the Antebellum South* (New York: Oxford University Press, 1978), and Joseph Holloweil, *Africanisms in American Culture* (Bloomington: Indiana University Press, 1990).

23. Davis, *The History of Black Catholics in the United States.*

24. Ibid., 88.

25. See, however, Jay P. Dolan, *Catholic Revivalism: The American Experience, 1830–1900* (Notre Dame, Ind.: Notre Dame University Press, 1978), and Diana L. Hayes, *And Still We Rise: An Introduction to Black Liberation Theology* (Mahwah, N.J.: Paulist Press, 1996).

26. These were the Paulist Fathers and Brothers. See Hayes, *And Still We Rise*, 42–43; see also Dolan, *Catholic Revivalism*.

27. Dolan, *Catholic Revivalism*, 25–52.

28. Ibid.

29. The first women's orders were established in 1828 (The Oblate Sisters of Providence) and 1842 (The Holy Family Sisters). A black men's religious order was never established, but there were several orders whose mission was to African Americans after the Civil War. They included the Society of St. Joseph, more commonly known as the Josephites, the Society of the Divine Word, and a women's community, the Sisters of the Blessed Sacrament.

30. See the discussion in Joseph A. Brown, S.J., *To Stand on the Rock: Meditations on Black Catholic Identity* (Maryknoll, N.Y.: Orbis Books, 1998), 128–130.

31. M. Shawn Copeland, "Methodology in Black Theology" in *Taking Down Our Harps: Black Catholics in the United States*, ed. Diana Hayes and Cyprian Davis (New York: Orbis Books, 1998), 123.

32. *Black Religion: The Negro and Christianity in the United States* (New York: Beacon Press, 1966). It is worth noting that James Cone was teaching at Adrian College, a Dominican college in Michigan, when he wrote his groundbreaking work on black theology, *Black Theology and Black Power* (New York: Seabury Press, 1970).

33. See James H. Cone and Gayraud Wilmore, *Black Theology: A Documentary History* (Maryknoll, N.Y.: Orbis Books, 1993), 1:19–40.

34. Hayes, *And Still We Rise*, 54. See also James H. Cone, *For My People* (Maryknoll, N.Y.: Orbis Books, 1984), Chapter 1.

35. Ibid., 54–55.

36. See Diane Batts Morrow, *Persons of Color and Religious At the Same Time: The Oblate Sisters of Providence, 1828–1860* (Chapel Hill: University of North Carolina Press, 1999), for the best account of how the first black women's religious community did this in the nineteenth century.

37. Copeland, "Method Emerging in Black Catholic Theology," 125.

38. They are the authors of several works, including Diana L. Hayes, *And Still We Rise: An Introduction to Black Liberation Theology* (1996), *Hagar's Daughters: Womanist Ways of Being in the World* (1995), and, with Cyprian Davis, *Taking Down Our Harps: Black Catholics in the United States* (1998); Jamie T. Phelps and Cyprian Davis, eds., *Stamped with the Image of God: God's Image*

in Black (2004); Jamie T. Phelps, *Black and Catholic: The Challenge and Gift of Black Folk—Contribution of African American Experience and Thought to Catholic Theology* (Milwaukee: Marquette University Press, 1998); Joseph A. Brown, *To Stand on the Rock: Meditations on Black Catholic Identity* (Maryknoll, N.Y.: Orbis Books, 1998); M. Shawn Copeland, *Enfleshing Freedom: Body, Race, and Being* (Minneapolis: Augsburg Press, 2010); and Toinette Eugene, *Balm for Gilead* (Nashville: Abingdon Press, 1998).

39. Diana L. Hayes, "We've Come This Far By Faith," in *Taking Down Our Harps*, 7.

40. Thaddeus Posey, ed., *Proceedings of the Black Catholic Theological Symposium* 1 (October 12–15, 1978).

41. Institute for Black Catholic Studies 1999 Handbook, 1.

42. "History of the Black Catholic Theological Symposium," www.bcts.org/history.htm (Accessed September 18, 2008).

43. M. Shawn Copeland, "Guest Editorial," *Theological Studies* 61 (December 2000): 603.

44. Ibid.

45. See James H. Cone, "Black Liberation Theology and Black Catholics: A Critical Conversation," *Theological Studies* 61 (December 2000): 741–757.

46. Father Tolton was ordained in 1884 for the Archdiocese of Chicago.

47. The first such congress was held January 1, 1889. It was followed by four more, ending in 1894 until resurrected in 1987 by black Catholics concerned about their status in the Church and affirming their centuries long presence as faith-filled Catholics. Since then, the Congress has met every five years.

48. Morrow's *Persons of Color and Religious at the Same Time: The Oblate Sisters of Providence, 1828–1860* won the Letitia Woods Brown Memorial Publication Prize for Best Book on Black Women's History in 2002, and in 2004 the Conference on the History of Women Religious also gave it its best book award.

49. Laurie Cassidy and Alex Mikulich, *Interrupting White Privilege: Catholic Theologians Break the Silence* (Maryknoll, N.Y.: Orbis Books, 2007), 4.

50. A few recent studies about or related to black Catholics by scholars who are not black Catholics include *Sisters of Selma*, a film released in 2006 by Jaysari Hart on the role of women religious in the civil rights movement; *A Precious Fountain: Music in the Worship of a Black Catholic Community* by Mary McGann (2004); *Soul on Soul: The Life and Music of Mary Lou Williams* by Tammy L. Kernodle (2004); *The New Nuns: Racial Justice and Religious Reform in the 1960s* by Amy Koehlinger (2007); and *A Mission for Justice: The History of the First African American Catholic Church in Newark, New Jersey* by Mary Ward (2002).

51. The Pew Forum on Religion and Public Life, "A Religious Portrait of African-Americans," http:pewforum.org/A-Religious-Portrait-of-African-Americans.aspx, January 9, 2009 (accessed May 9, 2010). Statistics elsewhere in this essay are also taken from this document.

13. Asian American Catholic Experience and Catholic Studies

LINH HOANG, O.F.M.

1. Jay P. Dolan, "The Immigrants and Their Gods: A New Perspective in American Religious History," *Church History* 57, no. 1 (March 1988): 66.

2. Sydney E. Ahlstrom, *A Religious History of the American People* (New Haven: Yale University Press, 2004), 1001–1002.

3. Ibid., 1002.

4. American Religious Identification Survey 2001, Graduate Center at the City University of New York.

5. Joseph Sadoc Alemany was a Dominican friar who became the first archbishop of California. He was born in 1814 and died in 1888. See John Bernard McGloin, *California's First Archbishop: The Life of Joseph Sadoc Alemany, O.P.* (New York: Herder and Herder, 1966).

6. United States Conference of Catholic Bishops, "Asian and Pacific Presence: Harmony in Faith," December 2001.

7. The term as defined by dictionary.com is dated and old-fashioned. It also has taken on the layered history of being "Eurocentric," and in some cases has become a means of objectifying. However, it is an old term that, even among Asian groups, is still used but possesses a pejorative punch.

8. Juanita Tamayo Lott, *Asian Americans: From Race Category to Multiple Identities* (Walnut Creek, Calif.: Altamira Press, 1998), 77.

9. Ian F. Haney Lopez, *White by Law: The Legal Construction of Race* (New York: New York University Press, 1996).

10. The Naturalization Act of 1790 was passed on March 26 under the 1 Statute 103–104. It was not until 1952, with the McCarran-Walter Act, that an immigrant was able to become a citizen without regard to race or sex.

11. Lisa Lowe, *Immigrant Acts: On Asian American Cultural Politics* (Durham, N.C.: Duke University Press, 1996), 19.

12. "The Senate's Declaration of War," *Japan Times and Mail*, April 19, 1924, 4.

13. Lowe, *Immigrant Acts*, 7.

14. The Hart-Celler Immigration Bill was issued on October 3, 1965, and eliminated the national origins quota that was issued in 1921. See www.cis.org/articles/1995/back395.html.

15. Martin E. Marty, "American Religious History in the Eighties: A Decade of Achievement," *Church History* 62, no. 3 (September 1993): 335–377.

16. Martin E. Marty, *Modern American Religion*, 2 vols. (Chicago: University of Chicago Press, 1986, 1991).

17. Pyong Gap Min and Jung Ha Kim, eds., *Religions in Asian America: Building Faith Communities* (Walnut Creek, Calif.: Altamira Press, 2002), 21.

18. Sidney E. Ahlstrom, *A Religious History of the American People* (New Haven: Yale University Press, 1972), 1051.

19. Edwin Gaustad, *A Religious History of America* (San Francisco: Harper & Row, 1990), 162–163.

20. Ibid., 187–188, 285.

21. R. Stephen Warner and Judith G. Wittner, *Gatherings in Diaspora: Religious Communities and the New Immigration* (Philadelphia: Temple University Press, 1998); Helen Rose Ebaugh, *Religion and the New Immigrants: Continuities and Adaptations in Immigrant Congregations* (Walnut Creek, Calif.: Altamira Press, 2000).

22. John B. McGloin, "Thomas Cian, Pioneer Chinese Priest in California," *California Historical Society* 48, no. 1 (1969): 45–58.

23. Jeffrey M. Burns, Ellen Skerrett, and Joseph M. White, eds., *Keeping Faith: European and Asian Catholic Immigrants* (Maryknoll, N.Y.: Orbis Books, 2000), 233.

24. Jay P. Dolan, *The American Catholic Parish: A History from 1850 to the Present*, vol. 2 (New York: Paulist Press, 1987), 72.

25. Ibid., 68–69.

26. Edwin B. Almirol, "Church Life Among Filipinos in Central California: Social Ties and Ethnic Identity," in *Religion and Society in the American West*, ed. David Alvarez, 299–315 (Lanham, Md.: University Press of America, 1987).

27. Ibid., 309.

28. John T. McGreevy, *Parish Boundaries: The Catholic Encounter with Race in the Twentieth-Century Urban North* (Chicago: University of Chicago Press, 1996).

29. Dolan, *American Catholic Parish*, 302.

30. A personal parish is one of three canonically approved parish styles. The other two types of parishes are territorial and multicultural. The territorial parish is understood as Catholics attending the parish located nearest to them. A multicultural parish is a composite of different masses and programs offered in native languages.

31. The 1.5 generation is a category of immigrants and refugees who come to a new country at 5–12 years old. They have some recollection of the home country but have been raised and are largely shaped by the new country of adoption.

32. Barry A. Kosmin and Seymour P. Lachman, *One Nation Under God: Religion in Contemporary American Society* (New York: Harmony Books), 1993.

33. The Catholic Church came to Korea through the efforts of laypeople.

34. Center for Applied Research in the Apostolate, http://cara.georgetown.edu/Overview200809.pdf.

35. Bryan T. Froehle and Mary L. Gautier, *Catholicism USA: A Portrait of the Catholic Church in the United States* (Maryknoll, N.Y.: Orbis Books), 2000.

14. Working Toward an Inclusive Narrative: A Call for Interdisciplinarity and Ethnographic Reflexivity in Catholic Studies

KRISTY NABHAN-WARREN

1. These works include Timothy Matovina, *Guadalupe and Her Faithful* (Baltimore: Johns Hopkins University Press, 2005), and *Becoming Latino: The Transformation of U.S. Catholicism* (Princeton: Princeton University Press, 2011); Roberto Treviño, *The Church in the Barrio: Mexican American Ethno-Catholicism in Houston* (Chapel Hill: University of North Carolina Press, 2006); Paul J. Vanderwood, *Juan Soldado: Rapist, Murderer, Saint* (Durham, N.C.: Duke University Press, 2004); and Luis D. León, *La Llorona's Children: Religion, Life, and Death in the U.S.-Mexican Borderlands* (Berkeley: University of California Press, 2004).

2. Such exemplary scholarship on apparitions includes William A. Christian, *Apparitions in Late Medieval and Renaissance Spain* (Princeton: Princeton University Press, 1981); *Person and God in a Spanish Valley* (Princeton: Princeton University Press, 1989); *Visionaries: The Spanish Republic and the Reign of Christ* (Berkeley: University of California Press, 1996); David Blackbourn, *Marpingen: Apparitions of the Virgin Mary in Bismarckian Germany* (Oxford: Clarendon Press, 1993); and Paolo Apolito, *Apparitions of the Madonna at Oliveto Citra* (University Park: Pennsylvania State University Press, 1998).

3. Michael Carroll, *Catholic Cults and Devotions: A Psychological Enquiry* (Montreal: McGill–Queen's University Press, 1989); *The Cult of the Virgin Mary: Psychological Origins* (Princeton: Princeton University Press, 1986); *Madonnas That Maim: Popular Catholicism in Italy Since the Fifteenth Century* (Baltimore: Johns Hopkins University Press, 1992); and *The Logic of Popular Catholicism in Italy* (Baltimore: Johns Hopkins University Press, 1996).

4. I am borrowing this phrase from my friend and colleague Sarah McFarland Taylor, who, in her recently published book *Green Sisters: A Spiritual Ecology* (Cambridge, Mass.: Harvard University Press, 2007), uses it to describe her status with the communities she was studying. As an empathetic non-Catholic who worked closely with her interlocutors, Taylor became close to

them in ways that blur traditional categories of emic (insider) and etic (outsider). "Intimate outsider" is a way to bridge the two worlds that are crossed when conducting deep ethnography.

5. Karen McCarthy Brown, *Mama Lola: A Vodou Priestess in Brooklyn* (Berkeley: University of California Press, 1998), 12.

6. James Clifford and George Marcus, *Writing Culture: The Poetics and Politics of Ethnography* (Berkeley: University of California Press, 1986).

7. Tod Swanson, "Through Family Eyes: Towards a More Adequate Perspective for Viewing Native American Religious Life," *American Indian Quarterly* 21 (Winter 1997): 70.

8. See Kristy Nabhan-Warren, *The Virgin of El Barrio: Marian Apparitions, Catholic Evangelizing, and Mexican American Activism* (New York: NYU Press, 2005), for more details.

9. Meredith B. McGuire, *Lived Religion: Faith and Practice in Everyday Life* (Oxford: Oxford University Press, 2008).

10. Excellent examples of recent scholarship include Robert A. Orsi, *Between Heaven and Earth: The Religious Worlds People Make and the Scholars Who Study Them* (Cambridge, Mass.: Harvard University Press, 2005); Thomas A. Tweed, *Our Lady of the Exile: Diasporic Religion at a Cuban Catholic Shrine in Miami* (Oxford: Oxford University Press, 2002); Michael Cuneo, *The Smoke of Satan: Conservative and Traditionalist Dissent in Contemporary American Catholicism* (Baltimore: Johns Hopkins University Press, 1997); Matovina, *Guadalupe and Her Faithful*; Taylor, *Green Sisters*; Julie Byrne, *O God of Players: The Story of the Immaculata Mighty Macs* (Columbia: Columbia University Press, 2003); Susan Ridgely Bales, *When I Was a Child: Children's Interpretations of First Communion* (Chapel Hill: University of North Carolina Press, 2005); and Deidre Sklar, *Dancing With the Virgin: Body and Faith in the Fiesta of Tortugas, New Mexico* (Berkeley: University of California Press, 2001).

11. Lynn Davidman, "Truth, Subjectivity, and Ethnographic Research," in *Personal Knowledge and Beyond: Reshaping the Ethnography of Religion*, ed. James V. Spickard, Shawn Landres, and Meredith B. McGuire (New York: New York University Press, 2002), 19–20.

12. Mary Ann Hinsdale, Helen Lewis, and Maxine Waller, *It Comes From the People: Community Development and Local Theology* (Philadelphia: Temple University Press, 1995) 3.

13. Kristy Nabhan-Warren, *De Colores! American Catholic and Protestant Cursillos and the "Fourth-Day" Christian Movement* (Chapel Hill: University of North Carolina Press, in press).

14. Rosita, interview, July 20, 2005.

15. Carmen, interview, July 21, 2005.

16. Arthur Kleinman, *What Really Matters: Living a Moral Life Amidst Uncertainty and Danger* (Oxford: Oxford University Press, 2007), 4.

17. Renato Rosaldo, *When Natives Talk Back: Chicano Anthropology Since the Late 1960s* (Tucson: University of Arizona Mexican American Studies and Research Center, 1986).

18. See Ann Taves's chapter in this volume.

19. Ibid.

20. Robert Orsi, *Between Heaven and Earth: The Religious Worlds People Make and the Scholars Who Study Them* (Princeton: Princeton University Press, 2005).

21. Michael Carroll, *American Catholics in the Protestant Imagination* (Baltimore: Johns Hopkins University Press, 2007), x. Carroll's reflexivity helps the reader to understand his fascination with Catholic culture that runs throughout all of his published work, yet it does little to explain his proclivity toward reductionist theories of religious experience that run through his other works, listed in note 3. As Carroll's work has shown, those who can claim an insider status to the tradition and faith do not necessarily exercise empathy or understand any better their informants, whether they be historical or ethnographic.

22. Rebecca Lester, *Jesus in Our Wombs: Embodying Modernity in a Mexican Convent* (Berkeley: University of California Press, 2005), 42.

23. Tres Dias is a "Fourth Day" nondenominational Christian movement that has its roots in Catholic Cursillos de Cristianidad. I discuss this movement at length in my forthcoming book *De Colores!*

15. Seeing Catholicly: Poetry and the Catholic Imagination

ANGELA ALAIMO O'DONNELL

1. Emily Dickinson, *The Complete Poems of Emily Dickinson*, ed. Thomas H. Johnson (Boston: Little, Brown, 1955), 667–668.

2. Gerard Manley Hopkins, *Selected Poetry*, ed. Catherine Phillips (Oxford: Oxford University Press, 1995), 129.

3. Andrew Greeley, *The Catholic Imagination* (Berkeley: University of California Press, 2000), 5.

4. Paula M. Kane, "American Catholic Culture in the Twentieth Century," in *Perspectives on American Religion and Culture*, ed. Peter W. Williams (Oxford: Blackwell, 1999), 402.

5. Ibid., 403.

6. Georges Bernanos, *Diary of a Country Priest*, trans. Pamela Morris (New York: Carroll & Graf, 1983), 298.

7. C. S. Lewis, *The Joyful Christian* (New York: Touchstone, 1996), 82.

8. Cormac McCarthy, *The Road* (New York: Knopf, 2006), 230.

9. Flannery O'Connor, "Letter to A," in *The Habit of Being*, ed. Sally Fitzgerald (New York: Farrar, Straus and Giroux, 1979), 90.

10. William Lynch, *Christ and Apollo: The Dimensions of the Literary Imagination* (Wilmington, Del.: ISI Books, 2003), 10–21.

11. Garry Wills, *Bare Ruined Choirs* (Garden City, N.Y.: Doubleday, 1972), 15.

12. Patricia Hampl, *Virgin Time: In Search of the Contemplative Life* (New York: Random House, 1993), 6.

13. Richard A. Blake, S.J., *Afterimage: The Incredible Catholic Imagination of Six American Filmmakers* (Chicago: Loyola Press, 2000), 25.

14. David Jones, "Art and Sacrament," in *Epoch and Artist*, ed. Harman Grisewood (London: Faber and Faber, 1952), 168.

15. James Joyce, *A Portrait of the Artist as a Young Man* (New York: Viking Penguin, 1976), 221.

16. Flannery O'Connor, "Catholic Novelists and Their Readers," in *Mystery and Manners*, ed. Sally and Robert Fitzgerald (New York: Farrar, Straus and Giroux, 1962), 171.

17. A. V. Christie, "A Conversation with Josephine Jacobsen," *Image: A Journal of the Arts and Religion* 23 (1999): 55.

18. Josephine Jacobsen, *In the Crevice of Time: New and Collected Poems* (Baltimore: Johns Hopkins University Press, 1995), 127.

19. Czeslaw Milosz, *New and Collected Poems, 1931–2001* (New York: HarperCollins, 2001), 569.

16. Cultural Studies Between Heaven and Earth: Beyond the Puritan Pedagogy of *The Scarlet Letter*

THOMAS J. FERRARO

1. The North American Religions Group (John Corrigan, presiding) kick-started this essay by inviting me (Tracy Fessenden, plotting) to respond to Orsi; it was a pleasure to address the group, who got the jokes, and to talk shop afterward, especially with the wonderful Catholic Studies mafia from Dayton. Of course it was the inestimable Jim Fisher who gave it life at the Curran Center again—accepting passion as something other than the death knell of cogency, inviting me to publish but pressing for more, and leading by example—with Maggie McGuinness shepherding as well. Thanks to all.

2. R. Marie Griffith and Melani McAlister, eds., "Religion and Politics in the Contemporary United States," *American Quarterly* 59 (September 2007).

3. *Between Heaven and Earth: The Religious Worlds People Make and the Scholars Who Study Them* (Princeton: Princeton University Press, 2005). Orsi is also the author of two major earlier monographs: *The Madonna of 115th Street: Faith and Community in Italian Harlem, 1880–1950* (New Haven: Yale

University Press, 1985) and *Thank You, St. Jude: Women's Devotion to the Patron Saint of Hopeless Causes* (New Haven: Yale University Press, 1996).

4. Orsi, *Between Heaven and Earth*, 12.

5. For a suggestive critique of the imperative, "always historicize!" (allied, too, to the Marxian, Freudian, and—yes—Nietzschean hermeneutics of suspicion) as, itself, wildly presentist, see Eve Kosofsky Sedgwick, "Paranoid Reading and Reparative Reading; or You're So Paranoid, You Probably Think This Introduction Is About You," in her edited volume *Novel Gazing* (Durham, N.C.: Duke University Press, 1997), 4–5.

6. Jenny Franchot, "Invisible Domain: Religion and American Literary Studies," *American Literature* 67 (December 1995): 834, 836.

7. For Orsi's account of the history of the academy's idea of "true religion," see the first half of "Snakes Alive: Religious Studies Between Heaven and Earth," *Between Heaven and Earth*, esp. 183–194.

8. Ibid., 74.

9. Richard H. Brodhead, "Manufacturing You Into a Personage: Hawthorne, the Canon, and the Institutionalization of American Literature," in *The School of Hawthorne* (New York: Oxford University Press, 1986), 48–66. I am a student of Richard Brodhead in more senses than one, including the profound and persisting counsel of his scholarship, which first suggested to me that Hawthorne himself might have had a hand in the religious bifurcation of his literary legacy: "There is what could be considered a Protestant line in the Hawthorne tradition, continuing his study of post-Puritan self-absorption and moral torment. (I think for instance of [Sarah Orne Jewett's story] 'Poor Joanna,' an 'Ethan Brand' with its cultural sources made explicit.) But there is also a Catholic line: it leads to [Flannery] O'Connor, whose Hawthorne is mediated partly by the Dominican Congregation she stayed close to in Atlanta—an order founded, as it happens, by Hawthorne's daughter Rose." *The School of Hawthorne*, 16.

10. Richard H. Brodhead, "Sparing the Rod: Discipline and Fiction in Antebellum America," in *Cultures of Letters: Scenes of Reading and Writing in Nineteenth-Century America* (Chicago: University of Chicago Press, 1993), 13–47.

11. Jane Tompkins, "Masterpiece Theater: The Politics of Hawthorne's Literary Reputation," in *Sensational Designs: The Cultural Work of American Fiction, 1790–1860* (New York: Oxford University Press, 1985), 3–37; Sacvan Bercovitch, *The Office of the Scarlet Letter* (Baltimore: Johns Hopkins University Press, 1991); Lauren Berlant, *The Anatomy of Fantasy: Hawthorne, Utopia, and Everyday Life* (Chicago: University of Chicago Press, 1991).

12. Nathaniel Hawthorne, *The Scarlet Letter*, in *Novels: Fanshawe, The Scarlet Letter, The House of the Seven Gables, The Blithedale Romance, The Marble Faun* (New York: Literary Classics of the United States, 1983), 163.

13. Ibid., 166.

14. Ibid., 286.

15. Jenny Franchot, "The Hawthornian Confessional," in *Roads to Rome: The Antebellum Protestant Encounter with Catholicism* (Berkeley: University of California Press, 1994), 260–269.

16. Herman Melville, *Billy Budd, Sailor (An Inside Narrative)*, ed. Harrison Hayford and Merton M. Sealts Jr. (Chicago: University of Chicago Press, 1962), 74; Orsi, *Between Heaven and Earth*, 158.

17. Paul Giles, *American Catholic Arts and Fictions: Culture, Ideology, Aesthetics* (Cambridge: Cambridge University Press, 1992); Tracy Fessenden, *Culture and Redemption: Religion, the Secular, and American Literature* (Princeton: Princeton University Press, 2007), 5; Franchot, *Roads to Rome*; Werner Sollors, *Beyond Ethnicity: Consent and Descent in American Culture* (New York: Oxford University Press, 1986). I first encountered Fessenden because of her trenchant revisiting of *Maria Monk* and the Ursuline Convent burning, "The Convent, the Brothel, and the Protestant Woman's Sphere," Signs: Journal of Women in Culture and Society 25, no. 2 (Winter 2000): 451–478.

18. James T. Fisher cautions against the kind of essentializing—the hypostatic projection of a "Catholic culture" or "analogical imagination"—that comes from not interrogating the power dynamics, the hard gender, race, and class questions constitutive of all institutions and their peoples. It is a warning that I take to heart, partly because I utterly concur (amen, brother) and partly because my coupling of flamboyant nomenclature ("Protestant Mariolatry") with explicatory coyness (say what?) runs the risk, in trying both to demystify and to remystify, of succeeding at neither. James T. Fisher, "The (Longed For) Varieties of Catholic Studies," *Listening/Journal of Religion and Culture* (Winter 2007): 54–67.

19. Julie Byrne, *O God of Players: the Story of the Immaculata Mighty Macs* (New York: Columbia University Press, 2003); James T. Fisher, *The Catholic Counterculture in America, 1933–1962* (Chapel Hill: University of North Carolina Press); Fisher, *Dr. America: The Lives of Thomas A. Dooley, 1927–1961* (Amherst: University of Massachusetts Press, 1997); and especially for me, Fisher, "Clearing the Streets of the Catholic Lost Generation," in *Catholic Lives, Contemporary America*, ed. Thomas J. Ferraro (Durham, N.C.: Duke University Press, 1997), 76–103; Paula M. Kane, *Separatism and Subculture: Boston Catholicism, 1900–1920* (Chapel Hill: University of North Carolina Press, 1994); Colleen McDannell, *Material Christianity: Religion and Popular Culture in America* (New Haven: Yale University Press, 1998).

20. Leo Braudy, "The Sacraments of Genre: Coppola, DePalma, Scorsese," in *Native Informant: Essays on Film, Fiction, and Popular Culture*, ed. Leo Braudy (New York: Oxford University Press, 1981); Peter Gardella, *Innocent Ecstasy:*

How Christianity Gave America an Ethic of Sexual Pleasure (New York: Oxford University Press, 1985); John Gatta, "The Sacred Woman: The Problem of Hawthorne's Madonnas," in *American Madonna: Images of the Divine Woman in Literary Culture* (New York: Oxford University Press, 1997), 10–31; Mary Gordon, *Good Boys and Dead Girls: And Other Essays* (New York: Viking, 1991); Frank Lentricchia, *The Edge of Night: A Confession* (New York: Random House, 1994), 39–113; Ellis Hanson, *Decadence and Catholicism* (Cambridge, Mass.: Harvard University Press, 1997); Camille Paglia, *Sexual Personae: Art and Decadence from Nefertiti to Emily Dickinson* (New Haven: Yale University Press, 1990), and *Sex, Art, and American Culture* (New York: Vintage Books, 1992), esp. 101–124.

21. Colleen McDannell, *Catholics in the Movies* (New York: Oxford University Press, 2008).

22. For an earlier account of the emergence of what we might have to call "Catholic Cultural Studies," see my "Not Just-Cultural Catholics," in *Catholic Lives, Contemporary America*, 1–18. For the movie case study I should have written for that volume, treating the interplay of parental sentiment, the science of disease, and Catholic devotionalism, see "Lorenzo's Chrism," *SAQ* 103 (Winter 2004): 235–263; for the essay most influenced by the contributors to that volume, especially Fisher and Orsi, see *Feeling Italian: the Art of Ethnicity in America* (New York: New York University Press, 1997), 181–197; and for a taste of the pagan/Catholic mythopoetics I have begun to investigate, as foreseen by Harold Frederic's rewrite of *The Scarlet Letter*, see "Of 'Lascivious Mysticism' and Other Hibernian Matters," *U.S. Catholic Historian* 23 (Summer 2005): 1–17.

23. The issue here of indebtedness runs deeper than my jeremiadic flourish, though all I can do here is embellish the rhetoric: In revisiting the canon, we reclaim, update (we do not feel the same as we once did about gender, race, and religious orthodoxy), sharpen, and redirect the work of earlier literary scholars working out of transatlantic comparative perspective, who thought of themselves not in the sectarian terms of the new (inter)disciplines—as practicing Catholic or Jewish or Protestant or Islamic Studies, as alas we must do here—but who understood that without accounting for the felt impress of G-d and the structural forces of Her Institutions both historically and persisting one could not enough account for society and culture, even after the rise of secularism and its hermeneutics of suspicion. They especially understood that without the Christian God we got nowhere with explaining U.S. culture and media arts, even when God is not thematized or conscious to reader or protagonist, and especially nowhere with explaining the main line of American novel and its twentieth-century rivals (Hollywood, pop lyric), which for all their seeming secularism remain knee-deep in those matters of

self, sex, and sanctity that *The Scarlet Letter* embodies and canonizes. So it gives me great pleasure to nominate as requisite to the evolution in Catholic literary studies the profound accomplishments of D. H. Lawrence (*Studies in Classic American Literature*, 1923), Denis de Rougement (*Love in the Western World*, 1940/1956), and the greatest of the postwar reading "secular" rabbis, Leslie A. Fiedler.

In his often-referenced "Come Back to the Raft Ag'in, Huck Honey," originally published in *The Partisan Review* in 1948, Fiedler sowed the seeds for the sexual revolution in American literary criticism by putting two key terms—race and gender—into play. Fiedler then discovered, during twelve years of prodigious labor, including a minor masterpiece on "The Jew in the American Novel" and culminating in his magnum opus, *Love & Death in the American Novel* (1960), that in order to deliver on both the analytical and synthetic promises of his ideas, he had to put a third major term into interpretative play—that of religion, particularly the distinction between Northern European Protestantism and Mediterranean Marian Catholicism. To approach Orsi as I do here is to begin the major task of revisiting Fiedler and reenvisioning—in the wake of queer theory, critical race and ethnicity studies, and (mind you!) the new religious history—his titanic achievement. Leslie A. Fiedler, "Come Back to the Raft Ag'in, Huck Honey," *Partisan Review* 15 (1948): 664–671; *The Jew in the American Novel* (New York: Herzl Press, 1959); *Love & Death in the American Novel* (New York: Criterion/Stein and Day, 1960).

24. Sollors, "Romantic Love, Arranged Marriage, and Indian Melancholy," *Beyond Ethnicity*, Chapter 4, esp. 110–112.

25. Denis de Rougement, *Love in the Western World*, trans. Montgomery Belgion (New York: Harcourt Brace, 1940).

26. Ferraro, "Of 'Lascivious Mysticism' and Other Hibernian Matters." I wrote this essay at the behest of Jim Fisher, and sotto voce in his honor and that of the other guerrilla Irish who have schooled me over many years, especially Tara Fitzpatrick and Tracy Fessenden.

27. Nina Baym, "Melodramas of Beset Manhood: How Theories of American Fiction Exclude Women Authors," *American Quarterly* 33, no. 2 (Summer 1981): 123–139.

17. Catholic Studies and the Sacramental Imaginary: New Directions in Catholic Humanism

MAUREEN H. O'CONNELL

1. Andrew Greeley, *The Catholic Imagination* (Berkeley: University of California Press, 2000), 1–12, 16.

2. John F. Haught, *What Is God: How to Think about the Divine* (New York: Paulist Press, 1986), 115–131.

3. Charles Taylor, *A Secular Age* (Cambridge, Mass.: Harvard University Press, 2007), 171.

4. Ibid., 25–89.

5. James J. Bacik, "Contemporary Spirituality," in *The New Dictionary of Catholic Spirituality*, ed. Michael Downey (Collegeville, Minn.: The Liturgical Press, 1986), 230.

6. Maxine Greene, *Releasing the Imagination* (San Francisco: Jossey-Boss, 1995), 28.

7. Michael J. Buckley, S.J., *The Catholic University as Promise and Project: Reflections in a Jesuit Idiom* (Washington, D.C.: Georgetown University Press, 1998), 119.

8. Michael Himes, "Living Conversation: Higher Education in a Catholic Context," *Conversations on Jesuit Higher Education* (Fall 1995): 21–27.

9. Ibid.

10. For descriptions of Catholic humanism, see ibid.; Buckley, *The Catholic University as Promise and Project*; and Margaret O'Brien Steinfels, "The Catholic Intellectual Tradition: Colleges and Universities," *Origins* 25, no. 11 (1995).

11. Buckley, *The Catholic University*, 117.

12. Ibid., 122.

13. See Mary Katherine Hilkert's analysis of Schillebeeckx's notion of "contrast experience," in "Grace-Optimism": The Spirituality at the Heart of Schillebeeckx's Theology," *Spirituality Today* 44, no. 3 (1991): 220–239.

14. Peggy McIntosh, "White Privilege: Unpacking the Invisible Knapsack," 1988, available as a PDF at http://ted.coe.wayne.edu/ele3600/mcintosh.html.

15. Mary Elizabeth Hobgood, *Dismantling White Privilege: An Ethics of Accountability* (Cleveland: Pilgrim Press, 2000), 7.

16. Margaret Pfeil, "The Transformative Power of the Periphery," in *Interrupting White Privilege: Catholic Theologians Break the Silence*, ed. Laurie M. Cassidy and Alex Mikulich (New York: Orbis Books, 2007), 130.

17. Bruce Springsteen, interview with Will Percy, *Double Take* 12 (1995).

18. Hobgood, *Dismantling White Privilege*, 10.

19. Taylor, *Secular Age*, 8.

20. Greeley, "The Catholic Imagination of Bruce Springsteen," *America*, February 6, 1988.

21. John Haughey, "From Tolerance to Engagement in Catholic Higher Education," *Woodstock Report* 87 (March 2007).

22. For an analysis of the generational differences among American Catholics see James Davidson, "The Catholic Church in the United States: 1950 to the Present," in *The Church Confronts Modernity*, ed. Leslie Woodcock Tentler

(Washington, D.C.: Catholic University of America Press, 2007), 177–207, and *Catholicism in Motion: The Church in American Society* (Liguori, Mo.: Liguori Publications, 2005). For an analysis of generational approaches to Catholic theology, see Roger Haight, "Presidential Address: The First 50 Years of Theology," *CTSA Proceedings* 50 (1995): 1–14.

23. Taylor, *A Secular Age*, 7–22.

24. For a discussion of the psychological impact of globalization, see Anthony Elliot and Charles Lemert, *The New Individualism: The Emotional Costs of Globalization* (Amherst, N.Y.: Prometheus Books, 1999); and Anthony Giddens, *Runaway World: How Globalization Is Reshaping Our Lives* (New York: Routledge, 2002).

25. Robert Wuthnow, *All in Sync: How Music and Art Are Reviving American Religion* (Berkeley: University of California Press, 2003), 185.

26. Christian Smith and Melinda Lundquist Denton, *Soul Searching: The Religious and Spiritual Lives of American Teenagers* (New York: Oxford University Press, 2005), 162–163.

27. Taylor, *A Secular Age*.

28. James Davidson, "Generations of American Catholics," *CTSA Proceedings* 63 (2008).

29. For an overview of method in Roman Catholic theology, see *Systematic Theology: Roman Catholic Perspectives*, vol. 2, ed. Francis Schüssler Fiorenza and John P. Galvin (Minneapolis, Minn.: Augsburg Press, 1991), which maps the contours of five central theological methods: transcendental, hermeneutical, analytical, correlational, and liberational. See also Mary Catherine Hilkert's assessment of the dualities inherent in many of these methods and the constructive role of the sacramental imagination in bridging the gaps in "Dialogue, Proclamation, and the Sacramental Imagination," *CTSA Proceedings* 61 (2006): 81–98.

30. John Donahue, S.J., *The Gospel in Parable: Metaphor, Narrative and Theology in the Synoptic Gospels* (Minneapolis: Augsburg Fortress Press, 1990).

31. Rowan Williams, "Christianity, Islam and the Challenge of Poverty," Archbishop of Canterbury Lecture, Bosniak Institute, Sarajevo, Bosnia, May 20, 2005.

32. Interview with Ras Malik, Philadelphia, March 15, 2007, emphasis mine.

33. I am indebted to Bryan Massingale, who shared these ideas members of the Fordham faculty at an invited lecture in December 2007.

34. James Wallis, *God's Politics: Why the Left Doesn't Get It and the Right Gets It Wrong* (New York: HarperOne, 2006), 20–30.

35. Hobgood, *Dismantling Privilege*, 14.

36. Michael Himes, "Living Conversation."

37. Richard Viladesau, "Theosis and Beauty," *Theology Today* 65, no. 2 (July 2008): 187.

38. Jane Golden, All Join Hands dedication ceremony, Benjamin Franklin High School, Philadelphia, October 26, 2006.

Contributors

UNA M. CADEGAN is Associate Professor of History at the University of Dayton. She holds a doctorate in American Civilization from the University of Pennsylvania and has published a number of articles on U.S. Catholic literary and print culture.

DEBRA CAMPBELL is Professor of Religious Studies at Colby College in Waterville, Maine. She is the author of *Graceful Exits: Catholic Women and the Art of Departure*. She is currently working on a joint biography of Kathryn Hulme, who wrote *The Nun's Story*, and Marie Louise Habets, "the real Sister Luke."

KATHLEEN SPROWS CUMMINGS is Assistant Professor of American Studies at the University of Notre Dame. She is also the Associate Director of the Cushwa Center for the Study of American Catholicism. She is the author of *New Women of the Old Faith: Gender and American Catholicism in the Progressive Era*.

THOMAS J. FERRARO is Professor of English at Duke University. He is the author of *Ethnic Passages*, *Feeling Italian*, and diverse essays, including a chapter in Colleen McDannell's *Catholics in the Movies*. He made his first foray into Catholic Studies through the writerly gifts of others, as editor of *Catholic Lives, Contemporary America*.

JAMES T. FISHER is Professor of Theology and American Studies at Fordham University. He is the author of *The Catholic Counterculture in America, 1933–1961*; *Dr. America: The Lives of Thomas A. Dooley*; *Communion of Immigrants: A History of Catholics in America*; and most recently *On the Irish Waterfront: The Crusader, the Movie, and the Soul of the Port of New York*.

JEANNINE HILL FLETCHER is Associate Professor of Theology and Faculty Director of the Service-Learning Program at Fordham University. She is the author of Monopoloy on Salvation? A Feminist Approach to Religious Pluralism. She researches and writes at the intersection of issues of Christian identity and religious diversity.

DIANA L. HAYES is Professor of Systematic Theology at Georgetown University. Her area of specialization is liberation theologies with an emphasis on Black and Womanist Theologies as well as Catholic Studies, Black Religious Studies, and World Religions. She has published seven books, including *Standing in the Shoes My Mother Made: A Womanist Theology* and, with Cyprian Davis, *Taking Down Our Harps: Black Catholics in the United States.*

LINH HOANG, O.F.M., is Assistant Professor of Religious Studies at Siena College and a Franciscan of the Holy Name of Jesus Province in New York. He earned a doctorate in historical theology from Fordham University. He is the author of *Rebuilding Religious Experience.*

RICHARD M. LIDDY is a priest of the Archdiocese of Newark and the University Professor of Catholic Thought at Seton Hall University. He is the Director of the Center for Catholic Studies and director of the program in Catholic Studies at Seton Hall. He is the author of Transforming Light: Intellectual Conversion in the Early Lonergan.

MARGARET M. MCGUINNESS is Professor of Religion at La Salle University, Philadelphia, and coeditor of *American Catholic Studies.* She is the author of the forthcoming book *Neighbors and Missionaries: A History of the Sisters of Our Lady of Christian Doctrine* (Fordham), among other works.

CECILIA A. MOORE is Associate Professor of Religious Studies at the University of Dayton, where she teaches undergraduate and graduate courses in U.S. religious history, African American religious studies, and U.S. Catholic history. She is also the Associate Director of the Master's Degree Program of the Institute for Black Catholic Studies at Xavier University of Louisiana.

KRISTY NABHAN-WARREN is Associate Professor of American Religions at Augustana College. She is the author of The Virgin of El Barrio and the forthcoming De Colores! American Catholics, Protestants, and the "Fourth-Day" Christian Cursillo Movement.

DAVID O'BRIEN is University Professor of Faith and Culture at the University of Dayton and Professor Emeritus of Roman Catholic Studies at the College of the Holy Cross. He has published a number of books, including *Public Catholicism* and *Isaac Hecker*.

MAUREEN H. O'CONNELL is Assistant Professor of Theology at Fordham University. She is the author of *Compassion: Loving Our Neighbor in an Age of Globalization* and the forthcoming *If These Walls Could Talk: Community Muralism and the Beauty of Justice*.

ANGELA ALAIMO O'DONNELL teaches English, Creative Writing, and interdisciplinary courses in American Catholic Studies at Fordham University, where she is Associate Director of the Francis and Ann Curran Center for American Catholic Studies. She is the author of a book of poems, *Moving House*, and two chapbooks, *Mine* and *Waiting for Ecstasy*.

MARY ELLEN O'DONNELL is Assistant Professor of Religious Studies at Chestnut Hill College.

CATHERINE R. OSBORNE holds a B.A. in art history from Swarthmore College and is currently a Ph.D. candidate in the Department of Theology at Fordham University.

ANN TAVES is Professor of Religious Studies and holder of the Virgil Cordano OFM Chair in Catholic Studies at the University of California at Santa Barbara. Her most recent book is *Religious Experience Reconsidered: A Building-Block Approach to the Study of Religion and Other Special Things*.

SANDRA YOCUM is Associate Professor of Religious Studies at the University of Dayton. She is author of *Joining the Revolution in Theology: The College Theology Society, 1954–2004* and coeditor, with William Portier, of *American Catholic Traditions: Resources for Renewal*.

Index